Dueling Harlows

ALSO BY TOM LISANTI
AND FROM MCFARLAND

Pamela Tiffin: Hollywood to Rome, 1961–1974 (2015)

*Glamour Girls of Sixties Hollywood:
Seventy-Five Profiles* (2008; paperback 2018)

*Hollywood Surf and Beach Movies:
The First Wave, 1959–1969* (2005; paperback 2012)

*Drive-in Dream Girls:
A Galaxy of B-Movie Starlets of the Sixties* (2003; paperback 2012)

*Fantasy Femmes of Sixties Cinema:
Interviews with 20 Actresses from Biker, Beach,
and Elvis Movies* (2001; paperback 2010)

BY TOM LISANTI AND LOUIS PAUL

*Film Fatales: Women in Espionage Films and Television,
1962–1973* (2002; paperback 2016)

BY GAIL GERBER WITH TOM LISANTI

*Trippin' with Terry Southern:
What I Think I Remember* (2009)

Dueling Harlows
The Race to Bring the Actress's Life to the Silver Screen

TOM LISANTI

McFarland & Company, Inc., Publishers
Jefferson, North Carolina

LIBRARY OF CONGRESS CATALOGING-IN-PUBLICATION DATA

Names: Lisanti, Tom, 1961– author.
Title: Dueling Harlows : the race to bring the actress's life to the silver screen / Tom Lisanti.
Description: Jefferson, North Carolina : McFarland & Company, Inc., Publishers, 2024. | Includes bibliographical references and index.
Identifiers: LCCN 2024004571 | ISBN 9781476692593 (paperback : acid free paper) ∞
ISBN 9781476651668 (ebook)
Subjects: LCSH: Harlow, Jean, 1911-1937. | Harlow (Motion picture : 1965 : Douglas) | Harlow (Motion picture : 1965 : Segal) | Motion picture actors and actresses—United States—Interviews. | BISAC: PERFORMING ARTS / Film / History & Criticism | LCGFT: Film criticism. | Biographical films.
Classification: LCC PN1997.H2594 L57 2024 | DDC 791.43/75—dc23/eng/20240206
LC record available at https://lccn.loc.gov/2024004571

BRITISH LIBRARY CATALOGUING DATA ARE AVAILABLE

**ISBN (print) 978-1-4766-9259-3
ISBN (ebook) 978-1-4766-5166-8**

© 2024 Tom Lisanti. All rights reserved

*No part of this book may be reproduced or transmitted in any form
or by any means, electronic or mechanical, including photocopying
or recording, or by any information storage and retrieval system,
without permission in writing from the publisher.*

Front cover images: publicity head shots of *left* Carol Lynley and *right* Carroll Baker as Jean Harlow (author collection); movie camera © zef art/Shutterstock

Printed in the United States of America

*McFarland & Company, Inc., Publishers
Box 611, Jefferson, North Carolina 28640
www.mcfarlandpub.com*

Acknowledgments

My heartfelt thanks go to the following people below who helped me with this book. Sadly, since the first edition was published in 2010, the following interviewees have passed away—Richard C. Bennett, Aron Kincaid, Carol Lynley, Robert Osborne, and Marvin Paige. I would like to thank again Michael Dante, David Permut, and Tim Zinnemann; and new interviewees Lindsay Bloom, Maureen Gaffney, Carol Hollenbeck, Lowell Peterson, Darrell Rooney, Nicholas von Sternberg, and Michael Westmore for sharing their stories and comments.

Thanks to James Hammond for coordinating my interview with Lindsay Bloom; Lis Pearson who, once again, went beyond the call of duty, to give my manuscript its first round of editing and for her encouragement; Shaun Chang for his continued support and for graciously letting me use a portion of his unpublished interview with Stella Stevens; and to TV historian Stephen Bowie for his permission to use a portion of his interview with Shirley Knight. A special thank you to author Foster Hirsch for reaching out to Carroll Baker, who declined to be interviewed, but directed me to her memoir for all she has to say about playing Jean Harlow.

A huge thank you to Marlin Dobbs, Lindsay Bloom, Lowell Peterson, and Wayne Schulman for sharing photos from their collections for use in the book. They greatly enhance the text.

As always, big thanks to Jim McGann, my web master. I will forever be your servant.

I couldn't have written this book without using the vast collections of the General Research Division at The New York Public Library, The National Film Information Service at the Margaret Herrick Library in Beverly Hills, and the Billy Rose Theatre Division at The New York Public Library for the Performing Arts, with a special thanks to librarian Jeremy Megraw.

Thank you to all my family and friends for their continued support with a special shout out to Ernie DeLia who has put up with my obsessions with Carol Lynley and *The Poseidon Adventure* to sixties starlets to soap operas to eighties New Wave music for the last 25 years.

Contents

Acknowledgments v
Preface 1
Introduction 3

1. Jean Harlow 5
2. The Return of the Platinum Blonde 11
3. Blame It on Irving Shulman 15
4. The Harlow Sweepstakes 22
5. Let the Race Begin 41
6. Harlow, Electronovision Style 56
7. Harlow, Paramount Style 87
8. And the Winner Is… 102
9. Last but Not Least… 121
10. The Aftermath 137
11. Harlow's Second Act: On Stage and Screen 151

Biographies—Post Harlows 183
Film Credits—Detailed 198
Chapter Notes 201
Bibliography 207
Index 215

Preface

The original version of this book came along by happy circumstance. In 2010, I did not set out to write a book about the making of the two competing *Harlow* biopics of 1965. Instead, I was writing a chapter on producer Bill Sargent's *Harlow* starring Carol Lynley for another book project I was working on. It was just going to be an opinion piece on the film. As a Carol Lynley fan, I always questioned why she agreed to play the thirties blonde bombshell. Not only was this a quickie black-and-white movie shot in a new process called Electronovision, but it was competing with a big budget, color version, also titled *Harlow*, starring Carroll Baker. This movie I had seen many times over the years and found very entertaining, though I knew it did not present a true portrayal of the star's life.

I was able to see the complete cut of Lynley's *Harlow* only recently on a bootleg DVD. The film was taken out of broadcast circulation years ago, where it would air on syndicated television mostly in the wee hours of the night. I rarely was able to stay awake past the part where Lynley, as Harlow, rips off her bra and throws it at Efrem Zimbalist, Jr. Back in 1965, the critics derided and lambasted the movie, but watching it now, I realized it wasn't the disaster they had labeled it.

Deciding my chapter needed some background information, I began doing some research and discovered numerous articles documenting the making of this *Harlow* and producer Joseph E. Levine's rival version with Baker. What fascinated me most was the war of words fought by each of the films' producers in the mainstream press. The more I delved into it, the more I was intrigued.

I culled together excerpts from many articles and then realized the chapter was now much too long for my book. It also now veered off-topic, extending into a discussion about the making of the Baker *Harlow* as well. I was going to edit it severely, but decided to see if I could obtain interviews with any actors or crew members associated with each movie. I soon discovered most were no longer with us, but I wrote to as many of the people still alive as I could find contact information for. I did my best in trying to get people to speak with me. Though I got a number of folks associated with Sargent's *Harlow*, I was only able to interview one person from Levine's production. Not getting to speak with Carroll Baker was my biggest disappointment, though she devoted a whole chapter to the *Harlow* saga in her 1983 autobiography. I am guessing their unwillingness was due to the film's failure and the unpleasantness in making it, which I totally understand. Of the people I did speak with, most only had negative things to say about both movies. And my questions regarding Carol Lynley's decision to star as Harlow were answered by the actress herself.

I decided to work on an expanded edition of the original *Dueling Harlows* because I was never satisfied with the original book. I self-published it through Amazon's now defunct CreateSpace subsidiary. The book was never professionally copyedited and the layout was wonky due to the insertion of photos that I had to do myself. There were also some sloppy mistakes in it that I take full responsibility for. I never expected the book to become popular due to its niche subject matter but it became one of my most reviewed books on Amazon. Most of the assessments were positive in terms of the text and storytelling, but I was rightfully taken to task for glaring errors and the obvious lack of editing.

For this expanded edition, I hope to correct all that was deficient in the first go-around. As for new material, I unfortunately could still not get Carroll Baker or anyone else who directly worked on her *Harlow* to speak with me. However, of the new interviewees all connected to Carol Lynley's *Harlow*, two of them had indirect connections to the Baker film. In addition, I discovered more research material about the making of both biopics. I replaced one chapter and added a chapter about Jean Harlow portrayed on stage and on screen in the 1977 film *Hughes and Harlow: Angels in Hell* with interviews with its leading lady, Lindsay Bloom, and two crew members. I also corrected a number of grammatical errors and factual mistakes; revised some text; and added new photos to enhance the book.

With that said, I hope you enjoy reading about the backstory of perhaps the only time in Hollywood history when two movies with the same exact title, about the same exact subject, starring two actresses with the same first name raced to the silver screen.

Introduction

In 1965, in a rare occurrence not seen before or since, two motion pictures with the same title, about the same subject, opened within weeks of each other. The film biographies were both called *Harlow* and endeavored to tell the story of legendary thirties blonde bombshell Jean Harlow's passionate love life and her meteoric rise from bit player to superstar, before her death at the young age of 26.

After Jean Harlow's passing in 1935, it was all quiet on the Harlow front for years although thousands mourned her death. During the fifties, there were on-and-off attempts in Hollywood to make a movie of her life but all went nowhere. Harlow then became all the national rage again in 1964 after the release of the biography titled *Harlow, An Intimate Biography*. The much-criticized book purportedly told the story of the movie star as observed through the eyes of her agent, Arthur Landau. The book was so popular that several studios announced rival movie projects about the thirties sex goddess. When the dust finally settled, only two remained standing.

In one corner was *Harlow*, a big budget Paramount Pictures production in color, produced by larger-than-life showman Joseph E. Levine and starring Carroll Baker (then age 34), as the legendary actress. In the other corner was *Harlow*, a low-budget, black-and-white, quickie production, shot in a new process called Electronovision, from young, upstart producer Bill Sargent and starring Carol Lynley (then age 23) in the lead. At the time it was unprecedented that an independent movie company would not only brazenly challenge one of the major studios in making a film about the same subject but would also use the same title and release it on the silver screen at the same time. Since Jean Harlow was a public figure and deceased, her life story was in the public domain and up for grabs, so let the better man or movie win.

The backstory of what it took to get these film biographies to the big screen is probably more interesting than the movies themselves, although both have taken on kitsch appeal today. Levine and Sargent fought a war of words in the press for months until both films were released. They even almost came to fisticuffs at the 1965 Academy Awards.

Instead of ranting at each other, the showmen should have been paying more attention to their movies. Sargent's quickie production was faced with major casting problems. His original leading lady, Dorothy Provine, was replaced just before rehearsals began. Judy Garland, playing the role of Harlow's mother, walked off the set two days before filming.

Levine's production was saddled with a poor screenplay and was being rewritten with new pages handed to the actors only a few days before they stepped onto the set. To the cast's dismay, the producer scrapped all rehearsals and was determined to rush production to have the film in the theaters shortly after his rival's. He even assigned an assistant director to shadow Carroll Baker everywhere she went on the set to keep things moving at a hurried pace.

After the two biopics were released, and for the most part skewered by the critics, the fun really began. Bill Sargent filed an anti-trust suit versus Joe Levine, Paramount Pictures, Technicolor, Inc., and others for conspiracy to restrain Electronovision in the production, distribution, and exhibition of its film, *Harlow*. Paramount countersued. Levine then filed a suit against Carroll Baker for not living up to her contractual duties to promote *Harlow* and for contributing to its box office failure. The actress countersued when the studio refused to let her work, resulting in her being blackballed in the industry. To the public's bemusement, a new round in the *Harlow* wars had just begun.

Meanwhile, Jean Harlow did pop up on stage and on film again. In late 1965, the controversial two-character play *The Beard* debuted in San Francisco telling a tale of Billy the Kid and Jean Harlow together in some sort of purgatory. Actress Billie Dixon played Harlow in various Northern California productions and Off Broadway, while movie starlet Alexandra Hay starred in a Los Angeles production. In between, Pamela Tiffin donned a platinum blonde wig to play Jean Harlow's Kitty Packard role in the Broadway revival of *Dinner at Eight* in 1966.

In 1977, producer/director/screenwriter Larry Buchanan, riding high from the surprise success of *Goodbye, Norma Jean* starring Misty Rowe as Marilyn Monroe, next took on Jean Harlow with Lindsay Bloom as the platinum blonde superstar in the low-budget, almost forgotten *Hughes and Harlow: Angels in Hell*. It was the last time Harlow was portrayed on the big screen as a central character for a long period of time, to the relief of her devoted fans, who were never pleased by any of the movies that attempted to tell her story or the actresses chosen to portray her.

1

Jean Harlow

Despite her brief career, Jean Harlow was one of Hollywood's most popular movie stars of all time. The cinema's original, platinum blonde bombshell was known for her unique appearance, her provocative dress (which usually did not include a brassiere), and for playing sexually uninhibited, liberated women in an era when most were not. She was the first to depict fair-haired gals who were not all sweet and perky like Mary Pickford. Many that knew Harlow claimed that the glamorous star could "flip a quip with an agile hip."

Film historian Robert Osborne of Turner Classic Movies described Jean Harlow as "a brightly gifted actress and comedienne" who was "the first in what became a long line of platinum blonde bombshells who have added sizzle, sensuality, and sassiness to the film medium."[1] Tom McQuade, director of the documentary *Harlow: Blonde Bombshell*, commented, "She was a woman far ahead of her time, in looks and behavior."[2]

Animator and director Darrell Rooney (whose credits include *The Lion King II: Simba's Pride, Aladdin, Curious George,* and *Hotel Transylvania 4: Transformania*) became a fan of Jean Harlow in the early seventies after discovering the glamour photography books by John Kobal that highlighted Hollywood actor portraits from the twenties through the forties. Now considered one of the leading authorities on the actress, he is the co-author, with Mark A. Viera, of *Harlow in Hollywood: The Blonde Bombshell in the Glamour Capital, 1928–1937* and posts on social media as jean_harlow_essential.

> **DARRELL ROONEY:** I bought the John Kobal books and loved all these gods and goddesses with their perfectly marbled faces in black and white. And then there was Jean Harlow who was smiling and radiant like sunlight. She was different from everyone else—she had humanity where everyone else was inaccessible or had a dramatic attitude. I think I just connected with her openness. I started watching her movies and collecting photos of her over the decades. I knew photographer Mark Viera and he noticed I was savvy about identifying locations where Jean Harlow was photographed. He thought we should do a book about her and eventually we did.

Harlow's popularity began because she had the ability to play amoral characters in a way that made them likable and not vulgar, using their sex appeal to better themselves and not meet a bitter end, as most big screen bad girls did back then. Sexually liberated, her characters still hold up and are well-liked to this day.

Jean Harlow was born Harlean Harlow Carpenter on March 3, 1911, in Kansas City, Missouri. Her father was Mont Clair Carpenter, a dentist, and her mother was the former Jean Poe Harlow. As a teenager, she moved to Hollywood with her young husband, Chuck McGrew, and began playing minor roles in many short films and two-reelers. She quickly ditched her young spouse and moved in with "Mother Jean" and her mother's second husband, Marino Bello. Harlow's relationship with her mother (who called her "the Baby") was always up for speculation.

DARRELL ROONEY: Mother Jean was nothing but dominating and controlling. Somebody said something to me about a new term that is being thrown around, "momager." That is Mother Jean all the way. She is the mother and she is the manager. There was a lot of friction that came out of that because the child is paying the bills. There is a certain demand there. To me, Mother Jean was a frustrated celebrity. I do not think that she wanted to be an actress—she wanted the attention. She never trained ... and she was not photogenic. Her daughter was freakishly photogenic. Mother Jean was in an unhappy marriage so she poured all her love into her daughter, who was completely devoted to her. Jean's mother wanted to become a movie star, so her daughter became a movie star for her mother. She even took her mother's name! They had an extremely close relationship but today we would call it co-dependent. At the time, it was considered charming, but there was a control method there. As a teenager you should be learning to psychologically separate from your parents. Finally, during Jean's last year of her life, she began to and that caused a lot of friction.

Jean Harlow, the original platinum blonde bombshell, ca. 1930s.

Harlow came to the attention of Howard Hughes when spotted in the Laurel and Hardy short, *Double Whoopee* by actor James Hall who knew that Hughes wanted a new leading lady for *Hell's Angels* (1930). When he decided to re-shoot the silent film using sound, his current actress had a thick Norwegian accent and was not acceptable for the part. With her platinum blonde hair and sexy persona, Harlow was an immediate sensation despite critical pans for her acting. Hughes took advantage of her appeal and sent the aspiring actress on a national tour to promote the movie.

Although Hughes was reluctant to release Harlow from her contract (Harlow's salary was $100 per week) despite not having a second movie for her, he eventually capitulated to MGM film executive Paul Bern and agreed to loan her out to other studios. During this period, one of her most memorable films was 1931's *Public Enemy* with James Cagney. Although the hard-hitting film received excellent notices, Harlow did not. Critics were still not impressed with her acting ability and she was panned in film after film. Even so, the public adored Harlow.

Her next movie, *Platinum Blonde* (1931), directed by Frank Capra, was a huge hit. Harlow played a snooty but likable socialite who marries a reporter (Bill Williams) who is secretly adored by a fellow reporter who only goes by the name Gallagher (a teenage Loretta Young). Although Jean's was really a supporting role, the film's original title was changed from *Gallagher* to *Platinum Blonde* to capitalize on the actress's hair color, which had become all the rage with women across the U.S. They flocked to their nearest drugstores to buy bottles of peroxide and to their beauticians to have their hair cut in the style of the actress. Although Harlow proclaimed at times that it was her natural hair color, it was not. MGM not only gave her platinum blonde tresses, but also her razor-thin eyebrows and a migrating beauty mark on her face. She originally added the mark herself in 1931 before being contracted to MGM. With their help, Harlow set the standard for the platinum blonde bombshell of the thirties.

> **DARRELL ROONEY:** Jean placed the beauty mark close to her mouth on the left side. Somehow it just accented her face that way. But sometimes it is on one of her cheeks. Sometimes it is near her eyes. Sometimes it was moved for a film role.

Seeing that the public couldn't get enough of her, Paul Bern was able to convince Hughes to let MGM pick up Harlow's option. Her first movie for the studio under this new contract (reportedly at $1,500 per week) was *Red-Headed Woman* (1932) in which Harlow hid her trademark blonde locks under a red wig. Expecting another diva with attitude à la Joan Crawford or Norma Shearer, Harlow surprised the crew by sweetly ingratiating herself—they adored her. She never played "the movie star" with them and once she stepped off the sound stage, she stopped acting.

After she officially divorced McGrew, Harlow married Paul Bern, whom she had begun dating prior to making *Red-Headed Woman*. An intellectual, Bern introduced Harlow to classic literature and the arts. He gifted his bride with a new house on Easton Drive in Beverly Hills. He did his best to wrest her from her controlling mother and stepfather, but to his dismay learned that Harlow wanted to deed the Easton Drive home to Mother Jean so Marino could invest in a gold mine. Despite the strain Bern's feelings towards the Bellos put on their marriage, to her friends and coworkers, Harlow seemed happy. But, two months after their nuptials, while Jean was working on *Red Dust* (her first movie with Clark Gable), Bern's butler found his employer naked and dead from a gunshot wound to the head. A note was found near the body that puzzlingly ended with, "You understand that last night was only a comedy."

Bern's unsolved death, the rumors of Bern having a common-law wife named Dorothy Millette (who allegedly paid him a visit at his home the day he died and may have run into Harlow), being impotent, and perhaps being a homosexual, swirled around Jean for months. Did Bern off himself or was he accidentally murdered by

Millette with his gun? A few days later, she committed suicide by jumping off a steamboat into the Sacramento River, so nobody will ever know for sure.

Although the public wavered in their sympathy for Harlow, they eventually came around. When *Red Dust* finally opened, it was a critical and box office hit—with Harlow getting rave reviews. Unfortunately, this was not enough to ease her grief over losing Bern.

Loving the chemistry between Harlow and Gable, not to mention the box office returns, MGM rushed them into the sex comedy *Hold Your Man* (1933), a very popular, pre-code, romantic crime drama with Gable as a conman and Jean as his loyal girlfriend. Harlow then won arguably the best reviews of her career with the prestigious *Dinner at Eight* (1933). Proving she was a gifted comedienne, the film featured Harlow (co-starring with Marie Dressler) as a wisecracking, adulterous wife constantly battling her older, tyrannical, businessman husband (Wallace Beery). They are just two of the many high society guests invited to attend the dinner party of a desperate New York City social climbing couple.

During the filming of *Dinner at Eight* and her next movie, *Bombshell*, Harlow began a romance with married, playboy boxer Max Baer, while he was in Hollywood shooting the film, *The Prizefighter and the Lady*. His wife filed for divorce on the grounds of adultery, naming Harlow as a co-respondent. This, unfortunately, coincided with the one-year anniversary of Paul Bern's death. The notoriety that this brought Jean worried the executives at MGM who were not sure she could survive another scandal. To head off any bad publicity, the studio was purportedly able to convince Mrs. Baer to postpone her divorce proceedings and then pressured Harlow into getting married immediately. She wed Harold Rosson, her friend, and the cinematographer on *Bombshell*. They eloped to Yuma, Arizona.

When *Bombshell* was released, it was a critical success but only a modest hit at the box office. In the comedy, a parody of Harlow's home life, she played Hollywood's reigning sex symbol Lola Burns, a tart-tongued actress always butting heads with a shifty, studio PR guy (Lee Tracy), a freeloading father and brother, a conniving secretary, and various servants.

Between her movies and all the gossip fodder about her, fans could not get enough of Jean Harlow. She burst onto the scene just when the public was looking for a new screen idol. With her trademark hair color and devil-may-care attitude, Jean was what they were craving and her antics were exploited by the press in film magazines of the day. Stories appeared around her never wearing a bra; posing naked for photos in Griffith Park; sleeping in the nude; and bleaching her pubic hair. Of course, most were exaggerations, but Harlow knew what her admirers wanted and lived the life they expected. She would usually be photographed clad in skintight, white satin dresses with a matching white mink, posing next to her white Cadillac or in her mansion. A friend was quoted once saying that Jean "Knew her image and she tried to live up to it, but only in a publicity way."[3]

Reportedly prodded by Mother Jean and Marino Bello, Harlow demanded more money from MGM, which balked and suspended the actress. With no work to be had, Jean penned a racy novel, titled *Today Is Tonight*, that was so sexually explicit that MGM forbade it to be published. Facing backlash from the public who were demanding more Jean Harlow movies, MGM signed the actress to a new contract starting at $3,000 a week. Shortly after, she and Rosson parted company on March 11, 1934.

In 1935, Jean Harlow began a romance with actor William Powell, whom she met casually while she was still married to Rosson. Louis Mayer was so delighted that two of his top stars were a couple that he was anxious to pair them in a picture,

Jean Harlow in one her most memorable roles as wisecracking Kitty Packard, seen here with Wallace Beery as her loutish, businessman husband in the classic film *Dinner at Eight* (MGM, 1933).

but first Jean was slated to reunite with Cark Gable in the romantic adventure *China Seas* (1935), costarring Rosalind Russell, who befriended Harlow. Decades later, while touring with her one-woman show, Russell remarked that Jean was one of the sweetest women she ever worked with—but she was sad. "With that mother, she couldn't help but be," she added.[4]

MGM replaced Powell's leading lady Joan Crawford with Harlow in the musical *Reckless* (1935) and they would go on to co-star together in *Libeled Lady* (1936). It was around this time when MGM allowed a more sophisticated Jean Harlow to appear on screen in *Wife vs. Secretary* (1936), *Suzy* (1936), and *Personal Property* (1937).

On the romantic side, Powell was called the love of Jean's life. They never wed, however, reportedly because of Powell's recent divorce from actress Carole Lombard and his admitted hesitation to marry another actress and especially one the entire world lusted after. Powell's stubbornness on the subject of matrimony frustrated Harlow, who desperately wanted a husband and family. She was devoted to him and reportedly came to his sets when she was not working just to be close to him. Even so, Powell held firm on not marrying. Allegedly, the frustrated actress began drinking more frequently (especially now that she was out from under the recently separated Mother Jean's watchful eye) and her friends began noticing a decline in her health.

Knowing the Harlow-Powell love affair was almost dead (they began seeing other people) and Harlow was still in recovery from mouth surgery, MGM shelved the couple's next film. Harlow then replaced Joan Crawford opposite Clark Gable in *Saratoga* (1937).

During the shoot, the cast and crew observed how ill Jean looked. She reportedly brushed off their concerns. Shortly after, she collapsed on set into the arms of Gable and was admitted to a hospital. She was suffering from an inflamed gall bladder and her kidneys began to weaken, perhaps caused by a bout with scarlet fever when she was a teenager. This was a time before kidney transplants and dialysis were the norm, so nothing could be done to cure her, despite the reported blood transfusions she received and her placement in an oxygen tent. Jean Harlow died from "cerebral edema and uremic poisoning, which is caused by a build-up of waste products in the blood" on June 7, 1937. A grieving William Powell commented, "She died in my arms. It was the saddest day of my life."[5] She was only 26.

Jean Harlow was dressed in a pink silk negligee that she had recently worn in *Saratoga* and laid out in an open casket for family members and close friends only. The coffin was closed for public viewing. She was then entombed in a private room in the "Sanctuary of Benediction" at Forest Lawn Memorial Park in Glendale. Jean Harlow's crypt reads simply, "Our Baby."

2

The Return of the Platinum Blonde

During the fifties, there were various attempts to bring the life of Jean Harlow to the silver screen, but all were aborted. The renewed interest in her may have had to do with the burgeoning popularity of a new platinum blonde to burst on the scene named Marilyn Monroe, who, after playing small parts in various films, scored three major box office hits in 1953 with *Niagara*, *Gentlemen Prefer Blondes*, and *How to Marry a Millionaire*. She became Hollywood's newest sex symbol and spawned a number of imitators including Cleo Moore, Mamie Van Doren, Joi Lansing, Jayne Mansfield, and Sheree North.

With the buxom platinum-blonde sexpot ideal in again, it may have been decided it was the perfect time to resurrect the original 1930s version onto the silver screen. The first reported by the press was in 1954 (17 years after Harlow's passing). Prolific producer Sam Bischoff announced that he was putting together a $2 million independent production to be called *The Jean Harlow Story*. He had produced many two-reel comedies, serials, and features including *Mixed Nuts* (1922), *Frisco Kid* (1935), *The Charge of the Light Brigade* (1936), *Angels with Dirty Faces* (1938), *A Night to Remember* (1943), and *South Sea Woman* (1953).

Bischoff was in negotiations with Mother Jean Bello to purchase the rights to her daughter's story for a sum of $100,000. She would come on board as technical adviser and Arthur Landau, Harlow's former agent, would be hired as associate producer. Confirming his participation, Landau announced that this picture would showcase the "true personality of a really wonderful girl."[1] To that end, clearances were purportedly received from all major personalities in her life and Bischoff was said to be seeking permission from MGM and Howard Hughes to use footage from Harlow's movies.

Bischoff was also in talks with William Faulkner and Robert Sherwood to author the screenplay, and George Sidney was touted as possible director. But the biggest mystery was who would get to play the lead role. The obvious choice was Marilyn Monroe, dubbed by many as "the new Jean Harlow." Columnist Sidney Skolsky, who was working on his own screen treatment about Jean Harlow, helped make the blonde newcomer a star. He wrote the popular column "Tintypes" that appeared in the *New York Post* and *Los Angeles Herald*, before being syndicated in newspapers across the country. Not as powerful as Hedda Hopper or Louella Parsons, Skolsky's claim to fame is that he was reportedly the first writer to use the term

"Oscar" in print when referring to the Academy Awards in a column he wrote in 1934. When he met Monroe, she confessed that Jean Harlow, whom he knew quite well, was her role model. Taking a quick liking to her, Skolsky would mention her name many times in his column and give her some much-needed publicity.

Monroe would have brought a sweet naïveté to the role that would have made her perfect for the part. The only problem was that she was under contract to 20th Century–Fox and since she was their hottest new star, it would be problematic in getting her for the movie. Landau did not discount Monroe, but added, "We would like to introduce a new girl if it is at all possible to find one young enough, about seventeen, with the combination of beauty and talent we are seeking."[2]

Beginning in 1952, when Columba Pictures signed her to a contract, Cleo Moore let it be known to whoever would listen that she was just right to play Jean Harlow. She remarked, "I'd like to play Harlow's life the way she lived it. She may have caused a lot of censorship but she was never tied down by it."[3] Two years later, Moore was still championing herself as the ideal choice for the role of Harlow although she was pushing thirty. Even so, columnist Mike Connolly concurred and wrote, "Maybe she is. There's a startling similarity between the two blonde sizzlers and the physical resemblance is more than slight. Cleo's measurements … are beguiling. And she can act too."[4]

Producer Sam Bischoff was never able to get his Jean Harlow production off the ground and abandoned his plans—no doubt disappointing Mother Jean's pocketbook. However, two years later she would get her $100,000 payment when 20th Century–Fox purchased the rights to her daughter's life as a film vehicle for Marilyn Monroe. The studio's head of production, Buddy Adler, closed the deal with the hope that Fox's biggest, most unpredictable star would agree to bring Jean Harlow to life on the silver screen. He assigned the film to producer Jerry Wald, and to help assure Monroe's commitment, Adela Rogers St. John, a personal friend of the late actress, was chosen to write the screenplay for *The Jean Harlow Story*. This turned out to be a mistake. Despite Monroe idolizing Jean Harlow, she declined the role due to advice from her then husband, playwright Arthur Miller, because he convinced her that the project was trash. She agreed and the disappointed actress was alleged to have commented that she hoped that when she died, they didn't do the same to her. If only!

With Monroe refusing to play Jean Harlow, other names were considered. Louella Parsons reported that Academy Award winner Eva Marie Saint was a hot contender for the role.[5] Though she was a fine actress, Saint arguably didn't have the sexiness and allure to play the blonde bombshell. Carroll Baker, who had wowed as the thumb-sucking *Baby Doll* in 1956, was also being touted at this time and was the first choice of columnist Sheila Graham who remarked, "only Miss Baker has Jean's sultry inner combustion."[6] Unfortunately, Baker was under contract to Warner Bros. at the time. Jayne Mansfield, who was under contract to Fox, campaigned mightily for the role. She fancied herself a combination of Jean Harlow and Mae West, so the studio cruelly used the script to keep her in line. Purportedly, Mansfield would agree to star in a movie she didn't want to make, such as *The Sheriff of Fractured Jaw*, thinking *The Jean Harlow Story* would be her next. Unfortunately for her, Fox had no confidence in Mansfield's acting abilities to carry such a high-profile role and never had any intention of casting her.

With no female lead in place, Fox put *The Jean Harlow Story* on the back burner, but plans to make the movie kept popping up for the next four years. Wald announced in December 1957 that, after producing the musical *Mardi Gras* starring Pat Boone, the Harlow movie would be his next to go into production in 1958 with an enthusiastic Kim Novak playing the part of the thirties superstar. This never happened, perhaps because she was under contract to Columbia Pictures and its notorious head, Harry Cohn, would not loan her out and wanted her to play Jeanne Eagles.

Wald once again postponed his movie but revealed in 1959 that he was receiving almost ten letters a week from friends and fans of the late actress offering their help with the making of the movie. Some even came with photos enclosed from women trying to impress the producer with their resemblance to Jean Harlow and explanations on why they should play her on the big screen. The flabbergasted producer remarked, "I am fascinated that people are so fascinated. It's a public barometer. I've been involved in a couple of hundred movie films, but I never got anything like this. It's an epidemic."[7]

With this continuing audience clamor, Wald once again pushed forward with *The Jean Harlow Story*. This time he turned to Academy Award–winning journalist-turned-screenwriter Ben Hecht to rewrite the screenplay, based on Adela Rogers St. John's story treatment. The renowned Hecht's movies included such classics as *Underworld, The Front Page, Scarface, The Scoundrel, Nothing Sacred, Gunga Din, Wuthering Heights, Angels Over Broadway, Spellbound, Notorious,* and *A Farewell to Arms*, among many others. Always a firm believer that Paul Bern's suicide was a frame-up by the studios, his script had Bern being murdered.

Fox tapped newcomer Stella Stevens to play Jean Harlow. She was working as a junior fashion model in a Memphis department store when she was noticed by a United Artists press agent, in town with Tina Louise to promote the movie *God's Little Acre*. With her hair bleached almost white, due to her playing the lead role in a local production of *Bus Stop*, Stevens took up the PR guy's offer to go to New York to be photographed. The Fox executives were immediately impressed and announced that Stella would star as Jean Harlow. She remarked to writer Shaun Chang:

> I thought I would be quite right for it. Then I met people who knew her and loved her, including William Powell, who said to me, "Stella, please, never play her. She wasn't really like what they tell people she was like. She was just this good ole' down home girl—a lot of fun with a great sense of humor. They bleached her hair white and made her this goddess, and she never was comfortable with that persona that they gave to her." I said to him, "Well, I think that, in itself, is pretty interesting." He repeated, "Oh, Stella, please. Never play her." So, I never did.[8]

In August of 1959, Hedda Hopper wrote that Lee Remick was cast as Jean Harlow.[9] This, unfortunately, never came to be. Remick, as evidenced by her performances in *The Long, Hot Summer* (1958) as a hot-blooded Southern vixen and *Anatomy of a Murder* (1959) as a trailer trash party girl, could be very sexy and she undoubtedly had the acting chops to play Harlow.

A few months later, Louella Parson reported that at Joanne Woodward's 30th birthday party, Fox studio head Buddy Adler offered the actress *The Jean Harlow Story* right on the spot. Parsons boasted, "Just goes to prove what I have been telling you, that Mrs. Paul Newman has developed into one of our top glamour girls—she's so beautiful these days."[10] This too never happened as Fox officially abandoned any plans to make *The Jean Harlow Story* in March 1960 when the Screen Actors Guild went on strike against the major studios for the first time in the fifty years of filmmaking. This was probably for the best. Though the Academy Award winner is an excellent actress, a glamour girl she is not—as demonstrated when she took the lead role, originally meant for Marilyn Monroe, in *The Stripper* (1963). As sensitive a performance as Woodward gave as the aging exotic dancer who falls for her friend's teenage son (Richard Beymer), she just did not have the fullness of figure or exceptional looks to be believable. Suffice it to say, this stripper could not entice many paying customers to watch.

Though his script for *The Jean Harlow Story* was shelved, it didn't stop Ben Hecht from proceeding with his cause to clear Paul Bern's name. He wrote an article about it and other Hollywood cover-ups for *Playboy* magazine in 1960. In it, he stated that the note found at the crime scene was a forgery, engineered by MGM studio executives to save face for their star Jean Harlow. Hecht's theory had the studio reasoning that having the husband of the world's most popular love goddess commit suicide for being impotent was better than reporting that he was murdered. Though Hecht did not name the culprit, it was strongly hinted that Bern was killed by another woman—a common-law wife, no less. Hecht called it a "suicide whitewash." Due to the writer's persistence, the case was reopened in October of 1960. As requested by Hecht, the District Attorney's office interviewed director Henry Hathaway but still could find no proof of foul play. It remained officially a suicide.[11]

During this period, Fox was not the only studio with the intent to make a movie about Jean Harlow. MGM announced their film biography which would star newcomer Barbara Lang, a brassy blonde bombshell in the vein of fifties B-movie stars Mamie Van Doren and Cleo Moore. This went nowhere, as did Sidney Skolsky's attempts in 1962 to get his screen treatment produced. The print columnist had a successful track record with movie bios, as he intermittently dabbled in filmmaking. He produced the Academy Award–winning film *The Jolson Story* starring Larry Parks in 1942 and produced and wrote *The Eddie Cantor Story* starring Keefe Brasselle in 1953.

Skolsky tried to revive interest in his story and convince Monroe to change her mind about playing Harlow. He reportedly lined up a meeting with the actress to discuss playing the star, but ironically, she died the day before. Though Monroe never got to play Jean Harlow on screen, she did pose as the actress for photographer Richard Avedon in 1958 as part of his screen goddess series of photographs.

3

Blame It on Irving Shulman

The *Harlow* film saga reignited in 1964 following the success of the Jean Harlow biography entitled *Harlow, An Intimate Biography* by Irving Shulman (with input by her former agent Arthur Landau). Shulman, who was born in Brooklyn to Lithuanian Jewish immigrants, was not the obvious choice to write the biographical story of the tragic movie star. He was most well-known for his notorious pulp fiction tales of sadistic juvenile delinquents, beginning with his first novel, *The Amboy Dukes* (published by Doubleday in 1947) about a teenage street gang whose members engaged in assault, rape, and murder. He wrote *Dukes* while teaching English at George Washington University. The violent, gritty book caused a sensation, as it was probably the first to address the tide of rising crime committed by urban youths from hard working families. It was so notorious that teenagers who got their hands on a copy had to read it in secret, lest it be taken away from them by overprotective adults.

Shulman followed *Dukes* with *Cry Tough* (1949) and *The Big Brokers* (1951), which chronicled the exploits of his teenage gang members into adulthood and more felonious crimes. Universal Pictures bought the rights to Shulman's first novel and changed the title to *City Across the River* (1949), which helped launch the film career of Tony Curtis. The author was then lured to Hollywood to turn his fourth novel, *The Square Trap*, about Mexican American youths living in the ghetto of Los Angeles, into a movie that was renamed *The Ring* (1952). Shulman's greatest success, though, was when he wrote the screen treatment for *Rebel Without a Cause*. It was loosely based on his novel *Children of the Dark* that was published in 1955 by Holt. Screenwriter Stewart Stern used the treatment as the basis for his script. The film, starring James Dean, Natalie Wood, and Sal Mineo, went on to become a classic tale of misunderstood, aimless, suburban youth, earning Shulman and Stern an Academy Award nomination for Best Story and Screenplay.

Next up for Shulman were the scripts for the B-movie *Terror at Midnight* (1957) starring Scott Brady; *Baby Face Nelson* (1958) starring Mickey Rooney as the notorious gangster; and Albert Zugsmith's exploitation melodrama *College Confidential* (1960) starring Steve Allen as a sociology professor surveying the sex habits of his students (including sexpot Mamie Van Doren and nymphet Tuesday Weld as coeds). *College Confidential* would be the last of his screenplays to be produced. Shulman's juvenile delinquent stories fell out of favor during the time when clean-cut, wholesome performers such as Sandra Dee, Troy Donahue, Fabian, and Shelley Fabares began to rule the movie and TV screens.

Irving Shulman was contacted by former Bantam Books editor-turned-movie producer Saul David in the spring of 1961 and asked if he would meet with Jean Harlow's former agent, Arthur Landau. David recalled, "Landau had some marvelous stories to tell of the old Hollywood days particularly of Jean Harlow. I thought they would make an interesting best-seller."[1]

During the fifties, Landau had tried to get a Jean Harlow film project going but failed. Now 71 years old and suffering from cancer of the larynx, the former agent-turned-producer, whose life savings had been depleted due to his medical expenses, told Shulman that "he felt the time had come to tell the story of Jean Harlow—the whole truth, as only he knew it."[2] He claimed to have been closer to the actress than any member of the family and boasted that she confided to him all matters professional and private. This was refuted later by many people, in particular long-time MGM publicity director Howard Strickling who exclaimed, "What a brazen lie! Hell, Arthur Landau wasn't even at her wedding."[3]

Once Shulman agreed to write Harlow's biography, Saul David arranged a deal with publisher Bernie Geis. Shulman and Landau were guaranteed $20,000 each. Bernard Geis Associates would receive half of the domestic sales, with Shulman and Landau splitting the other half 65 percent to 35 percent.

Irving Shulman's *Harlow: An Intimate Biography* played fast and loose with the facts of the beloved movie star and, not surprisingly, Arthur Landau comes across as the hero in her short, tragic story. Landau was not even a big part of the actress' life during her last few years, as agents Frank and Vic Orsatti handled her affairs once she was working at MGM. But, grateful to Landau for getting her career kick-started, the generous actress still gave him ten percent of her salary.

People alive at the time who knew Harlow felt that her agent had betrayed and maligned her, not to mention giving himself much too much credit for her success. Most of Harlow's friends and co-workers steered clear from speaking with Shulman. The only people, other than librarians, thanked for their help with the biography were Landau's wife Beatrice, Saul David, Harlow's former press agent Kay Mulvey, Harlow's friend Ruth Hamp, and Frank Whitbeck, the former head of publicity for MGM.

The publication received scathing reviews from the press, including Milton Esterow of *The New York Times* who found it "tasteless." Hedda Hopper called it "a horror," and revealed, "Shulman treats the living in this septic epic with gloves, but what he does to the dead! Ugh!" Richard G. Hubler of the *Los Angeles Times* remarked that it was "a hack job" and "garbage in print." Brendan Gill of *The New Yorker* exclaimed, "A disgusting book, disgustingly written." *Time* magazine dismissed "the truth," as presented by Shulman and Landau, and commented, "What they didn't know between them, they improvised." Marjory Adams of the *Boston Globe* called it "sordid."

The biography, written in a somewhat snide fashion, was rightfully criticized for a lot of reasons, but, in particular, for reworking the facts in a sensationalistic fashion, à la such rags as *Confidential* magazine, just to titillate the reader. Episodes in her life were fabricated; dialog was made up; coarse language spewed from the mouth of Jean Harlow throughout; and even the actress' thoughts were presented without any explanation as to how the author knew this information.

By the early sixties, a few people felt Paul Bern had been murdered by his mentally disturbed common-law wife, Dorothy Millette, who flung herself off a ferry boat two days later. Another theory was that Bern committed suicide after Millette, newly arrived in Los Angeles, threatened to reveal their marriage and he didn't want to ruin Jean's career. The studio fabricated the impotence story thinking that it would be less of an embarrassment to the world's reigning sex goddess than her husband's being a bigamist.

Although Shulman addresses both theories in his book, he gives them short shrift and sticks to the idea that Bern committed suicide due to impotence, hinting perhaps due to his homosexuality. In Shulman's view, after not being able to perform sexually on their wedding night, the frustrated Bern beat his new bride with a cane. The next morning, she fled to her agent's home and cried, "The little bastard's a maniac! A dirty rotten Goddamned sex fiend."[4] An apologetic, sobbing Bern explains to Landau later that day, "Every man … every man I know gets an … erection…. Just by talking about her, other men get them. Arthur, didn't I have the right to think Jean could help me at least that much?"[5] Not only does Shulman present Bern as a sexual deviant, but as a potential murderer, blaming the caning for Harlow's kidney trouble that eventually killed her.

As badly as Paul Bern is portrayed, the biggest complaint is how the author totally annihilates the character of Jean Harlow. People who knew and worked with her found the actress to be an honest, somewhat shy, sincere, kind, bright, fun-loving girl. That is *not* the picture Irving Shulman painted. Instead, he went the opposite route—no doubt to arouse reader interest. Lloyd Shearer remarked that the biography disgustingly presents Jean Harlow as "a sordid, foul-mouthed nymphomaniac, married to a fiend, who beat her so badly that she later died of the wounds." Marjory Adams added in her review of the book that the author makes Jean out to be vulgar, corrupt, and licentious, and then rightly states if that were the case, "she would scarcely have won the love and devotion of such a fine actor and gentleman as William Powell."

Giving credit where credit is due, critics felt that in one passage of the book, Shulman accurately summed up Jean Harlow's immense popularity with both sexes at the time. He opined, "The incandescent good humor Jean radiated from the screen made her the choice of all men. Women reproved her for behaving wickedly with her body but loved her for not being wicked in mind."[6]

Despite the critical pans and barbs, readers rushed to the bookstores and made the sensationalized claptrap a bestseller. It was high-grade trash, right up there with Harold Robbins' *The Carpetbaggers* and Grace Metalious' *Peyton Place*. By the end of the year, it topped *The New York Times* best seller list in the General category for 1964.

Friends of the actress were outraged by the biography. At first, most ignored it, not wanting to give it any more publicity and hoping it would disappear quickly. But when it became such a huge hit with the general public and it seemed movie studios were moving ahead with rival film biographies, many thought it was time to speak out against it and stand up for Jean Harlow. William Powell, of course, defended his former lover, while Howard Strickling called it, "one of the most nasty, filthy, sordid, vulgar, untrue hatchet jobs I've ever read."

Kay Mulvey and Adela Rogers St. John, who wrote a number of articles on Jean Harlow and also authored an unproduced screenplay, appeared on the debut airing of *The Les Crane Show* to debate the merits of the book with Irving Shulman, there to defend his tome. The ladies took the author to task, calling his bio "ghastly." Rogers St. John asked, "How can you report conversations between Harlow and her husband?" Shulman replied, "It is a new theory of biography."[7] Some would call that fiction. Years later, Robert Osborne would opine that the public indignation was because Jean Harlow was "an extraordinary person" and "seemed at heart, a kind, sensible, immensely likable human being."[8]

Irving Shulman defended his book numerous times. Per columnist Harry MacArthur, Schulman "got involved … while in pursuit of information to refute a recurring rumor that Miss Harlow's second husband, Paul Bern, had been murdered, possibly by the actress herself. His aim in the book, he says, was to expose the inhumane treatment Hollywood gives young girls who become stars without being prepared for all that adulation."[9] Addressing his critics, Schulman remarked to MacArthur, "Sure it's a dirty book, it's about a dirty business."[10]

Columnist Sheila Graham did a multi-part story investigating the truth about Jean Harlow, as compared to what Shulman presented in his biography. Her first interview was with Arthur Landau, who defended the work and claimed that 99 percent of what was written was true. He stuck to the story that Paul Bern was impotent and, out of frustration, beat Jean with a cane on their wedding night when he could not perform sexually. When Graham presented testimony from Harlow's maid, who was there the next morning and found the actress to be in glorious spirits with no visible signs of injuries, the former agent exclaimed, "The maid is a liar."[11]

Kay Mulvey remarked that Jean Harlow had a difficult time talking about her sex life with her mother, to whom she was devoted, so she found it very doubtful that the actress would share details with any man, especially one who was no longer her agent. Landau insisted that she did and said, "I was her Father Confessor. She told me things she would not tell anyone else." He added, "Actually the book could have been more sordid. I did not give all my material."[12]

Graham was taken aback by Landau's attitude and asked him why he was saying such terrible things about Jean when she was so kind to him, even giving him a commission long after he stopped being her agent. He angrily replied, "The retainer story is a lie."[13] He also accused Ben Lyon of not telling the truth when the actor's story of how Jean got cast in *Hell's Angels* contradicted Landau's version. According to Lyon, her agent did not engineer Jean's audition for *Hell's Angels*. Co-star James Hall recommended Jean to Howard Hughes, who agreed to test her. It seems in Arthur Landau's world everybody was a liar except him.

Howard Strickling was very vocal with Sheila Graham, denouncing Irving Shulman's book and Arthur Landau, in particular. As the studio's head of publicity and close advisor to Jean Harlow, he swore that after the actress was signed by MGM, her agent never set foot on the lot. He raged, "The only time I ever saw Landau at Metro was recently, when I told him he was a filthy liar, and to get out, or I'd throw him out."[14] He also dismissed Irving Shulman's claim that he tried to contact Strickling for an interview without success. "Shulman never called me for information about his book. He said he tried to reach me three times and I couldn't be reached. That's a lie. As most of the 'facts' in his book are lies."[15]

Addressing some of what he deemed were fabricated or embellished stories presented in the book, Strickling began by vowing that Jean was devoted to her mother and loved her dearly. He also asserted that Mother Jean did not deny medical attention to her daughter after she collapsed on the set of *Saratoga* and that she was immediately rushed to the hospital. He revealed that shortly after Paul Bern's death, Jean implied to him that they did not have sex on their wedding night, but there was no mention of a fight, yet alone a caning. He opined, "Jean was a strong, healthy woman who took a lot of exercise. What was *she* doing while Paul was supposedly beating her black and blue with a cane? If I knew Jean, and I did, she would have taken the stick from a man twice the size and beaten *him* with it."[16]

Strickling blames all the salaciousness in the biography on Arthur Landau's greed and desperation for money. His prior attempts to sell a screenplay on the actress had failed. The former agent was flat broke and badly in need of a bestseller, thus making up shocking stories about the beloved actress to sell more books.

As the backlash from Jean Harlow's friends continued and the bad reviews piled up, Arthur Landau began to distance himself from Shulman's book—even after going on the record with Sheila Graham. Now he began telling columnists that he was not part of the writing process. He claimed that he saw the author only four times in three years and that Shulman would send him a questionnaire from time to time, in which he would answer some, but not all, of the questions put forth. Not privy to any drafts or galleys, he professed to have read the biography for the first time after it was published. He declared that he too was aghast and swore he never stated that Jean Harlow was promiscuous or that she used vulgar language.

> **DARRELL ROONEY:** Arthur Landau took too much credit for Jean's success. I have been to the Academy [of Arts and Sciences] a couple of times and have researched letters between Landau and Irving Schulman. A lot of the letters are Schulman berating Landau for giving him conflicting information. My understanding is that Arthur had an illness and had a lot of medical bills. He was doing this because it was his only solution to pay for hospital stays and things. I think he was throwing as much wood on the fire as he possibly could, hoping that Schulman could make something of it. Irving certainly did do something with it but he manufactured a lot of incidents and changed people's characters. That is *not* Mother Jean's character in any way. She is a dynamo and not somebody who was controlled by sex with this Latin guy. She called the shots.

Despite his new objections to the way Irving Shulman treated Jean Harlow in his book, this didn't stop Landau from collecting his royalties or exploiting the dead superstar further. He helped Jean's friend Ruth Hamp publish Harlow's novel *Today Is Tonight* with Grove Press in 1965. Landau claimed that Harlow told him in 1933 or 1934 that the story, about a socialite reduced to performing a sleazy nightclub act after her wealthy Wall Street broker husband is blinded in a horseback-riding accident and loses his money, came to her in a dream. Though the actress did come up with the idea, it was alleged that Hollywood publicist Tony Beacon actually wrote it and then it was re-worked by screenwriter Carey Wilson.

Others upset by *Harlow: An Intimate Biography* took a different approach than slamming the book in the press, and court actions began almost immediately after the book was released. Kay Mulvey led the charge and sued the author for $1 million for using her name, even though she willingly helped Shulman and was thanked in the acknowledgments for her contribution. The star's father, Dr. Mont Clair Carpenter, filed a lawsuit versus Shulman, Dell Publishing Co., Random House, Bernard Geis Associates, and the Ward Parkway Book Shop, Inc. in November 1964, asserting that the book "destroys his right of privacy, holds him up to humiliation, disgrace and ridicule and exposes him to public contempt."[17] He also claimed "that it blackens and vilifies the memory of Jean Harlow and scandalizes and provokes her surviving relatives and friends."[18] His petition asked for $1 million in damages for each of these three accounts.

A few months later Violette H. Bello, the widow of Harlow's stepfather Marino Bello, filed a $5 million suit claiming that the author and publisher "willfully and maliciously published false, defamatory and libelous printed matter"[19] about her late husband. At first, it was reported that she would file in Utah, the only state to have a statute "that holds it's as wrong to defame the dead as it is the living."[20] However, the suit wound up in the state of Missouri, where the Jackson County Court dismissed the action. The decision was repealed, but it was held up by the Missouri Supreme Court, which ruled in December 1967 that the alleged libel could only be applied to Mr. Bello and not his widow.

The lawsuits continued to fly, as Shulman, Arthur Landau, Bernard Geis Associates, and Dell Publishing, owners of the paperback rights to *Harlow, An Intimate Biography*, filed an injunction in New York against Popular Library, a publishing house that planned to release, in softcover, *The Jean Harlow Story* by John Pascal. At 132 pages, with 32 of them photographs, some felt it did bear a superficial resemblance to Shulman's biography.

The dueling Harlow books foreshadowed what was to happen with the movie productions about Jean Harlow. The complainants argued that this new book was an imitation of Shulman's, and that the publisher was planning on misleading the public with its cover, advertising, and promotion to trick the readers into thinking it was a paperback reprint of Shulman's *Harlow*. A month later, the injunction was denied by Justice Owen McGivern whose opinion stated, "Defendant's book, publication of which is herein sought to be restrained, is from even the most cursory examination of its physical appearance completely different from the plaintiff's book and it is difficult for the court to conceive how any confusion may arise between the two."[21]

Due to the publication of *The Jean Harlow Story*, Dell Publishers felt inclined to push up the release date of the softcover version of *Harlow: An Intimate Biography* lest the public get confused. They paid an additional $30,000 to get permission to do so. This was less than three months after the release of the hardcover retailing at $5.95 a copy, which now had competition from two paperbacks priced at less than a dollar. Despite the lower cost, *The Jean Harlow Story* did not sell as well as the Harlow biography, but it did receive its share of bad notices, just like its rival. For example, reviewer Clarence Petersen remarked in the *Chicago Tribune* that this "pot boiler could be read in an hour and hardly could have taken much longer to write."

Of course, with the biography a runaway bestseller, the public condemnations of Irving Shulman and Arthur Landau, and the lawsuits flying fast and furious, Hollywood couldn't help but notice the renewed notoriety of Jean Harlow. Always on the lookout to make the fast buck, they quickly leapt into the fray.

4

The Harlow Sweepstakes

By the summer of 1964, four major motion picture studios (20th Century–Fox, MGM, Columbia, and Paramount) and one independent producer announced that they were in preproduction on movies about the legendary Jean Harlow, the hottest property in Hollywood due to the success and notoriety of Irving Shulman's biography. All were jockeying for publicity to help move their projects along.

First out of the gate in late August was 20th Century–Fox—naturally. Producer Aaron Rosenberg proclaimed that the studio was dusting off Adela Rogers St. Johns' screenplay and rushing *The Jean Harlow Story* into production. The writer was ecstatic when she learned of the news because, as a friend of the late movie star, she thought Shulman's book was an atrocity and made sure everyone knew it. She felt her script was a truer portrait of Harlow's life and career despite the bashing it got by Arthur Miller and Marilyn Monroe almost ten years earlier.

Stella Stevens was unfortunately now out of contention for Fox's film, because she was under contract to Paramount. Kim Novak was back in the running, along with sophisticated Angie Dickinson, who had made a splash in *Rio Bravo* (1959) and *Ocean's Eleven* (1960). The most ridiculous contender was Hollywood's newest Euro sexpot, Elke Sommer, who won kudos for her co-starring role opposite Paul Newman in *The Prize* (1963) and Peter Sellers (as Inspector Clouseau) in *A Shot in the Dark* (1964). How they were going to explain a Jean Harlow with German accent is anyone's guess. The world, luckily, will never know.

MGM, Harlow's studio, also cryptically announced their movie version about the private life of the blonde bombshell. Hinting only that an unnamed, prominent actress had been approached to play the glamorous movie star, they released no other details. This idea was quickly abandoned (possibly due to the competition from the other studios) in favor of a 90-minute documentary on the actress to be produced by MGM executive Ralph Wheelwright. It was to include excerpts from her movies and newsreel footage of the actress at various functions, plus on-camera interviews with friends and co-workers.

The persistent Sidney Skolsky was able to get Columbia Pictures interested in his screen treatment and the studio was very keen to proceed. Sir Carol Reed (whose previous credits included *The Third Man* and *Our Man in Havana*) was slated to direct. With Monroe dead, none of her successors (such as Jayne Mansfield or Mamie Van Doren) were considered for the role. By 1962, the big-busted platinum blonde had become a caricature and these actresses, who continued posing for *Playboy* and appearing in sexploitation movies with titles such as *Promises! Promises!* and *Three Nuts in Search of a Bolt*, were not taken seriously. Instead, the studio wanted Carroll Baker, whose name had come up for the part a few times over the years.

* * *

Carroll Baker was born in Johnstown, Pennsylvania. As a teenager she danced in high school productions and then failed her tryout for the Pittsburgh Civic Ballet, but her dancing was good enough to land her chorus girl work. She was also a magician billed as Carroll Carroll, her shtick being to do a reverse striptease, plucking an evening gown from a plastic box. She moved to New York and began appearing in commercials after being hired and then fired as a weather girl. After a sojourn to Hollywood, she landed a bit role in the Esther Williams' comedy *Easy to Love* (1953). With no more film offers and her quickie marriage (to a man named Louie Ritter) at an end, she took a job with Russ Morgan's band, which brought her back to New York where she auditioned for Lee Strasberg at the Actors Studio. She stayed two years before returning to Hollywood with husband number two, director Jack Garfein, in tow and snagged a contract at Warner Bros., beginning with a featured role in George Stevens' Academy Award-winning epic *Giant* (1956) starring Rock Hudson, Elizabeth Taylor, and James Dean.

However, it was the sex-filled *Baby Doll* (1956), based on an original screenplay by Tennessee Williams, that made her a star. Baker, in a role intended for Marilyn Monroe, was simply scintillating as Baby Doll Meighan, the childish nineteen-year-old bride of much older Archie Lee (Karl Malden), a cotton gin owner. Baby Doll sleeps scantily clad in a crib-like bed and sucks her thumb, driving her husband into a sexual frenzy. Though they are married, he can't lay a hand on her until she is "marriage ready," as he vowed to her father. A newly arrived competitor, Silva Vacarro (Eli Wallach), forces Archie out of business and in a fit of desperation Baby Doll's husband burns down Vacarro's cotton gin. Vowing revenge, the tempestuous Sicilian focuses his charms on Baby Doll, hoping to seduce the nymphet and get her to confess Archie's crime.

Recalling the shooting of her evocative scenes in *Baby Doll*, Baker confessed, "In my efforts to be real…. I worked myself into a combustible, near-volcanic state of desire—so much so that it wasn't all released on celluloid. I was still smoldering after the 'takes,' so that if anyone inadvertently touched me it was difficult to suppress a moan."[1]

An overnight sensation, Baker won raves from the critics with her natural ease in the part culminating with a Golden Globe Award for Most Promising Newcomer—Female, an Academy Award nomination for Best Actress, and a BAFTA Award nomination for Best Foreign Actress. The role, however, had its downside. Baker bemoaned, "That part caused so much hoopla that I couldn't walk around without people treating me as if I were Baby Doll. I wanted to be thought of as an actress who created the part, not as a weird character who portrayed herself on the screen. I could have made a whole career posing in Baby Doll pajamas and sucking my thumb."[2]

Warner Bros. also only wanted her to play the seductive nymphet, but the newcomer stood up to the studio heads and refused. Since she turned down roles in *God's Little Acre,* as the sexy farm nymph Griselda (Tina Louise got the part and a Golden Globe Award) and *Too Much, Too Soon,* as alcoholic actress Diana Barrymore (Dorothy Malone stepped in), the studio would not lend her out for *The Three Faces of Eve* (Joanne Woodward took the part and won an Oscar) or *Cat on a Hot Tin Roof* (Elizabeth Taylor steamed up the screen instead).

With Baker holding steadfast to her convictions and abandoning her sex kitten persona, she opened the door to a new batch of Baby Dolls—Sandra Dee, Tuesday Weld, Yvette Mimieux, Carol Lynley, Connie Stevens, Diane McBain, and Sue Lyon. They ruled Hollywood from 1959 (the year the Barbie Doll was first released, with many feeling the doll was modeled on the character) to 1964. They were the "It" girls of the time, especially with younger audiences as they were usually cast as the virginal teenager, the knocked up good girl, or the innocent looking nymphet who could be naughty or nice in glossy overwrought melodramas or romantic comedies such as: *The Restless Years, Because They're Young, A Summer Place, Where the Boys Are, Parrish, Claudelle Inglish, Return to Peyton Place, Susan Slade, Palm Springs Weekend, Diamond Head, The Pleasure Seekers,* and *That Funny Feeling.*

As the studios were now focused on creating their own imitation Baby Dolls, Baker was able to buy her way out of her contract for a reportedly whopping $250,000. On the big screen, she was part of an all-star cast in the western *The Big Country* (1958), playing the spoiled, shallow daughter of land baron Charles Bickford. Her other movies from this time period were romances with mismatched lovers. In the comedy *But Not for Me* (1958) Baker played a secretary smitten with her boss, Clark Gable, a much older Broadway producer. For *The Miracle* (1959) she dyed her hair black to essay the role of a postulant nun fighting her attraction to British soldier Roger Moore. Neither film was a box office hit.

Dejected over the path her career was taking,

Publicity photograph of Carroll Baker from *The Carpetbaggers* (Paramount, 1964).

Baker returned to New York and joined the Actors Studio. She remarked, "I really didn't know how to handle it. So I ran away from everything and hid."[3] An overseas trip to Rome brought Baker out of her depression when she reluctantly posed in a bikini for an Italian photographer and became the sensation of the Continent.

A new, more provocative and secure Carroll Baker returned to films in 1961. She smoldered on screen playing a haunted, suicidal rape victim saved by lonely mechanic Ralph Meeker, who takes her home and becomes her jailer, in the controversial *Something Wild* (1961) and as a sexy blonde who vamps the men at an isolated desert oil drill station in *Station Six-Sahara* (1962). In between, she played a demure Southern girl who impetuously marries Japanese diplomat James Shigeta and relocates to his home country after World War II breaks out in *Bridge to the Sun*. None of these films were hits, so Baker then joined the all-star cast in the epic Cinerama western *How the West Was Won* (1963), playing a strong-minded pioneer woman. It was the highest grossing movie of the year and picked up three Academy Awards including Best Story and Screenplay—Written Directly for the Screen. Still, Carroll was not happy about the roles she was being offered. "I'm interested in playing the modern woman. They have become so liberated they've given way to all sorts of passions and desires. It's an interesting character to play."[4]

A year later Baker got the dramatic part she craved after she was introduced to producer Joe Levine at the Queen of the Ball gala charity event at New York's Plaza Hotel. Wearing a strapless evening gown with her cleavage on display, the glamorous Baker dazzled the producer and by evening's end he had decided that she would be starring as the sexy Rina Marlowe in *The Carpetbaggers* (1964), which was based on Harold Robbins' sexsational, bestselling novel. Per Baker, Levine had seen her before on stage in *Come on Strong*. She said, "This play, with Van Johnson, had great reviews, but it only lasted a few weeks. A Boston reviewer wrote, 'Never since Jeanne Eagles walked the boards of the American stage has there been such a combination of beauty and talent.'"[5]

Baker's big screen co-stars were to be George Peppard, as the cold-hearted, Howard Hughes–like tycoon Jonas Cord, and Alan Ladd, as his mentor and cowboy-turned movie star Nevada Smith. Baker admitted that when she read the novel, she did not see the character of Rina as a part she would care to play. After it was offered to her, she had a change of heart because "I considered the fact this would be one of the most important movies to come out of Hollywood this year."[6]

Before *The Carpetbaggers* was even released, the buzz surrounding Baker and the movie was so great that it landed her on the cover of the November 1963 edition of the *Saturday Evening Post*. She was a spitting image of Jean Harlow right down to her honey-blonde hair dyed platinum, the thin, arch-shaped eyebrows, and draped in a white fur coat over a white satin dress. It was a promising start—or was it?

DARRELL ROONEY: Carroll Baker had a lot more lead time and did these shoots with thirties makeup so there is a hope that the movie is going to look authentic to the period. The way she looked on the cover of the *Saturday Evening Post* was not what she looked like in the movie. My understanding is that when the film went into production, they decided the film could not look like the thirties because it would not appeal to the public. It had to have a sixties reflection. Carroll lost that battle.

Obviously, the role of blonde sexpot Rina was a test run for Baker as the character was very loosely based on Jean Harlow. In a story set in the twenties, Rina is Cord's former flame now married to his rich daddy. After her husband dies suddenly, she dons a sexy black negligee, which she calls her "widow's weeds," and puts the sexual moves on the vengeful Jonas, who rejects her. The rest of the movie shows the tug of war between them as their love-hate-love relationship rules their personal lives. The comparison to Jean Harlow comes into play when Nevada Smith, now a major star in silent film westerns, needs Jonas to save his self-produced western epic that has been shelved by the studio due to the advent of talkies. Jonas does but takes complete control, investing in a talkie remake with Rina as the new leading lady, replacing the nasal-voiced actress originally cast. Beefing up her role, knowing she will become a star, he diminishes Nevada's part. Disgusted with Cord's callousness, Rina tries to break away from him, but their destructive, dysfunctional attraction leads them to bed, despite Rina's upcoming wedding to Nevada. Her new husband and stardom don't bring Rina any happiness and she only finds solace in the bottom of a liquor bottle. Speeding down the highway with the police on her tail, the drunken actress loses control and plunges off a cliff. She makes it to the hospital still alive but dies before Jonas can make it to her bedside.

Carroll Baker looked spectacular in her Edith Head-designed wardrobe and made quite the seductive vamp. Although the script gave her some ridiculous

Photographs comparing Jean Harlow to Carroll Baker as Harlow. The makeup and wig shown were scrapped when Paramount's *Harlow* began production.

dialogue, Baker was able to project the angst felt by Rina with regards to her warped attraction to the cruel Jonas. Between Baker's looks and performance, it was no wonder Joe Levine felt she would make a wonderful Harlow. Audiences loved Baker as well and she was a sensation partly due to her well-publicized, brief nude scene in which she emerges from her bath, walks into her dressing room, sits down with her back to the camera, and after hearing footsteps, calls to her maid for her robe. She is handed the white satin and feathers frock, but by George Peppard's lecherous Jonas. The scene was shot on a closed set with only director Edward Dmytryk and cameraman Joe MacDonald in attendance. It was Baker's idea to do the scene nude because she felt her amorous character was not the type to immediately reach for her robe while alone in her dressing room. Baker was proud of this segment and was dismayed that most of it was excised when the film was released in the States.

Although her scene was shot tastefully and American audiences only saw Baker's bare back, it created quite the controversy with old guard Hollywood led by Hedda Hopper and Louella Parsons. Even officials of the Screen Actors Guild came after Baker, charging that her willingness to appear nude "would lead to an epidemic of movie nudity and set back the social position of actresses a hundred years."[7] Baker defended her lovely self and said, "If a script calls for nudity, if it seems to be an inherent part of the character that I'm playing, then why shouldn't it be done that way?"[8] She was prophetic when she stated that she believed in the next ten years nudity would be the norm in American movies and that she personally felt that it would not injure the country's character.

Baker took her free spiritedness with regard to nudity one step further when she disrobed for the pages of *Playboy* in their December 1964 issue. Her pictorial titled "Baker in the Boudoir," featured the scintillating star provocatively posing in sexy lingerie and topless. A few years later, she commented in *Coronet* magazine, "I love posing in the nude. I even say, 'let's take some more'—if the pictures are beautiful and not vulgar. And to think—I was once insulted when a photographer asked me to pose in a bikini!" This was quite the attitude change for the actress. A few years prior, she had even dyed her hair black to escape being typecast in sexy nymphet roles, à la *Baby Doll*, which she loathed to play.

Carroll Baker's new on-screen persona did not go unnoticed by producers and she was in talks to appear in movies with producer/director George Stevens and was in talks to appear in movies from producer Martin Ransohoff, who was especially eager to work with her. He commented, "The movie going public still goes for glamour and sex. And Carroll has that in spades."[9]

Surprisingly, since Baker seemed to be reaching for the sex symbol crown recently vacated by Marilyn Monroe, she accepted the role of a Quaker schoolmarm in director John Ford's sprawling western *Cheyenne Autumn* co-starring Richard Widmark, Sal Mineo, and Dolores del Rio. Commenting on the disparity of her roles, her husband Jack Garfein opined, "Carroll is cast most successfully as a sinner or a saint. There's this thing about her—combination of purity and beauty and yet a corruption. Audiences get satisfaction out of seeing something pure being corrupted."[10]

While the public, especially the male kind, were enjoying Carroll Baker's new openness with regards to her body, her film performances were getting recognized in an unflattering way. *The Harvard Lampoon* voted her the Worst Actress of 1964 for *The Carpetbaggers* and *Cheyenne Autumn*. As most actors did when being "honored" by *The Harvard Lampoon*, she ignored it.

Determined to exploit Baker's success in *The Carpetbaggers* and build her up as Hollywood's newest sex symbol, Paramount signed Baker to a non-exclusive contract. Her first movie for them was *Sylvia* (1965) directed by Gordon Douglas. Baker portrayed a mysterious blonde with many personalities and aliases. Her millionaire husband (Peter Lawford) hires a handsome detective (George Maharis) to find out who Sylvia really is. The film was not a hit and Baker's reviews were along the lines of "her performance here is at least respectable as her role isn't."[11]

* * *

Carroll Baker readily agreed to play Jean Harlow for Columbia and was eager to work with director Sir Carol Reed. She wrote, "Sir Carol's enthusiasm and his brilliant concepts of re-creating the mood of the 1930s, especially that gung-ho slapstick quality of Jean's early movies, convinced me that he was the ideal man for the project."[12] Baker had already completed her first film for Paramount and to her knowledge had an oral agreement with studio head Jack Karp to make one movie outside of the studio before starting her second film. She felt very confident that she could play Jean Harlow for Columbia Pictures.

At the same time, the *Los Angeles Times* reported that artist and independent filmmaker, Gino Hollander, was rumored to be going forth with a movie about Jean Harlow to be titled *The Rise and Fall of a Star* with Abigail Shelton cast as the platinum bombshell. She was a blond beauty seen playing decorative roles on many TV shows during the late fifties and early sixties including *Peter Gunn, The Tab Hunter Show, Bonanza, The Donna Reed Show, Perry Mason,* and *The Fugitive*, etc. Her film appearances were scarce with her largest role being a "young old maid" in the comedy western *Mail Order Bride* (1964) starring Buddy Ebsen and Keir Dullea. Nothing seems to have ever happened with this proposed production.

The final entry into this box derby (and definitely not a rumor) was independent producer/exhibitor/distributor Joseph E. Levine, who revealed that he was in talks with Gordon Douglas to direct a movie about Jean Harlow for Paramount Pictures. The short (5'4"), heavyset producer quickly proved to the Hollywood community that he had a flair for picking properties with big box office appeal. One of the last of the movie moguls, in the showman mold of Louis B. Mayer and Sam Goldwyn, Levine was flamboyant, shrewd, and one of the most successful and powerful men in the film business. He usually didn't make the movies himself, relying on producers and other talent, but took responsibility in selling his pictures to the public with his unique flair through old-style ballyhoo, showmanship, imaginative promotion, and merchandising. In 1964, *Fortune* magazine dubbed his world "super colossal" and praised him for giving the movie industry "a much-needed lift."

* * *

After holding a series of jobs including clothes shop owner, dress salesman, drummer, and café owner, Joseph Edward Levine entered the movie business in 1938 as a movie exhibitor, buying a small arthouse in Connecticut. When foreign films began to become popular, he formed Embassy Pictures in 1956, registering the name for $153. He became extremely successful pairing similarly themed films with the same stars into double bills or just changing the title of a movie on the theater's marquee to get the audience to fill the seats. And fill them they did. He acquired the U.S. distribution rights to the Japanese horror movie *Godzilla* in 1956 and the Italian adventure film *Hercules*, starring former bodybuilder Steve Reeves, in 1958 for $125,000. Despite its shoddy color and cheap production values, Levine took a chance because "it had everything: muscle men, broads, and a shipwreck and a dragon for the kids."[13] He oversaw the exploitation of *Hercules* (which he called "a cornucopia of corn"), spending over $1 million on all types of publicity, and negotiating a deal with Warner Bros. to distribute the film. Saturating the market with over 1,000 prints (at the time the typical number of prints circulated was approximately 375 to 400) and an advertising budget of $1.5 million, *Hercules* went on to gross close to $5 million in the U.S. alone. Its success spurred a torrent of foreign-produced sword-and-sandal pictures (or "peplums," as they were called in Europe), usually with an American muscleman in the lead role. A number of them were big successes in the U.S., causing Levine to opine, "So I figure I did a little to hurt as well as help the Hollywood film industry. Because of me business was good and because of me business was bad."[14]

Levine's company then expanded rapidly into the distribution of more distinguished foreign movies and was responsible for bringing such acclaimed fare (some co-produced with Carlo Ponti) as *Two Women* (featuring Sophia Loren in her Academy Award-winning performance—the first for an actor in a foreign-language film), *Divorce, Italian Style*, *Boccaccio '70*, *8 ½*, and *Yesterday, Today, Tomorrow* to arthouses across the country. Due to his marketing savvy, all the films turned a profit. An unidentified publicity agent at a competing studio remarked, "Joe's a master at exploitation. He'll spend a lot of money to get his movies in the papers and whether you like him or not, he's a dynamic, exploitation-minded guy."[15] His success also spurred a number of critics who complained that the producer had no heart for filmmaking but was only in it to make a fast buck and was just lucky in his choices.

One example of Joe Levine's outrageous exploitation ideas was when he held a luncheon for exhibitors to promote *Jack the Ripper* (1959), a movie Embassy had picked up for distribution. Knowing that just telling the room full of jaded theater owners in Boston that Embassy was going to invest $1 million in advertising would not be enough to get guests to lift their heads from their free plates of food, Levine got city banks to "rent" him the cash. With armed guards surrounding the money, he not only got their attention, but made all the newspapers as well, generating much free publicity for the movie. Despite the hoopla, it was one of Levine's rare failures, as was *Long Day's Journey into Night* (1962) starring Jason Robards, Jr., and Katharine Hepburn. Although director Sidney Lumet called the producer "a vulgar vulgarian," he nonetheless respected his devotion to the movie and remarked, "I ended up having a real affection for him—he really stuck by the film when it was doing no business."[16]

Joseph E. Levine is congratulated by Natalie Wood and Dana Wynter after accepting three Golden Globe Awards at the Hollywood Foreign Press Association's ceremony in 1965 (Billy Rose Theatre Division, The New York Public Library for the Performing Arts).

Levine stayed committed to *Long Day's Journey into Night* because he thought it was "…superb. This was the artiest of the art." However, he went on to say, "This was a big, big flop. When you have a dead art film there's nothing deader than that."[17]

After conquering distribution (his New York office went from four people including himself and his wife to 106 employees in just under five years), the final step for Joe Levine was to go into moviemaking. He signed a long-term, twenty-three picture production deal with Paramount Pictures in July 1963. Even though speculation was that the two organizations would merge, the savvy Levine kept his own sales organization, precluding any exclusive tie to Paramount, while making Embassy Paramount's largest film supplier. According to the terms of the contract,

Embassy would receive a producer's fee for each movie and would split the profits equally with Paramount after they recouped their expenses. For certain films, Embassy would retain domestic distribution rights with Paramount distributing most films worldwide. Commenting on why he kept Embassy independent from Paramount, Levine candidly said, "They're too big for me to swallow, even with my big belly. They'd swallow me. It would frighten me. I like complete autonomy to do what I like, which I know is impossible to do with a public company."[18]

Their first joint motion picture was the historical epic *Zulu* (1964), whose posters exclaimed, "Dwarfing the Mightiest! Towering over the Greatest!" This was followed by *The Carpetbaggers* (1964), a fictitious look at the life of Howard Hughes adapted from the bestseller by Harold Robbins. Levine bought the rights to the book for $300,000 and then paid screenwriter John Michael Hayes $125,000 to deliver a "cleaned-up" script. He brought the package to Paramount. The film was allocated a $3.3 million budget while Levine was paid $250,000 as producer and promoter. Discussing his arrangement with the studio, Levine explained, "There are different schools of thought on what a producer is. If you are a working producer, which we are not, you're on the set every day tending to the business of the picture. Here Paramount is really doing the production, although I'm listed as producer and it's presented by me."[19]

The Carpetbaggers had all the ingredients that Levine was looking for in a property—sex, action, and relatable characters. The film's director, Edward Dmytryk, liked working with Joe Levine a lot because he did not interfere on the set and was only focused on the financial aspects of the production. Dmytryk commented, "[Levine] made it a point, more than once, to let me know that he was only interested in the picture's sales values and the creative end was entirely in my hands. He's a good producer in that he gives a director complete freedom and autonomy and I must say I've never enjoyed directing more."[20]

With sales of over 5 million copies of Robbins' novel, *The Carpetbaggers* came "pre-sold." With its all-star cast and marketing push orchestrated by Levine, who shamelessly felt that you could fool people if the advertising is right, the movie could not help but succeed. Taking in $14.5 million at the box office, it was the second highest grossing motion picture of 1964, behind *It's a Mad, Mad, Mad, Mad World*.

Keeping with exploitative-themed movies, he quickly followed up with *A House Is Not a Home* (1964) starring Shelley Winters as notorious thirties madam Polly Adler and *Where Love Has Gone* (1964) starring Susan Hayward as a famous artist whose teenage daughter (Joey Heatherton) stabs her lover to death. The latter was loosely based on the real-life Lana Turner/Johnny Stompanato/Cheryl Crane murder scandal that had taken place a few years prior. To give his movies an edge, Levine was known for previewing them at his New York City office, which contained a posh screening room in Greco-Roman décor, seating up to forty people comfortably. Cocktails and food were always served afterwards in the reception area next door. Lucky VIPs were then treated to a cruise on the mogul's 96-foot yacht anchored in the East River.

* * *

Trying to trump the other studios, even though his official announcement about his Jean Harlow movie trailed theirs, Joe Levine stated that his plans to bring the movie star's life story to the silver screen dated back over a year—even before production began on *The Carpetbaggers*. At that time, Embassy and Paramount had begun researching Harlow's life. He also claimed that the idea to cast Carroll Baker hit him after photographer Philippe Halsman shot portraits of the actress, including one that appeared on the cover of the *Saturday Evening Post*, which so resembled Jean Harlow that Baker became his only choice to play her on screen.

With four major studios now vying to be the first to go into production with a film about Jean Harlow, the publisher of Irving Shulman's bio put the screen rights up for sale at $400,000. Levine purchased the rights to *Harlow, An Intimate Biography* for a reported fee of $100,000. He explained that he bought the rights for two reasons. First was for the title, since the book had been on the bestseller list for a long period and was well known to the public. Second was because the book was only going to be used as research into the star's life. He explained: "The legend of Jean Harlow has survived more than thirty years…. We are exploring every facet of this legend through intensive and exhaustive research wherever that legend leads us. We will present Harlow as truthfully and honestly as she lived her own complex life."[21] If only this held true, considering the fairy tale that Levine eventually hoisted onto the big screen.

With the bestseller in his pocket, the determined producer set out to make sure Carroll Baker starred in his production. When he heard that she had verbally committed to Columbia Pictures' Harlow biopic, Levine raised bloody hell with Paramount's executives in New York, claiming that they all knew in advance that he had purchased the rights to the Harlow biography with only Carroll Baker in mind for the lead. Unfortunately for the actress, Jack Karp had been recently removed as head of the studio and their oral agreement, allowing her to work at Columbia, was not recognized. She was told that her agent had to put in writing her request to do a movie for any other studio. In the meantime, Paramount expected her to honor her contract and intended her next project to be Levine's movie about Jean Harlow. Baker was furious and vented, "I felt double-crossed and miserable about losing the rare opportunity to work with Sir Carol Reed. I felt outraged by the injustice: had they shuffled out an honorable man like Karp, just to pull a fast one? I stormed around the house, but there seemed nothing I could do about it."[22]

During the time that Carroll Baker was hesitating about playing Jean Harlow for producer Joe Levine, another Carol, aspiring, blonde starlet Carol Hollenbeck, whose stage name was Carol Holland, revealed to her manager that she felt a strong connection to Jean Harlow. This gave him an idea.

CAROL HOLLENBECK: My manager was getting me loads of press in Hollywood. I was getting into the papers as Miss Moulin Rouge appearing here and Miss That appearing there. It was unbelievable and so fantastic. Besides that, I was a fan of Jean Harlow and had many psychics tell me I was her reincarnated. I researched her—especially after I read that they were doing a movie on her. I became a student of Jean Harlow and studied anything about her that I could get my hands on. My manager encouraged me because he felt that I may have had a good chance to play her. No matter how slimy Hollywood was when I was there—it was a cesspool with people being passed around—I just love the Golden Age of Hollywood. Now, I should feel terrible about all that stuff that happened to me and other young girls, but when that Hollywood sign comes on, I melt—it is so addictive to me.

Regis Philbin had a talk show that he took over from Steve Allen. My manager got a call from Regis to send me over to the show because they wanted to keep me on hold in case Carroll Baker did not sign for the Jean Harlow film. If so, they wanted me to go on that night looking like Harlow. That was a disappointment. I was rushed over to the show. I sat with Regis. They had a white outfit ready for me to wear on the show if it worked out. He told me, "Be dressed and ready to go on tonight." Then a phone call came in saying that Joe Levine had signed Carroll Baker. That was it and I did not go on.

Publicity photograph of actress Carol Hollenbeck, then known as Carol Holland, ca. 1964 (courtesy Carol Hollenbeck).

Baker's then-husband, Jack Garfein, was the one who convinced his wife to sign on with Levine. He acted as her manager and made Baker's unhappiness with the turn of events quite clear to Levine and Paramount. To appease the actress, Joe Levine gifted her with a platinum necklace studded with shimmering blue-white diamonds. Baker confessed that she was "ashamed to admit that I did enjoy holding it to the light and marveling at the beauty of those brilliant sparkling gems. I also hated myself for being so dazzled by it; for trading my self-esteem for a bauble; and, ultimately, for propagating the myth that a woman could indeed be bought."[23]

By accepting the peace offering, Baker stopped bad mouthing the studio and agreed to star in the movie. Levine proudly announced to the press that "Jean Harlow presents a tailor-made subject for Carroll Baker's fiery talents and is the logical successor to her role of Rina in *The Carpetbaggers*, the biggest grossing non-road show film in history."[24] Despite the praise for his star, all of Hollywood knew of the extravagant necklace Baker was given and gossip mongers had a field day speculating as to whether she was now the producer's mistress, which she was not. Despite his bravado in business, Levine was not a womanizer (unlike other powerful studio men of the time, such as Darryl Zanuck and Harry Cohn) and remained true to his wife of many years, Rosalie.

It was reported that to make Baker's decision to play Harlow official, Levine hosted a press conference at the Beverly Hills Hotel. With much fanfare, Levine announced, "This is my star," and a curtain slowly opened revealing Carroll Baker, whom Peter Bart described as being "seated in a sleek, yellow Isotta Fraschini [an Italian luxury car manufacturer] and wearing a Harlow-like costume."[25] Levine also officially announced that Gordon Douglas would direct the film.

Interestingly enough, Stella Stevens had been working at Paramount since 1959 and was interested in playing Jean Harlow. Reportedly, she was so disappointed at being passed over that she obtained an early release from her contract and jumped to Columbia Pictures. Stella would have been an excellent choice for the role. She was more than curvaceous enough and exuded sex appeal—a requirement for the part. She also had the proven dramatic chops, as evidenced by her turns as a voracious alcoholic in *Man-Trap* (1961) and as a singer who comes between jazz musician Bobby Darin and his band members in *Too Late Blues* (1962).

Stevens was very pragmatic about losing out on playing Jean Harlow yet again and remarked, "At the time, the publicity helped to get me started in Hollywood. It didn't break me up too much when the movie was cancelled. And I honestly do not feel any disappointment or bitterness because I was overlooked when someone finally did get around to doing the Harlow story. It's just part of the game."[26]

Since Joe Levine now had the rights to Shulman's biography, and a director and star were in place, Paramount was way ahead of the competition in getting their movie into production. Soon after, MGM dropped their plans to make their Jean Harlow documentary film.

Fox was still in the running and an unnamed executive remarked, "We have nothing to worry about. We don't care that Levine will start his movie next month. We'll still beat him to the screen."[27] A starting date of October 15, 1964, was announced, though no actress had yet been cast as Harlow. Reportedly, the studio was in talks with Kim Novak. Columnist Sheila Graham speculated that actress Terry Moore (whose films included *Mighty Joe Young*, *Come Back, Little Sheba*, and *Peyton Place*) was angling for the role, since she was determined to shake her eternal ingénue image. She even dyed her brown hair a silver-platinum, perhaps to prove she looked the part. Graham mentioned that Elke Sommer still had a shot for the part and she felt Jayne Mansfield would be suitable for the role if "she would trim some of her fore and aft. Jayne could use a good role. And she is a better actress than what we give her credit for."[28]

Another contender being pushed by her agent was Pamela Curran. The thirty-three-year-old, statuesque blonde had many television appearances under her belt and had a small role in the hit comedy *Under the Yum Yum Tree* (1963) with Jack Lemmon and Carol Lynley.

Columbia Pictures had ceased their production plans shortly after losing leading lady Carroll Baker to Paramount, but then had a change of heart and re-entered the race. Sidney Skolsky was still scheduled to produce and Marguerite Roberts was hired as screenwriter.

4. The Harlow Sweepstakes

There was one late entry in the Harlow sweepstakes, though at the time none of the major studios paid it any mind. Just days before Levine purchased the rights to Shulman's biography, producer Bill Sargent declared that he was moving ahead with a movie about Jean Harlow for his company Electronovision, Inc. It was to star an unnamed newcomer and he promised that his version would stay clear of the sensationalistic aspects of Shulman's biography. He remarked, "We want to show Miss Harlow as Miss Harlow the public was in love with."[29] Vowing that his version would be perfect family viewing, Sargent boasted, "I intend to take my children to see it, that's how good and clean it's going to be."[30]

* * *

Bill Sargent, only thirty-seven years old at the time and once described as "a heavy-jowled, curly red-haired fighting Irishman" and "red-haired, rotund and rambunctious," was taking a big gamble going ahead with filming *Harlow* in Electronovision because the first two attempts were not technical successes. Sargent was an electronics expert from the time he was a child when he ran a radio repair shop from his family's garage. He held patents on tape heads, secondary heads and distribution amplifiers for CATV systems; on a single channel sound system for movie theaters; and on 20 individual parts of electronic cameras. Sargent had his first major financial success installing public address systems in schools and hotels. From 1954 to 1960 he headed up Electronic Industries, Inc., specializing in the installation of commercial sound and antenna systems and the manufacturing of electronic equipment. It was during this period that he developed the first commercially viable pay–TV system. Sargent considered himself a concept man who didn't compete. Instead, he claimed that he came up with ideas to put his competitors out of business.

In 1961, as Executive Vice President of the Home Entertainment Company of America, Sargent presented a pay–TV event—a closed-circuit boxing match between Cassius Clay and George Logan that was shown in movie theaters around the country. His system was soon expanded to homeowners when he sold it for $973,000 (making a nice profit) to Subscription Television, Inc., which had close to 20,000 subscribers in the Santa Monica, California, area. Soon after, he formed Electronovision, Inc.

The Electronovision process was like shooting a live TV show or stage production, as it did not need the extra illumination that normal movie lights provided and could operate with only available light. It employed multiple electronic cameras (resembling television cameras), sometimes up to fifteen, which were similar to television cameras in that they shot a scene continuously, getting all the angles simultaneously and in sequence, then transmitted them electronically to a monitoring board where the director was positioned to select the best angle on the spot. This eliminated not only retakes, shooting the same scene over and over from different angles, but also the wait in viewing daily rushes for selection. The chosen shots were then transferred by cable to a mobile station for recording on a modified motion picture camera. Kinescope tape was used then transferred in the film laboratory to 35 mm prints. In contrast, most motion pictures are filmed using one camera, which shoots a scene a number of times at different angles to obtain a smooth continuous production. The film is then "edited and spliced, necessitating weeks of or months of post-production, involving dubbing, sound and special effects work after the shooting has been completed." While shooting in Electronovision was just as costly as the ordinary filmmaking method, it was infinitely quicker.

The Broadway stage production of *Hamlet*, starring Richard Burton and directed by Sir John Gielgud, was the first production chosen to be shot in Electronovision. Their concept for this stage revival was to perform it in casual dress. "A startling idea at the time," opined Tony Award-winning co-star Hume Cronyn, "but it wasn't fully thought through. If you have a guy in sneakers and jeans also wearing a sword belt, his get-up becomes as distracting as the most elaborate costume."[31] The play opened at the Lunt-Fontanne Theater on April 9, 1964. Even though they were charging the highest ticket prices at the time it still had a large advance sale. Reviews were mixed, but it ran for 138 performances.

While the play's producer Alexander Cohen was mulling various film and broadcast offers, Sargent swayed him and Burton to permit a live performance filmed in Electronovision, arguing for the cost savings with Warner Bros. distributing. With the promise of 75 percent of the studio's 70 percent of the box office receipts to be split evenly amongst Cohen, Burton's company Atlantic Programmes Ltd. (the actor purportedly negotiated a percentage of all future films released in Electronovision as well), and Sargent with the agreement that after its initial run all prints would be destroyed, it was an offer Cohen and Burton couldn't turn down.

William Colleran, formerly of *The Judy Garland Show,* was hired to direct and a budget of $1.1 million was allocated for production, prints, and exploitation. Due to AFTRA and Actors Equity rules, Colleran had only two nighttime performances and one matinee to capture the play on tape. Two of those tapings were only to secure "protection footage and backstage shots."[32] Essentially, Colleran only had one performance to get it right.

Five cameras were used and Colleran edited as he shot, under extreme pressure from Bill Sargent to get the film completed in time for its theatrical distribution

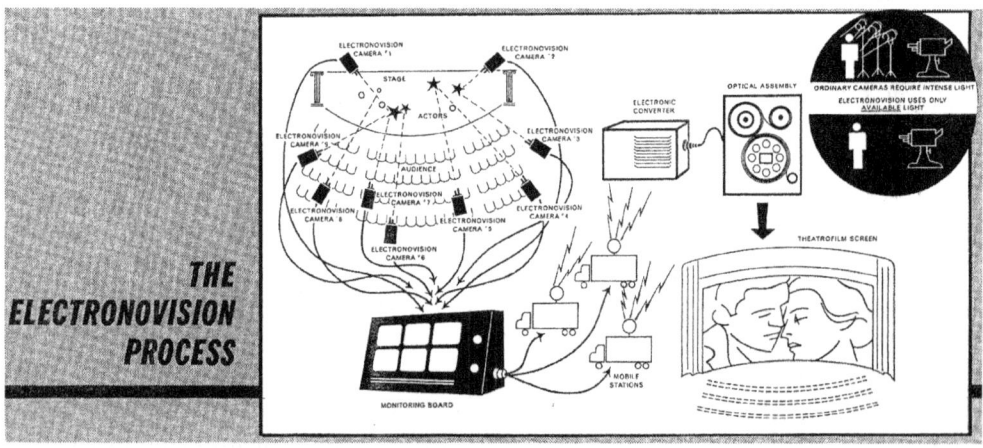

Diagram explaining the Electronovision filming process (Billy Rose Theatre Division, The New York Public Library for the Performing Arts).

deadline. Praising the Electronovision process that eliminated special lighting and the conventional techniques in shooting close-ups, and long and medium shots, the director raved, "This new process will totally eliminate the necessity of waiting for dailies. Since the process involves the simultaneous exposure on tape as well as ordinary motion picture film, the director can immediately see what is on film, and if necessary, re-shoot immediately."[33] Years later Sargent remarked, "Bill Colleran did a good job, after we beat the shit out of him!"[34]

Bill Sargent was so confident in this Electronovision production of *Hamlet* that he predicted the film would gross $6.5 million, despite allowing only four screenings in two days (and then withdrawing the print from distribution). *Hamlet* opened nationwide on September 23, 1964, in more than 1,000 theaters ("the largest print order in motion picture history," boasted Sargent[35]) with ticket prices at $1.50 for matinees and $2.50 for evening showings. At the time, the average ticket price was a little less than one dollar. The higher price was justified due to the film's very limited run. Despite the critics' jeers regarding the film's gaffes, including audience members' heads popping into the frames; audio glitches in some spots owing to Burton's distorted line delivery; lack of close-ups; and the flat, grainy, sometimes dark look (due to a lab error where a portion of the film was placed in a wrong bath), moviegoers still made *Hamlet* the 23rd highest grossing picture of 1964 with a box office take of $3.1 million. It was less than half of Sargent's prediction and the disappointed producer blamed Warner Bros. for not touting the movie enough as "an event." However, it was still a very respectable gross and reportedly set a record for the highest gross over a two-day period. Ultimately, the movie turned a profit (thanks to the inexpensive shooting in Electronovision) as sophisticated moviegoers flocked to it to get their chance to see the esteemed Richard Burton play Hamlet in his theatrical triumph. As he was contractually bound, Sargent withdrew the movie from theaters after two days. All prints, save for a very few deposited with with colleges, were destroyed—but were they?

Despite its first success, Electronovision, Inc. went though some growing pains. It lost its executive vice-president (whose settlement included $100,000) and its first film as collateral while dealing with unhappy shareholders suspecting stock fraud. The company also lost Warner Bros. as its distributor. It was planning on shooting *Who's Afraid of Virginia Woolf?* in Electronovision, but *Hamlet*'s disappointing production values discouraged the studio to continue.

Bill Sargent chose to shoot a rock concert called *The T.A.M.I. Show* as the next Electronovision production. At the time this was a novel idea. Since the mid-fifties, rock 'n' roll performers were getting top billing in such films as *Rock Around the Clock* (1956), *Don't Knock the Rock* (1957), *Twist Around the Clock* (1961), *Get Yourself a College Girl* (1964), etc. These movies all had actors and a plot with the rock acts providing musical interludes. *The T.A.M.I. Show* was determined to give teenagers what they really wanted—uninterrupted music. With a $1.4 million budget, it was shot live at the Santa Monica Civic Auditorium in front of an estimated 2,700 screaming teenagers, most of them girls. T.A.M.I. stood for Teen-Age Music Awards International, a proposed international, nonprofit foundation that was supposed to produce a series of yearly concerts and televised award ceremonies to benefit music students with scholarships. None of this, except for the initial concert, ever took place.

Popular singing duo Jan and Dean, who topped the charts in 1963 with their huge hit "Surf City," were tapped to host *The T.A.M.I. Show*. Directed by Steve Binder, they snuck in a few songs including "The Little Old Lady from Pasadena" and "Sidewalk Surfin'." The eclectic array of rock acts assembled to perform came from the music worlds of R&B, Motown, surf music, the British Invasion, garage rock, and girl groups backed up by a session band that included Glen Campbell on guitar, Leon Russell on piano, Hal Blaine on drums, Jack Nitzsche on electric piano, and backup singers Darlene Love, Fanita James, and Jean King. Choreographer David Winters' team of go-go dancers included Teri Garr, Anita Mann, Carlton Johnson, and Suzie Kaye.

Bill Sargent, ca. 1975 (Billy Rose Theatre Division, The New York Public Library for the Performing Arts).

The concert opens with Chuck Berry and Liverpool rockers Gerry and the Pacemakers. They take turns performing and the crowd goes wild when Berry sings "Sweet Little Sixteen." The Pacemakers match him with their hit "How Do You Do It?" They are followed on stage by Lesley Gore, singing some of her most popular tunes including "You Don't Own Me," before giving way to the number one Girl Group at the time, The Supremes. Close-ups of Diana Ross singing "Baby Love" and "Where Did Our Love Go" are truly something to behold. They are followed by the British band Billy J. Kramer and the Dakotas, garage band The Barbarians, the Beach Boys (who rock on "Surfin' U.S.A." and "I Get Around," amongst other songs), Smokey Robinson & the Miracles, and Marvin Gaye. The fabulous James Brown & the Famous Flames is the second to last act to perform and they tear the house down with three songs including "Please Please Please." The closing act is the incomparable Rolling Stones who had not yet hit it big in the U.S. Still, they drive the audience into a near frenzy, singing such songs as "Time Is on My Side" and "It's All Right," closing the show on a high note.

Lee Savin did well as producer of *The T.A.M.I. Show* and Sargent hired him in the same capacity for *Harlow*. Steve Binder skillfully directed, overcoming some of the shortcomings of the previous Electronovision production, such as lack of close-ups, by distributing the cameras in such a way as to ensure they captured a variety of angles. He successfully conveyed the excitement of a live concert, including at times the screams and cheers from the audience (including AIP Beach Party regular Mary Hughes) sporadically drowning out some of the performers. The film was also helped by the improvement Bill Sargent brought to the video signal, resulting in a superior, sharper image than was the case with *Hamlet*.

To sell *The T.A.M.I. Show*, Sargent booked his film into thirty-three select theaters in Southern California for a single test-day screening. It grossed $32,000, impressing exhibitors so much that many booked the concert film for a Christmas release. Once again, he cautioned moviegoers that they would only have this one-time opportunity to see the film because after its initial run it would be pulled from circulation forever. However, with Sargent needing funds, he sold first a portion and then his entire stake in the film to Screen Entertainment Company with the stipulation that *The T.A.M.I. Show* had to be billed as an "Electronovision Film." They in turn sold the distribution rights outright to American International Pictures. The movie went on to outgross their then-biggest hit, *Beach Party*.

Critics were kinder to the technical facets of *The T.A.M.I. Show* than they were with *Hamlet*, as the improvements in the quality of the Electronovision filming process were noted and applauded. This may have given Sargent the extra nudge he needed to attempt a full-blown original motion picture and he voiced his enthusiasm to take on the major film distributors.

The T.A.M.I. Show did show up again years later on VHS, but excluded the entire set performed by The Beach Boys, whose manager demanded that they be excised from all prints when he learned that Richard Burton was able to pull *Hamlet* from circulation. In 2010, it was finally released on DVD with the restored Beach Boys footage (obviously they were not deleted from every existing print, just as not every print of *Hamlet* was destroyed) as well as many other deleted segments.

Sargent next wanted to film the stage musical *High Spirits*, a musical version of Noël Coward's *Blithe Spirit*, starring Beatrice Lillie and Tammy Grimes. Salaries were agreed upon by the cast. The actors' union, however, sank the production by demanding that scale performers be paid nine times the weekly minimum rather than double, which is what Electronovision was offering. Not able to meet their demands, Sargent cancelled his plans. He also vigorously pursued the rights to film Sir Laurence Olivier's stage production of *Othello*, but that too never came to pass.

An attention-grabbing publicity stunt (courtesy Carol Hollenbeck).

Despite these setbacks, Hollywood was still interested in Electronovision. Bill Sargent held no patent on it and freely shared the intricacies with the public. However, it was noted that the studios allocated large sums of money for some of their top technicians to figure out the Electronovision process, to Sargent's bemusement. He remarked, "But all they have to do is pick up a phone and ask us about it. We would tell them. In fact, we'll even let them use our equipment."[36] He then went on to elaborate that his company was still perfecting the process and promised that in a matter of three months Electronovision's film quality would surpass the studios.

Sargent promised that filming of his Harlow biopic would commence on December 10, 1964, with a shooting schedule of ten days. He then added that his movie would be theatrically distributed in January with one performance a day on Mondays and Tuesdays for four consecutive weeks, keeping it along the lines of an "event" as with *Hamlet* and *The T.A.M.I. Show*.

* * *

It is quite surprising that four movie studios and one independent production company would scramble against each other to make a film about Jean Harlow, especially since Hollywood's track record with nonmusical movie biographies a few years prior to 1964 (*The Buster Keaton Story* starring Donald O'Connor as the comic in 1957, *Too Much, Too Soon* with Dorothy Malone as Diana Barrymore in 1958, and *The George Raft Story* with Ray Danton as the lead in 1960) was dismal to say the least. Only *Man of a Thousand Faces* (1957) starring James Cagney as screen legend Lon Chaney was considered a success both creatively and at the box office.

Two biopics closest to the *Harlow* films that, in particular, exploited deceased stars who had died young were the big budget, colorful *Valentino* (1951) starring newcomer Anthony Dexter as the matinee idol and the low-budget, black-and-white *Jeanne Eagels* (1957) starring Kim Novak as the troubled young actress. Both actors' eventful lives were ripe for storytelling. However, the highly publicized movies, both from Columbia Pictures, turned out to be critical and financial failures due to all the inaccuracies contained in their scripts.

Despite all of Columbia's attempts to avoid being sued, they were. *Valentino* was hit with two lawsuits—one from Valentino's brother and sister, who maintained the movie was unauthorized and that the film caused them "shame and humiliation." The other came from director Rex Ingram's wife, actress Alice Terry, who was part of the Joan Carlisle composite character. Both cases were settled out of court. *Jeanne Eagles* was mired in lawsuits (not surprising, considering the liberties the film took with the truth) as the actress' surviving family members sued for portraying the actress as depraved and immoral.

These not-so-long-ago movie bios did not deter the remaining studios from moving forward with their Jean Harlow projects, but they made them vigilant (especially Paramount Pictures) in terms of their screen portrayals of the actress and possible lawsuit threats from the still-living people from her life.

5

Let the Race Begin

The Jean Harlow sweepstakes became a case of David versus Goliath when Columbia Pictures and 20th Century–Fox, despite the latter's executives' bravado about taking on Joe Levine, dropped their plans to make their movies. It was reported that Paramount struck deals with both studios to cancel their Jean Harlow projects. The Fox agreement reportedly went one step further and forbade them to produce a biopic on any platinum blonde actress for at least another three years, most likely to keep the studio from doing a movie on the life of the recently deceased Marilyn Monroe, which Paramount would consider direct competition to its *Harlow*. It must have cost the studio a big penny to get this deal with Fox.

Although Joe Levine, in essence, was a novice in producing movies, he hit a home run on his second try with *The Carpetbaggers* and was considered a very formidable opponent. Considering how savvy he was with exploitation, and how expensive it would be to challenge him, the idea that these two studios took a payout to drop their planned films sounds totally plausible.

Bill Sargent, after his *Harlow* was released, admitted that his associate went to Paramount's then-studio head Howard Koch with Sargent's offer to cease his plans to make the movie for $22,000. The studio ignored the offer.[1] This too sounds credible since Electronovision had never produced a real theatrical movie before. Perhaps nobody at Paramount perceived it as a serious threat because they believed it would never get off the ground. In hindsight, they must have been kicking themselves, since they had a chance to make Sargent go away for such a small amount of money.

With two studios still in the game, Paramount allocated a budget of $4 million ($2.5 million for production and $1.5 million for promotion) for their *Harlow*, going up against Electronovision's "instant movie" (as some journalists dubbed it) which had a $1.5 million budget ($800,000 for production and $750,000 for promotion). It then quickly turned into one of the nastiest, dirtiest feuds that Hollywood had ever witnessed. Writers had a field day reporting on the "Harlow Wars," describing the volatile situation as everything from a "name-calling rumpus" to "a ding dong-no-holds barred brawl."

The feud reached a feverish pitch when Joe Levine and Bill Sargent both proclaimed that they were going to title their films *Harlow*. Levine was outraged and claimed that he had registered the title *Harlow* with the Motion Picture Association of America (MPAA). It was accepted practice by the studios, basically a gentlemen's agreement, not to use an already registered title. Sargent refuted Levine's claim and stated, "I've bothered to check with the title registration office and that title [*Harlow*] isn't registered. What is registered is the name of the book, *Harlow, an Intimate Biography*."[2] Even so, since Electronovision was technically not a movie company and wasn't a member of the MPAA, Sargent could use whatever title he chose.

A similar situation arose in 1960 with two films about notorious writer Oscar Wilde. Distribution rights for *Oscar Wilde*, a British production starring Robert Morley, were picked up by 20th Century–Fox. United Artists acquired the rights to release theatrically in the U.S. another British film called *The Trials of Oscar Wilde* (1960) starring Peter Finch. These films tried to distinguish one from the other in the press by playing up their differences, as the first was a general biography on Wilde's life, while the second concentrated on the courtroom drama when the writer was brought up on a morals charge. The second film was also re-titled and released in some areas as *The Man with the Green Carnation* to avoid audience confusion. While the competition between these two films was fought with decorum by the respective studios, that was certainly not to be the case with the two *Harlow*s, especially with Levine and Sargent's big egos involved.

Joe Levine was known throughout the industry for picking up films for a cheap price and spending lots of money on advertising and promotion to get bodies into the theaters. He never had any real competition in this matter and was not used to being openly challenged. Reportedly he boasted that he was "a colossus towering above the lesser moguls of filmdom."[3] It is no surprise then that he was outraged, accusing Sargent of thievery, and doing everything short of bringing him to court regarding the *Harlow* title. Had he done so, he would have lost, as titles cannot be copyrighted and there is no infringement case for two filmmakers creating screen treatments about a deceased person since it falls under public domain. Sargent also used an original screenplay that had no connection to the biography, so he had every right to make his film any way he chose to.

The powerful showman did have a number of supporters in the film industry, but many remained silent and did not come publicly to his defense. Most likely his competitors secretly reveled in the fact that a young upstart was driving the mogul mad. Columnist Martin Quigley, Jr., though, defended Levine's outrage and felt that Sargent's *Harlow* was piggybacking on Levine's expensive marketing campaign for his *Harlow*, purposely trying to confuse the public. In the end, he felt the moviegoer would be the injured party and warned what would happen if this continued. "If the practice of selling one picture on the fame of another becomes common, the public will turn their backs on theater box offices in disillusionment and disgust."[4]

The ironic thing was that Bill Sargent was so similar to Joe Levine. Both were "big as life" and scrappers who had worked hard to get where they were in Hollywood. Earlier on, Sargent struck a conciliatory tone, even complimenting Levine and calling him "the best showman in the business" and praising the producer for "creating more jobs and furor than anyone else in the history of Hollywood."[5] He remarked that the notoriety his *Harlow* was causing, due to the new filming technique Electronovision, would only help increase the interest in Levine's movie. But Sargent's attitude toward the producer quickly changed, as he felt that Levine was using his power and influence to stymie his *Harlow* at every turn. Later, Sargent attributed all his production and distribution difficulties to "the long arm of Joe Levine."[6]

Producer David Permut met Bill Sargent during the seventies, when he was a teenager selling maps to the stars' homes. After graduating college, he began his career working for the producer. Their first successful project was videotaping the stage production *Give 'em Hell, Harry!* in 1975 and releasing it theatrically. Permut was not shocked at all that Sargent would take on someone as powerful as Levine.

> **DAVID PERMUT:** Bill was a renegade, a rogue, a visionary, and a maverick. He had no fear. He was a combination of P.T. Barnum and Mike Todd. I think there are very few people you can say that about today in or out of the industry. It was his idea to videotape and release *Hamlet* in a new process called Electronovision. He then videotaped the first rock concert with *The T.A.M.I. Show*. I will have been surprised if he *didn't* take on Joe Levine who represented the establishment. Bill was a fiery red-haired Irishman from Oklahoma and always considered the outsider. A dreamer with a glint in his eye, he instilled in the people around him to believe in dreams. He was a Pied Piper of sorts.

With Columbia Pictures out of the running, Bill Sargent then brought on Sidney Skolsky as associate producer, story consultant, and writer after purchasing his treatment for Electronovision's *Harlow*. Sargent remarked, "I am jumping on a bandwagon of a good thing—the bandwagon of Skolsky, who has been preparing this property since 1946."[7] The showman then went on to boast that Electronovision would release twelve films in 1965. That was pure hyperbole since the studio was barely able to handle this one production.

Carroll Baker, meanwhile, had one more hurdle to climb before she could play Jean Harlow. She reportedly had an oral commitment with producer Martin Ransohoff to star in a picture for him. She then announced to the press, "I hereby cancel our verbal agreement to make a movie for you. We did have a contract but that was for a cameo role in *The Loved One*. When that didn't come off, we agreed that any time I wanted out, all I had to do is tell you. I'm telling you."[8] Seeming to have resigned herself to making *Harlow* for Joe Levine, Baker said, "If [it] does as well as *The Carpetbaggers*, I could make $3 million."[9] Unfortunately, that turned out to be a pie-in-the-sky dream.

With that out of the way, Joe Levine was determined to have audiences accept Carroll Baker as his Jean Harlow. He had the actress immerse herself in the mannerisms and behavior of the thirties blonde bombshell. Then, to introduce her as Jean Harlow to the world, he and his star sailed across the Atlantic on the *Queen Mary* for the opening of *The Carpetbaggers* in London. Paramount Pictures took over the entire first-class section of the ship for its executives and publicity team at a reported cost of over $30,000. Also aboard were twenty-one invited members of the press, including two syndicated columnists, television crews from the U.S., Canada, and Germany, and renowned photographers Jean-Pierre Sauer of *Paris Match* magazine and Pierluigi Praturlon. It was a spectacular, over-the-top promotion—typical of Joe Levine.

Traveling with hair, makeup, and costume designers, the lissome Baker emerged from her stateroom looking and dressing more and more like the famed thirties sex symbol. "Operation Harlow," as it was called, also had Baker perusing publicity clips and photographs of Harlow and reading Shulman's biography in preparation. Of the latter she opined, "It's fascinating, but sometimes phony. I mean the 'third party' dialog the author made up because he wasn't there behind closed doors. But our screen writers will improve the lines." She also promised that she would portray Jean Harlow "with great compassion."[10]

Levine's publicity stunt culminated with "Harlow Night" at the Captain's Gala where every table was stocked with champagne and a copy of Irving Shulman's *Harlow, An Intimate Biography*. After working with prolific hair stylist Nellie Manley (whose film credits included *The Carpetbaggers*, among many others) and the makeup team, the metamorphosis was complete. A transformed Carroll Baker made her debut on the arm of Joe Levine at the huge celebration in her honor. An immediate hush ran through the crowd and for one moment not a sound was heard. Baker, standing by a large column, welcomed the guests as 500 white balloons fell from the ceiling as the orchestra began playing and caviar was served. Recalling the moment, Manley said, "A spotlight was thrown on her, and you never heard so much whistling and hollering in your life! She really looked marvelous. The photographers took hundreds of pictures!"[11]

Publicity stills showing Baker, clad in a white satin robe with fur sleeves, striking "a Harlowesque pose" and sitting in a chair in front of a huge blowup of the real Jean Harlow ran in all the newspapers and magazines of the time. Baker recalled, "There were people on board who had personally known her. When I entered the room … some of these people actually cried."[12]

"Operation Harlow" seemed to be a huge success. However, years later, Baker bemoaned that the entire experience was exhausting, as she worked steadily throughout the trip without a moment to rest. "I wasn't able to use the swimming pool, walk on deck, or even eat a single uninterrupted meal. On the third day out, Levine and the publicity coordinator urged me to work faster in order to take advantage of all the press coverage. I burst into hysterical tears."[13]

Returning from London in early December, a tired Carroll Baker's time off was disrupted when her Beverly Hills home was burglarized while she and her family were dining at a nearby, upscale cafe. Reportedly, the thieves made off with $11,500 worth of furs and costume jewelry. Luckily for Baker, they overlooked a diamond necklace valued at $75,000. Four days later, the burglars were caught and it emerged that Baker was the latest victim of an elaborate robbery scheme—an assistant maître d'hôtel at the swanky restaurant where Baker had dined would collect reservation information and then would telephone his partners in crime to rob the homes of unsuspecting diners after they arrived to enjoy their night out. Baker recovered most of her valuables. Since none were insured, the relieved movie star commented that it was "like a Christmas present to get it back."[14]

Despite both Sargent and Levine's boasting and bragging, December 1964 came and went and neither *Harlow* was in production. Rumors soon circulated that Levine was going to scrap his venture, but in January 1965 he emphatically denied the reports and spent $250,000 before one frame of film was shot—to outfit eight offices on the Paramount lot for himself and his staff, and to commence the creation of sets. Keeping to the sex and sensationalism that made *The Carpetbaggers* a huge hit, Levine announced that with *Harlow*, "We will go as far as we can and stay out of jail."[15] To titillate the public even more, he even stated that he would release the movie without a seal of approval from the MPAA.

Exhibitors were relieved that Levine was proceeding with the movie since he was on a roll, turning out a succession of box office hits due to his exploitation expertise. One theater chain executive remarked, "By the time Levine gets finished plugging this film, there'll be so much notoriety about it, it will have to be real great box office."[16] While the gentleman was prophetic in how notorious *Harlow* would become, he was far off on how that would translate into ticket sales.

Bill Sargent was facing his own set of problems and the rival *Harlow* was the least of them. He still needed a leading lady and a distributor to get the picture into movie theaters nationwide. Warner Bros. released *Hamlet* but had no interest in becoming involved with Sargent's new movie, even though they had made a tidy profit from his first. This is not surprising since Warner Bros. was the only major studio that never even entered the Harlow sweepstakes to begin with. Going head-to-head with a rival studio was probably not acceptable to them. With the major studios out, Sargent needed an independent distributor. American International Pictures had distributed *The T.A.M.I. Show*, but it is unclear if Sargent approached them again. Instead, he struck a deal with Magna Pictures Distribution in February of 1965 even before casting had begun.

The head of Magna was Marshall Naify, a Lebanese businessman whose father had founded United California Theaters in 1920. Naify and his brother Robert worked in the family business their entire lives, starting out as ushers and projectionists. In 1963, the company merged with the United Artists Theater Circuit. Shortly after, the then-current president George P. Skouras resigned and recommended Marshall Naify as his replacement. Like Joe Levine, Naify also wanted to get into the distribution side of the movie business rather than just running theaters. They had previously dabbled in distribution, releasing the hit musical *South Pacific* in 1958. Naify's company owned a 50-percent stake in Magna Pictures (as well as a sizable interest in the Todd-AO Corporation), which began acquiring rights to European movies just as Embassy Pictures had done in the late fifties. In 1964–65, Magna released in the U.S. *High Infidelity/Alta Infedelta* with Charles Aznavour and Nino Manfredi, *Mata Hari, Agent H21* with Jeanne Moreau, and *I malamondo*, a documentary about the "way out" activities of European youth, such as nude skiing. Branching out into American movies in 1965, Magna chose *Harlow* as its first release. As stipulated, the movie was credited as "Marshall Naify Presents Bill Sargent's *Harlow*."

Despite all the media excitement and publicity that he was able to generate, Levine was livid that young upstart Sargent had obtained a distribution deal and was still going ahead with his movie *Harlow*. The mogul remarked, "What he's doing is against the ethics and the code of the industry."[17] He didn't stop there and came at Sargent with personal attacks, labeling him "a leech who lives on other people."[18] Levine's indignation rang hollow as he had announced his plans to make a movie about Jean Harlow after 20th Century–Fox, MGM, and Columbia had already moved ahead with their eventually abandoned projects. All his huffing and puffing couldn't blow the Electronovision *Harlow* house down. Was it real or just bluster to get publicity for his *Harlow*? Either way Sargent seemed to enjoy antagonizing the producer and promised, "We're going to drive Levine out of his mind. He's got it coming."[19]

With the war raging in the press between the producers, complete with continuous name-calling, the race to the silver screen really hit its stride when their films competed against the deadlines of their promised opening dates. Electronovision's *Harlow* was scheduled in theaters on May 12 and Paramount's version was due on June 25, moved up from a late August date. Unfortunately, both were both plagued by problems, beginning with the screenplays—making those dates questionable.

When Joe Levine purchased the rights to Irving Shulman's biography on Jean Harlow, he declared his *Harlow* would be very sexy. It was highly speculated that Academy Award nominee Shulman would be hired to adapt his work into a screenplay. However, due to all the bad press the book received for being inaccurate and exploitative, Paramount got cold feet and wanted to create some distance from it. Levine went along and quickly switched gears with the media. He proudly announced that he never met or even spoke to Shulman and that he "isn't writing a single line in the picture…. This will not be a crude or crass film—we want no vulgarity in it. Just the truth. The wheat from the chaff."[20] Irving Shulman, though, revealed that he had been hired by Joe Levine to "make up stories to create controversy"[21] as a way to help publicize the movie. This was a claim that the producer vehemently denied many times, yet there is a good chance Shulman was telling the truth. When Levine first purchased the rights to the book, he didn't say a bad word about it and he had boasted at how sex-filled his film would be. Prodding Shulman to help promote the movie would not be so far-fetched for the master of exploitation.

Going forward, Levine was sure reviewers were chomping at the bit to bring his biopic down, even though he was not going to use Shulman's biography as a singular reference source for the screenplay and promised a "cleaned-up" movie. He said, "I can promise you, no matter what the production turns out to be, certain critics have their reviews already written. And they won't be good ones."[22] His assumption was that many critics loathed his prior movies that were full of sex and sensationalism. They were peeved that the general public ignored their criticism and made the movies box office hits. He remarked, "Today people like to refer to me solely as a purveyor of *The Carpetbaggers*. Have they already forgotten *Two Women*, *Fellini's 8 ½*, and *Yesterday, Today and Tomorrow*, which are just a few of films I have brought here."[23]

Prospective screenwriters for Levine's movie were instructed to eliminate all the tawdry portions of the book for any commissioned screenplays. Sydney Boehm was the first writer hired. His films ranged from the sci-fi classic *When Worlds Collide* (1951) to the thriller *The Atomic City* (1952), for which he received an Academy Award nomination. He also was known for his hard-hitting dramas such as *Union Station* (1950), *The Big Heat* (1953), and *Violent Saturday* (1955). Ironically, his most recent credits, just prior to *Harlow*, were the melodrama *Shock Treatment* (1964) starring Carol Lynley and the mystery *Sylvia* (1965) starring Carroll Baker.

It was reported that Boehm was using the Schulman biography and "original source material"[24] for the basis of his script. Once word got out that he was writing the screenplay, it seemed every wacko in town—from cab drivers, to salesmen, and even a scientist—claimed to have had a love affair with Jean Harlow and was eager to share his tale—for a price. After listening to some of their stories, Boehm put an end to it after three weeks. The exasperated screenwriter exclaimed, "It's ridiculous. Some of these guys claim to have spent the weekend with Jean long after she was buried."[25]

Boehm was present at a press conference where Joe Levine lambasted Shulman's biography and vowed he would be presenting an accurate biopic done in good taste. Boehm also trashed Shulman's tome asserting that it was fifty percent fiction. When reporter Dick Kleiner asked him what percentage of his script was fictitious, the screenwriter replied, "About the same—but in a different way."[26] Based on this answer, you can tell Boehm was learning a lot from Joe Levine, the master double-talker.

According to Paramount Pictures' production memos, Boehm's first draft required a number of changes that were immediately ordered by the studio, due to notes it received from the MPAA. Jean Harlow's penchant for going braless was to be toned down and racy words like "castrate" were to be deleted from the script. In late 1964, the writer submitted a final second draft. Before leaving the project, Boehm warned Levine that if he was not happy with the final cut of the movie, he would publicly ask for his name to be removed from the credits.[27]

Irene Kamp, a Paramount staff writer, was then given the assignment of "polishing" Boehm's screenplay. Her credits were slim and included *Love in a Goldfish Bowl* (1961), *Paris Blues* (1961), and *The Lion* (1962). At a story conference meeting with the writer, Howard Koch, and other executives, Levine voiced concerns about Boehm's draft being too sexual, even though the producer's prior films were notorious for their racy content. The MPAA had been criticized for giving its Seal of Approval to sensational films like *The Carpetbaggers*, while denying the seal to more serious adult fare like *The Pawnbroker*, so it was scrutinizing new movies even more. This development, coupled with all the lawsuits swirling around Irving Shulman's biography, prompted Paramount Pictures to want a nice, clean, non-controversial motion picture. Levine agreed and feared a sexsational *Harlow* would hurt his movie's acceptance even more. The producer remarked, "Normally, we go pretty far. But never has a picture been on a spot like this one. This is the most publicized picture in the business."[28] Examples of elements he singled out as unacceptable included hints of lesbianism and the insinuation of Paul Bern's homosexuality, as explicitly revealed in Shulman's biography.

Kamp's revised version of the screenplay also had the producer questioning whether the audience would like Jean Harlow as presented. He wasn't so sure. When he left the room, according to studio minutes, Kamp remarked, "Everyone who knew Harlow knew she had a rough life and will feel cheated if they don't see some of it."[29] Despite the defense of her work, Kamp's draft was also deemed too sensationalized and unacceptable, especially by Carroll Baker. The search for a satisfying script continued.

Commenting on Levine's problem-laden screenplays, a bemused Bill Sargent remarked, "As for the script ... we always intended to make something kids could see, and they started out with sex and sensationalism. Now I hear they're going to make a nice, clean picture. They're following me."[30] He was right, of course, although it is quite ironic that both film companies were after the family audience with a story about one of the screen's most desirable sex goddesses. But all was not rosy for Sargent either, as he was also having screenplay woes. He did not pick up the option on Sidney Skolsky's script because it contained only "three or four percent dialog" and was written more as "a Sidney Skolsky story than a Jean Harlow story. Right now, I'm not making a Skolsky film, but I might sometime later."[31]

Outraged, Skolsky filed a $140,000 lawsuit against Electronovision—$40,000 for services contracted and $100,000 for mental suffering and damage to reputation. He also complained that the first check bounced, but conceded it was made good shortly thereafter. Sargent countered that the second payment for $40,000 was not owed because Skolsky's option was not exercised and that the writer was lucky that he wasn't being counter-sued for the return of $5,000 due to "misrepresentation." Sargent opined, "Sidney Skolsky has not got a chance to get any money so obviously he's after publicity."[32]

Needing a script, Sargent purchased what he called a "much better screenplay"[33] (compared to Sidney Skolsky's, no doubt) submitted by prolific screenwriter Karl Tunberg. He was well known in the industry for co-writing musicals and comedies including *Hold That Co-Ed*, *Down Argentine Way*, *Tall, Dark and Handsome* (Academy Award nominee), *Orchestra Wives*, and *Count Your Blessings*. His best-known work was the historical epic *Ben-Hur*, for which he received his second Academy Award nomination (though people associated with the movie claim Gore Vidal and Christopher Fry rewrote most of it without official credit).

With a screenplay in place, savvy Sargent knew he would need a director who could work fast in this hybrid filming method and who could double as an editor. The assignment was awarded to the extremely talented, Peabody Award-winning, and three-time Emmy nominee Alex Segal (he'd go on to win an Emmy Award in 1967 for directing *Death of a Salesman*), who was considered one of the very best directors working on stage and in live television during the fifties. His resume included episodes of such esteemed anthologies as *Actors Studio, The U.S. Steel Hour, Producer's Showcase, Kraft Theater, Playhouse 90,* and *The DuPont Show of the Month*. A tough, tense director, he was described by colleagues as being "explosive" and dubbed by one critic as "TV's shrieking genius."[34] Segal copped to the shrieking part and admitted, "Actually, when I am under stress, I'm a bit of a screamer. I've lived under this curse for years. I suddenly find an actress I'm working with terrified of me."[35] Although his cast and crew were victims of Segal's ire, it was mostly aimed at meddling, on-set network executives always demanding changes. "What do you think Van Gogh would have said if someone stood behind him and said, 'You can't paint that face yellow.' Yet that's what everyone in the studio does to the director. Why the hell don't they wait until he's finished and let him be judged for the color he chooses?"[36]

Actress Shirley Knight worked with Alex Segal and described him as "a great director, another crazy person who could be not very nice at times. But never to me." She went on to add, "He had such insight. He would never direct you, in a sense, but he would say, 'Think about this. Think about that.'"[37]

Segal's work away from live TV was slim prior to *Harlow*. During the early sixties he began directing TV anthologies such as *Alcoa Premiere* and *Bob Hope Presents the Chrysler Theater* that were shot on film in Hollywood. His feature debut was the touching *All the Way Home* (1963) with Robert Preston and Jean Simmons, who described Segal as "one of the finest craftsmen I ever worked with."[38] The movie won the Best American Film Award at the Lincoln Center Film Festival. He followed this with the less successful romantic melodrama *Joy in the Morning* (1965) with Richard Chamberlain and Yvette Mimieux as mismatched newlyweds in the 1920s. Since *Harlow* was going to be shot in the style of a live TV program, Segal, with his experience, seemed a wise choice to bridge the two mediums.

Twenty-seven sets were constructed on four sound stages at the Desilu Cahuenga studios for Electronovision's *Harlow*. Bill Sargent's goal was to achieve twenty minutes of film per day and to shoot most scenes straight through, like a stage play, with no interruption in the action. Segal seemed perfectly up for the challenge.

With a distributor and director set, and an approved screenplay, next to do was to hire actors. *The Hollywood Reporter* stated in January 1965 that Jill St. John, Barbara Loden, and a third, unnamed actress were in the running. Jill St. John began her career as a child actress, then progressed to teenage ingénue roles in such films as *Summer Love* (1958) and *Holiday for Lovers* (1959). She blossomed into a curvaceous redhead and reached sex symbol status beginning with *The Lost World* (1960) as Jennifer Holmes, the Victorian heroine, in Arthur Conan Doyle's classic tale. On the strength of that performance, St. John then played dramatic roles in *The Roman Spring of Mrs. Stone* (1961) and *Tender Is the Night* (1962), but comedy proved to be her forte. In *Come Blow Your Horn* (1963) she received a Golden Globe nomination for Best Actress in a Comedy or Musical, playing Frank Sinatra's kooky neighbor. Other "sexy dumb broad" parts followed in *Who's Minding the Store?* (1963) with Jerry Lewis, *Who's Been Sleeping in My Bed?* (1964) with Dean Martin, and *Honeymoon Hotel* (1964) with Robert Morse and Robert Goulet. St. John undoubtedly had the shapely body to play Harlow and would have brought out her humor (if the script allowed for it, which it did not), but it is questionable if she could pull off the dramatics.

Former model and pin-up girl Barbara Loden had just won a Tony Award for Best Featured Actress in a Play for her role as the Marilyn Monroe-ish Maggie in Arthur Miller's *After the Fall*, directed by Elia Kazan, who had discovered the blonde actress in the late fifties. She became his protégé and eventually his wife. No doubt her acclaimed performance playing the sex symbol brought her to Bill Sargent's attention. Her previous movies included two directed by Kazan—*Wild River* (1960) as Montgomery Clift's secretary and *Splendor in the Grass* (1961) playing Warren Beatty's reckless sister. Loden definitely had the looks and talent to pull off playing Harlow, but she had no box office draw.

Neither actress got the part. Instead, Sargent cast pretty, leggy, blonde Dorothy

Provine, a talented actress, singer, and comedienne. Her acting career began after she left the University of Washington with a degree in Theater Arts and accompanied a friend to Hollywood. Almost immediately, she landed a small role in the B-movie *Live Fast, Die Young* (1958). More low-budget fare followed, including *The Bonnie Parker Story* (1958) playing the title role of the gun-toting criminal; *Riot in Juvenile Prison* (1959) as a tough teenage blonde named Babe; and *The 30 Foot Bride of Candy Rock* (1959) as Lou Costello's girlfriend who grows to gigantic proportions. It was one of the comedian's rare appearances without partner Bud Abbott.

Warner Bros. then signed Provine to a seven-year contract and began to exploit her comedic and singing talents. She guest-starred on the debut episode of *77 Sunset Strip* and made appearances on a few of the studio's other series before landing her own with *The Alaskans*, which lasted only one season (1959–60). She played a saloon singer and friend of Gold Rush fortune hunters Roger Moore and Jeff York. Her second series, *The Roaring Twenties* (1960–62), was more successful and made her a star for her portrayal of kooky flapper Pinky Pinkham, romanced by two adventurous news reporters—played by Donald May and Rex Reason. When the show ended, Provine returned to films, but of the big budget kind, appearing to good effect in two box office hits—the zany *It's a Mad, Mad, Mad, Mad World* (1963) as Milton Berle's wife and *Good Neighbor Sam* (1964) as Jack Lemmon's better half.

Based on her prior performances, the thirty-year-old Provine seemed a good choice to interpret Jean Harlow on the screen despite being a bit too long in the tooth. Sharing a vivaciousness and gregariousness that was needed to bring Harlow to life, she also had the physical requirements to meet the challenge. To prove the latter, Sargent had Provine made up as Harlow and dressed to the nines in a slinky gown typical of the bombshell's style. Together they attended a Hollywood party sponsored by MacFadden-Bartell publications in February 1965. Besides touting his *Harlow*, the ambitious producer also boasted to anyone who would listen that Electronovision would be shooting three additional movies, mostly unnamed, filmed stage productions—two in New York and one in London.

The biggest casting coup for Sargent was signing Judy Garland to play Harlow's overbearing mother. Garland had an ambitious mama herself so it was going to be interesting to see how she would interpret the role. Since the fifties, Garland had only worked in films intermittently, instead choosing to concentrate on concert appearances and TV. She won an Oscar nomination for her heartbreaking performance in *Judgment at Nuremburg* (1961). This was followed by starring roles in *A Child Is Waiting* (1963) as a music teacher who forms a special bond with one of her autistic students, and in the melodramatic *I Could Go on Singing* (1963) as a performer who, years earlier, chose her career over her son and husband (Dirk Bogarde) and now wants to rebuild a life with them. It was also reported that Garland's new younger husband, Mark Herron, would play one of Harlow's directors.

As for Dorothy Provine's leading men, José Ferrer (Academy Award winner for *Cyrano de Bergerac*) was announced to play Harlow's second husband, the tragic Paul Bern, but he eventually dropped out and was replaced by Hurd Hatfield—best known for his leading role in *The Picture of Dorian Gray* (1945). It was his second movie role and so successful in bringing the character to life on the big screen that

Judy Garland, flanked by her children Lorna and Joey Luft, is shown a poster advertising *Harlow* by her co-star, Barry Sullivan (UPI Telephoto, March 21, 1965).

he was typecast as "Dorian Gray." Hence, his movie career stalled and he spent most of the fifties on TV. He returned to the big screen in such historical epics as *King of Kings* (1961) and *El Cid* (1961). Hatfield was hesitant about taking the role and said, "After trying to live down 'Dorian Gray' for 20 years, I wasn't sure, then decided if Peter Lawford [cast as Bern in the rival version] could do it, I could."[39]

Efrem Zimbalist, Jr., was signed to play the fictitious William Mansfield, very loosely based on actor William Powell, Harlow's true love in the last years of her life. The actor had a slick and debonair persona about him, coupled with a soothing speaking voice. Arriving in Hollywood in 1956 and signed to Warner Bros., he began co-starring in such films as *Band of Angels* (1957) with Clark Gable and Yvonne De Carlo, *Bombers B-52* (1957) with Natalie Wood, *Too Much, Too Soon* (1958) with Dorothy Malone, and *Home Before Dark* (1958) with Jean Simmons. Though he shared the Golden Globe for Most Promising Newcomer—Male in 1958 (with Bradford Dillman and John Gavin), it was television that brought him fame as suave private eye Stuart Bailey in the enormously popular detective series *77 Sunset Strip*, which aired from 1958 through early 1964. *Harlow* was his first feature after the series was cancelled.

Strapping six-foot, two-inch Michael Dante was hired to play Jean Harlow's fictitious paid lover Ed, who gives the blushing bride what her new husband cannot on their wedding night and on lonely evenings to follow. Dante (born Ralph Vitti) grew up in Stamford, Connecticut, and became a professional baseball player, who signed with the Boston Braves at age seventeen. He moved on to play shortstop for the Washington Senators. In the off season, he studied drama at the University of Miami. His baseball career was cut short when he developed chronic bursitis in his throwing arm and before he could even bemoan his bad luck, orchestra leader Tommy Dorsey (his roommate's friend) arranged an audition for him in Hollywood with MGM. In 1955, the studio signed the tall, rugged, and extremely good-looking Dante and cast him in a number of minor film roles, most notably in *Somebody Up There Likes Me* (1956). Three years later he was working at Warner Bros. and quickly became a fixture in their TV westerns, with multiple appearances on *Sugarfoot*, *Colt 45*, *Cheyenne*, *Maverick*, *Death Valley Days*, and *The Texan*. Dante also began landing bigger roles in motion pictures including *Seven Thieves* (1960) as a safecracking member of Edward G. Robinson's gang that plan to rob a Monte Carlo casino and *Kid Galahad* (1962) as boxer Elvis Presley's sparring partner.

MICHAEL DANTE: This was not my first movie biography. I played a small role without any billing in *Jeanne Eagels* with Kim Novak, who was a beautiful actress, and when made up looked like the real Jeanne Eagels. I was brought in by the executive producer Lee Savin to read for Alex Segal. Lee worked for Desilu and I appeared in an episode of *Desilu Playhouse* called "The Killer Instinct" with Rory Calhoun and Janice Rule. Lee thought I was great in it and got me a contract with 20th Century–Fox.

I auditioned for Alex and got the role. I was thrilled because I heard of Bill Sargent's new process of Electronovision where the movie would be shot on tape and then transferred to film. It was going to be like doing a play and it was exciting because we had a very experienced and talented cast.

I also really wanted to play the role of Ed because, even though he was a gigolo, he was more sophisticated and elegant than the gigolo roles I played previously. Satisfying ladies was just a business for him. The character had substance and was just not some idiot who had sex with women for money. He had intelligence and was very seductive. For example, he knew what Harlow was and what she wanted. He didn't go at it like an animal, but with finesse.

The rest of *Harlow*'s supporting cast included such fine thespians as Lloyd Bochner, an actor with numerous dramatic TV guest appearances, as fictitious actor Marc Peters, who discovers Harlow; Barry Sullivan as Marino Bello; Hermione Baddeley (Academy Award nominee for *Room at the Top*) as Marie Dressler; John Williams as fictitious director Jonathan Martin; and Celia Lovsky as Maria Ouspenskaya.

Probably just to rile up Joe Levine even more, Sargent sent him a telegram with an offer to play the role of gruff MGM studio head Louis B. Mayer. Receiving no response as expected, Sargent cast Jack Kruschen (Academy Award nominee for

The Apartment) instead. A few weeks later, on Mike Wallace's radio show, a miffed Levine addressed Sargent's proposal and remarked, "I would like to say what's on my mind about this man, but I can't say it. You'll cut it off the air."[40]

More publicity stunts to get *Harlow* press included casting former world boxing heavyweight champion Sonny Liston as a fighter sparring at the old Hollywood Legion Stadium, which Jean Harlow and others from the film colony heavily frequented, and Fred Klein, publisher of *Photoplay* magazine and reported Electronovision, Inc. investor, to play himself, as he presents an award to Jean Harlow on her triumphant return to Hollywood after studying in New York.

Publicity photograph of Michael Dante as Ed from *Harlow* **(Magna, 1965).**

* * *

Back on Joe Levine's *Harlow* set, casting was proceeding as well. Shelley Winters, who had just worked with the producer in *A House Is Not a Home*, told columnist Earl Wilson that Levine wanted her as Mama Jean. "I'm not anxious to play Carroll Baker's mother unless I can get Marcello Mastroianni as my husband," Winters stated.[41] She didn't and she passed on the film. Academy Award winners Joan Fontaine, Patricia Neal, and Olivia de Havilland were also mentioned as contenders for Mama Jean. Rita Hayworth claimed she was offered the role, but turned it down because "nobody would let me see a script."[42]

The role eventually went to Angela Lansbury, only six years her "daughter" Carroll Baker's senior. A few years later, she told Rex Reed, "I played all the roles nobody wanted."[43] On a roll with mother parts, Lansbury had recently portrayed Elvis Presley's southern-fried, scatterbrained mama in the hit movie musical *Blue Hawaii* (1961) and she received her third Academy Award nomination for Best Supporting Actress as the cunning, cold-hearted mother of brainwashed soldier-turned-assassin Laurence Harvey in *The Manchurian Candidate* (1962). She exuded pure evilness in the role and deserved all the praise she received.

As for Marino Bello, Vittorio Gassman (another Italian actor with a connection to Shelley Winters, being her ex-husband) was considered for the part but he did not get it. Taking it in stride, he remarked to Sheila Graham, "I was somewhat too young for it anyway. I'm 40 and Carroll is 33."[44] Instead, Raf Vallone (stepping in for the previously announced Mexican actor Gilbert Roland) won the role.

Carroll Baker's leading men were Peter Lawford (her co-star in *Sylvia*), as Paul Bern and Michael Connors (who had previously worked for Joe Levine in *Where Love Has Gone*) as the fictitious character Jack Harrison, the equivalent to Efrem Zimbalist, Jr.'s role in Electronovision's *Harlow*, with the exception being that Connors' Harrison character is closer to Harlow's frequent co-star Clark Gable than her true love William Powell.

British actor Peter Lawford was a former young heartthrob at MGM during the late forties with a long resume of films, including *A Yank at Eton* (1942), *Good News* (1947), *On an Island with You* (1948), *Easter Parade* (1948), *Little Women* (1949), *Royal Wedding* (1951), and *It Should Happen to You* (1954). By the early sixties, he seemed to alternate between playing sophisticated military officers and politicians in such films as *Exodus* (1960), *Advise and Consent* (1962), and *The Longest Day* (1962), and more comedic roles in *Ocean's Eleven* (1962) and *Sergeant's 3* (1962) as a member of Frank Sinatra's Rat Pack (due to his marriage to John Kennedy's sister Patricia).

Dark-haired Michael Connors, of Armenian descent, began acting in low-budget B-movies under the name "Touch" Connors—his nickname from his college basketball days. He starred in a slew of sci-fi, teenage exploitation, and western films during the fifties before landing his own TV series called *Tightrope* (1959–60) in which he played an undercover cop who infiltrates organized crime gangs. When the show ended after only one season, he began concentrating on his movie career again (now billed as Michael Connors). He co-starred in three 1964 releases: *Panic Button*, *Good Neighbor Sam*, and *Where Love Has Gone* as the father of troubled teenager Joey Heatherton, on trial for the murder of her mother's lover.

Due to his dark, good looks, Connors was being groomed to become Hollywood's next romantic leading man—along the lines of Rock Hudson. However, he was not worried about being typecast as a matinee idol, due to the fickle popularity of the types of leading men who were briefly popular over the years, from Latin lovers such as Valentino, to rugged he-men like Clark Gable, to the rebel such as Marlon Brando. Connors remarked, "The challenge for me right now is to become a big enough box office name so that no producer could ever turn me down on the basis of me not being bankable. But no matter what type or how talented you are it takes twice as much drive to succeed in acting as it does in any other profession."[45]

Although George Jessel wanted the part, Academy Award-winning actor and comedian Red Buttons won the role of Harlow's agent Arthur Landau, a character who was noticeably absent in the rival version (no doubt due to legal reasons). Other cast members included Martin Balsam (Academy Award winner for *A Thousand Clowns*) as fictitious studio head Everett Redman and Leslie Nielsen as producer Richard Manley, a disguised Howard Hughes.

Aspiring actress Julie Parrish was cast in the small role of Jack Harrison's young bride Serena. The pretty brunette was a Paramount contract player, who had previously played a college student in the hit comedy *The Nutty Professor* (1963) with Jerry Lewis. She would go onto have a prolific career in television, starring in her own sitcom *Good Morning, World* (1967–68); co-starring in the daytime soap *Capitol* as

Maggie Brady (1982–87); and playing a recurring role on *Beverly Hills, 90210* as Peach Pit owner Nate's wife (1996–98). In her *Harlow* scene, an unhappy Jean descends on Harrison's home hoping to rekindle their flirtatious romance, unaware that the matinee idol has wed Serena. Recalling the movie, Parrish commented, "I only met Carroll Baker briefly, but she seemed sweet. Mike Connors was okay *then*, but not when I did an episode of *Mannix*. I think actors, who are stars of shows, get used to women coming after them. Well, that generation of actors anyway. So, if you were friendly, they just assumed you wanted more."[46]

Other sixties starlets to grace the movie in minor roles included voluptuous Edy Williams (*The Secret Life of an American Wife, Beyond the Valley of the Dolls, The Seven Minutes*) hidden under a platinum blonde wig as a girl working in the studio's mailroom; prolific TV actress Roxanne Berard as a studio executive's secretary; kewpie-doll blonde Susan Holloway (*When the Boys Meet the Girls, Angels from Hell*) as a Harlow look-alike riding a bus; and *Playboy*'s Miss August 1954, blonde bombshell Arline Hunter (*The Angry Red Planet, Sex Kittens Go to College, White Lightnin' Road*) as another imitation Harlow seen outside a movie theater.

6

Harlow, Electronovision Style

With the casts in place, preparations for filming began on both movies. Electronovision's *Harlow* began shooting in early April. Richard C. Bennett, who began his career in live television, was hired to work on the film as an assistant director. It was during a break from working on the *Dr. Kildare* TV show that he took on *Harlow*. However, he did not receive screen credit, perhaps in part because *Harlow* was a mutant production—using TV cameras that videotaped the action, which was then transferred to film. The unions did not know how to categorize it, causing all sorts of confusion.

RICHARD BENNETT: I was unable to get into movies until the Film Directors Guild merged with the Live Directors Guild, but I had to start all over again as second assistant director. I don't know for sure why I did not receive credit. I didn't care then or now, but suspect it was the handiwork of the then representative for the Assistant Film Directors in the Film Directors Guild. When they merged with the Television Directors Guild, he feared that the associate directors and stage managers would be a threat to the assistant film directors. It resulted in some very unsavory goings on for a while. I was President of the Associate Directors and Stage Managers Council, and it's just possible that is why I got involved in *Harlow*.

Harlow was taped somewhat in the TV-style that needed what "live TV" called stage managers and associate directors as assistants to the director. Though this production was being shot in some ways as a "live" production, it really was going to be shot partially as a film production and released in theaters as a feature motion picture. This was virgin territory, loaded with grey areas and at the time caused some painful moments at the Directors Guild, which is an absolutely fabulous organization.

I look back on this as something very sad. There were good intentions on the part of the cast and crew, but the producer [Bill Sargent] didn't know what he was doing. As somebody who loves movies and was just starting to work in the film industry after being in live television, I think I blocked out a lot of what happened here because it was just a depressing experience. It was one of those exceptions. Most films you look back on and even though they may have been hard work and all that, it was a joyful experience with good memories. With *Harlow* it was not and unfortunately there was nothing good about it.

Days before production was set to begin, Bill Sargent's agent Freddie Fields was reportedly contacted by Paramount to see how much Sargent would accept to abandon his movie. Having to cover contracts with actors and Desilu, whose soundstages were booked for the movie, Sargent asked for $325,000 or $350,000 depending on the source. In addition, he requested financing for a $1 million production of *Candy* from a screenplay by its novelist Terry Southern (after the writer's deal with director Frank Perry and United Artists lapsed), and three future movies. He also required that the titles for Paramount's *Harlow* read, "Joe Levine and Bill Sargent present *Harlow*." He never heard a word back, which is not surprising considering his outrageous demands. Being snubbed by the major studio a second time, an indignant Sargent, playing the victim being set upon by the big bad wolves of Hollywood, exclaimed, "I guess they thought I was just a smalltime operator trying to get as much as I could from something I had no intention of going ahead with. I have made every possible overture I can make to try to get some order out of this chaos. Now I'm ready to fight."[1]

With all the hoopla in the press and back-and-forth barbs with Joe Levine, some thought Bill Sargent was just out to make a quick buck off the other *Harlow*, rather than a good movie.

RICHARD BENNETT: Yes, that was my impression of him all along.

MICHAEL DANTE: I loved Bill Sargent. I like renegades. To me, he was a maverick and was trying to do something new. Unfortunately, he didn't have the money to back up his creative and inventive ideas that he wanted to promote. I admired Bill Sargent because he tried to do a stage play with experienced actors on film. However, the budget and other circumstances hampered the picture. He also had a great deal of love and respect for his cast, which was a wonderful group of actors.

With the cast set (or so they thought) for the Electronovision production, rehearsals were scheduled to begin, but then Dorothy Provine dropped out of the picture stating that the role didn't suit her. Newspaper columnists, however, reported that she was "dumped" by Sargent. The wily producer never confirmed Provine's firing but insinuated it and revealed that her departure cost him $25,000. He remarked, "I signed Provine, but I just couldn't see her dying—I couldn't feel sorry for her."[2] A third reason for the actress's abrupt departure was also floated in Hollywood. Purportedly, the distributor had financing trouble and bankers felt that Provine was not a big enough draw to attract ticket buyers. They wanted someone with more box office clout to play Jean Harlow.

Needing to find a replacement quickly, it was at this point that he met young actress Maureen Gaffney. Originally from Cambridge, Massachusetts, she arrived in Hollywood, via Tucson, after studying ballet and singing. To make ends meet, she took a job dancing at The Booby Trap, a strip joint next door to the old Playboy Club on Sunset Blvd. near La Cienega. It was run by a man named Freddie Ray who was good friends with comedian Shecky Greene. Working the club at night left her free during the day to pursue acting work. She landed a small part in a skit on *The Red Skelton Hour* and was so liked that the producers kept inviting her back. She then did a takeoff on *Goldfinger* in a skit with Johnny Carson on *The Tonight Show* and was cast as a beach girl in *A Swingin' Summer* (1965) with James Stacy, William Wellman, Jr., and newcomer Raquel Welch. Frankie Ray then introduced her to Bill

Sargent and Greene's agent, Irving Schacht. This was the beginning of her friendship with the wily producer.

> **MAUREEN GAFFNEY:** Irving Schacht was very tall and handsome. He and Freddie Ray bought me dinner and we had a lot of laughs. They remained friends with me for many years—even Frankie until he died.
>
> Bill Sargent was loud and spoke fast in a high-pitched voice. At the time, I just thought he was a crazy character. Afterwards, Frankie called me and said Bill and Irving wanted to meet with me. Sargent had an office on Sunset Blvd. on the south side just before you entered Beverly Hills. Next door was The Cock and Bull. Bill had the whole building and you went up this round staircase to the second floor. He interviewed me and said, "You'd be perfect for Harlow—but can you act?" He liked that I had the big eyes and the body for it. I was new in the business so I didn't say a word. I should have said, "Of course I can act!" I am always honest so I just didn't respond. He wanted me for the part but instead cast someone else. But he did have them write me in a cameo part because he liked me.

Gaffney was not the first newcomer Sargent purportedly considered to play Jean Harlow. Carol Hollenbeck, who was promoted for the Carroll Baker *Harlow*, also caught Sargent's eye due to a publicity stunt her manager concocted during early November 1964.

> **CAROL HOLLENBECK:** My manager said, "Why don't we have you looking like a glamorous Jean Harlow and send you to various polling areas?" My slogan was "Vote for me for *The Jean Harlow Story*." He came up with this idea after he found out that they were doing a second movie about Jean Harlow. Of course, I went along with it. I wore my long, gold sequin dress. I stood outside the voting places and handed out these ballots with that slogan. We handed out lots and lots of ballots. It got me into Hedda Hopper's column who wrote, 'Carol Holland took a tip from the politicians and paid for an ad in a trade paper—"Vote yes on Carol Holland for The Jean Harlow Story." That mention by her got me a lot of interest. After that, Bill Sargent contacted my manager to set up a time to meet with me. I am not sure if his wanting to meet me was just for publicity or he was really going to consider me for the part.
>
> Bill Sargent was a very charming man. Of course, I did not know the ins and outs of him, but as far as meeting with him at his office, he treated me well. Sometime in Hollywood you don't get treated so well—you may get attacked. That happened to me many times in so-called agents' offices. Bill interviewed me. He said, "I wanted to meet and talk with you." We had a nice chat but I did not get the part.

It is not surprising that Sargent did not go with a newcomer with more seasoned actresses available with bigger names that the distributor craved. One of them was former Warner Bros. contract player Diane McBain. She began her career on television making guest appearances on all the studio's top shows beginning in 1958 and then co-starred in the hit TV series *Surfside 6* for two seasons. On the big screen, she was part of that baby doll blonde brigade consisting of Sandra Dee, Tuesday Weld, Carol Lynley, and Yvette Mimieux. Diane, however, had more of a sophisticated persona about her making her ripe to play the bad girl or the snobbish rich bitch in such films as *Parrish*, *Claudelle Inglish*, *Mary, Mary*, and *A Distant Trumpet*. Wanting the role of Jean Harlow, McBain bleached her hair a whitish blonde and agreed to wear nothing underneath the lacy costume she was given. Her uncomfortableness shown and she wrote in her memoir,

> The test was shot on a television stage, and director Alex Segal was hidden away in the control booth. The inability to see the director—a rare experience on movie sets—made me unable to get a feeling for what he wanted. My dependence on his negligible direction was all too apparent, and I clumsily fumbled my lines. Momentarily, I heard the voices of Segal and producer Bill Sargent coming from the control booth.
> "You don't think she's going to do it like that, do you?" the director asked Sargent. Stunned silence gripped the sound stage where everyone could hear what he said. Thunderstruck, and feeling very naked in my negligee, I flatly said in response, "I can hear every word you are saying, you know." I needed reassurance at that moment, rather than callous criticism.[3]

Not surprisingly, Diane McBain did not get the part and instead they offered the role to fellow baby doll blonde Carol Lynley. She had a recent track record of box office hits and her casting no doubt satisfied the moneymen.

> **CAROL LYNLEY:** At the time that I did *Harlow* I had a vague notion of Jean Harlow. I knew her name, but that is all I knew. My agent wanted me to do it so I did.

* * *

Carol Lynley was born Carole Ann Jones on February 13, 1942, in New York City. She grew up in the then Irish neighborhood of Inwood in northern Manhattan. Her mother and father were separated when she was two, and she and her younger brother, Daniel, were shuttled between relatives in Massachusetts, New Jersey, and New York. Ballet training at an early age led to a modeling career when she turned ten. Using the name Carolyn Lee, she quickly became one of the highest paid pre-teen fashion models in New York along with her friendly rivals Sandra Dee and Tuesday Weld. At age twelve, she began acting beginning with the touring production of *Anniversary Waltz*. It was then that she learned that another Carolyn Lee was registered with Actors Equity—hence the change to Carol Lynley that was suggested by Moss Hart. After appearing in a number of live TV dramas, Lynley made her Broadway bow in Graham Greene's *The Potting Shed*, playing Dame Sybil Thorndike's granddaughter, for which she received a Theater World Award. Hollywood beckoned and she made an auspicious debut in *The Light in the Forest* for Walt Disney in 1958, playing an indentured servant girl in love with James MacArthur, who was raised by Indians. She captivated critics with her tender performance and received a Golden Globe nomination for Most Promising Newcomer—Female. She passed on an offer from Disney to make a second motion picture so she could return to Broadway to play an unwed, pregnant teenager who has an abortion in the hit drama *Blue Denim*, directed by Joshua Logan. Lynley received kudos for her sincere performance and become much sought after by the major studios. She chose to sign a seven-picture deal with 20th Century–Fox.

With the studio grooming her to be another Sandra Dee, Lynley's early films were aimed squarely at the teenage market. In 1959, she played Clifton Webb's hip-talking daughter ("What's rocking? Roll?") in *Holiday for Lovers*; reprised her role as the high school girl, who goes all the way with Brandon de Wilde in his parents' basement, in a watered-down *Blue Denim* (due to censorship abortion was out, so her mortified father buys the naughty Carol a one way ticket out of town to have the baby); and then a small town girl who favors the charms of scalawag Stuart Whitman to that of popular teen idol Fabian (causing her adolescent fans to scratch their heads in bewilderment, no doubt), in *Hound-Dog Man*.

In the underrated western *The Last Sunset* (1961), directed by Robert Aldrich and penned by Dalton Trumbo, she was chosen by Kirk Douglas (whose production company was producing the movie) to play Dorothy Malone's teenage daughter, who falls for a black-clad outlaw (Douglas) while on a cattle drive from Mexico to Texas. What the poor gal doesn't know is that he is her biological father! Rock Hudson and Joseph Cotten also starred.

After being harangued for months by Fox, she begrudgingly took over for actress Diane Varsi (from the original *Peyton Place*) as young author Allison MacKenzie whose scandalous book about her hypocritical small town causes quite a stir in *Return to Peyton Place* (1961). The residents of Peyton Place are outraged. Her own mother, Connie (Eleanor Parker), finds it "cheap and dirty and vulgar," while a disgusted town matron (Mary Astor) calls it a "lurid piece of trash" and tries to ban it from the high school library. Discovering that her daughter is also in love with her married editor (Jeff Chandler), Connie berates her and Lynley, as Allison, woodenly retorts, "What you're afraid is like mother like daughter." Infuriated, Connie slaps Allison who hisses, "I hate you for that," in one of the film's many over-the-top moments that were reviled by the critics but loved by moviegoers, propelling it to become Fox's highest grossing movie of the year.

After taking a break from acting to marry publicist Mike Selsman and have a daughter, Lynley returned to Hollywood and was forced by Fox to play a high school student whose boyfriend, Richard Beymer, falls for exotic dancer Joanne Woodward in *The Stripper* (1963). Lynley separated from her husband and concentrated on her career with a vengeance, alternating between film and television.

On the big screen, the pretty blonde began to blossom, graduating to more mature roles, beginning with the hit comedy *Under the Yum Yum Tree* (1963). She played an enterprising college coed living platonically with her boyfriend (Dean Jones) to see if they were marriage compatible while staving off the lecherous advances of her playboy landlord (Jack Lemmon). Producer/director Otto Preminger spotted her on the Columbia Pictures lot while she was making *Yum Yum* and asked her to test for the role of the ill-fated Mona Fermoyle in his epic *The Cardinal* (1963). She got the part, beating out Ann-Margret, Dolores Hart, Shirley Knight, and Pamela Tiffin. In the film, Lynley plays Father Fermoyle's (Tom Tryon) sister, Mona, who after her family rejects her Jewish fiancé (John Saxon), runs off to become a tango-dancing prostitute. She ultimately dies in childbirth when her brother makes the choice to save the baby and not the mother. Preminger was so impressed with Lynley's acting that he also offered her the role of Mona's daughter, Regina. Most actors hated working with "Otto the Ogre," as he was called—but not Carol, who was a tough New York City kid at heart. She recalled,

> Otto was a cineaste and I think he saw the end result before it was actually filmed, which most people really into cinema do. And he would lose his temper with the execution of it. He could tell you what he wanted done. He needed it done instantly. If you could not translate that instantly, he had no in-between. He'd go from very charming to Mount Vesuvius … if you couldn't execute his ideas instantaneously that would create tension.
>
> On the set, it had to be done his way. If not, he would start getting agitated. Then when he got agitated you could see the veins start to pop on his quite bald head. When I would see that, I would think, "Oh, God!" Then he'd turn bright red and start shouting and the actor would just fall apart. Otto's idea of a joke when the actor was quivering was that he'd come up to them and yell into their ear, "relax!" The actor would fall apart even more. People were led away by assistants quite a lot.[4]

Publicity photograph of a wholesome Carol Lynley from *Under the Yum Yum Tree* **(Columbia, 1963).**

Both *Under the Yum Yum Tree* and *The Cardinal* were huge box office hits. Lynley was now in high demand by big time producers such as Robert Mirisch who described the actress as being "a very warm, wonderful person" and as "unaffected, down-to-earth."[5] Unfortunately, the actress owed 20th Century–Fox two more movies on her contract and the studio was holding her to it. The more mature Carol was determined to continue shaking her ingénue image and wound up playing the sex kitten in her next two films. In *Shock Treatment* (1964), she portrayed a manic depressive who falls for struggling actor Stuart Whitman, hired to feign insanity to catch a killer in a nuthouse. *The Pleasure Seekers* (1964), a remake of *Three Coins in the Fountain* (by the same director Jean Negulesco), featured Lynley, Ann-Margret and Pamela Tiffin as single gals out to trap themselves men while living in Madrid. Lynley's character pines for her married boss played by Brian Keith (his wife Gene Tierney, catching them together at a private soiree, slaps her in the ladies' room, calling her "a little tramp") while ignoring Gardner McKay's protective playboy reporter.

Lynley then took her sexy persona to the next level and posed semi-nude in the pages of *Playboy* in a pictorial entitled, "Carol Lynley Grows Up." It was a daring move for the time, but she did it under advisement from her agent, who felt it would help her progress to adult roles. The issue was released in March 1965, shortly before Sargent began looking for his new Jean Harlow. Coincidentally, Lynley's photo spread appeared four months after Carroll Baker disrobed for the magazine. It seems that both of them were vying for the vacant sex goddess crown once owned by the deceased Marilyn Monroe. The Hollywood establishment was not surprised with Baker's nudie pictures after her sexy role in *The Carpetbaggers* and her appearance at a press conference in a see-through dress, but they were shocked about Lynley's. The pretty actress was taken to task, with Louella Parsons leading the charge, calling her "young and foolish."[6] Feeling she didn't do anything wrong, Lynley frankly admitted that she posed just because she wanted to and felt just wonderful wearing not a stitch of clothing, adding, "There's nothing vulgar or immoral about nudity."[7]

Years later, Carol was still defending her decision to pose nude and remarked, "I still cannot believe the hoopla that surrounded that pictorial. My agent suggested I do it because it would be good for my career. Growing up in Manhattan, I'm very liberal so I agreed. It was very tame—before they started to show pubic hair. I firmly believe there is no evil in nudity."[8]

* * *

After it was announced that Carol Lynley was Sargent's new Jean Harlow, Joe Levine quickly pounced. He accused the producer of only casting her because she shared a first name with Carroll Baker, alleging that Sargent wanted to confuse the public even more. Sargent maintained it was truly a coincidence, and quipped years later, "Had Carol Lynley's name been 'Big Shit,' I still would've used it prominently in the ads."[9]

Although Lynley accepted the part of Jean Harlow, she didn't know what led them to cast her. She took the role with the prodding from her agent, and because Judy Garland was already signed to play Harlow's mother. According to Sargent, Lynley got the part after he had "an artist go through the Players Directory and draw Harlow's platinum-blonde tresses on each actress who might be right for the part. And when he came to Carol, they fit. What was even more extraordinary, when we measured Carol, we found she was identical with Jean!"[10] This proved to be pure publicity nonsense.

RICHARD BENNETT: There was a hassle about whether or not Carol Lynley's breasts were large enough to play Jean Harlow. There was a discussion about having her wear falsies. Somebody said, "That won't work because Harlow never wore a bra." So, they just went ahead with what they had.

Breasts aside, there were vastly different opinions of whether Carol Lynley looked like Jean Harlow.

RICHARD BENNETT: Carol Lynley looked nothing like the real Jean Harlow, who had a very distinct look, especially her hair, which people remember more than anything.

MICHAEL DANTE: Carol Lynley looked much more like Harlow than I think anybody in the world. When Carol put on the wig, she was absolutely gorgeous, while being seductive and sexy. They couldn't have cast anybody more perfect for the role.

A lot of the credit for Lynley's resemblance to Jean Harlow is due to makeup man Michael Westmore. His father, Monte Westmore, was the eldest son of George Westmore, who created the first studio makeup department and brother to Bud, Perc, Wally, Ern, and Frank, who all followed in their father's footsteps. All worked for different studios with three of them heading makeup departments—Bud at Universal, Perc at Warner Bros., and Wally at Paramount. Mike went into makeup as well.

MICHAEL WESTMORE: I was under contract to Universal from 1961 to 1972. I started with a three-year apprenticeship studying under all these makeup artists at the studio. I was working on *McHale's Navy* in 1964 and I got a call from the production company to see if I was interested in working on *Harlow*—but I do not know why they chose me. They told me it was in this new process called Electronovision and that Bill Sargent was producing it. Carol Lynley was going to be the star of it. Now, I did not know Carol at all. I had gotten some publicity because I was running the tours at Universal and I met a lot of people including my future wife, who was a model for an Edith Head fashion show.

When they called me, it was a slow time at Universal. My Uncle Bud was the department head at the studio. He gave me permission to go do it after I kind of begged him. Also, it was not a long shoot—maybe three or four weeks away from Universal.

To this day, Westmore does not have any idea why Bill Sargent chose him to be his film's makeup artist.

MICHAEL WESTMORE: I was twenty-seven and Carol Lynley was a few years younger. We may have crossed paths prior at Universal [Carol appeared on *The Alfred Hitchcock Hour*, *The Virginian*, and two episodes of *The Bob Hope Chrysler Theatre*]. Looking back, if Carol worked a lot at Universal and knew and liked my Uncle Bud, I am sure that had something to do with him giving me permission to work on *Harlow*. Knowing both of them, I am sure they got along greatly. And I just slipped right into the movie.

Carol and I met and immediately clicked. Carol was probably the second largest movie star I had worked with up to that point. The first one was Shelley Winters. Carol and I did this one project and we never saw each other again.

Regarding Bill Sargent, Westmore liked his personality and never had any problems working for him. He felt that the producer let everybody to the jobs they were hired to perform without interference.

MICHAEL WESTMORE: Bill Sargent was full of life. You would think he was a movie mogul the way he would show up on set with his limo and accompanied by two or three good-looking girls. It was kind of like a joke. He just wanted to come and look. He really did not have much to do with the filming process on the set—maybe behind the scenes.

Of course, I did makeup tests on everybody when they were first hired. He probably would have looked at them. If there was something he didn't like or needed to be changed, word would be sent down. Since we were shooting in that particular period [the thirties], I did research on it—how the eye makeup was done and the color of lipstick used. It wasn't difficult in finding color pictures of Jean Harlow. All my uncles were running makeup departments during Harlow's time, so it was easy for me to research even though none of them worked at MGM. I would add my two cents to what was historical. I don't remember having to change anything.

Prior to rehearsals commencing, casting consultant Marvin Paige was hired to fill the supporting and minor roles. His prior motion picture credits included *Breakfast at Tiffany's* (1961) and *Dime with a Halo* (1963), while for television he worked as the casting director on the series *Mickey* and *Combat!*

MARVIN PAIGE: I believe Efrem Zimbalist, Jr. was already cast, but I brought in Hurd Hatfield, Audrey Totter, Barry Sullivan and the rest.

One of the minor players hired for the movie was actor Rad Fulton. He was a discovery of agent Henry Willson, whose clients included Rock Hudson, Tab Hunter, Troy Donahue, and Guy Madison. He made his film debut in *Come Next Spring* (1956) with Steve Cochran and then was signed to a contract with Warner Bros. where he played some uncredited parts in films and guest starred on several of their TV westerns. He landed his first movie lead in the juvenile delinquent programmer *Joy Ride* (1958). In 1963, he and his agent had a falling out and parted company. In an unusual twist, Willson demanded the name "Rad Fulton" back since he created it. The actor put up a fight but eventually gave in so he could move on with his career. He then decided to use his real name, James Westmoreland.

The actor realized he had to start over since no one in Hollywood knew him by that name. He recalled on his website,

> I picked up *The Hollywood Reporter* and I busied myself reading. I came to a part in the magazine listing casting calls for up-coming films. There was a film titled *Harlow*, starring Carol Lynley. I knew the casting director and fortunately for me he took my call. I explained my predicament to him and asked if he could find me something to do to get started with my new name. He gave me a nice little part and said I'd start next week.
>
> Here I was on top of the world starting all over again.... When I got to the set, I saw Carol Lynley who I had worked with in *The Last Sunset*. She said, "Rad, are you working on this film?" "Yes, I am and it's nice to see you. I've had a few changes in my life. I've taken back my real name, James Westmoreland, and I'm beginning my career over." Carol smiled and said, "I've got it in my mind now, Jim. Knowing you and your abilities, you will make it happen. Good luck, Jim." Carol's kind words relaxed me and I enjoyed my first day of shooting.[11]

Considering that she was the star of the movie, it is nice to hear that Carol had no airs about her and did not play the diva. The fact that she had a lot going on and still found time to stop and chat with Westmoreland is a credit to her personal character, especially with all the attention focused on her to turn her into Jean

Harlow—beginning with her appearance. The hair stylist on the movie was named, coincidentally, Mary Westmoreland. Mike Westmore had never worked with her before but she had with Carol Lynley on the films, *Under the Yum Yum Tree* and *Shock Treatment*. There were two very different styled wigs worn by Lynley. A very short, cropped wig was used in the opening scenes and in publicity photos of Lynley as Harlow, including the one used for the LP soundtrack cover. In the movie, once she hits it big in *Hell's Angels*, Lynley, with a fuller wig, came closer to resembling Jean Harlow, especially her *Dinner at Eight* look. What remained constant was the small beauty mark added just below Carol's mouth on the left side.

> **MICHAEL WESTMORE:** The fact that Mary worked with Carol on two previous movies, I would guess that Carol brought her in. That is common in the business and that is why I was surprised that Carol did not bring in some other makeup artist that she worked with.
>
> **MARVIN PAIGE:** I think some of the wigs they gave Carol to wear were too twenties looking. They always had a soft hairdo on Jean Harlow, except in the very, very early days. The hair styles for Carol had a little bit of tightness to them.
>
> **MICHAEL WESTMORE:** Carol and I hit it off very well. Carol was easy to work with and if it looked good on her, she was happy. If the hairdresser was doing something that did not look quite right, Carol would speak up. We had to match Carol's Harlow look day to day. I would have liked to have worked with her later on, but our paths never crossed again.
>
> I don't recall if I was part of these [publicity photo] shoots. If it was shot way after we finished the film—probably not. If the wigs were different, they probably did not have Westmoreland there either because she would have gotten the originals and duplicated the look. Another hair stylist must have come in at that point, think they were doing it correctly but were not and the look was off. It is not uncommon where that has happened before. When somebody else takes over, they just don't have the same finesse or feel for what was done prior.

Costume designer Nolan Miller was hired to attire Lynley in white satin gowns, which were the trademark of Jean Harlow. This was years before Miller became famous for his stylish fashions worn by Joan Collins and Linda Evans on the eighties TV phenomenon *Dynasty*. He began designing clothes for such TV shows as *The Dick Powell Show* in the early sixties. Impressed with his creations, the show's guest actresses, including Joan Crawford and Barbara Stanwyck, asked him to design for them in private. He opened his own shop, and his list of clients grew to include Susan Hayward, Eleanor Parker, Natalie Wood, Ann-Margret, and Suzanne Pleshette, among many others. *Harlow* was one of the first movies he worked on, and despite the meager budget, his designs for Lynley looked expensive and stood out beautifully. However, it seemed he only costumed the leading ladies.

> **MAUREEN GAFFNEY:** I did not get any star treatment. I believe Nolan Miller just designed Carol and Ginger Roger's costumes. I cannot remember if I brought the dress I wore or the wardrobe department supplied. I had many low-cut dresses because I wanted to be Marilyn Monroe and a sex symbol. Boy was that the biggest mistake I ever made.

Michael Westmore: Even this early in Nolan's career, he was a genius in his designs—they were so notable. He put a lot of creativity in his costumes. I liked working with Nolan. All of a sudden, for example, if he decided to go with a scoop neck on a dress and the actress needed body makeup, I was there to do it. We all had to work together. I have done that my whole career. I worked with Nolan a couple of more times after *Harlow*. We became good friends.

With the shooting start date fast approaching, the cast (including Judy Garland, who had reported to the set on time after completing a ten-day engagement at the Fontainebleau Hotel in Miami Beach) would gather around a large table on the soundstage to rehearse their lines. Her coworkers had various opinions about her condition and her ability to play the role.

Carol Lynley: I rehearsed for three and a half weeks with Judy, who was playing my mother. I spent almost the entire time with her. She was in very good shape and was doing really well with the role. Like everybody else, I heard all the horror

Above and opposite: **Publicity photographs of Carol Lynley as Jean Harlow wearing the tighter hair-styled wig (above) and wearing the wig used in the film (opposite) (above photograph courtesy Marlin Dobbs).**

stories about working with her, but she was in fine health. I've been around actors my entire life and if something was off kilter with her, I would have spotted it in a minute. She was happy and married to a nice guy named Mark Herron. She was just the sweetest person in the world and would talk about her children—Lorna, Liza, and Joey. Judy was also one of the funniest people I ever met in my life. She didn't tell jokes—she just had to talk and she'd have you laughing. Most of the people who knew her would say the same thing.

Michael Dante: Judy Garland read with us and she was terrific, but you could see that she was just not comfortable or perhaps having personal problems. She was very nervous and overly sensitive.

Richard Bennett: I remember her reading the part, but she was almost a zombie at that time. She looked ghastly, shaky, and thin. It was tragic to see her in person and it was obvious that she wasn't strong enough to do it.

Marvin Paige: Judy was in pretty good shape at that point, but I think she felt the project was not going the way she hoped.

Carol Lynley: After we had finished up rehearsals on a Friday and were going

to start shooting on Monday, Judy came to me and said, "Sweetie, I really like you." I replied, "Well, I am crazy about you Judy." Then she said, "I've got to tell you something. I'm quitting. This is going to be a piece of shit. I know the press will write that I am crazy and drunk and couldn't handle it, but I don't care. I just wanted you to know first that I am leaving and this is a piece of shit." I begged her not to quit. That night I thought of calling her. I didn't and thought maybe she was testing my love.

Garland was AWOL the next workday, so Sargent called her agent Freddie Fields and warned if she wasn't there in ten minutes she was out. She didn't show. According to Michael Dante, her press agent Guy McElwaine came to the set and apologized for her. He explained that Garland was not physically capable of doing the role. Sargent told David Permut that he then went to Fields' office to get him to change his client's mind. Infuriated with Judy Garland's unprofessional behavior, the producer overturned his desk in anger.

The press was told by Judy's representatives that due to "a commitment conflict" Garland had to bow out of the production. Seasoned columnists, including Dorothy Kilgallen, did not believe this for a second. She opined, "Anyone in the trade knows there is no such thing if you have a booking agent or a personal manager—a star's contract has more pages than the scenario, everything is spelled out … it's not likely that someone would suddenly say, 'Oops! Sorry. We just noticed that Judy's supposed to be doing four weeks at the Olympia in Paris.'"[12]

Sargent, meanwhile, alleged to the press that "billing problems"[13] introduced by Fields were the cause. However, unnamed insiders at the time revealed to Kilgallen that Garland "became incensed and irate" because she felt that she wasn't being treated as a professional.[14] This was most likely closer to the truth, considering what the actress confided to Lynley the day before she quit.

CAROL LYNLEY: I consider my *Harlow* experience my three weeks with Judy. I truly appreciated having spent that time with her.

Scrambling to recast the key role of Mama Jean, Sargent announced Eleanor Parker, who had previously played Lynley's mother in *Return to Peyton Place*, was

Garland's replacement, but she quickly backed out after reading the script. Ginger Rogers then stepped in as Mama Jean. She was eager to play the role, since, as with Jean Harlow, she too had entered show business at a young age with a stage mother in tow.

After arriving in Hollywood in the late twenties, Ginger Rogers began landing small roles and finally broke out from the background with *Gold Diggers of 1933* (1933). Super stardom came as Fred Astaire's most popular dance partner in such hit musicals as *Flying Down to Rio* (1933), *Roberta* (1935), *Top Hat* (1935), and *The Story of Vernon and Irene Castle* (1939). She proved to be an excellent dramatic actress as well, winning an Academy Award for *Kitty Foyle* (1940). Surprisingly, her career began to slow in the fifties with such unmemorable films as *The Groom Wore Spurs* (1951), *The First Traveling Saleslady* (1956), and *Oh, Men! Oh, Women!* (1957). Her only sixties film prior to *Harlow* was the barely released *The Confession* (1964), produced by her husband William Marshall, where she played a madam of a bordello. She hadn't had many offers of late and commented, "They usually say I dance. I seldom get dramatic roles except on the Chrysler show [*Bob Hope Presents the Chrysler Theater*]."[15]

> **MICHAEL DANTE:** Ginger Rogers was absolutely fantastic. We began shooting right away and she knew all her lines verbatim. She was a hell of a pro and I had just so much respect for her. She came in cold and just did a wonderful job.
>
> **CAROL LYNLEY:** Ginger Rogers was very sweet. She showed up and did a beautiful job despite having no rehearsal time whatsoever.
>
> **MICHAEL WESTMORE:** I remember when they told me that Ginger Rogers was coming in. I was in awe of her as if it was the President of the United States. You start doing her makeup, and you're hoping you are doing it right. When you have a star like that, they are very used to having a certain look. If they ask to go over their lip line or want a certain color eye shadow, you do it. We got her done and made up. I was always starstruck having to stand by to powder her nose and fix her lipstick while we were filming. She did have an aura about her. You're there for them and never far away—right there at their beck and call. However, we did not have much social conversation—it was all business. We did exchange pleasantries. "Good morning." "How are you?" We worked together for such a short time.

While the two previous Electronovision movies were taped, live events, *Harlow* would be the first time the new process was being used under controlled conditions on a soundstage, with the film shot entirely in sequence. Unfortunately, problems arose from the start. Screenwriter Karl Tunberg was miffed because director Alex Segal was rewriting portions of the dialog. He claimed Bill Sargent's associates blocked him from sharing concerns with the producer. "Their strategy seemed to be to get me alone when Sargent wasn't present. Someone was always talking me out of seeing Sargent. Sargent would call up and say 'meet me and Carol Lynley in my office in ten minutes' and a few minutes later [Lee] Savin would call and say it was off."[16] Frustrated, he walked off the picture.

Due to the rushed production, *Harlow* employed a number of assistant directors who juggled many tasks, from maintaining the production schedule, to keeping the actors happy, to supervising extras.

Richard Bennett: You had to get there really early in the morning before the actresses arrived for makeup. You'd run errands and keep the filming schedule on track for the director. You also had to take care of the actors and make sure everything ran smoothly for them. I have such admiration for actors, but I didn't baby them. I made sure that I was able to make life as easy for them on the set as I could, so they could perform at their best and not worry about things. I had spent a year doing this on *Dr. Kildare*.

Despite filming in this new process called Electronovision with its intense lighting, it is surprising to learn it did not affect the makeup process.

Michael Westmore: The lighting used for Electronovision did not cause a change in the way I did the makeup. I followed how I was taught—using Max Factor pan-cake and stick—and it was not a problem.

I did not make everybody up. For the actors who I did not personally work on, I would check their makeup. It had to be to my liking. Nobody went to the set without my okaying them and getting the director's approval.

Technical mishaps began right from the start as "the intense lights washed out many of the sets, the movement from one sound stage to another sapped actors' energy and concentration."[17] Then, in the middle of the shoot, Carol Lynley finally learned about the other *Harlow* with Carroll Baker. This is surprising, since the entire crew knew about the rival version due to all the press it was receiving.

Richard Bennett: I knew. It was hard to ignore. It brought a competitive spirit to the set.

Michael Dante: I was well aware of Joe Levine's film. It was quite obvious to everybody in the industry, and a conversation piece every day, that two pictures, with the same title about the life story of Harlow, were being filmed at the same time.

Well, it wasn't obvious to Electronovision's leading lady, and it is very odd that Lynley's handlers didn't inform her before she accepted the role. Perhaps thinking it was a smart career move for their client, they withheld that tiny fact. Conversely, Carol Lynley was not happy about it at all.

Carol Lynley: When I agreed to do *Harlow*, I didn't know anything about the other one. I really had no idea. Sometimes the actor is the last to know. If I had known, I would have passed on playing Harlow. After learning about the other film, I said to my agent, "This is not going to work. I've got to get out of this." Traditionally, in show business, which is basically still true today, if you do two movies based on the same subject, they cancel each other out. Neither one does very well. I didn't want to be part of it anymore and thought it was rather shoddy. I then tried to quit, but they threatened to sue me, so I finished the picture.

Michael Westmore: Carol did mention to me when she learned about the other *Harlow*. It upset her that they were doing it. Thankfully, I was not the one who carried the bad news to her. I had known about the other movie and I was perturbed that these two movies called *Harlow* were being made at the same time. To me, this *Harlow* was special because I was able to leave Universal and thought it was going to be a big deal and then all of a sudden, you hear about the other one that was a bigger picture with a bigger budget.

CAROL LYNLEY: I also thought our script wasn't factual at all. At the time I didn't know much about Jean Harlow. As I was doing it, people who did know her would come up to me and talk about her. My impression was that nobody knew Jean Harlow deep down. She worked constantly and I don't think had any good friends from what I could see. The only people who knew the real Harlow, from what I could gather, were her mother and Bill Powell, and that's about it. There was no true story to tell. What she died of and why she died so young is open to speculation. I don't even presume to know. If she lived today, she'd be ... in the UCLA Medical Center. They take better care of people nowadays.

It seems Bill Sargent only had an unhappy leading lady and not an ill one, as Carol refutes the stories that she had pneumonia during filming. Ginger Rogers was also having a rough go of it and it was speculated that she would never make another film for Electronovision because "Miss Rogers gave them more trouble than Carol [Lynley] and that was plenty."[18] This seems to be vicious gossip drummed up to only to entice readers.

RICHARD BENNETT: Neither actress was difficult to work with. They were good and tried their best. Ginger Rogers was very hard working and I think grateful for the role.

MICHAEL DANTE: Certainly, Carol's unhappiness did not hurt her performance. I thought she was absolutely fantastic and looked so beautiful.

Perhaps more of a prima donna than any of the actors was boxer Sonny Liston. He reported to the set, but then refused to lift a glove when he read that his scene had him being knocked out in the ring by an actor (Nick Dimitri) playing his opponent, who attracts Harlow's attention. Obviously, Dimitri was supposed to be prizefighter Max Baer, who had a love affair with the actress despite his marriage. The scene had to be quickly re-written before he would go before the cameras.

Despite the problems, Bill Sargent made sure to invite Hollywood's most important columnists to watch the making of the movie. One was writer Philip K. Scheuer of the *Los Angeles Times*. He sat with Sargent at his office at Doheny Drive and Sunset Boulevard, outfitted with five television screens. There they watched both the rehearsals and the takes from the soundstages at Desilu over three and a half miles away. Per columnist David Lewin, "He sees his picture as it is being shot by using a micro-wave link, which is in fact Big Brother's big eye."[19]

Sargent had access to a two-way intercom, so he was able to hear the goings on from the set and could communicate with director Alex Segal. Sargent remarked, "And when I don't like what I see, I holler into this microphone, and even without it, they can hear me at the studio."[20]

After rehearsing his actors to the point of his satisfaction, the director, per Sargent, "retires to a control board in the mobile-truck unit to watch it play—same as in television."[21] This process also allowed Segal, working with a film editor, to choose and cut the best takes as they happened, saving valuable postproduction time. As Sargent explained, "Thus we gain all the advantages of TV and come out with the quality of a motion picture. The artistic quality is not lost."[22]

What fascinated Scheuer the most was that, not only was the image clearer and sharper than he expected, but "the image came through in the 1.85 to 1 aspect ratio in which the picture will be released instead of in the usual 4x3 shape of the home TV set."[23] This gimmick was due to Sargent's expertise in electronics.

Perhaps all the good and bad publicity the movie was garnering began to annoy its leading lady who quipped in one interview, "All this interest in a dead woman is unhealthy and necrophilia, and I don't mind who knows it."[24] This was not the first or last time Carol Lynley was so openly vocal with the press.

Meanwhile, studio heads were closely monitoring what Sargent was accomplishing with Electronovision. One hopeful, anonymous executive remarked to writer Harold Heffernan, "I think we could be reaching the crossroads. I saw some of the shooting on Electronovision—it was a revelation in speed and efficiency. They rehearse everything and then they shoot. No retakes! No standing around waiting for high-salaried craftsmen to spend hours lighting the set while at the same time others in the huge ensemble play gin or knit. This new deal eradicates all that. No wonder they can shoot a full-length feature in 10 or 12 days!" The executive, however, was savvy enough not to get his hopes up too much and concluded, "About quality, we don't know yet—but it will be well worth watching closely."[25]

It was reported that the Electronovision process allowed the feature to use the minimum amount of production crew as the unions would allow. Normally the total number of electricians, carpenters, stagehands, makeup, costumers, etc., totaled up to more than one hundred people. Here it was a fraction of that amount.

According to Michael Dante, Bill Sargent made one of his smartest moves in selecting Alex Segal to direct. However, his castmates and some of the crew begged to differ.

MICHAEL DANTE: Alex was probably the greatest director in the history of our business with multiple cameras from his live TV days.

He worked in the booth where he directed and edited from. He'd come back to the soundstage if there was something that needed to be worked out. He was the boss on the set so much so that producer Bill Sargent left Alex alone to direct. We didn't see much of Bill on the set.

I remember the day we were just finishing up rehearsing the scene where my character is about to make love to Harlow by the fireplace. As far as I'm concerned, that is the best seductive love scene I've ever had the pleasure of doing because the only thing I did was to take off my bow tie. Everything else is left to the imagination. It was choreographed and directed beautifully. For me, it was like a ballet move as my character starts turning out the lights, moving closer to the fireplace, and then taking Carol [wearing a gorgeous white satin gown, Harlow's trademark] and putting her down gently on that beautiful polar bear skin rug.

By the way, we rehearsed with laborers hammering away with noise so loud due to the low-budget and rushed timetable. We were behind schedule before we even started due to Judy Garland bowing out as the mother. Anyway, Alex came to me and said, "Michael, I need for Ed to say a line just as he sets Harlow down on the rug. Go home and think about it." I did and that weekend I put on the fireplace in my first house in Encino. I tried to recreate the scene and then it came like magic to me. It was such a creative moment and I got the biggest kick out of it. When we started filming again, Alex asked me if I had something for him and I said yes. Carol Lynley was there. I turned to her and said, "Carol don't be frightened. I am not going to do anything physical to you, but I am not going to tell you. I would rather just do it and have Alex shoot the rehearsal." As we began filming, I slowly placed her on the rug as rehearsed. She looked up at me with her beautiful eyes, and I said, "Do you like ffff-fireplaces?" I held on the "ffff." After we finished the scene, Alex, who was an emotional guy, came running down from the booth screaming, "That was the greatest ad-libbed line I ever asked an actor to do." He grabbed me and kissed me on the cheek. That is what I loved about Alex—he had so much passion for his work.

CAROL LYNLEY: Alex Segal was just kind of there. I don't think much of anything when I hear his name. I don't think anything good—I don't think anything bad. I just remember he had very dark circles under his eyes—I guess for good reason!

MICHAEL WESTMORE: I, too, don't remember much about him. My job, as I was trained, was to stand by the camera with my powder puff and any lipstick or makeup at the ready if anything needed to be done. I think because I do not remember anything specific about Alex Segal or the cinematographer it was very congenial. If we had had a problem, those are the things you remember.

MARVIN PAIGE: Alex Segal had a lot of ego though he didn't seem totally secure in what he was doing. At times, he got demanding and I thought he was like Otto Preminger. In fairness, he had a big job to do in this new process. He had done a lot of live television prior to this and that is why they brought him in.

Maureen Gaffney did not receive much help from Alex Segal when the time came to shoot her small role of a dumb starlet who is William Mansfield's date and encounters Jean Harlow at the Clover Room.

MAUREEN GAFFNEY: I was never introduced to anybody in terms of the stars of the movie. I had just a little part. I couldn't even say what the atmosphere was like for the actors because I was on my own. I was sitting in a corner waiting for my scene. I can say I do not think Carol Lynley was very happy. They had her climb onto the craps table and throw the dice. I watched that scene because she goes from there into the other room where I was going to be. I knew what was going to happen next. That was all one continuous shot with the cameras placed in both rooms.

They explained the shooting procedure a little bit. They set up cameras like doing a play. I don't remember how many they used but they were set up in every angle and in the right sequence. It cut down on the production time and made it shorter than a regular movie.

I had no rehearsal time and did not know what I was going to do until I got there. They said, "Can you sing 'Love, Love, Oh Careless Love'?" I looked it up and did the best I could. I only remember the name Alex Segal but I recall meeting [producer] Brandon Chase on the set. He and Bill Sargent remained friends with me.

The only direction I received from Segal was to go stand in front of the mirror and sing my song. Then to come out, turn around and, after seeing Jean Harlow, go ask for her autograph. That is all I was told.

I am in a room just off the casino and as they [Carol Lynley and Michael Dante] enter I am there singing. I come out to leave with Efrem Zimbalist Jr. and turn to see it is Jean Harlow on the sofa. I go over to her and exclaim, "It's Jean Harlow! May I have your autograph?" I bent over and I hear Bill and Frankie Ray laughing because I had a low-cut dress on and my boobs kind of filled the screen. Carol did not like it and said her line, "Get out of here!" And she really meant it so I was not a hit with Carol Lynley—or Raquel Welch [in A Swingin' Summer] but that's another story.

Carol Lynley and Michael Dante (whom Carol liked and declared, "We got along just great.") both have fond memories about working with Hermione Baddeley, who played Marie Dressler. Lynley found her "always prepared and funny." They worked together again in the episode "Eve" on the TV anthology series *Journey to the Unknown*. Dante also found the British actress to be "wonderful and so professional." He knew her Marie Dressler saw right through his character and thought he was a bum using Harlow, even though she sought him out.

Hedda Hopper visited the Desilu soundstage one day to watch the "quickie movie" in action. The columnist got to witness a scene between Carol Lynley (whom she found to be just beautiful as Harlow), Barry Sullivan, and Ginger Rogers. It seems the antsy stars couldn't wait to finish filming as Hopper reported (perhaps they sensed a bomb?). Sullivan was scheduled to fly off to Rome to shoot *Outlaw Planet* (released as *Planet of the Vampires* in the U.S.) and Lynley would soon be jetting to London to film *Bunny Lake Is Missing* for director Otto Preminger.

Ginger Rogers later confessed in *Newsweek* that she "didn't know what I was getting myself involved in, but you have to be prepared for all kinds of onslaught." When asked her opinion of the Electronovision process of filming she answered, "It could be a boon to inexpensive picture making." However, she felt more money should have bene spent on pre-production in terms of having the cast properly prepared with more rehearsals.[26]

Writer Bob Thomas, of the Associated Press, was another invited guest. He reported that Carol Lynley greeted him with, "Welcome to the nuthouse. It is so nice to see someone from the 'outside.'"[27] The columnist got to view the scene of Lynley's Jean Harlow storming into the office of MGM executive Paul Bern and demanding better scripts. Between takes, while in full Harlow makeup and costume, Lynley claimed to the writer that she was only trying to give an impression of Harlow and was not trying to imitate her. She also admitted many times over the years that she didn't know anything about Jean Harlow but did view some clips of her movies after being signed for *Harlow*. This is in great contrast to Carroll Baker, who was immersing herself in the ways of Jean Harlow for almost a full year before filming began on her movie.

Co-star Ginger Rogers, though, had not only heard of Jean Harlow, but was friendly with her as well. "Sure, I knew Jean and liked her. I met her through Bill Powell when we were making *Star of Midnight* together. I used to go up to his house for dinner, and Jean would be there. She adored him, needed his stability. And her gaiety brightened his life. She was always gay, always sparkling. When she entered a room you couldn't keep your eyes off of her. Maybe that gaiety was to hide the hurt she had known, I don't know. But I do know that she loved life and lived it to the fullest."[28]

On another day of filming, writers witnessed the party scene thrown on the MGM soundstage welcoming Jean Harlow back to Hollywood. Director Alex Segal boasted to the onlookers that he would be shooting twenty-three pages of the 121-page script that day. This included a scene where Harlow and William Mansfield share a surprisingly tender moment up in the rafters. Carol Lynley commented, "I never climbed a ladder before in my life and I am terrified of heights."[29] She would have to face that fear again seven years later when she was cast as Nonnie in the hit disaster movie *The Poseidon Adventure*. Efrem Zimbalist, Jr., countered that ladder climbing was "easy for me. In the army, I had lots of practice."[30]

Actor Aron Kincaid also visited the set that day. At the time, the handsome blonde newcomer had the All-American appeal of Tab Hunter and Troy Donahue. He co-starred with John Forsythe and Noreen Corcoran on the last season of the popular TV sitcom *Bachelor Father* and had just completed two starring roles in the *Beach Party* knockoffs, *The Girls on the Beach* and *Beach Ball*. Kincaid was friendly with Nancy Anderson, the West Coast editor of *Photoplay* magazine. Her office was on Rodeo Drive in Beverly Hills. When she proved too busy to pick up her boss, Fred Klein, at the airport, Aron volunteered as a favor. After settling the publisher into his hotel, Kincaid then drove him to the studio, and hung around while he filmed his scene.

> **Aron Kincaid:** I told him that he was very believable. He replied, "I doubt that." We laughed about it. I remember watching Carol Lynley and Efrem Zimbalist, Jr., but for the life of me I don't know why I didn't see Ginger Rogers.
>
> **Michael Westmore:** I remember that day because there was one scene in the movie where Efrem and Carol had their first kiss. Carol's skin was so light we had to use a darker white makeup on her but applied very lightly. His skin was dark because he must have been in the outdoors a lot, so we had to use a darker makeup. When they stood together, it was such a contrast—like between black and white, almost. When they kissed, it wasn't a light peck on the lips. This was a big, big smooch—possibly a tongue swapper. Their lips were pressed in so tightly. It was the only time I remember something like this happening. When the director yelled, "Cut!" and the two separated, Carol's makeup had rubbed off on his face—he had pale white makeup all around his mouth. And his makeup rubbed off on her. She had dark makeup all around her mouth. The makeup was literally smeared all over them. It was a good thing they did not have to go into a conversation because it wouldn't had worked. I had to clean them both up and touch up the makeup. I knew it would happen again because we had to shoot another take on it. This time I was ready for it when it happened.

Even though Carol Lynley and Richard Bennett were not impressed with the Electronovision processing of shooting, Hurd Hatfield and Jack Kruschen were. Hatfield extolled the fast-shooting schedule and remarked, "Just to give you an idea, there was one group of scenes that Carol and I did without a single cut or break; that was about five-and-a-half pages of dialogue, which would normally take two or three days to do; we did it in less than one morning's work."[31]

Kruschen, who did immense research on MGM studio mogul Louis B. Mayer in preparation of portraying him, also had high praise for filming in the

Electronovision process and disputed naysayers, who claimed it would cost many jobs in Hollywood. As with Hurd Hatfield, he liked that the movie came as close to a stage production as possible. Championing the new filming process, he said, "An actor has a good opportunity in Electronovision because he can properly prepare himself and with the proper technical people he can do a role in continuity, thus maintaining a character through a scene, or for that matter, an entire picture."[32] He envisioned future productions shot even quicker than eight days after three to four weeks' rehearsal with cast and crew, and that the film editors should be in attendance so that editing could begin immediately after the director yelled, "Cut and print!"

Barry Sullivan concurred in praising Electronovision due to the speediness and remarked, "This is a great way to do business. An actor like me can knock off this picture and do other things. I didn't think I could do a picture in Italy because of this one, but now I can."[33]

It seems most of the cast were challenged by working in Electronovision and some even liked the fact that it was like doing a live play. They had to learn more pages of dialogue because of the continuous shooting without as many takes for different camera angles. Most, though, had stage experience so it was not too difficult for them.

> **RICHARD BENNETT:** If you know actors, they are a remarkable strain of people. They really are. I have tremendous respect for them, because they have such courage and take chances baring their emotions and their bodies throwing themselves into their roles. I am a big fan of actors, but this was not a joyful production or one where the cast was at the top of their form in any regards—makeup, acting, production. The actors seem to just get the job done.
>
> **CAROL LYNLEY:** I tend to like actors—female actors, male actors I've know them my entire life. I admire and respect their work, because I know how difficult it is since I have acted three quarters of my life. I loved working with Ginger Rogers and Efrem Zimbalist, Jr., whom I especially adored, and thought was just great.
>
> **RICHARD BENNETT:** I later worked with Efrem Zimbalist, Jr. on another project. He is an excellent human being and such a splendid chap. I know making *Harlow* was not a happy experience for him or the rest of us for that matter. He would never say anything bad about anybody from what I know about him.
>
> **MICHAEL WESTMORE:** Efrem Zimbalist, Jr. was such a nice, nice, pleasant man to work with. Actually, all the actors on this film were wonderful and I did not have any problems. We were shooting so fast with all those cameras positioned around. On a regular movie, you are lucky to film ten pages in a day.
>
> **CAROL LYNLEY:** I knew Barry Sullivan over many years. We worked together a lot. He was a journeyman actor with an enormous amount of experience. He was extremely articulate and a gentleman but wasn't as funny as Judy. Even so, it was always a joy to come to a set and to see Barry. It was the same with Efrem. It made me happy to be working with them. The whole cast was wonderful and we did the best we could—considering.

As for the crew, perhaps it was quite another story, since technically there were vast differences in shooting via Electronovision versus regular film—from the lighting to the multiple cameras, trying to keep booms and mikes out of the frame, etc.

Knowing that the Electronovision *Harlow* would be in theaters over a month before his own movie, Joe Levine began placing ads in all the trade papers proclaiming that "In 1965, there is only one Harlow…. Carroll Baker"—just as the rival version began shooting. To counter, Sargent rented a blimp to fly over the theater hosting the 1965 Academy Awards urging TV viewers to "See Bill Sargent's *Harlow* starring Carol Lynley."

DAVID PERMUT: Bill loved telling that story and said that when Levine looked up and saw the blimp, he grabbed his heart. Bill just reveled in touting their rivalry to promote his film. Bill went with his instincts and often said, "You need to sizzle to sell the steak." I think with his relationship with Joe Levine, the sizzle became the contentious relationship of who was going to beat whom to the box office.

The two showmen almost came to fisticuffs at the Oscar ceremony when Sargent went to shake Levine's hand to congratulate him on his Best Foreign Language Film win for *Yesterday, Today and Tomorrow*. Levine didn't recognize him but did notice the excessive popping of flashbulbs from surrounding photographers. Then the stranger uttered the dreaded words, "Mr. Levine, I'm Bill Sargent."[34] Levine raged and called him an "S.O.B." Pulling his hand away, Sargent threatened, "Another crack like that and I'll slap you down right here and now."[35] The heated exchange continued, so Paramount executive Howard Koch and others quickly stepped in to separate the warring rival producers.

Sargent defended himself in the press against Levine's accusation that he had tipped off the photographers beforehand just to get a rise out of him. "I made sure that there were no photographers about and I shook hands sincerely. I admire this man, but I don't need his handshake."[36] Continuing his attack on Mike Wallace's radio show, Sargent belittled Levine's purchasing of distribution rights to films rather than making them. He remarked, "You know when he accepted the award at the Academy, I just looked at him with one comment: 'Keep buying 'em. I can make 'em faster than you can buy 'em.'"[37]

Life magazine reported the incident in a story it did on the two rival *Harlow* movies that featured photos of the actresses as Jean Harlow. It prompted a reader named L. Harkins to write in and comment, "I just finished reading in your May 7 issue that Carroll Baker and Carol Lynley expect to portray Harlow on the screen. Know any more good jokes?" This person may have represented the true feelings of the general public. Despite all the publicity Sargent and Levine were drumming up for their movies with their allegations and name calling, their leading ladies were not generating much excitement or confidence from skeptical moviegoers. Most felt that neither could bring the thirties blonde bombshell to life fully on the silver screen.

Despite the public's waning interest in the movies, accusations between the two producers continued raging and reached ridiculous levels. An outraged Joe Levine lambasted Bill Sargent on the radio for making his version of *Harlow*. He railed, "I think that he's violated every rule of fair-trade practice … he's started a thing that could well end the motion picture business as we know it."[38] He then went on to claim that he had been in production with his *Harlow* for over two years and that Bill Sargent just came in and stole everything.

Levine continued with his tirade against Sargent, warning that he could co-opt any public domain topic for a movie even if another producer had poured millions of dollars into their production. He specifically referred to Dino De Laurentiis' upcoming *The Bible* as a prime example.

The angry Levine also had very strong words for Marshall Naify, whose company, Magna Pictures, was distributing the movie. Having had a prior business relationship with Magna, Levine was surprised that Naify would agree to do business with Electronovision. He then went on to mention that he had read that Naify was going to produce a multi-million-dollar production of *Don Quixote*. Reminding Wallace that the property was in the public domain, Levine revealed that he held the rights to an already produced Italian version that was supposed to go directly to U.S. TV, but now under the circumstances, he was going to hold on to it. He wondered aloud how Naify would feel if he released it to theaters at the same time. When Wallace asked Levine if he was trying to get Naify to withdraw from releasing *Harlow*, Levine, quickly responded, "I'm not suggesting anything. I just want to know how Mr. Naify would like it."[39]

Bill Sargent reminded Mike Wallace that when he jumped into the Jean Harlow sweepstakes there were three other studios also planning movies about her. He went on to say, "We spent about five weeks adapting it [Karl Tunberg's screenplay] to the technique—the Electronovision technique—seventeen days later we had a picture. There's no use making a picture costing $3 ½ million if someone can beat you to it, like I beat Mr. Levine, and my intention was not to beat Mr. Levine; it was to make a good picture."[40]

Even the marketing campaigns were fodder for the bitter *Harlow* wars. Levine contended that he had been using the color pink and pink hues for months in all of the marketing for his *Harlow,* from the gowns worn by Carroll Baker in promotional appearances to all of the display ads. He became enraged when Bill Sargent took out an ad in *Daily Variety* featuring Carol Lynley in "a here-to-there cutaway black gown—the whole thing four-dimensioned by the pinkest pink background."[41] Defending his use of the color, Sargent flippantly remarked, "Pink's in public domain too."[42]

The out-of-control Levine's accusations that Sargent co-opted Paramount's marketing campaign inadvertently gave the Electronovision movie even more free publicity. Regarding Sargent's ads, Levine railed to Mike Wallace, "He has taken the title, he has used the coloring that we have used in our ads, he has used the title of the book, copied it exactly—the figures—and he's using it in his ad. Additionally, his ad reads, 'The movie that the world is waiting for.' Well, you know, Mike, nobody in the world knows about his film. But I've publicized mine for two years worldwide."[43]

In actuality, Sargent's ad proclaimed, "The picture the world has been waiting to see!" For some reason, though, the official movie poster did not feature Carol Lynley despite the numerous publicity photos they took of her in costume. Instead, it had a close-up image of the real Jean Harlow. Perhaps it was a way to confound moviegoers who were waiting for the Baker movie. Sargent flooded the newspapers with preview ads featuring a full-length shot of Lynley as Harlow in silhouette accompanied by the title of the movie and its opening date. When the movie was released, the ads had pictured a bra-less Lynley (who arguably never looked sexier) in full Harlow makeup and clad in a low-cut evening gown perhaps in hopes of getting the public—especially of the male kind—into the theaters. A close-up from her waist up was used for smaller ads.

It is a mystery why Bill Sargent chose not to feature Lynley on the movie poster.

Pressbook cover, featuring the film's official movie poster with an image of Jean Harlow, for Electronovision's *Harlow*.

He even had a horizontal ad of her as Harlow (clad in a skintight, satin evening gown) lying across a fainting couch while holding a white fur coat that was partially on the floor. It would have made quite a stunning half-sheet poster.

Defending his poster choices against Levine's allegations, Sargent claimed he had his lawyers review the two ads and they felt they were not similar. He then went on to explain, "The type for their title is nothing like ours. Theirs is straight up and down, ours has little curlicues on it. We have the color pink, but we used that before Levine did. His first ad—the only one that came out before our first ad—was red. If we stole the color pink, we got it from *The Pink Panther*, and if we stole the string of light bulbs we use, we got it from *Mary Poppins*, not from them."[44]

While the two producers continued to battle it out in the press, the filming of Electronovision's *Harlow* came to completion with a splash. The last sequence to be filmed was the mud bath scene where a submerged Carol Lynley, as Harlow, flings mud at her director to show her distaste for being subjected to yet another bathtub scene. When a satisfied Alex Segal yelled "Print it," the jubilant crew (probably glad to be done with this mess) grabbed the director and threw him fully clothed into the mud. Hopefully they waited until Lynley removed herself from the bath.

As filming wound down, Michael Westmore caught the ire of one of the ADs.

MICHAEL WESTMORE: Carol and I would meet in the makeup room at around 5 a.m. because we needed to get her makeup exactly like we wanted to. It wasn't just thrown on. She had to be on the set by 7:30 or so. Carol was kind of a health nut. She would bring her own breakfast—a little bowl of something. The second AD would always come in every morning and ask Carol what she wanted for breakfast. She would order a big breakfast with, say, pancakes, bacon, orange juice, coffee, and more. There was no commissary where we were filming so the AD had to run out to Denny's or somewhere. When he came back, he would lay it all out for her. This happened every morning of the shoot.

On the last day of filming, he came in and he said to Carol, "I don't understand how you eat all this food and you don't gain weight." She replied, "I don't eat it—Mike does!" Well, he turned around and glared at me. If a look could kill, I would be dead. He'd lay out this breakfast buffet daily and I would eat it.

The actual filming of Sargent's *Harlow* took eight and a half days, including two days of rain delay, plus re-shooting some scenes because of the mysterious disappearance of film footage. It was finished in the same time that it took Joe Levine to complete less than thirty minutes of film.

Another time-saver and a way for Bill Sargent to cut corners on *Harlow* was that the film's musical score was already composed by Al Ham, with Nelson Riddle conducting the orchestra, before filming began. Normally, the scoring is done after the picture has been completed. It was reported that the composer created different themes for seven major characters for when they appeared on screen. For example, Harlow's theme was called "I Believed It All" and for Paul Bern it was "With Open Arms." A prideful Bill Sargent predicted that critics would hail the music score as "the greatest ever written."[45] All that had to be done after shooting commenced was for the musical tracks to be laid down on the soundtrack and in a rare occurrence, the soundtrack LP could be released at the same time as the movie rather than weeks or months later as happened with most movies.

The rushed production, however, was not a total success as it contained filming errors, which Sargent promised that the audience would not be able to notice. Despite the mistakes in his quickie movie, Sargent exclaimed, "Look at the savings in film alone. George Stevens came into my office the other day and told me he uses over 100,000 feet of raw film on an average production. We used less than 26,000. There's savings on wardrobe, on cable men and laboratory and cinema crews, and what with labor so high as it is today it all mounts up. And you don't need to sacrifice quality just because it all goes so fast."[46]

Despite Sargent's boasting, some of his cast and crew were not impressed with this new filming technique.

> **RICHARD BENNETT:** It was an experiment to make a feature film with TV cameras. They were taping it instead of filming and then transferring to film. It was a mess. They hadn't perfected those skills at the time and they were not very successful. They weren't working with a very good script to begin with, so that didn't help matters. It was a disaster and kind of sad since everyone worked so hard.
>
> **CAROL LYNLEY:** I found the whole filming process bizarre. It was such a shoddy production. When you walked by the sets, they would waffle back and forth. They even hid the cameras behind things. You'd be standing there saying your lines and then a painting would slide away and a camera would come in on you. I had no idea what for and did not care why.

This was most likely because the Electronovision process used TV cameras placed in a variety of spots in order to obtain different angles of the action in one take, so director Alex Segal could make his decision on which one was best to use.

Sargent then announced that he would not be submitting his film for a Motion Picture Production Code Seal. This was the industry's censorship board that would give its seal only to films that they deemed acceptable. It was standard practice by studios to only release movies with this seal and they would cut scenes to meet the guidelines. By 1965, more and more films with adult subject matter were being released without the seal and still making money. The Production Code was fully abandoned two years later.

To celebrate the completion of *Harlow*, Bill Sargent threw a wrap party on the studio's soundstage. According to Michael Dante, after director Alex Segal yelled his last "Cut and print," tables were immediately brought out with food and drink. There was no in-between time as the actors in attendance were still in costume and makeup. Bill Sargent and Alex Segal gave thank you speeches.

> **CAROL LYNLEY:** I wasn't there for long—maybe about ten minutes—for good reason.
>
> **MICHAEL DANTE:** The first time that Ginger made her appearance there wasn't much attention given her. She was still in her film wardrobe, as she walked around and kind of blended in with everybody else. Shortly thereafter, she changed into a beautiful dress and made a grand entrance to the party. She turned every head in the

place and got all the attention especially of the photographers. Ginger looked lovely and it was very clever of her, or whoever told her to do this, to grab the spotlight.

ARON KINCAID: I accompanied Fred Klein to this and it was the oddest one I ever went to. I didn't see a single cast member, only the crew. [By the time he arrived most of the cast had already departed.] I knew the director, Alex Segal, and I don't even remember him being there. I heard the shooting had been just a disaster with all sorts of problems and everybody could hardly wait until their bit in it was done so they could clear out.

I recall it was about five o'clock and dark already with the rain pouring down. People were drinking and mingling, and they had a bunch of girls, who sort of looked like Jean Harlow, but not really, wandering about. One of the girls resembled Lesley Ann Warren in *Victor, Victoria*. She was rocky and shaky on her heels, and I think she had thrown back a few. It was very weird—almost like an episode of *The Twilight Zone*. You'd look and there would be a girl dressed in white satin standing over in the shadows underneath a klieg lamp. I knew several people from past things I worked on. I was having a good time chatting and walking around stepping over these rain puddles as the water had seeped in under the soundstage doors. All of a sudden, we heard this loud fracas with glass breaking, chairs being broken and then some woman screamed. There was a fight and some guy said, 'we've got problems.' A grip or electrician slugged somebody and this huge Islander maybe from Samoa or Tonga punched the guy in the throat killing him. The man was dead on the floor with his blood mixing with the flowing rainwater. An ambulance was called and soon the police were swarming all over the place. The Islander guy was taken away in handcuffs. I turned to Fred Klein and said, "Does this mean the party's over?"

RICHARD BENNETT: I try to forget it. It was tragic seeing that sort of thing. It was frightening and awfully sad. Usually, the crew members get along fine, especially film crews. They are a remarkable bunch, but one of the problems with this movie was that it was a hodgepodge of electronic crew and film people. The film unions wanted to work in tape because this was being touted as a feature film, but the live engineers [from TV] didn't want them there, so there were battles over that from the beginning.

ARON KINCAID: A few days later I went to a party thrown by Mark Goddard. I was surprised to see the drunken Harlow gal on the arm of Paul Lynde. They both arrived tipsy. Mark's wife was upset with their behavior and they were asked to leave. Soon after, Lynde came bursting through the front door screaming that he had killed his date. Mark and I ran outside and found her lying practically in the gutter. We carried her over to the lawn and I felt a pulse. I said to Paul, "She's going to be all right—she's just drunk." He replied, "What do you know about it—you, you blonde, you!" We got her into the car and instructed Paul to take her to the hospital emergency room. That I was the last I saw of them and never knew what happened to Miss Harlow look-alike.

Since he did not attend the wrap party and immediately returned to Universal, Michael Westmore has nothing but fond memories of *Harlow* and found his whole time working on the picture to be positive.

MICHAEL WESTMORE: Working with Carol Lynley was great. And overall, it was a very good experience for me. With some of the actors playing characters that were known, I was able to research to see what they looked like. I have done this throughout my whole career."

Shortly after *Harlow* finished shooting, a seemingly exhausted Bill Sargent commented, "I don't intend to do anything like this again, and I wouldn't have done it this time if someone had asked me." This sounds very suspect, especially since he went on to say defiantly, "People tell me that he [Levine] announced his picture before I announced mine, but I made my announcement before he acquired the book. And at the time I started work on production I wasn't at all sure that his project was for real. Every one of the majors had been talking about a similar project."[47]

All of Sargent's fighting with Joe Levine in the press did not sit well with some of his cast and crew.

> **CAROL LYNLEY:** That's not about making movies, that's stupidity. It did more harm than good.
>
> **MARVIN PAIGE:** The public feuding between Bill and Joe Levine did not help either movie. However, I believed the producers thought the publicity would have intrigued moviegoers to see both versions. It didn't.
>
> **CAROL LYNLEY:** Bill Sargent was full of bluster. He wasn't that well versed in show business. I didn't find him to be a bad guy, but he was a promoter and not a filmmaker. And it shows with *Harlow*.
>
> **MARVIN PAIGE:** I thought Bill Sargent was a rough and tough guy. He was also soft-hearted. I liked him and we got along very well. I think his intention was to make a good movie, but he invested so much in Electronovision thinking it would skyrocket and revolutionize the industry. Unfortunately, the movie was shot like a Kinescope in black and white and the quality was not as good as it should have been.

When Bill Sargent wasn't trading barbs with Levine, he was dealing with the many problems that crept up in post-production. Technicolor Corporation, the preeminent photo lab in Hollywood, refused to print the film and Sargent was sure that Joe Levine and Paramount had pressured them not to work with Electronovision, Inc. Then to Sargent's shock and dismay, exhibitors refused to schedule the movie despite his offering them a fifty-fifty split of the box office take with distributor Magna Pictures. *Harlow* was then booked into secondary movie houses and drive-ins. However, one major chain that did book it was, ironically, Paramount Pictures Corporation's former subsidiary Paramount Theaters.

Frustrated and furious, Bill Sargent accused Paramount and Joe Levine of "pulling every dirty trick in the book,"[48] including pressuring the big chains from booking his *Harlow* even though the movie was set to open in 1,200 independent theaters. Sargent bemoaned, "Some 80 percent of the theater business is controlled by seven chains and not one of the seven chains has booked our picture, except AB-PT, which has it in only one house in Salt Lake City. And AB-PT owns 10 percent of Electronovision stock!"[49]

The one remaining sticking point that could have derailed the release of *Harlow* altogether was the continuing Sidney Skolsky lawsuit. To prevent a lien on the film negative, Electronovision had to post a $35,000 bond. With that settled, it should have been clear sailing for Bill Sargent, but then the Screen Actors Guild cancelled

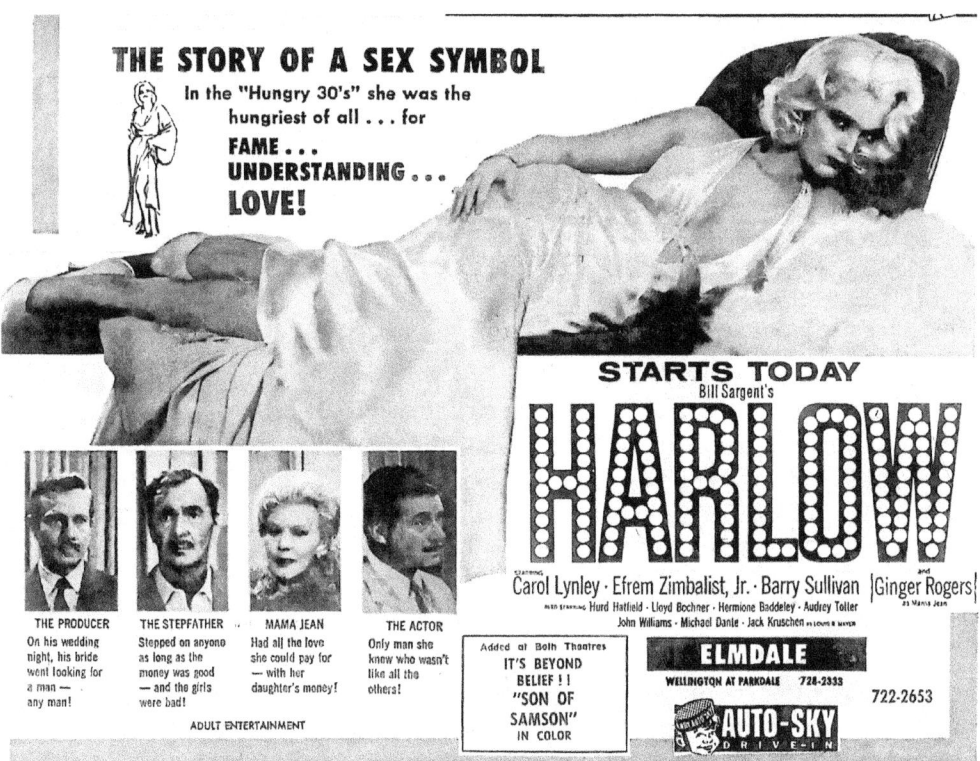

Newspaper ad for *Harlow* with Carol Lynley as Jean Harlow front-and-center.

its pact with Electronovision (allegedly without notice) because it had failed to pay some of its actors including Hermione Baddeley and Jack Kruschen for their services. Baddeley was most upset at not receiving the money owed her (about $3,000) and went public about it (as did Jack Kruschen declaring he was due $7,000) giving Sargent's *Harlow* more bad press. Electronovision claimed it was all a mistake due to clerical errors and that all union members had received their pay. Certified checks were reportedly mailed to the actors still owed their salaries a day after the cancellation. Money from the company's New York account in the Bank of Israel was supposed to be wired to the account in the Santa Monica Bank, but because the latter did not have wire service, the check to cover the salaries had to be mailed, causing the delay.

Bill Sargent was taken aback by the Guild's quick action and remarked that the money owed was "only 10% of the salaries" and that his actors "had been paid 90% of their fees."[50] He and Electronovision, Inc., trying to uphold their reputation, released the following statement:

> Electronovision has paid all monies due to performers in its production of *Harlow*. The payments to Hermione Baddeley and Jack Kurschen were made on a delayed schedule according to dates agreed upon by their representatives. The action comes

as a complete surprise to Electronovision as no notice or complaint was received by the company prior to the hearing. Furthermore, all production monies were dispersed by Electronovision within hours of their receipt from the distribution company. There seems to be a misunderstanding in regard to this entire matter. Electronovision's past record speaks for itself. During the first nine months of the company's existence, more than $650,000 has been paid to SAG members without a single complaint.[51]

After the matter was finally settled, a perturbed Sargent, tired of his actors' bellyaching, railed, "I don't know how any of these actors had any cause for complaint. They all got more money than they'd made before for the same time [eight days of shooting], and the leads got more money than they'd ever got regardless of time."[52]

While Sargent was dealing with Electronovision's fiscal problems, Magna was concentrating on marketing its film. It was during the time when movie companies would produce a pressbook to be sent to distributors to help them promote the movie. Pressbooks contained plot summaries, cast and crew credits, biographies of the major players, different size poster ads and newspaper inserts using various versions of the movie's film poster, and promotional gimmicks to create buzz for movies and help get paying customers into theater seats.

One of Magna's pressbook marketing ideas was having theaters get their local radio stations to play the movie's end title song or opening credits' theme music. Because the score was composed and recorded before the movie was shot, the LP was already released by Warner Bros. Records and available in record shops.

Magna also came up with an advance promotional idea to send four aspiring starlets on a multi-city tour to hype the movie. The "Harlow Girls" as they were described were four blonde Hollywood beauties: Bobbie Whilby, Janet Day, Jackie Andre (all of whom purportedly appeared in the movie without screen credit), and Maureen Gaffney (the only one to have received screen credit for her role as Miss Larsen). Conspicuously missing from this list, despite Sargent's fondness for her, was Carol Hollenbeck. Reportedly, the one direction the girls received was that when mentioning the film to call it "Bill Sargent's *Harlow*" to differentiate it from the rival version.

> **MAUREEN GAFFNEY:** After the movie was produced, Bill said we are going to invent the Harlow Girls. I was chosen to be the spokesperson to speak about the movie and he hired three models from Cole Bathing Suits. I was a dancer and studied fashion modeling so I was good at it, although I had never done any professional modeling. They sent us out on a seventeen-state tour. It was like one night in every state. I did most of the speaking because I had a part in the movie.
>
> **CAROL HOLLENBECK:** I was not surprised that Bill Sargent did not ask me to become a Harlow Girl. I had the look but I may not have had the outgoing personality he was looking for. I was rather shy and not the type to do promotion. Today, I am the complete opposite.
>
> **MAUREEN GAFFNEY:** We were sent to New York for the world premiere and Bill also opened the movie the same night in theaters across the entire United States. Most movies did not open nationally at the same time back then.

Publicity photograph of Maureen Gaffney from *Harlow*, 1965 (courtesy Maureen Gaffney).

We were on *The Mike Douglas Show* and some other talk shows. I had not seen the movie at this time. I was involved with the making of it and knew the answers to the questions because I hung out with Bill Sargent and the guys. I would sit in his office for hours and hang out. I would listen to them talk about the movie.

We would dress in thirties dresses like Jean Harlow and I also got to model Cole Bathing Suits. I was too bosomy so the designer would always put me in one-piece suits until we got to the Mormon state of Utah. She did not have time to sort out the swimsuits. I jumped in there and put on a bikini because I was tired of the one-piece. I came out wearing this bikini in the middle of a department store and all the Mormon women gasped. The designer yelled at me, "Don't you ever do that again!" I knew she could not get rid of me because I was the spokes-model who knew how to talk about the movie. We generated a lot of newspaper publicity wherever we went. I even got a write up about me in a Boston paper because that is where I am from.

After the tour ended, we had our picture taken with Bill Sargent at the Hollywood Wax Museum. It was hanging up there for many years in the front entrance under glass. The problem was that all the models were looking into the camera and stupid me leaned over and kissed Bill Sargent on the cheek. My profile is only visible and not my full face. I was not polished yet and still learning. I had no one teaching me the ropes. You make a lot of mistakes but know what to do the next time.

The pressbook also suggested that each theater have their own Harlow Girl contest in conjunction with Cole Swimsuits. Some theaters turned the contest suggestion into full-fledged beauty pageants. For instance, in San Antonio, Texas, the

```
┌─────────────────────────────────────────────────┐
│              ENTRY BLANK                        │
│                                                 │
│  Harlow Girl Contest                            │
│  Woodlawn Theater                               │
│  1020 Fredericksburg Road                       │
│  San Antonio, Texas                             │
│     Yes, I would like to be made up as a Harlow Girl │
│  and I will be at the Woodlawn Theater for the judging │
│  at 10 a.m. Saturday, May 8.                    │
│           Name ..................................│
│           Street and Number .....................│
│           Telephone .............................│
│           City and State ........................│
└─────────────────────────────────────────────────┘
```

Entry blank to become a Harlow Girl.

Harlow Girl contest was co-sponsored by the *San Antonio Express and News* newspaper, radio station KTSA, and the Woodlawn Theater. Entrants, who had to be age 19 or older and unmarried, had to submit a form by the deadline date. They were judged by beauty and personality. Among the prizes showered on the winner were a 100 percent human-hair blonde Harlow wig; a $150 diamond necklace; a $150 wardrobe from the Chez Louise Dress Shoppe; and an all-expense paid, three-day trip to Houston.[53]

Other tie-ins suggested working with local car dealers to have the Harlow Girl winner and three runners-up ride around in a convertible with a banner promoting *Harlow* and to work with beauty salons advertising the new, short Harlow hairdo. Nowadays these marketing ploys seem desperate and laughable, but in the sixties, it was the norm as the goal was to get a movie mentioned in the press as much as possible leading up to its opening.

To help support the movie, Bill Sargent, Carol Lynley, and Ginger Rogers guested on *Hollywood '65*, a local Los Angeles program hosted by John Willis. And on the national late-night program *Nightlife*, hosted by Dave Garroway, a scene from this *Harlow* was screened as a sneak preview for the audience.

7

Harlow, Paramount Style

Days before Bill Sargent's *Harlow* was released, Joe Levine issued a prepared statement to the press. Without mentioning Electronovision, Inc., or Bill Sargent, it defended the fair, upstanding business practices and ethics of the producer and Paramount Pictures, and how they had been wronged. This, according to Levine, resulted in loss of public trust. He built the case that they did the right thing by registering their title with the MPAA, an organization created to safeguard its members (though it had no control over nonmembers). He explained how they had made deals to book their *Harlow* in numerous topflight theaters only to see some renege on showing the movie. Though not actually stated, the implication was that it was due to rival Sargent's *Harlow*.

Levine ended with how the industry was losing the support of the public. Here is where he blamed Electronovision, Inc., and Bill Sargent without actually mentioning them. He stated, "As an industry, we have never confused the public ... at least we haven't confused them until now. At a time when everyone is trying to build the industry's public image the development of the past few months can do nothing but destroy that image."[1]

Levine makes a good case in his press release, but he fails to take any blame or responsibility for his own actions. As was suggested to him, he could have just ignored Bill Sargent's quickie movie (his star Carroll Baker begged him to) and concentrated on producing a good picture. Instead, he feuded with his rival in the media creating bad press for both of their movies. Obviously, the showman's ego could not handle that another producer, a novice in Hollywood, would dare to not back down to the mighty Joe Levine, who acted like a longtime movie mogul but in actuality had only just begun producing films two years before. His decision to race Sargent to the silver screen, and the vitriol that stemmed from that competition, would seriously hurt his movie.

Levine made one last Blitzkrieg assault on Sargent's *Harlow* in the days before it opened. He reportedly paid $100,000 for one hundred ad pages in *Variety* and placed additional ads for his own movie in all the major newspapers nationwide using the catchphrase, "It's the Only *Harlow*." Full page advertisements contained a variety of combinations of the below:

Let There Be No Confusion

The only *Harlow* produced by Joseph E. Levine and Paramount Pictures.
The only *Harlow* with Carroll Baker.

> The only *Harlow* filmed in Technicolor.
> It's *all* the *Harlow* you've ever heard about!
> It's *all* the *Harlow* you've ever pictured!

In hindsight, Levine should have been paying more attention to the filming of his *Harlow* and he should have adhered to the advice his leading lady gave him. Carroll Baker felt quality would trump speed and that audiences were smart enough to know that, but the prideful producer ignored her. He plugged ahead with getting his *Harlow* completed and in theaters no later than five weeks after Sargent's *Harlow*.

When Baker begrudgingly agreed to make *Harlow* for Paramount, she was hoping that Paddy Chayefsky would write the script and Academy Award winner George Cukor, who had a wonderful reputation for working with actresses, would direct. She actually spoke with them about it and disclosed, "We intended *Harlow* to be a portrait of the 1930s. Here was a period when Hitler was rising in Europe, we had a depression in this country, and everybody was glorifying this blond symbol."[2] Much to her disappointment, her input was ignored. Levine had already announced the hiring of director Gordon Douglas, who had previously worked with Carroll Baker on the movie *Sylvia*.

Douglas began his directorial career working on Our Gang and Laurel and Hardy shorts before progressing to feature films. His post–1950 movies included *Come Fill the Cup* (1951), *The Charge at Feather River* (1953), *Young at Heart* (1954), *The McConnell Story* (1955), *Yellowstone Kelly* (1959), *Claudelle Inglish* (1961), *Follow That Dream* (1962), and *Robin and the Seven Hoods* (1964). Baker later agreed that Douglas was a good choice to helm *Harlow* due to the speediness of the shoot.

Troubles began on Levine's *Harlow* right from pre-production. Carroll Baker had agreed to give columnist Sheila Graham a thoroughly honest interview about her life and career for an unnamed popular women's magazine. Per Graham, the magazine only agreed to publish the piece if the byline read, "By Carroll Baker, as told to Sheila Graham." Per the writer, Baker and her husband were quite open talking about the actress' childhood (especially her relationship with her father), her new life in Hollywood living with her husband and children in a $300,000 mansion for hopefully the next six years, and her career. At one point, though, Baker told Graham that she was making her nervous and promised to put it all down on tape to send to her. She did, but it was not up to par. After writing the article, the magazine had Graham send it to Baker for her approval. Per Graham, "There were three handwritings on the copy she returned—Carroll's, her husband's and her press agent's. There was barely a word left of the original. The story was refused."[3] This was a sign of the difficulties Baker would face making this *Harlow*.

This incident must have really angered the columnist, who wrote a scathing opinion piece about why she felt that Baker was wrong for the part of Jean Harlow even though in the late fifties Graham thought Carroll was perfect for it. She viciously remarked, "The betting in Hollywood is that Carroll Baker will never make it as a sex goddess of the screen. She can take off all her clothes, she can try to copy Marilyn Monroe until the cows come home, Joe Levine can spend all his zillions in publicizing her, but in my opinion and the opinion of all those with whom

I discussed the subject, Carroll simply does not have what it takes to set the screen on fire. She was like a wax effigy in *Sylvia*, and I don't really expect much more from her as Jean Harlow. Jean had warmth and candor. Baker has calculation. You need the former for popular success. Carroll did have something long ago in *Baby Doll*. Where oh where did it go?"[4]

The actress had more pressing troubles than being bad-mouthed by a vengeful Sheila Graham. Most of the Paramount executives she had dealt with in the past had been let go. Howard Koch was supposedly now in charge of the studio but was more of a figurehead. Baker desperately wanted *The Carpetbaggers*' screenwriter John Michael Hayes to write the script. During the fifties, Hayes won Academy Award nominations for *Rear Window* and *Peyton Place*, and his other films included *To Catch a Thief*, *The Man Who Knew Too Much*, *Butterfield 8*, *The Children's Hour*, and *Where Love Has Gone*. At first, Levine refused to pay Hayes' asking price, but just days before principal photography was to begin, the actress learned that Hayes had been hired after all. She was even more surprised when her husband, Jack Garfein, told her that he had formed a new production company to co-produce *Harlow* and that he was to receive a producing fee, although he would not receive screen credit. How did they come up with the extra money to pay Hayes? It was to come from Baker's percentage. Too perplexed and exhausted to fight, Baker went along with it, especially when Hayes shared with her that he wished to rewrite Sydney Boehm's script and present Jean Harlow as an innocent, who had to fight her way to the top while keeping her integrity.

The controversy surrounding all the litigation over the Shulman biography worried Paramount Pictures with regard to the final shooting script. The studio was overly cautious so as not to suffer the same fate and went overboard (as outlined in a five-page memo from Eugene H. Frank, one of Paramount's presidents) from not identifying MGM as Harlow's studio (it is called Majestic in the film) or using anything close to its roaring lion logo, to naming the studio head Everett Redman, even though Louis B. Mayer had been dead for almost ten years. People still alive that were associated with Jean Harlow, such as her father, her first husband, and even her doctor, were not to be portrayed. Neither was William Powell, who had filed an injunction against 20th Century–Fox preventing the studio from depicting the actor "by name, appearance, personality or characterization" as stated in a Paramount interoffice communication. Since Paramount had purchased the project from Fox to stop their film production, they had to abide by this as well.[5]

The one living person that Paramount made an exception for (besides Arthur Landau and his wife, whose permission was most likely granted) was Howard Hughes—who was turned into the fictionalized, powerful, womanizing Richard Manley in the film. He is the only sinful character portrayed and he is sort of like the Big Bad Wolf to a fictionalized, virginal Jean. Even Marino Bello and especially Mother Jean became watered-down versions of themselves. Harlow's mother is presented as a caring, selfless parent, who put the love of her daughter above all else and whose love was equally returned by Jean. There is no trace of her greed or selfishness, as there was in Sargent's version.

With Hayes' script ready to film, Joe Levine reiterated that his *Harlow* would be fit for family viewing. He again justified not adapting *Harlow: An Intimate Biography* into a screenplay, even though he held the rights to it. "We have never at any time said that our picture will be a literal translation of the Shulman book. There are things in it, of course, that we will want to use, but we have also gone to a multitude of other sources. We have spoken to hundreds of people who knew Harlow."[6] This was no doubt Levine's attempt to save face for buying such a reviled book and to keep distancing his movie from it.

In the interim, Carroll Baker was fielding a multitude of confusing phone calls from unhappy cast members and crew. Angela Lansbury's husband wanted to know why Carroll didn't want his wife to play her mother. She did want her. Howard Koch wanted to know why she was demanding Angela Lansbury for Mama Jean. Debbie Reynolds inquired why Baker didn't hire her brother to be her makeup man. She had specifically requested him. An actress whom she had befriended from another picture wanted to know how many assistant directors she'd have to have sex with to get a part. The head of makeup wanted to know the size of her nipples.

That makeup artist charged with transforming Carroll Baker into Jean Harlow was Michael Westmore's esteemed uncle, Wally Westmore.

> **MICHAEL WESTMORE:** Wally was the department head at Paramount for over forty years. He always seemed to have a smile on his face and, among my uncles, he is the only one who got married only once. The rest all had multiple wives. His work goes back far in special effects makeup and beauty makeup. He had a wonderful lab man that worked for him named Charlie Gemora, who was an unsung hero in special effects makeup. Wally did the makeup for *Dr. Jekyll and Mr. Hyde.* He and the director of photography came up with a technique of filming with a red lens and used red hair on Fredric March's face when the hair was growing. It was how they lit it and how the lens was rotated that it made it look like the hair was really growing on his face. That was a kind of a first. Now, of course, you have CGI.
>
> The other thing Wally became known for was with the heads of Tweedledee and Tweedledum during the filming of *Alice in Wonderland* in 1933. They were gigantic

Publicity photograph of Carroll Baker as Jean Harlow, 1965.

latex heads and the producers wanted to get movement in them. Wally devised the technique of putting sponges on the insides of the heads glued to the skin, so when they moved their face that movement would be projected to the surface. I can't say that was the greatest thing in the world, but it worked—the timing was fantastic. It was so different and innovative that Wally took out a patent on it. Later on, Wally most famously worked on *Breakfast at Tiffany's* and created Audrey Hepburn's look. You could see the range of his talent. Literally, every picture that came out of Paramount during those forty years had his name on it.

It was never an issue between us [working on competing films]. We both knew about the other and what was going on—but what are you going to do about it? You go ahead and you do it—it's been greenlighted and the money is there. When it comes out, you see what happens.

As for the nipple issue, Wally Westmore had false ones made for Mae West and was instructed to do the same for Baker since Jean Harlow wore the same type of slinky, sheer dresses. His nephew speculated that it could not be done at Paramount so they sent her off to another studio.

MICHAEL WESTMORE: I remember meeting Carroll Baker in one of the makeup rooms at Universal. Whether this was reported anywhere or if anybody else said it, I do not know. However, I seemed to remember that somebody—I believe it was John Chambers—did a chest cast for her, probably because they needed to make her boobs larger or wanted to make nipple covers for her. I believe that is why she was there for the day to do. Wally did not have a lab man there at Paramount at that time or somebody who could do it. Chambers was the lab man at the time at Universal. Everybody came to him independently from all the studios for special creations.

DARRELL ROONEY: In Baker's *Harlow*, there is one evening gown with fake nipples in it. I get it—Carroll Baker was not big breasted but neither was Jean Harlow. She had a much more symmetrical body and had a sensuality to her. It never bothered me that Baker's breasts were smaller but it is distracting seeing these nipples bursting through her costume.

Even though production was going to be rushed, no expense was spared by Joe Levine and Paramount to duplicate the background and setting of thirties Hollywood. $100,000 alone was budgeted for Carroll Baker's 65-costume wardrobe, designed by multi–Academy Award winner Edith Head, remembered by most for her iconic appearance—dark sunglasses and an Anna May Wong hair style with flat bangs in front and a chignon in the back.

Head seemed to try to reimagine, with a sixties style, rather than replicate some of Harlow's most iconic looks from her films. Jay Jorgensen, Edith Head's biographer, reported that the film's producers wanted the reluctant designer to expose more of Carroll Baker's flesh with her costumes, which flew in the face of her design aesthetic to create drama and mystery by keeping the actresses stylishly covered up. Describing the finished look of Head's designs for the movie, Jorgensen wrote, "Baker's silk gowns were cut on the bias, in which the fabric is placed on a forty-five-degree angle to the straight of the grain, causing it to shape itself to the body. Edith added plenty of rhinestones and marabou feathers to give audiences the illusion of the way they thought movie stars should dress."[7] Unfortunately, Head's outfits may have been too form-fitting, as they exposed the shortcomings of Baker's figure, which was not as curvy as Jean Harlow's. Nevertheless, the costumes were stunning.

Edith Head also created the Oscar-nominated costumes for Joe Levine's next production for Embassy, *The Oscar* (1966). Jean Hale played a vile and self-absorbed Jean Harlow–like sexpot in the film and described the designer's working process. She recalled in the book, *Fantasy Femmes of Sixties Cinema*:

> Edith was an absolutely amazing woman and a creative genius. She had an office about sixty to seventy feet long. At the entrance to it there was a light panel with a great number of switches. At the other end of the room, she'd have you stand on this pedestal with mirrors three quarters of the way around it. Three or four of her assistants would then take a piece of fabric and with their hands create all different looks for the evening gowns she was designing for me—from various necklines to all types of skirt styles. They would literally create the dress on you while you were standing there. Edith could see you from every angle in every type of light and would decide your finest look. I remember her telling me that my best look was a scoop neck. She designed three gowns for me and all of them had a variation on that type of neckline.[8]

Levine boasted that Carroll Baker had the exact same measurements as Jean Harlow (just as Carol Lynley supposedly did) and that Edith Head had used Harlow's actual dress form to design Baker's gowns for the movie. Most likely this was studio produced hyperbole. According to one source, MGM listed Jean Harlow's measurements as 34–24–36. Baker came close, but supposedly measured in at 34½–26–36½. While Carol Lynley wore a variety of wigs to get the Jean Harlow look, Baker did not. According to the film's hair stylist Nellie Manley, they decided to make the actress' blonde hair blonder. This was exactly as MGM did with the real Jean Harlow, who didn't dye her hair platinum blonde until she was fairly well-known.

Just as the cameras were set to roll with the expensive sets constructed and costumes designed, Levine's leading lady began experiencing extreme neck pain. She flew to New York to see her family physician. Diagnosed with nervous exhaustion (some sources claimed it was a virus), Baker was ordered on immediate hospital bed rest for a few days. This delayed the start of production and the elaborate kickoff celebration that had been arranged by the producer. Furious with his leading lady, Levine accused her of deliberate sabotage.

After Baker regained her strength and returned to Hollywood, Levine proceeded with the "Opening of the Golden Gates" ceremony at Paramount Studios on February 24, 1965. It was the first time in about twenty years that the ornate DeMille gates would be used as an entrance onto the lot. Levine hosted a champagne and caviar breakfast at the studio with close to 250 print and photo journalists. All of Paramount's top brass were there, including the studio's patriarch, 97-year-old Adolph Zukor, studio head Howard Koch, and Y. Frank Freeman. John Michael Hayes was in attendance, as well as cast members Mike Connors, Raf Vallone, and Red Buttons.

The event was wisely filmed for prosperity by Paramount. It began with the stunning Carroll Baker, clad in a very tight, white, beaded gown, that was equally reflective and transparent, and a white ermine fur coat, emerging from her studio bungalow. As she posed for photographers at the top of the landing, there was no big smile from the actress, just a forced grin that reeked of trepidation. Waiting for her was a 1930 or 1931 (depending on the source) white 16-cylinder, open Cadillac Touring Special and two pure-bred, white Russian wolf hounds. She and the dogs got into the chauffeured car and rode to the Paramount Gate.

A red carpet was rolled out and Baker stepped out to be met with flowers held by Howard Koch. Looking very nervous, she removed her fur coat and stepped over to where Levine was standing in front of a block of wet cement. Both the producer and his leading lady left their footprints and autographs in it to be placed in the forecourt of the iconic Grauman's Chinese Theater. A publicist stood nearby holding an extra pair of black loafers in case Levine needed them. Most producers would let their stars bask in the glory alone, but not a showman with an ego as big as Levine's. He had to share the spotlight, while light bulbs from photographers' cameras flashed consistently. The duo was surrounded by Koch, Zukor, Hayes and some of the *Harlow* cast all standing in front of a huge blowup of Carroll Baker in costume as Jean Harlow sitting in a chair with a picture of the real Harlow hanging behind her. Most likely this was one of the many photos taken during the "Operation Harlow" sea cruise. During the festivity a Dixieland jazz band, clad in striped blazers and straw hats, played "Love Is Just Around the Corner."

The celebration then moved indoors as the press was invited onto Stage Four. Waiters from Chasen's, one of the hottest restaurants in Hollywood, raced around serving caviar, champagne, and strawberries to the invited guests. Baker, seeming extremely uncomfortable, sat on the dais looking as if she couldn't wait until the event was over. Howard Koch introduced Levine as "the producer of the year—the producer of any year."[9] Levine gave a short speech, proudly asking the press to stay to watch the filming of *Harlow*'s first scene, which he had been waiting to shoot for almost two years. He also assured the press, again, that although he had purchased the rights to the book they would use portions, but not be faithful to it because "it will not be a dirty picture or a salacious picture."[10] Taking another shot at the biography and Irving Shulman, Levine went on to say rather candidly, "I've never met Mr. Shulman and if I never meet him it'll be a pleasure. He's a liar."[11]

The first scene, directed by Gordon Douglas, was a huge Busby Berkeley number, featuring a number of floor levels with forty or more tap-dancing chorus girls. Carroll Baker was not part of this. Instead, her debut scene as Harlow was set on the musical's soundstage, where she is part of a lineup of nubile young girls vying for a part and, not surprisingly, she is selected. Despite an exploding floodlight, the filming went smoothly and was completed on time.

Stories about the event ran in all the newspapers. Some of the press noted how ravishing Carroll Baker looked and some suggested that she wasn't wearing any undergarments—a trademark of the real Jean Harlow. This could be true, as the Mae West false nipples wouldn't stick to Baker's flesh, so they had been discarded.

Most reporters were awed by the day's events, but not all. Regarding the actress and all the pomp and circumstance, Philip K. Scheuer described it as the "most depressing event of the week."[12] As for Carroll Baker, he opined, "A reasonable facsimile of Harlow? Maybe. It was the time, as Shakespeare might have said, that seemed out of joint."[13] He was not alone. A photographer reportedly bemoaned, for all to hear, that Baker was lacking Jean Harlow's mole on her cheek and a wire service reporter called her "awfully boney," to which a female reporter snapped, "She's also a damn good actress."[14] Later, columnist William E. Sarmento would go further with the insults and decried, "Miss Baker, who is a pretty poor actress, has all the sex appeal of a bowl of oatmeal."[15]

Hedda Hopper was also dubious about all the fanfare and remarked, "In the old days when we had something to sell that we didn't think was very good, we used to do stunts like that. But Louis B. Mayer never found it necessary to go to that expense for any of his pictures. In fact, he never even gave a caviar and champagne breakfast for Jean Harlow while she lived."[16]

It must be noted that the powerful columnist was not a fan of Joe Levine's movies, though she found him to be a personable and likable guy. She wrote in one of her columns about running into him at a publicists' luncheon where the producer was being honored for his "showmanship":

> **LEVINE:** Here's the woman that I love, but she hates me.
> **HOPPER:** Not at all—I just don't like dirty movies.
> **LEVINE:** But you won't see my good ones.
> **HOPPER:** If you let me know which they were, I'd go and see them.[17]

Prior to starring in *The Carpetbaggers* and her professional involvement with Joe Levine, Baker was liked by the media and never received bad press. Friends were surprised that she let Levine talk her into such outlandish publicity and that she had gone "movie star." She had always shunned the Hollywood scene and lived modestly with her family. The look on Baker's face during the entire first day of shooting and celebration showed that the actress really was not at ease playing that role in real life. A neighbor commented, "I can't believe she's a movie star. She is a home-loving, family-loving housewife."[18] However, she was prodded by Levine to adopt a new lifestyle. He remarked, "Stars should live like stars. They should create excitement and glamour about themselves."[19] He went on to boast that he advised Baker to buy an expensive wardrobe, never travel without a secretary, and always be driven to the studio in a white, chauffeured Rolls-Royce.

Baker reluctantly heeded his advice. She moved into Harold Hecht's former Beverly Hills mansion, completely designed in white, from the walls to the rugs, to the furniture. A few years later, she blamed her husband, "[He] wanted to maintain a certain kind of lifestyle. We'd been very poor when we started out at the Actors Studio in New York … [now] I was making a lot of money, but there was never anything left because when you make that much all you can do is live well and the rest goes to taxes."[20]

In the press, Levine made it sound like all was peaches and cream between him and his star, commenting, "She's a tremendous showman. She's a very hardworking girl. She'll do anything to help a picture."[21] However, behind-the-scenes their relationship was frosty at best before filming began and became really strained after the "Opening of the Golden Gates" ceremony. The producer became furious with his leading lady for posing in photos with the wolf hounds instead of him, as he had planned. Wearing a heavy beaded dress and trying to control the huge dogs, Baker was in no position to wrestle the mongrels away.

When asked to compare herself to Jean Harlow and comment on the deceased movie star, Baker replied, "Jean Harlow was a sex goddess and I'm certainly not like that. Her romantic vanity drove her on and her life was like an old Hollywood script. I know what being a movie star means—it means being lonely. I have compassion for Harlow because she was very, very lonely and in this business, you get lonelier as you get on."[22] Baker then added, "She was not a good actress, but she had great charm and a wonderful toughness."[23]

Shortly after filming of *Harlow* began, Carroll Baker discovered that the screenplay was still not fully completed. John Michael Hayes was turning in script pages only a few days before scenes were to be filmed. There was no rehearsal time scheduled for the actors and director, so some of the cast took it upon themselves to rehearse with each other on their lunch hours or on their own time after shooting stopped for the day. Angela Lansbury would arrive on the set two hours before she was due in makeup at seven a.m.; Red Buttons skipped all his lunch breaks to rehearse; and Peter Lawford worked with Baker until the wee hours of the night to help her learn lines. Despite having to pay overtime, the cast and crew even filmed on Saturdays due to Joe Levine's dogged determination to get his movie into theaters on June 24—one month after the rival version's scheduled release. An exhausted Baker commented, "I've been saying I think it's impossible to make that date—but Joe Levine does the impossible every day." The rotund producer jokingly added, "Yeah, that's right. I get up."[24]

On a lighter note, it was reported that each day on the set Michael Connors would pretend, for a laugh, to be one of Jean Harlow's lovers. One day he would pretend to be Clark Gable, one day William Powell, and so on. During a scene where his character had to embrace Baker, he unintentionally delivered "a real rib-cracker." The surprised actress was able to wiggle away and, though in pain, reportedly quipped, "Since when did Jean Harlow play opposite King Kong!"[25]

With regards to Wally Westmore's makeup process on the film, his nephew Michael was not there but could only surmise.

MICHAEL WESTMORE: As I did on my *Harlow*, Wally probably did the makeup only for Carroll Baker and the bigger stars and had assistants do the rest with his approval needed before they could go on set. Like every one of my uncles, no matter what studio they were working at, everything outside of straightforward makeup on a TV series or a supporting actor on a movie, they would just approve the makeup. Being around my uncles during these times when I was at different ages, I followed their work ethic (for the eighteen years I worked on different *Star Trek* TV shows, I was on set, and not hiding somewhere, and approved makeup for every single person before they could step on set) and became good friends with them. Wally due to his talent and personality (he got along with producers, directors, and everybody else) just had a successful career and a great reputation. He was not the type of person, like me, just standing on the side thinking, "I am bigger than poop." Wally would work with the people, just like I did no matter who they were. We both were open to suggestions like, say from the director, who would bounce them off of us.

In the interest of fair play perhaps, Joe Levine invited reporters back to the *Harlow* set to watch more scenes being shot, just as Bill Sargent did, to drum up publicity, as if the public didn't already have their fill of the *Harlow* wars. A number of writers witnessed the filming of the scene where Leslie Nielsen's big shot producer tries to seduce Baker's Harlow in his opulent master bedroom suite. This lavishness came with a hefty price tag of $100,000 and a portion of the Ponderosa set from the TV western series *Bonanza* had to be dismantled to make room for it. Cinematographer Joseph Ruttenberg described the sets as "old-time glamour at its best."[26] Critic Judith Crist wittily described the boudoir as "a lecher's laboratory."[27] With the push of a button, walls slid aside to reveal separate ladies' and men's dressing rooms and a bathroom with a sunken bathtub; curtains moved to uncover a tropical garden populated by orchids, and music waffled through the room. The centerpiece was a huge round bed covered with a fur spread. How could a girl resist? She does, as Gordon Douglas described: "He gets angry, tries to force her. Her dress is torn in the struggle, but we won't show too much of Carroll. This is not a dirty picture. It reveals Jean as a good kid."[28]

Writer Bob Thomas viewed the takes where Harlow, with torn dress, rushes from Manley's mansion into the waiting car of her agent, Landau. He thought Baker "looked wan, but believable" in the scene. Though interviews were prohibited with the recuperating actress, she made a perplexing comment to him. "When it becomes recurring, it's awfully hard to kick," she remarked.[29] Was she talking about her illness or playing Harlow? Thomas reported that insiders suspected that she didn't have a virus at all but was suffering from "scriptitus."

A delusional Red Buttons had more to say: "This is a good one. I got a feeling about it. You usually tell about a picture when you're doing it, whether it's going to be good or not. Like I knew *Sayonara* was going to be a dog."[30] It wasn't and won him an Academy Award for Best Supporting Actor.

Director Gordon Douglas knew the real Jean Harlow when he worked in the casting office at Hal Roach Studios. At the time, the platinum blonde newcomer was playing minor roles in Roach slapstick comedies, getting whipped cream pies in the face or getting buckets of water dumped on her by comics. He commented that Harlow, "was a great gal. The crew loved her." He also defended Carroll Baker from the bad press she was receiving for being difficult with regard to the script and lamented, "I don't know why people pick on this girl so much. I'm telling you, Carroll is the one who doesn't want to change the script. I change the start or finish of a scene to get a little heart, a little laugh, and she asks me if it shouldn't stay as it is."[31]

Determined at all costs to meet Levine's completion deadline, the studio assigned an assistant director to shadow Carroll Baker everywhere she went on the set. Perturbed by this, especially since she prided herself on her professionalism and always being on time, the exasperated star wrote, "I was never a second late, so why had they ordered him to hang over me every moment of the day? When I changed costumes, I could hear his walkie-talkie outside my dressing-room door. 'We're about fifteen minutes away, what's she doing now?'"[32]

Tim Zinnemann was that assistant director and, like Richard C. Bennett, he also did not receive on-screen credit for his work. The son of Academy Award-winning director Fred Zinnemann, Tim began his career in the movie industry as an assistant film editor in Rome. When he returned to Hollywood, he began working as a second assistant director. He would go on to work as first assistant director and production manager on such films as *The Happening, Bullitt, The Reivers, The Great White Hope, Carnal Knowledge, The Cowboys, Day of the Locust*, and *Smile*. In 1975 he began producing movies including *Straight Time, The Long Riders, Fandango, The Running Man, Pet Sematary*, and *The Island of Dr. Moreau*. *Harlow* should have been a pleasant experience for the novice AD, but the combination of Carroll Baker and worrying about being drafted interfered.

> **TIM ZINNEMANN:** I was hired by Paramount and Dave Salven who was the first assistant director on the film. My duties included taking care of the cast, giving calls, setting background action, dealing with extras and crew, etc. And I had a lot to do with Carroll Baker. I would come to bring her to the set—not spy on her. She was always late and always having temper tantrums. Her husband was around a lot. She was a DIVA—completely out of control most of the time. Neither man nor beast seemed able to tame her.
>
> Gordon Douglas was an old studio pro and seemed oblivious to the conflict around him. He was able to laugh it off and stick to business. Howard Koch was the studio head at that time and he seemed to be taking the heat.

Tim Zinnemann seemed to be the victim of Carroll Baker's misplaced anger. After coming off the epic western *The Hallelujah Trail* starring Burt Lancaster and Lee Remick, he was obviously surprised by her behavior. As a second AD, Zinnemann was assigned to Pamela Tiffin.

> **TIM ZINNEMANN:** I remember Pamela Tiffin with great fondness. She was very sweet and approachable. She was nothing at all like Carroll Baker. I did spend time with Pamela occasionally ... I remember her as just being part of the crew.

According to studio memos, Carroll Baker's absences and lateness cost the studio $58,113.99.[33] Perhaps her on-set behavior was out of frustration. Carrying the weight of the movie on her shoulders, she was going to feel the success or failure of *Harlow* more than Tiffin, who did not have this type of pressure working on *The Hallelujah Trail*. A lot of critics were chomping at the bit to take Baker down, and she knew this was due to the bad publicity she was receiving. Most of the ideas she suggested to make the film better were ignored by a producer who was obsessed with racing the rival version to the silver screen, even if it meant a rushed production and cutting corners. The pressure may have been too much for the overworked, bothered actress who lashed out. If Baker was being unprofessional on the set, it was kept secret at the time, and her co-stars only showed admiration for her in the press.

In the middle of the shoot, trying to diffuse the bad publicity between the production and its leading lady, Paramount Studios took out a trade paper ad that brought a laugh to Hollywood insiders who knew better. It gushed, "Joe Levine and all of us at Paramount greatly appreciate the magnificent job you are doing in the role of Harlow." Columnist Dorothy Kilgallen quipped, "It should have had one more line like, 'When you show up on the set' or 'When you are not battling with Joe.'"[34]

To achieve Joe Levine's goal to get the movie in theaters quickly, scenes were shot chronologically (unheard of for a major studio production) and in one or two takes. The disappointed actors never got a chance to see the rushes. This allowed the film to be scored by composer Neal Hefti as it was being shot, rather than after completion, cutting down on post-production time. A team of editors were assigned to splice the film immediately after the words "cut and print" were uttered by Gordon Douglas. This rushed schedule may have prodded cinematographer Joseph Ruttenberg to praise the competition: "I think that the Electronovision process should be encouraged. It's the only new technical thing we've had in Hollywood for years. In the hands of professional photographers, Electronovision could be a significant step forward."[35] Heaven knows how Joe Levine reacted when reading this, with one of his own giving props to a filming technique used by his rival.

Michael Connors also had good words for Sargent's *Harlow*, and was disappointed to hear about its bad reviews. However, it wasn't that he felt particularly sorry for the rival cast—it was more self-interest. He stated, "It would be better for us if it was good and if it was doing well. That would help us at the box office. As it is, people will hear bad things about *Harlow*, and they won't stop to wonder which is which. They just won't go to either."[36]

Carroll Baker was in practically every scene of the movie and literally worked nonstop. She even refused to accept a body double and took custard pies in the face, had pails of water dumped on her, and was even knocked into a water fountain. This impressed her castmates, in particular busy Italian actor Raf Vallone. He was working in Hollywood for the first time in a career that began opposite Silvana Mangano in *Bitter Rice* (1949), though he did have one U.S. production under his belt, Otto Preminger's *The Cardinal* (1963). Praising Baker, he raved, "I do not like flattering people, but I am really surprised by the temperament, the strength, the [he groped for the word] penetration she showed in the first scene we had together."[37]

Reflecting on the character of Marino Bello, Vallone remarked, "Bello is a new type for me. I cannot identify myself with him—a gigolo—but in a certain way his irony in front of life is something that I like to express and will try to express."[38]

Shooting on *Harlow* finally came to an end. Like fellow assistant director Richard Bennett, who disliked working on the Electronovision production, Tim Zinnemann did not enjoy his time on Joe Levine's version.

> **TIM ZINNEMANN:** The set was mostly tense and unpleasant due mainly to Carroll Baker. Joe Levine was not a presence as I remember. I never had much to do with him and did four movies for his company.
>
> The one bright spot for me was Leslie Nielsen. He was funny, professional, and easy going.

Once shooting on *Harlow* wrapped, the Associated Press reported that an extravagant, thirties-themed, celebratory soirée hosted by Carroll Baker, wearing one of her Edith Head–designed costumes, was thrown at her lavish mansion with a hundred guests dressed to the nines. A sumptuous dinner was catered by Chasen's. Vintage champagne flowed, Laurel and Hardy shorts were screened, and the live band played Charleston music, with the cast and crew dancing away their stressful experiences while making the movie. Attendees included Charlton Heston, who reportedly rode up to Baker's house on a horse; Peter Lawford, clad in knickers; Susan Oliver seriously resembling Carole Lombard; Michael Connors; Leslie Nielsen; Michael Callan; Barbara Rush; and hairstylist Sidney Guillaroff, who remarked,

7. *Harlow, Paramount Style* 99

Japanese magazine publicity photographs of Carroll Baker as Jean Harlow side-by-side with the real Jean Harlow, 1965.

"This party takes me back 30 years. It's the kind Jean herself always tossed—a real swinger."[39]

With *Harlow* in the can, Carroll Baker let it be known to anybody within earshot what an exhausting shoot it had been for her. She remarked, "It was the first time I have done a picture that was glamorous and heavily dramatic. That meant two or three hours of being made up and then going into emotional scenes all day."[40] Perhaps trying to let bygones-be-bygones, Joe Levine presented his worn-out star and her husband with an all-expense-paid holiday to the Cannes Film Festival in the South of France in late May. Hedda Hopper advised Baker to be smart and reject the offer and stay home to get much needed rest. Baker replied, "I can't resist the temptation—it's too exciting."[41]

It is unclear if Baker and her husband stayed in Levine's villa on the beach or on a yacht that the couple rented themselves. While she should have spent her time relaxing, Baker was a trooper and promoted *Harlow*—no doubt to the delight of her producer. However, the couple's extravagant ways reportedly caused Levine to rage, "I told them to visit France, not buy it!"[42] He had no cause to complain, when it was he who instructed Baker how to live life as a movie star—no expense spared. The

A page from Paramount's pressbook for *Harlow* featuring various promotional ads.

student learned well from her teacher. This trip would become part of the lawsuit between the star and her producer when Baker was shocked to learn that she had to foot the bill and would not be reimbursed.

Angela Lansbury went right from playing Mama Jean to the outrageous Auntie Mame in the Broadway musical *Mame*. After its smash opening, she remarked to playwright Christopher Isherwood, "I told Joe Levine I'd do *Harlow* again—but this time I get to play Harlow!"[43]

Meanwhile, Paramount's marketing machine was in overdrive and it should come as no surprise that its pressbook for *Harlow* was as lavish as they come. While the cover for Sargent's *Harlow* pressbook was in color, it was a flimsy three-page foldout with an insert containing various size newspaper ads. Paramount and Joe Levine's pressbook was 18 pages, bound by a gold cover that said, "Joseph E. Levine Presents HARLOW ... A Golden Opportunity for Showmen!" and a back cover that had a picture of the Paramount Pictures logo. Besides the usual pressbook entries, it included a number of different poster ads all asking the same question, "What was Harlow really like?" A bold statement to make considering the film was totally off the mark in presenting the real Jean Harlow.

Among the marketing gimmicks were the typical TV and radio spots plus a trailer in gorgeous Technicolor. For local functions, Paramount pushed "Harlow Parties" where guests would dress in the styles of the thirties; a Movie Clue Contest where newspapers or radio stations would give a clue and the reader/listener would have to identify the Jean Harlow movie and her co-star; and a Harlow Dance Party where contestants would have to perform popular dances of Harlow's day such as the Peabody, the Shag, or the Lindy Hop to win.

Levine also had his stars get on the promotional band wagon. Carroll Baker posed for print ads for Foster Grant sunglasses ("Isn't that Carroll Baker behind those Foster Grants?") and Coppertone tanning lotion where *Harlow* was prominently mentioned. Michael Connors did a photo spread for popular men's wear manufacturer Channel Ltd., modeling an overcoat. The ad's tag line read, "Who does he think he is ... he's Michael Connors! He's the man in the Channel coat, starring in 'Harlow.'"

Joe Levine had one last decision to make. He was facing a dilemma with the screenplay credit. He decided to give John Michael Hayes sole recognition, despite his use of Sydney Boehm's second draft. This was to block Boehm from publicly distancing himself from the movie, as he threatened, if he disliked it. Levine didn't want to take that chance and stir up more bad publicity. As expected, Boehm filed a complaint with the Writers Guild of America (WGA). In a letter he claimed that, although he disliked what they did to his script, he was really fighting to protect all writers from bullying producers like Joe Levine, who dole out writing credits to anyone they choose such as friends or family. After review, an arbitration board of the WGA sided with Levine, and Hayes received lone acknowledgment for the script.[44] And despite all of Levine's declarations of not using Shulman's book as the basis for the screenplay, the final screen credit read:

Screenplay by John Michael Hayes
Based upon the book by Irving Shulman in collaboration with Arthur Landau

8

And the Winner Is...

Not surprisingly, considering all the corners he cut, Bill Sargent's *Harlow* won the race to the silver screen, beating Levine's *Harlow* into theaters by over a month. Unfortunately, speed won out over quality as the reviews would soon suggest. The movie opened nationwide on May 12, 1965. With much fanfare, it premiered in New York City's Paramount Theater paired with a live rock-'n'-roll revue hosted by Clay Cole and including performers Mary Wells and The Marvelettes. One glaringly missing attendee at the premiere was its star, Carol Lynley.

The title credits for Bill Sargent's *Harlow* feature a montage of cast photos, with the emphasis on Carol Lynley as Jean Harlow, accompanied by a jazzy theme. This *Harlow* version begins after Jean Harlow has been working in Hollywood for a while, playing bit roles in many shorts. The opening scene has the actress, wearing only a very sexy black slip, emerging from a car in a scene from a Laurel and Hardy short. After the director yells cut, the cast and crew break for lunch. Jean immediately attracts the attention of suave actor Marc Peters, who is there to meet the comic duo. Mama Jean (as she is called in this and the rival version rather than Mother Jean) shows up and makes plans to rendezvous with her daughter at a local diner where all the studio folks eat.

At the eatery, Harlow and her mother sit at the counter side-by-side but pretend not to know one another. A distracted counterman is more interested in Harlow's cleavage than taking food orders. Jean asks for a cup of coffee, while her mother orders steak ("a big one"), fries, two scoops of ice cream, and a chocolate malted. After they are brought their separate tabs, they nonchalantly switch them. Mama Jean hurries out of the diner, paying for the coffee, while Jean causes a distraction complaining about her bill. "Isn't it a little overpriced," she exclaims. "$2.60!? What's that—the cover charge?" As the counterman goes to chase down Mama Jean, the actress stops him, demanding her rightful check. Bemusedly watching the whole episode from a table nearby, an impressed Peters declares to Al Jolson (complete in blackface) and Laurel and Hardy that Jean Harlow is the girl for *Hell's Angels*—if she can act.

The next morning, Mama Jean's loutish husband, Marino Bello, berates his stepdaughter for giving up a day's pay on a whim. Mama Jean comes to her daughter's rescue, defending her decision to audition for *Hell's Angels*, and exclaims, "If you were any kind of man, she wouldn't have to work!" Bello, finding an excuse, asks, "Have you not heard of the Depression?" His miffed wife snipes back, "I heard of it. For the first time after I married *you*." After yelling at them to both shut up, Jean goes off to the studio.

As they walk to the soundstage, Peters questions Harlow about her home life, and she tells him about her father, a dentist in Kansas City, her wonderful grandparents, and her former husband. After apologizing for being late due to the bickering Mama Jean and Marino, Peters suggests she move out and live in better emotional surroundings. A stunned Jean stops in her tracks and replies, "I just couldn't leave Mama."

Publicity photograph of Carol Lynley as Jean Harlow from *Harlow* (Magna, 1965) (courtesy Marlin Dobbs).

Peters then introduces the novice actress to the screen test's impatient director, Jonathan Martin, before leading her to makeup and wardrobe. Harlow is then informed that she must wear a bra, but she refuses. After he convinces her that she has to don one ("It inhibits me," she protests as she reluctantly slips it on), the audition proceeds, but it is a disaster. Clad in what was to be her trademark look, a skintight white silk evening gown, Harlow looks stunning, but is terrible and

Jean Harlow (Carol Lynley), looking quite uncomfortable, during a press party for her new movie *Hell's Angels* in *Harlow* (Magna, 1965).

amateurishly wooden in the test. She only comes alive when she rips off her brassiere (or as she calls it, "a straitjacket") and throws it at Peters. She then blasts actor William Mansfield, observing from the wings, for putting "the evil eye" on her and jinxing her chances. It is revealed that he had her thrown off one of his pictures. Unimpressed with her audition, Mansfield suggests that Harlow "find a husband and raise a family," infuriating her even more as she storms off the set.

After getting sympathy from her mother the following morning, a dejected Jean is berated by Marino for waking him. She tells her step daddy dearest to "drop dead." It won't be the last time she insults this freeloader. Harlow finally cracks a smile when Peters arrives with the news that she, surprisingly, got the part. The cameras kept rolling as she gave her tongue lashing to him and Mansfield, which impressed the film's producer, Mr. Hatcher (who is never seen but assumed to be a disguised Howard Hughes). An elated Jean hugs Peters, while Marino, seeing dollar signs, demands that she be paid adequately and that as a businessman he will be looking after Jean's financial matters.

Hell's Angels makes Jean Harlow a star, as her billing goes from "introducing Jean Harlow" below the title, to third billing behind the film's two lead actors, to top billing. At a press conference, in an expensive hotel suite in New York City, Harlow poses provocatively, lying on a couch in her low-cut evening gown for photographers, as she takes questions from reporters. When one suggests that she would like to write a human-interest story on her, an annoyed Jean retorts, "I don't feel very human at the moment." Uncomfortable with the attention, she is further unnerved by the presence of William Mansfield, which sends her fleeing into a bedroom. As

Upset with a last-minute bathtub scene slipped into the script, an irate Jean Harlow (Carol Lynley) barges into a meeting with actor William Mansfield (Efrem Zimbalist, Jr.) and studio executive Paul Bern (Hurd Hatfield) in *Harlow* **(Magna, 1965).**

her delighted mother becomes the center of attention and beguiles the press with exaggerated tales of how she spent a week by the side of her terribly ill daughter, Mansfield is once again giving unwarranted advice to her daughter. Telling her that "girls with remarkable chests are a dime a dozen in Hollywood," he recommends that she study and maybe she will succeed as an actress. Torn about her sexpot image, she admits to him her desire to be taken seriously as an actress. He departs, impressed with her attitude.

Not wanting to see their meal ticket disappear, however, Marino tells Jean to ignore the actor's advice and not rock the boat. He wishes that "she never wake in the small hours of the night knowing that you are a failure." A touched Mama Jean thanks him for being kind to the Baby. She then gives Jean a pep talk, about becoming the screen's newest sex goddess and the responsibilities it entails. "Can you live *up* to it," asks Mama Jean, to which her daughter replies, "You mean can I live down to it!" With renewed energy, Harlow goes back to face the journalists. Smiling and posing ("Do you want a bigger smile," she asks, as she sticks out her bosom), Jean Harlow decides to play the sexpot game.

Jean Harlow is soon a huge star of the silver screen. However, we see her frustration grow because every movie contains a bathtub scene. Off-screen, she lives with Mama Jean and Marino in a sumptuous mansion complete with servants and a long, curved staircase in the main entry for those dramatic entrances (almost the identical set, albeit a much cheaper version to be sure, from the rival *Harlow*). After making a string of sexy comedies, Harlow is elated to be making a prestige film with Marie Dressler and not having to disrobe for a bath. Jean is introduced to the esteemed actress on the set by the director, Jonathan Martin, who gushes over Jean's professionalism and her lack of temperament. He is buttering her up, though, to get her to jump into a goldfish bowl for a scene just inserted into the script. Livid, she storms off the set swearing, while Dressler remarks facetiously to the director, "*no temperament!?!*"

Jean interrupts a meeting in the studio's executive suite with a not-too sympathetic William Mansfield and producer Paul Bern. After Mansfield exits, an enraged Harlow is miffed that she agreed to one script and then "behind my back you sex it up." She begs for a chance to play a role other than a tart. The soft-spoken producer says he doesn't think her public would accept her "in a picture that wasn't based upon sex." He also doubts that she could handle a part that wasn't dependent on "her physical attributes." After a long diatribe on how for some people sex is a religion, he convinces his star that the movie is a step up for her and that being the personification of sex, she is an important person. He goes on to explain that the girl in the script is not a tart, but a girl "who uses sex like a surgeon uses a scalpel." Once she regains her composure, the actress not only consents to do the scene, but she also agrees to a dinner date.

Sometime later, Jean reveals to Mama Jean and Marino that Paul Bern has proposed marriage, but she is unsure about accepting due to the age difference ("he is almost twenty-five years older than I am"). At first, they are against it, until Jean assures her greedy mother and stepfather that they can remain in her house in the lifestyle they have become accustomed to, and that Bern would find a job for Marino

After calming down, Jean Harlow (Carol Lynley) agrees to go on a date with Paul Bern (Hurd Hatfield) in *Harlow* **(Magna, 1965) (courtesy Marlin Dobbs).**

at the studio so he could earn an income. She decides to go away to think about it, claiming she is tired and needs a rest. Mama Jean is taken aback and asks, "Stop working?" After Marino badgers the Baby for being irresponsible, Mama Jean comes to her defense and tells her not to do anything that she does not want to do. After Jean exits, Marino is afraid of the financial uncertainty, especially since he just purchased a new car and needs Jean to pay the bills. His manipulative wife assures him that Jean will marry Bern because "she knows that I know what's best for her and she will do as I tell her." The couple has a celebratory embrace and then fall onto the couch to make love.

Just before the wedding day, a woman named Marilyn visits Mama Jean claiming she is Bern's mistress, but not in the usual way a man is with a woman. She reveals that though Bern supports her, there is nothing physical in their relationship because "there never is with Paul." She has come forth to stop Jean from making a terrible mistake. Mama Jean dismisses her innuendo and throws her out. She then rushes up the stairs to warn her daughter, but stops suddenly, turns around, and slowly walks down the staircase thinking better of it.

Paul and Jean's marriage ceremony is a lavish affair at his palatial home, with her parents and Louis B. Mayer standing up for them. Jean is so happy that she even accepts a congratulatory kiss from William Mansfield. Her elation soon dissipates as Bern's impotence is revealed on their wedding night. At first, Jean is sympathetic, thinking it is a one-time occurrence. When Bern admits it isn't, and that he married

At their wedding ceremony, Paul Bern (Hurd Hatfield) and Jean Harlow (Carol Lynley) receive congratulations from guest William Mansfield (Efrem Zimbalist, Jr.) in *Harlow* (Magna, 1965).

her thinking the world's biggest sex symbol could cure him, he begs for her help. Calling him a "pathetic cripple," an enraged Harlow flees into the night.

At the Clover Club, a Sunset Strip casino, a boisterous Harlow plays craps and falls into the arms of suave manager Ed. As he leads her into a private VIP room, Harlow comes face-to-face with Mansfield, who is there with a chatty Miss Larsen who is singing as she primps in the mirror. When she sees Jean Harlow, she makes a beeline for her and asks for an autograph but Jean barks at her to get lost. After the pair exit, Harlow asks Ed, "Well, what are your intentions tall, dark and handy?" Bemused by her troubles and self-pity, the gigolo schools her and says, while handling Jean's fur coat, "You're luckier than most, Miss Harlow. You've got problems? At least you can afford them." Later, he seductively walks around the room, turning the lights off, as he removes his tuxedo bow tie. Leading her to a bearskin rug in front of a roaring fireplace, he gently lays her down as they begin to make love.

Despite Bern's pleas for Jean to stay with him at night to listen to music, Harlow continues to hit the town. At a boxing match, she catches the eye of one of the prize fighters, whom she makes plans to meet with afterwards. Soon after, Bern kills himself with a gunshot to the head.

Devastated by her husband's death, Harlow refuses to work. She goes into seclusion instead, despite the pleas of Mama Jean and Marino. They are panicked after an encounter with Louis B. Mayer. Paying a visit with flowers in hand, the gruff studio head issues a veiled threat and says, "Up to a point grief is to be respected. Beyond that, it becomes a luxury, even for great corporations, Mrs. Bello. If we don't start Jean's picture soon, we will suffer a substantial financial loss. People will be laid off—some lose their jobs permanently—I'm sure Jean would not want that to happen." Reading his message loud and clear, Mama Jean promises to speak with Jean. When she thanks the departing Mayer for the flowers, he makes sure that she knows they were from the Board of Directors and not from him personally.

Panicked that MGM may drop Jean and they will lose their fabulous lifestyle, Mama Jean tries to sweet talk her daughter into returning to work. However, Jean catches Marino outside her bedroom door holding a new script, knowing it was a setup. When Mama Jean suggests they all go to Palm Springs for the weekend and forget about the studio, Jean tells her that she and Marino should go. Seeing them embrace as Mama Jean says they don't want to leave her, Jean says, "You love him—

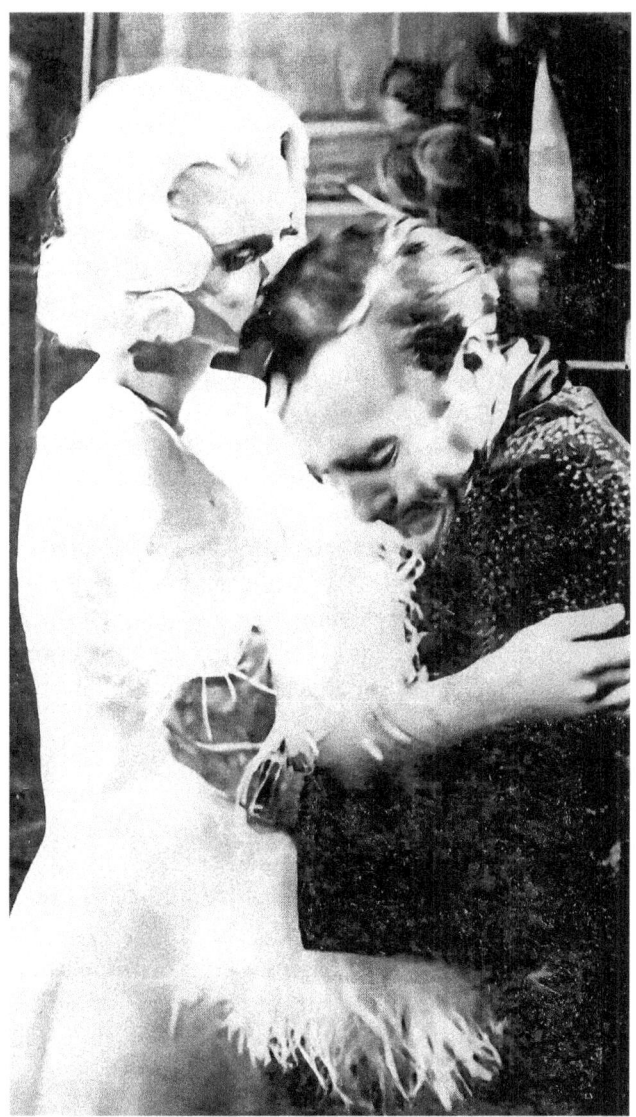

After failing to perform on his wedding night, a distressed Paul Bern (Hurd Hatfield) admits to this recurring sexual problem and receives no sympathy from his duped bride, Jean Harlow (Carol Lynley) in *Harlow* (Magna, 1965).

don't you Mama? You two you fight all day and tear each other to pieces. But at night, the white flag goes up and you jump into bed like two happy crickets—God, how I envy you."

About a year later, a rejuvenated Harlow turns up at the Sunset Strip casino now divorced from hubby number three. She tries to get a roll in the hay on credit from Ed who can't believe she is broke. "You make $10,000 a week." She replies, "My mother and Prince Albert spend eleven." Not caring that she is *the* Jean Harlow, he won't front her credit. She yells that neither he nor any man has ever satisfied her anyway, and says, "Isn't that a laugh? The captain hates the sea. America's sex symbol hates sex." Left crying, she is comforted by Marie Dressler. The actress advises Jean to sacrifice her fame, her current career, and her family so she can study to gain confidence and become her own person. "You've got to get rid of the leeches," Dressler declares. "Throw out your mother and her husband."

Taking the older actress' advice, a determined Harlow nonchalantly informs a shocked Mama Jean and Marino that the house is going up for sale and that she is departing for New York to learn the craft of acting from Maria Ouspenskaya. Mama Jean tries to guilt her daughter into not leaving and says, "What will happen to me?" Jean replies it is now up to her husband to take care of her.

After working with the esteemed Ouspenskaya for a short period, Jean heeds the desperate pleas from Mama Jean to come home. She is now separated from Bello and living in their old rundown apartment. A distraught Mama Jean claims that she is ill, has paid no rent, and has lied to the landlord that Jean will be sending monthly checks. Jean has no money either. Mama Jean presumes her daughter will return to work, but she doesn't want to. Jean laughs at their predicament but does remark about an upside—at least Mama Jean has finally realized what a louse Marino Bello is. Her irate mother responds with a slap across the face.

Knowing she needs to restart her career, Harlow triumphantly returns to MGM and is warmly welcomed back by Louie B. Mayer. A party is thrown in her honor, where she is presented with a *Photoplay* magazine award by its publisher, Fred Klein. A contrite William Mansfield is in attendance, and he apologizes for his past behavior. They have a quiet moment in the rafters above the party dwellers. They discuss their past behavior toward each other and their current true feelings. It ends with a long kiss. Working with Mansfield on a new film, Jean confesses to Hank, one of the stagehands, that she has been feeling out of sorts lately, perhaps due to the flu. As she and Mansfield rehearse a scene, the stunning actress collapses in his arms. In her bedroom, a doctor sets up an oxygen tank for her but informs her family and friends that she will not survive. She dies shortly after with Mansfield at her bedside. As the end credits roll, Mary Mayo sings the mawkish ballad "I Believed It All" by Alan and Marilyn Bergman and Al Ham.

Despite the free publicity that rival producer Joe Levine's outrage brought to Sargent's film, and the hubbub Lynley herself drummed up with her *Playboy* pictorial, this *Harlow* only played in most theaters for seven days or less. It did better business at drive-ins, no doubt because the indiscriminate teenage audience really didn't care what film was showing on the screen. At the time of big screen epics filmed in Technicolor and Cinemascope, the poor production values offered by Electronovision (akin to watching a live, early fifties variety show or soap opera on Kinescope) doomed its box office chances. Critics attacked the movie from all fronts pointing out "extraneous noises, gaffers' shadows, fluffed lines, and focusing errors."[1] One critic moaned that the inferior sound and image quality was "quite appropriate to the '30s." Tunberg's dialogue was called "atrocious" and Segal's direction "rambling."

Production was so rushed that Bill Sargent was taken to task, and deservedly so, for allowing a flubbed line to remain in the final print. While on the set, concerned makeup woman Thelma, played by Audrey Christie, goes to Harlow's

Jean Harlow (Carol Lynley) informs the "leeches," her stepfather Marino Bello (Barry Sullivan) and Mama Jean (Ginger Rogers), that they need to find their own place to live in *Harlow* (Magna, 1965).

co-star William Mansfield and says that the actress "has been taking pains for her pain." Though Christie blew the line, director Alex Segal did not call cut and had his actors continue with the scene. Perhaps no one caught it at the time or perhaps they were just too rushed to finish the film. In any event a retake was not called for—tsk, tsk.

Reviewers were a bit kinder to the actors (even Carol Lynley to an extent) knowing they had little time for rehearsal and that scenes were shot in one or two takes due to the hurried production schedule. Columnist Herb Michelson went one step further and quipped, "They didn't have enough time to READ their roles [since] Bill Sargent was in such a rush to get this monstrosity on the screen" and he dubbed it the worst movie of the year in his annual "Terrible Ten" poll.

Of the supporting players, Ginger Rogers generated the most buzz for her performance. The love Mother Jean had for her daughter comes through. However, the veteran actress also expertly presented the character's greed and selfishness, as presented in the screenplay, while trying to keep control over the Baby. Sanford Lewis of the *Los Angeles Sentinel* in particular raved that Rogers "is outstanding. As a matter of fact, this is her best performance to date."

Receiving the most consistent praise was Hurd Hatfield, for his sensitive turn as the tragic Paul Bern ("strongly acted," *Los Angeles Times*; "played with much decorum," *New York Daily News*; and "delivers a sincere performance," *Variety*). Michael Dante also survived *Harlow* unscathed and was singled out in the reviews when being complimented ("adding his talent," *Newark Evening News*, and "delivers a good performance," *L.A. Herald-Examiner*).

As expected, though, most of the reviews for the movie (from the Hollywood trades to the major national newspapers, to even smaller cities' locals) were scathing:

"*Harvard Lampoon*, look no further. The worst movie of the year is here."—R.M. Hodgens, *Film Quarterly*

"The cheap, lusterless and excruciatingly dull picture spares the late actress—and the audience—nothing."—Howard Thompson, *The New York Times*

Full page newspaper ad for *Harlow* with the tagline that infuriated Joe Levine and, ironically, on a double bill with a Carroll Baker film, *Sylvia*.

8. And the Winner Is...

"This cheap attempt to cash in on the late movie star's tragic life is a contender for all-time worst."—*Cue*

"Sargent was able to wrap up the entire movie in eight days. How could it have taken so long to make such a rotten picture."—Al Cohn, *Newsday*

"The picture looks terrible and sounds worse. The sets are jerrybuilt, the lighting flat, the camera's movement rudimentary and awkward—all adjectives that might be applied as aptly to Karl Tunberg's anachronistic screenplay."—Arthur Knight, *Saturday Review*

"It's not really a movie, but sort of a crossbreed, something like watching a drama on a TV set with poor reception."—Kathleen Carroll, *New York Daily News*

"'Harlow' is so bad it's almost a satirical triumph."—Joan Quarm, *El Paso Herald-Post*

"Tasteless, tawdry screen biography.... The film has been prepared ... with all the taste the Skid Row Players might muster in staging 'Peyton Place.' And the acting! The great 'Method' teacher Maria Ouspenskaya, who is portrayed in the film ... would rip apart Forest Lawn if she could see what Mr. Sargent hath wrought."—Herb Michelson, *Oakland Tribune*

"The script ... is in almost unbelievably poor taste and is extremely difficult to sit through. The acting is poor without exception..."—Jack Baker, *The Montreal Gazette*

"Carol Lynley looks at least as much like the late Miss Harlow as Levine's Carroll Baker, but Sargent's film does not conjure up so much an image of the celebrated 'Platinum Blonde' ... as it does of the old Monogram movies—a prewar product characterized by cardboard sets, painted backgrounds and near-amateur acting."—John Bustin, *The Austin Statesman*

"The film's lack of clarity is hard on the eyes and its violation of the dead proves repulsive to the standards of common decency."—Barney Glazer, *Jewish Advocate*

"[Jack] Kruschen is called upon to say, as Harlow lies on a deathbed, 'This is terrible. It's like losing a daughter.' He should have stopped at: 'This is terrible.'"—E.C., *The Spokesman Review*

Sargent's *Harlow* did have its few fans, if you looked hard enough to find them, and did pick up some good notices:

"Surprise of the month.... *Harlow* with Carol Lynley is not too bad. In fact ... despite its technical flaws, worth seeing."—Michael D. Unger, *Newark Evening News*

"Fairly or unfairly, this *Harlow* ... has a high audience potential. It makes the platinum-blonde bombshell a sympathetic if bewildered figure."—Philip K. Scheuer, *Los Angeles Times*

"As an entertainment, there's nothing much notable about 'Harlow' ... but the film is interesting for at least a couple of other reasons."—Dorothy Stanich, *Corpus Cristi Times*

As for Carol Lynley, some critics understood that this *Harlow* was such a quickie production and under those circumstances lauded her for a gallant effort:

"Bill Sargent's Electronovision 'Harlow' ... turns out to be a powerful drama, which reveals Carol Lynley, playing the title role, as a first-rate actress with far more talent than Jean Harlow herself ever displayed."—Gerald Ashford, *San Antonio Express/News*

"Carol Lynley ... does a very good job considering what she had to work with."—Sanford Lewis, *Los Angeles Sentinel*

"Miss Lynley's Harlow is almost soft and almost sophisticated. Taken by itself her performance is capable and appealing."—Michael D. Unger, *Newark Evening News*

"Carol Lynley struggles valiantly against sweeping odds in the shape of an almost ludicrous script."—Kathleen Carroll, *New York Daily News*

"To those who never saw the blonde.... Carol Lynley gives a lusty, busty performance."—John G. Houser, *L.A. Herald-Examiner*

"Carol Lynley ... tries valiantly, but the outcome altogether is not a triumph."—Whit., *Variety*

"She [Carol Lynley] flounders about bravely.... At least it was a valiant try, considering the odds were all against her, including bad direction and a poor script."—Nadine M. Edwards, *Hollywood Citizen-News*

"She [Carol Lynley] is totally inadequate, remote from the moods of fun, anger and brooding that characterized Hollywood's sex symbol of the 30s.... Faulting Miss Lynley is unfair. Neither she nor her co-stars have an opportunity to develop character in this shoddy treatment."—B.F.W., *The Philadelphia Inquirer*

"While Miss Lynley at times seems all baby face and nothing more, her limpid eyes do exert a spell and her surrender to one outburst of loneliness is touching."—Philip K. Scheuer, *Los Angeles Times*

Most reviewers, however, were not so compassionate and some were downright cruel. Among the most vicious being:

"Miss Lynley, faced with the challenge of depicting a performer who is admittedly a bad actress, is equal to the demands of her role."—Larry Jonas, *Film Daily*

"There is front, center and anything but alluring Carol Lynley.... She squeaks, occasionally furrows her youthful brow and twitches her nostrils."—Howard Thompson, *The New York Times*

"The only time Carol Lynley resembles the late Jean Harlow ... is at the end when she is dead."—Sheila Graham, *The Evening Star*

"Even if she is alone in the belief, at least Levine's Harlow, Carroll Baker, thinks of herself as a sex symbol. Sargent's Carol Lynley has neither the pretensions ('I'm not trying to impersonate Harlow'), nor the goods. Holding her mouth down at the corners, parading around in platinum-blonde wig and low-cut silk dress, Miss Lynley looks like a pretty little girl dolled up with mother's wardrobe and makeup kit. Harlow she isn't."—Al Cohn, *Newsday*

"The logical actress to impersonate her [Jean Harlow] is Marilyn Monroe, and the most unlikely is Carol Lynley.... Miss Lynley is a baby-faced actress with a great deal

Publicity photograph of Carol Lynley as Jean Harlow, 1965.

of assurance, but she lacks warmth and understanding for the character."—Frank Morriss, *The Globe and Mail*

"Miss Lynley, in addition to being way out of her depth, comes about as close to Jean Harlow's style as Margaret O'Brien would."—Emerson Beauchamp, *The Evening Star*

Beauchamp could not control his contempt for *Harlow* and continued, "The Electronovision people claim *Harlow* was shot in eight days; if that's true, they must have spent seven playing Poker. Except for the fact that it talks, it looks like something that was ground out 50 years ago."[2]

On a lighter note, columnist Earl Wilson weighed in on this *Harlow* and jokingly wrote, "The Electronovision version premiered in L.A. and viewers weren't sure whether Carol Lynley looked like Jean Harlow—but she certainly looked like Carroll Baker."

During its first week in release, business for *Harlow* was below par, to say the least, and it did not crack the top ten film box office grossers. Heading the list for that week was *The Sound of Music* followed by (2) *My Fair Lady*; (3) a reissue double bill of *Dr. No* and *From Russia with Love*; (4) *The Greatest Story Ever Told*; (5) *How to Murder Your Wife*; (6) *Synanon*; (7) *The Train*; (8) *Lord Jim*; (9) *Zorba the Greek*; and (10) *Cheyenne Autumn*.

Describing the box office take for *Harlow*, *Variety* reported, "Sargent's Electronovision version is a major disappointment. Rated mild in Denver, pic is slim in L.A., bad in Cleveland and light in N.Y."[3] In Los Angeles, *Harlow* grossed $13,800 in three major theaters but did better in multiplexes earning $147,000 in 24 theaters. It played the Hippodrome in Cleveland and grossed a paltry $5,000 for the week. In

New York, where it played at the Paramount Theater, accompanied by a rock and roll show, its weekly gross was $26,000, which, per *Variety*, was below average for the venue. In Denver, at the Denver Theatre, it took home $7,000.

In Cincinnati, *Harlow* opened in two theatres with a combined gross of $9,200. *Variety* reported that Paramount Pictures played offense and ran an ad in both of the city's daily newspapers announcing that its "only Harlow" by Joseph E. Levine would be opening in six theaters on July 28. It would actually open a full month earlier.

During its second week of release, *Harlow* still failed to crack the top ten grossers and languished as a runner-up. A spokesperson for Magna Pictures reported to *Variety* that the film "is still doing only fair or worse in various spots." They added that response to the film has been "'so-so' in conventional theatres, 'okay' in drive-ins, which represented majority of initial bookings." *Variety* than concluded, "whether tepid public reaction is due to Paramount-Embassy wait-and-see-ours campaign or to generally poor reviews is moot."[4]

Magna received some good news from Detroit where *Harlow* opened and brought in a healthy $21,000 for its first week, but it was dampened by a return of only $3,500 in Seattle. Overall, per *Variety*, business surprisingly improved for *Harlow* due to "saturation play-dating." However, it was not enough to propel it to the top 12 box office grossers for the month of May. It was during this period when Bill Sargent and Magna Pictures filed suit against Joe Levine, Paramount Pictures, Embassy Pictures, and a number of major theatre chains, blaming them for the disappointing box office returns by blocking theatres from showing the Electronovision *Harlow* with threats of withholding any future Paramount/Embassy releases.

Despite the drubbing it took in 1965, Sargent's *Harlow* is not that bad and actually surprisingly entertaining, especially for Carol Lynley fans. She looks glamorous as the blonde bombshell and projects a smoldering sexiness (not usual for her) in some of her scenes and in publicity photos. Watching it today, the lambasted Electronovision film process with its flat, grainy quality actually creates an aura for the time period, as does the opening jazzy theme music that evokes a speakeasy. You think you are about to watch a movie (albeit low budget) made in the thirties when Jean Harlow was a living goddess of the silver screen. Yet, there are numerous production faults that are distracting, giving the film a very amateurish feel. It is badly shadowed, has extreme floodlighting that makes the film look washed out, and lacks depth.

This *Harlow* is fast moving and gets right to the point, following the edited facts of the blonde bombshell's life, as Jean Harlow quickly progresses from unknown extra in a Laurel and Hardy short to overnight sensation in *Hell's Angels*. To emphasize her rise in popularity, the film smartly flashes through Jean Harlow's billing, as it goes from "Introducing Jean Harlow" after her two leading men to eventually top billing over them. The press party is an interesting scene, as it shows Mama Jean's love of the spotlight when she steps in for the Baby who needs to take a break from all the reporters. Then it addresses Harlow's lack of confidence in terms of her acting, which she confesses to her mother.

Jean Harlow was described as being an optimist, generous and lovable, but that's no fun to portray. Instead, Carol Lynley's Harlow is erroneously written as more of a tough, bewildered, unhappy woman battling her materialistic mother (whom she loves deeply), her stepfather, and the studio over her sexpot image, while looking for love. Lynley never comes close to projecting a Jean Harlow persona. The script does not give her much of a chance to do so. With that said, Lynley resembles the actress at certain points in the movie while clad in Nolan Miller's beautiful white, tight-fitting, satin gowns and other outfits, and tries hard to pump life into the character. She is better than her negative reviews would lead you to believe and her portrayal arouses sympathy throughout most of the movie. Carol comes off best in some of the earlier scenes, especially when she and Mama Jean scam a lunch or when she strips off her bra during her audition for *Hell's Angels* while ripping into William Mansfield. She does well when insulting her loafing stepfather with lines like "drop dead." Arguably Lynley's best scene is not where she vents her anger, but where she laments her loneliness. While mourning the death of Paul Bern, she is touching as she admits how she envies the rocky, but loving, relationship between Mama Jean and Marino, and longs for the same with any man.

Earlier scenes where Lynley is irate with the impotent Paul Bern fall flat. The viewer should be more sympathetic to her than Bern due to his deception. This is more the script's fault rather than Lynley's, so her Harlow comes off petulant and much too heartless, shifting the compassion to Hatfield's pained Bern. It was reported that Harlow took Bern's death hard and turned to gambling (craps was her game) and drinking to numb the pain. Here, they show Harlow's love of playing dice but instead of booze she turns to men, including a boxer whose name is never mentioned but who obviously was supposed to be Max Baer. Lynley's most embarrassing moment, though, is the audition scene for *Hell's Angels* with Lloyd Bochner. Trying to give a purposely bad performance, she is so embarrassingly shrill delivering the fake script's lines that you have to hope that this was on purpose. She is much better when ripping into the Mansfield character for putting the evil eye on her.

The film's most entertaining scenes are Harlow's interactions with "the leeches," Mama Jean and her husband Marino, as the film shows them as greedy and controlling—worried more about their standard of living than the needs and happiness of the Baby. They are more combative here with each other than how they were portrayed in the rival version. Marino's sexual virility is played down here, but not Jean's dislike of him, as she tears into him with a great amount of ferocity. Ginger Rogers, in particular, is very good (especially since she was a last-minute replacement) as a calculating, clinging Mama Jean.

Equally well-played are the scenes with Marie Dressler who, according to sources, really did befriend Jean Harlow. Hermione Baddeley gives a rollicking good performance as the compassionate actress and enlivens the film immensely. She and Lynley play off each other well, making their friendship very believable.

Screenwriter Karl Tunberg's biggest mistake was in the strange character of William Mansfield. Considering he was at least trying to follow the facts of the actress' life, this character is just used as a plot device to create conflict. It was also Tunberg's way of disguising the character to not resemble William Powell too much, as the threat of a lawsuit from the still living actor hung over the film (and Paramount's version as well).

Because of this, the Mansfield character is like Jekyll and Hyde. At the beginning,

Publicity photograph of Carol Lynley as Jean Harlow, Efrem Zimbalist, Jr., as William Mansfield, and Ginger Rogers as Mama Jean from *Harlow* (Magna, 1965).

he seems to be a one-man Greek Chorus watching from the periphery and constantly bombarding Harlow with snide comments and putdowns of the actress' acting ability—just as the critics of the day did. He brings out Harlow's hostility, whereas the actress was not known for that type of behavior. There is never a shred of friendship between the two, as Mansfield is continually condescending towards Harlow—even when trying to offer her advice. Obviously, after Harlow's grand return to Hollywood, William Mansfield morphs into a loving William Powell. It is a transformation that doesn't succeed fully because there was never a hint of affection between the two characters, although Mansfield is contrite for his past actions and begs forgiveness. Acting the sophisticated and superior actor, Efrem Zimbalist, Jr., does well—first purposely coming off smug and pompous tempered by his quiet delivery of his lines. Then, once he falls for Harlow, he becomes looser and much more likable.

Portraying a more affable character is Hurd Hatfield as the tragic Paul Bern. He plays the role sensitively and you feel for him. He elicits much sympathy, as he confesses his sexual inadequacy or when he desperately begs his bride to spend the evening with him talking about music instead of going off to the casino to see her paid lover. In contrast, Michael Dante, as the gigolo, is quite virile and seductive in the part.

Does Bill Sargent's *Harlow* tell the real truth about the blonde bombshell? No. But although it fictionalizes portions of the star's life, Sargent's film is truer to the then-known facts than Levine's version would be and makes a much better attempt to bring Jean Harlow's story to life—faint praise though this is.

In this version, Harlow reveals her failed teenage marriage and when asked what happened to her husband she quips, "I gave him back to his mother." There is no mention of her agent Arthur Landau (obviously due to legal reasons) and a fictitious Marc Peters gets her the audition for *Hell's Angels*. This follows Ben Lyon's remembrance that his fellow actor, James Hall, prodded Howard Hughes to screen test Jean—not Landau. However, this *Harlow* gives short shrift to Jean's early life in Hollywood pre–*Hell's Angels*, as she quickly jumps from bit player to auditioning badly for and then getting that movie anyway, which made her a star. Levine's *Harlow* does a far better job showing the struggle Jean had to go through playing many sexy, uncredited roles in short films and two-reelers before getting her big break. Here, during the screen test, Harlow also professes her distaste for wearing brassieres. The rival version steers clear of this topic.

Harlow is sent out on a national tour to promote *Hell's Angels*, but due to immense budget constraints, she is seen at only one press party in New York City. There is no mention that she was under contract to Howard Hughes, who was badgered by everyone, including Paul Bern at MGM, to loan her out to other studios and or that he kept her on tour for over a year promoting his movie where she and her family racked up huge expenses. Hughes eventually sold her contract to MGM. In this *Harlow*, she immediately jumps from *Hell's Angels* right to Metro without explanation and is seen getting frustrated after playing one bathtub scene after another, but no actual scenes from any of her movies are reenacted.

Harlow was what they called a real "crew gal," and the stagehands just loved her. At least here they make some attempt to show that, as there are a few scenes of Harlow backstage playing dice or up in the catwalk chatting with the guys. These scenes present a truly happy Jean Harlow, as she just loved hanging out with them. There are, actually, many soundstage scenes—perhaps since producer Bill Sargent was working on the cheap, it saved a lot of money because sets did not have to be specially built.

Paul Bern gets a bad rap in both versions. Although he is portrayed as a gentle and caring man, here, unlike in the rival movie, they introduce a mystery character named Marilyn, who is based on Bern's alleged common-law wife. She warns Mama Jean about Bern's lack of sexual performance in an ambiguous way that could be interpreted as he is impotent, homosexual, or both. At least, he isn't accused of beating his wife, which contributes to her death years later, as he is in Levine's film. After Bern's demise, Louis Mayer did keep Harlow under wraps and the depressed actress didn't work for a time, but once she did, it was non-stop. Harlow was known to hit the town after being widowed, but it is highly unlikely that she had a gigolo as she does here. The real Harlow, however, did have an affair with boxer Max Baer, who was separated from his wife. In this version it is alluded to, as Jean is seen front row at a boxing match flirting with a handsome boxer.

The story then jumps about a year, and when she returns to the casino to see her paid lover, he mentions that he read that she got married again and just got divorced, but there is no mention of husband number three's name, Harold Rosson. There is no truth in Jean Harlow's going to New York to study with Maria Ouspenskaya (where and why they came up with this is mindboggling) but her mother did separate from Marino Bello, as presented. Here, Jean takes Mama Jean back into her home out of pity because her mother has become a pathetic mess. In reality, it was reported that, out of her own loneliness and the love for her mother, Jean asked her to move in again.

It was at this point that she connected with William Powell, who would become the love of her life. The film then jumps to the making of her last movie *Saratoga* with the duo still a happy couple. It does not address and skips over Jean's frustration with the marriage-averse Powell. As depicted here, Harlow did collapse on the set of a movie (but her co-star was Clark Gable and not William Powell). By this time, Harlow and Powell had drifted apart but here they are shown happy and in love to the bitter end. Harlow dies in an oxygen tent (which is true) at home with Powell at her bedside and surrounded by family and friends, but in reality, it was at the hospital. This change was probably to save money on constructing another set. Although a bit off from the truth, this version's ending is miles closer to what happened than Levine's *Harlow*.

Despite the film's faults (including cheap sets, bad lighting, and grainy filming due to the Electronovision process), Bill Sargent's *Harlow* is not nearly as rotten as the reviews from the sixties indicated. Tunberg's screenplay, even with only sporadically showing the more sweet and playful side to Jean Harlow's personality, tried to stick to known facts about her life and his script is not that awful when compared to the claptrap John Michael Hayes thought up for Joe Levine's *Harlow*. The film remains an interesting curio that deserves to be resurrected and remastered on Blu-ray, not for being a great biopic about Jean Harlow, but for being the lone feature film to be shot in Electronovision—the failed process that was supposed to revolutionize the industry.

9

Last but Not Least…

Carol Lynley was in London filming *Bunny Lake Is Missing* with Sir Laurence Olivier when the rival *Harlow* was about to debut. When asked to comment, she replied, "I saw an ad in a trade paper about the REAL Harlow being released. Otto Preminger [*Bunny Lake*'s producer/director] said the rival company should take an ad for the day after and say, 'So what?'"[1] So what, indeed?

Before its premiere, it was reported that Joe Levine screened his *Harlow*, with Carroll Baker in attendance, to his friends in the press at his new 23rd floor office in the J.C. Penney building in New York City. The relocation was spurred on because Levine's company had grown from three people from when he first started to 120 staff members and more space was needed. The office included "a posh projection room … unique in Greco-Roman décor (it can seat about 50); [and] a nearby cocktailery-lounge [that] can entertain press and other VIPs comfortably, with 'groceries' to match." Levine remarked that he wanted a plush, comfortable screening space to save money and wanted his pictures "shown under the most favorable projection circumstances."[2]

After the *Harlow* screening, Levine threw a champagne party on a bus that took his guests to the pier where they boarded his lavish yacht for a sumptuous feast. Seems the wily producer was doing everything to garner good word of mouth for his movie.

To get maximum publicity (as if anymore was needed), Levine premiered his *Harlow* in Chicago. On Wednesday June 23, the day the film opened, five weeks after Sargent's *Harlow*, he took out a two-page spread in *Variety* with a photo of the throngs of moviegoers underneath the marquee. The text, in part, proclaimed, "The word is out—and it is HARLOW! Last Friday night Chicago had the chance to see the long-awaited Joseph E. Levine–Paramount multi-million-dollar Technicolor production. From the first announcement of this paid preview, they just barreled in. Talk about explosive excitement! Talk about want-to-see! They came. They saw. They ate it up!"[3]

In conjunction with the premiere, Levine hosted a luncheon in the Windy City with Paramount executives, heads of theater chains, and theater owners to review the promotional plans to make *Harlow* the box office champ of the summer. In his opening speech, it was reported that Levine knocked his rival when he assailed "quickie and cheapie productions" as being "detrimental to the health of the film industry."[4] He received a big round of applause but there were a few naysayers in

Publicity photograph of Carroll Baker as Jean Harlow, 1965.

attendance. One theater owner defended his decision to run Sargent's *Harlow* and quipped that he would "take any picture with a prospect of profit."[5] An allegedly intoxicated head of a theater circuit began heckling Levine, prompting the exasperated producer to exclaim that he had not "flown all the way from Glasgow to Chicago to be interrupted by a drunkard bum."[6] The luncheon ended with Paramount's sales chief predicting that *Harlow* would be as huge a box office hit as *The Carpetbaggers*.

In another pre-release interview, Joe Levine proudly boasted that he didn't use a word from Irving Shulman's biography except "the" because "I didn't want to malign Jean Harlow and I didn't."[7] The critics would soon disagree.

As the opening credits begin in Paramount's *Harlow*, we see a Hollywood movie studio awaken from its slumber. Employees begin walking through its gates

Mama Jean (Angela Lansbury) comforts her daughter, Jean Harlow (Carroll Baker), who just got fired from a picture because she would not give in to the advances of the film's lecherous AD, while Marino Bello (Raf Vallone) looks on in *Harlow* (Paramount, 1965).

and punch their timecards. The camera follows some young women as they go from wardrobe, to makeup, to hair dressing. They then emerge as glamorous showgirls.

On one soundstage, a choreographer is rehearsing a Busby Berkeley–type dance routine, while at another, a number of pretty girls are lined up in hopes of landing a small role as a fashion model. The director picks a platinum blonde named Jean Harlow for the bit. While she poses for a photographer on the street in a long, tight, black evening gown, a police officer, chasing a man, runs by, ripping her dress off. This leads to another bit where she is having a bubble bath and a window washer pulls the plug from the drain with a fishing rod. As the water begins to seep down, she notices him ogling her through the window. She flings her washing sponge and knocks him off his ladder.

After she lands yet another minor role in a musical, an assistant director named Hanson invites Harlow to a private dressing room. He instructs her to remove her robe so that he can see the costume underneath—a slinky slip for her bedroom scene. He then pulls the casting couch routine on Jean, promising her five days on the picture. He says, "Honey, I picked you out special. You play ball with me—I'll keep you working." When a nervous Jean won't put out and insists that she'll get ahead on her talent alone, he makes a call and has her fired from the picture.

Harlow returns home, where she lives with over-protective Mama Jean and her lazy husband, Marino Bello. "Oh, Mama, all they want is my body," she wails. Her mommy replies, "I knew you were too young for this business. It's rotten and evil." Marino berates Jean for losing out on the part and insinuates that she should have obliged the frisky assistant director for the sake of the family. An irritated Jean mocks him for not finding his own job, calling him, "King Liar. Prince Loafer. Count Ne'er-Do-Well. Baron Loudmouth." Insulted, he says Jean is wrong to think she is too good to sleep with a man to get a part. The outraged actress hisses, "The day I make love, Marino Bello, it will be for myself—not for you—not if I starve to death!"

Mama Jean gently suggests to her husband that he needs to find employment as the bills are piling up and they need to eat. Not motivated in the least, Marino tells her he wants something better for them and can achieve it, as long as Jean keeps working a little while longer. He then pulls his wife onto the couch and seductively says, "If I took a job, what would you do for your pleasure in the daytime?"

Harlow's luck changes when she meets beady-eyed Arthur Landau. The minor agent observes her as she tries to snag a free box lunch after sneaking onto a Western movie set. She's caught, but he rides to her rescue. Once he wins the skeptical actress' trust, she agrees to have Landau represent her. He is prophetic, telling her one day she is going to resent his ten percent. She scoffs, and Landau insists, "Human nature."

Landau then arranges an introduction to big movie star Jack Harrison at his pool party. While Jack plays cards with some of his studio buddies, Jean goes for a swim and learns from another woman of Harrison's playboy reputation. The naïve Jean panics when left alone with the handsome leading man. "Oh, please don't touch me," she pleads, as she calls, *"Arthur! Arthur!"* She embarrasses herself and angers Landau. Although Harrison is miffed, he knows he won't be able to forget the beautiful blonde.

Despite this incident ("You have the body of a woman and the emotions of a child," he remarks), Landau keeps Jean as a client and begins to get her constant work. Playing the sexy girl in short after short, she is usually the brunt of a joke, with a pie in the face or falling, elegantly dressed, into a pool of water. After one exhausting day on the set, Jean comes home to find Marino hosting a party with his friends with food and drink paid for with her money. She is infuriated, especially when she sees that he bought imported wine at three dollars a bottle. Mama Jean follows her into the bedroom and pleads with her daughter to stop being cruel to Marino. She admits he is an impractical man, but the party is in honor of their wedding anniversary. Jean apologizes for not remembering and agrees to join the celebration.

Landau, meanwhile, laments to his wife, Beatrice, his failure in getting Jean Harlow bigger roles. Although he has a whole reel of film of her to present to the studios, there is not one line of dialog on it. Her success means his success, and he tells Beatrice that he is determined to make her a star. He gets Jean's reel to producer Richard Manley who wants to test her to see what she sounds like on film. However, he won't finance it unless they have an agreement first. Jean lands the movie, titled *The Allegheny Trail*, and a contract. Landau makes a verbal pact for $200 a week when she is not working and $250 a week when she is, with $50 raises the second and third years. Because she is under 21 years old, Mama Jean needs to co-sign the contract, but Marino forbids her. He feels that the producer is taking advantage and demands $1,000 a week with $500 raises. After explaining the movie business to him, Landau gets up to leave when the stubborn Marino refuses to back down. Horrified about losing out on this picture deal, Jean threatens to tell her mother about the sexual advances she's had to endure from Marino. Not wanting to hear another word, Mama Jean asks Arthur for the agreement and signs it.

Jean runs from the premiere of her first starring movie in tears. "I was terrible," she wails. "I walked scared, talked scared, and I was scared." Manley points out to her agent that the film received good reviews, but Harlow did not. The critics trashed Harlow's thespian skills, or lack thereof, but heralded her as Hollywood's newest sex symbol. The producer is determined to get a return on his investment in Jean Harlow, so he sends her out on a whirlwind, national, personal appearance tour accompanied by Mama Jean and her husband. After screenings of the film, Jean, clad in silk, tight dresses, entertains the crowds by acting sexy and talking in double-entendres.

Harlow makes a huge splash with the public and triumphantly returns to Hollywood. Arthur takes note that she and her parents look like movie stars in their fancy new clothes, and that he has the unpaid bills to prove it. He then drives Jean to the home of Richard Manley, who has demanded to see her. As they ride over, Landau plots to get Jean released from her meager $200 a week contract, as he senses the billionaire is smitten with the actress. When Jean asks why she should break the contract, Landau explains that Manley is notorious for his slow pace in producing movies and that Jean could sit around for months before he has another project for her.

Jean arrives dressed to the nines in a lovely white evening gown. Manley wants to give Jean a lead role in his life, as Landau suspected, and invites her into his lavish bedroom—complete with a sunken Roman bathtub and a rain forest. He asks, "Do you think you can be comfortable here?" She turns down his amorous advances by throwing her drink at him. This leads to his slapping her face and tearing her gown, as he viciously throws her onto his bed. She gets away by kicking him in the stomach. It is an ugly scene but accomplishes the goal of having her fired, as he yells after her, "You can't even act. You're a physical curiosity." Landau is waiting for her and an anguished Jean tells him that their plan worked. He is surprised to hear that Manley got her up to his bedroom, but even more so when she confesses, "Arthur, I really didn't want to leave. Oh, I hope you know what you're doing."

With Jean now a free agent, the wily Landau tries to persuade mogul Everett Redman to sign her to Majestic Studios. At first, the studio head balks at the $60,000 price tag attached to acquiring Harlow's contract. However, knowing that the public craves adult stories with sex and that studio executive Paul Bern champions signing her, he changes his mind. Jean Harlow becomes Majestic's newest star with her own bungalow right next door to fellow contract player Jack Harrison. He advises her to get out of the business pronto, "Don't even sit down. Turn right around and walk out of here." But a determined Jean has no intention of giving up her career, even after Harrison kisses her and proposes marriage. Before she can answer they are interrupted by Paul Bern, who has stopped by to meet her.

Angry producer Richard Manley (Leslie Nielsen) assaults Jean Harlow (Carroll Baker) after she refuses to go to bed with him in *Harlow* (Paramount, 1965).

Jean goes through her paces at Majestic, taking dance classes and being transformed by the makeup and wardrobe departments into a glamorous sex goddess, complete with the requisite beauty mark added to her face, as she poses for publicity photographs. Titles of her movies such as *Yukon Fever*, *Wild Journey*, and *Luscious Lady* flash by on theater marquees or billboards. Marino stops by to pick the Baby up from the studio wearing a new jacket and driving a brand-new car. He then informs her that he and her mother have taken over the management of "our mutual income" and invested their money in a new house. Jean is rightfully angered, considering it is all her hard-earned income, but Marino convinces her to give him a chance because he was right that Jean would be a star and he makes her mother happy. "Anyway, it's only money," says Jean flippantly, as she gives in.

Jean is attracted to the flirtatious Jack Harrison, but she is distracted by the soft-spoken Paul Bern, who brings some culture into her life. She dates both men, alternating between spending time at boxing matches and jazz joints with Harrison, and attending classical music concerts and dining in upscale restaurants with Bern. Self-serving Everett Redman encourages Harrison to propose to Jean because he feels her pairing with Paul Bern would make her too worldly and perhaps more difficult to work with. "The day Jean Harlow becomes Lady Harlow, she becomes worthless to us—and we lose money," he remarks.

One night in her bedroom after dinner, Jean laments to her mother about being alone and says woefully, "A bedroom with one person in it is the loneliest room in the world." She then admits her envy for Mama Jean's relationship with Marino and how her public would laugh if they knew how lonely she was. Her mother advises her "to find somebody you love, marry him, and let nature take its course."

Taking her mother's words to heart, Jean weds Paul Bern, disappointing both Jack Harrison and Everett Redman. After a lavish wedding, the newlyweds retreat to Paul's home. At four in the morning the doorbell rings at Arthur Landau's house. A distraught Jean, wearing a fur coat over her nightgown, enters and relives her horrible wedding night. She tells Arthur and Beatrice how she and Paul argued and how

Jean Harlow (Carroll Baker) accepts an invitation from studio executive Paul Bern (Peter Lawford, standing) to tour Majestic Studios after being caught in a romantic clinch with movie star Jack Harrison (Michael Connors) in *Harlow* **(Paramount, 1965).**

Newlyweds Paul Bern (Peter Lawford) and Jean Harlow (Carroll Baker) are about to cut their wedding cake, as studio head Elliot Redman (Martin Balsam), Beatrice Landau (Hanna Landy), Marino Bello (Raf Vallone), and Mama Jean (Angela Lansbury) look on in *Harlow* (Paramount, 1965).

he beat her. When a confused Landau asks why, Harlow cries, "He didn't want a wife. He wanted a mother, a companion, a decoration. He couldn't make love. He's never been able to. The man I waited for—saved myself for—didn't even want me. I prayed for it to be beautiful. *It was ugly! It was so awful!*" Landau's wife wants to call a doctor to examine Harlow's bruises, but her husband forbids it, thinking of the scandal that could erupt if the news got out to the public.

The next morning Landau and Jean meet with a desperate Bern. He begs Jean to remain his wife. "I'll give you love in every way," he promises. "Except the one that counts," she snaps back. He pleads for her patience and her support, so that he can conquer his demons. She refuses and demands an annulment before leaving. A dejected Bern kills himself three days later.

Jean refuses to go to the funeral and has to be coaxed by her mother and agent to attend. Declining to take time to mourn, a hardened Harlow immediately returns to the studio and begs Everett Redman for a picture. She plays up the public's curiosity with her. "I'm a woman so hot that her husband killed himself because he couldn't satisfy her. Look how they'd line up for that. Doesn't that excite that ticket window you call a heart?"

In her dressing room, Harlow begins boozing while perusing scripts. Six months later, she has completed two pictures and "two cases of whiskey," as pointed

A distraught Jean Harlow (Carroll Baker) describes her wedding night nightmare to her agent Arthur Landau (Red Buttons) and his wife Beatrice (Hanna Landy) in *Harlow* (Paramount, 1965).

out by Marino. She decides to make a play for her step daddy and, taken aback, Marino is insulted with her come-on and scolds her for it. Desperate, Harlow then tries to reconcile with Jack Harrison only to learn that he has a new young bride. Next, she pays a visit to Richard Manley, telling the surprised producer she owes him one, as they make their way to his boudoir. Still not satisfied, the insatiable glamour girl glides from one cheap hookup to the next, waking up in strangers' hotel rooms.

After being berated by Landau, due to out-of-control behavior that is jeopardizing her career and embarrassing the studio, a boozy Harlow tells him off. Standing up for himself, he says, "You hired my judgment, which I just gave you," to which she replies, "For a very pretty price, I might add." He calls her out on the fact that she resents his commission, reminding her that he had predicted she would when he first became her agent. Screaming that she made everyone around her wealthy, she kicks him out of her bungalow demanding to be left alone.

A soused Harlow then drives off and winds up at the beach where she stumbles onto the sand and passes out with liquor bottle in hand. The police find her the next morning and take her to the hospital where she is put into an oxygen tent to help combat her pneumonia. As life fades from her, Mama Jean pleads with the doctor to help the Baby, but Jean expires with her family and Arthur Landau at her bedside. "She didn't die of pneumonia, she died of life," sighs her agent. Bobby Vinton then begins singing the love ballad "Lonely Girl," as a montage of Baker photos as Jean Harlow flash on the screen.

When the reviews for Joe Levine's *Harlow* came forth, raves were few and far between. One of the better notices came from Donald Zec, of *The Daily Mirror*, who commented, "*Harlow* is a well-scripted movie that packs a hefty punch." Most notices, though, were as negative as Electronovision's:

"Cheap, vulgar and hardly believable."—Leo Mishkin, *Morning Telegraph, N.Y.*

"'Harlow' ... is a dud. The problem is ... the charge derived from a bad formula—Irving Shulman's book with sweetness replacing obscenity"—Philip Kopper, *Washington Post*

"Rambling and dull entertainment, without character or style"—Bosley Crowther, *The New York Times*

"*Harlow* ... is the best movie to be made this year about Hollywood's legendary platinum blonde—which means simply that it is bad in a big, bold way."—*Time*

"*Harlow* is as phony as a Hollywood movie set."—Bruce Dunning, *St. Petersburg Times*

"Not bad enough to be funny, just stupid enough to be pathetic."—Gregory P. Pressman, *The Harvard Crimson*

"Lots of dazzle, but ... is really just one more, rather feeble version of the common horse."—Clarius Backer, *Chicago Tribune*

"Hollywood, in raising its own ghost, has produced a dull movie."—Ann Pacey, *The Sun*

"*Harlow* is a glossy depiction of Hollywood's legendary shortcomings."—F.H.G., *Christian Science Monitor*

Critics Philip Scheuer and Judith Crist, in particular, were extremely disappointed in this version of *Harlow*. Scheuer felt "cheated" because Joe Levine and scriptwriter John Michael Hayes "have presented her as more sinned against than sinning. Which must have taken some doing by Levine, who started out, at least, by using the scandalous book by Irving Shulman.... Even Levine & Co. chicken out at the finish, as if confessing doubts of the validity of their whole operation."[8]

Crist was expecting so much more from Levine's *Harlow*—due to the time they had to work on it, the big buildup Carroll Baker was given as the sex goddess, and the generous budget afforded the lavish sets and costumes. Another turnoff for her was the theme that perpetrated the myth that "everybody and everything in Hollywood was dream-peachy-marvelous except Jean Harlow, who was a crazy mixed-up girl sex-wise." She then delivered a backhanded compliment to Sargent's *Harlow* in the *New York Herald Tribune*, "Strangely, that first inept, tasteless, threadbare, illiterate sudsily sensational film, which at very least made an obeisance to the biographical facts of the star's career, doesn't seem quite so awful compared with the Levine effusion which, in turn, is the thuddiest of what now becomes his trash tetralogy."

In her review of Levine's movie, Crist continued refuting her pan of Bill Sargent's *Harlow* and commented, "In retrospect, we have to credit the quickie *Harlow* with at least suggesting that the star's mother and stepfather were interested in money, that venality was rampant, that studios did exploit their stars and that

Movie poster for *Harlow* (Paramount, 1965).

stars can become victims of their stardom, and that.... Carol Lynley, did ... exude a youthful sexuality and attempted a vulgarity not alien to the very young Harlow."

Acting honors in Levine's *Harlow* were bestowed mostly on Raf Vallone for his performance as oily Marino Bello. He received a few raves like those from *Variety* ("lends a persuasive presence") and from the *Chicago Tribune*: "Only Italian import Raf Vallone ... really crackles filling the screen with a three-dimensional portrait of lovable villainy that is an absolute joy to behold."

Like Carol Lynley, Carroll Baker also received unnecessarily mean-spirited reviews, arguably the cruelest being the ones that not only attacked her performance, but her physical appearance as well:

"[Baker is] a thin, chaste, lachrymose, scratchy-voiced, and altogether unvoluptuous creature."—Brendan Gill, *The New Yorker*

"Carroll Baker portraying the sex goddess of the 1930s is a pretty funny idea … but in this movie she is even more sexless than ever."—Bruce Dunning, *St. Petersburg Times*

Overall, though, most of Baker's reviews were more positive and some were quite complimentary, certainly more so than the ones Lynley had received. Baker did have much more time to prepare for the part and had studied up on the actress, which was a benefit to her.

"Miss Baker fizzles but not as badly as I expected."—Donna Lange, *The Valley Independent*

"Miss Baker does her best to elicit a jot of sympathy … but her best is not enough."—Philip Kopper, *Washington Post*

"Carroll Baker is a fairly reasonable facsimile although she lacks the electric fire of the original. She delivers well."—Whit, *Variety*

"Carroll Baker … is the only truly pleasing part of the movie."—Gregory P. Pressman, *The Harvard Crimson*

"Carroll Baker gives a racy, competent performance …"—Donald Zec, *The Daily Mirror*

"The role seems a close fit with Carroll Baker's abilities and one is hard put to imagine it better played."—Allen Eyles, *Films and Filming*

"Carroll Baker handles herself very well."—R.M. Hodgens, *Film Quarterly*

"Despite Carroll Baker's credible impersonation, 'Harlow' is essentially just another expensive epic about Hollywood …"—F.H.G., *Christian Science Monitor*

One particularly positive review for Carroll Baker came from critic Wanda Hale of *The New York Daily News* who dissed Carol Lynley in the process. She commented, "Miss Lynley's performance is not in the class of Carroll Baker's…. In almost every scene, Miss Baker gives a good account of the late actress." She then added about the film as a whole, "For all the money and effort put into *Harlow*, the result is a sudsy melodrama, a tear-jerker about a famous actress who apparently never knew happiness, never had peace of mind, never had a friend, except her loyal, enterprising agent, Arthur Landau."

By the end of the year, Harry MacArthur, the drama critic at *The Evening Star*, was touting this *Harlow* as one of the worst pictures of 1965. He wrote, "The leading candidates are *What's New, Pussycat?*, *The Sandpiper*, and *Harlow* with *Sylvia* a close runner-up. Deciding which of these was more painful than all the others will not be easy. There may be a clue, though, in the fact that Carroll Baker is running as an entry, having starred in both *Harlow* and *Sylvia*."[9]

Years later, when the film was shown on television, *The Evening Star*'s opinion had not changed, unlike the rival *Harlow*, and its review stated, "Not a definitive biography of the late film star, but a gross story full of slush and nonsense. This was not Jean Harlow!"

Box office-wise, although *Harlow* opened mid-week, *Variety* reported that the film was "making great showings on initial showings this round."[10] *The Yellow Rolls-Royce* topped the week in grosses, followed by (2) *The Sound of Music*; (3) *My Fair Lady*; (4) *Von Ryan's Express*; (5) *The Greatest Story Ever Told*; (6) *Cat Ballou*; (7) *The Art of Love*; (8) reissue of *Dr. No* and *From Russia with Love*; (9) *The Sandpiper*; (10) *In Harm's Way*.

Opening in more cities, *Harlow* took in $23,000 in Philadelphia prompting *Variety* to comment, "Big campaign plus personal promotion of Joe Levine and heavy ad budget is showing big results."[11] It also grossed $15,000 in Kansas City; $33,000 in Chicago; and $20,000 in Detroit. Despite outperforming its rival, *Harlow* just missed out on being part of the ten highest grossing films for its first full week in release, coming in 11th place per *Variety*.

Joe Levine received more disappointing news when *Variety* reported that the John Wayne western *The Sons of Katie Elder* was now anticipated to be Paramount's "big summer picture" with projected rentals of $9 million. Box office predictions of *Harlow* earning $13 million, like *The Carpetbaggers*, were scaled back to $6 million, but even that would be an over-estimation.[12] This coincided with *Harlow* slipping to 12th place among box office grossers during its second week of release. By the third week, the film had completely dropped off the charts and was listed as a runner-up. However, due to new playdates, the film rebounded the following week and climbed to sixth place. The following week it slipped to seventh. This last-minute surge was enough to land *Harlow* on *Variety*'s list for "July's 12 Hottest Grossers" placing at number ten. Top honors went to *What's New Pussycat?* Although the box office gross was nowhere near what Levine had boasted it would be, his film achieved a fairly decent take and made the list, unlike Sargent's *Harlow*, which was a box office misfire.

As a biography of Jean Harlow, Paramount's *Harlow* stinks. The story is pure fiction. Harlow was married three times, not once as indicated here. The titles of her films are all made up for some reason. She died of uremic poisoning and not pneumonia as she does here. The film also takes itself *much* too seriously and wallows in maudlin sappiness at times—poor Jean can't find love, poor Jean hates the roles offered her, poor Jean is so unhappy despite being adored worldwide. It tries to be sincere, despite all the inaccuracies in the script. Instead, it should have reveled in the sensational aspects of Irving Shulman's biography and presented the story as unadulterated, high gloss, cotton candy trash à la *The Carpetbaggers*. Especially since almost everything in the movie is untrue and unintentionally kitschy anyway. At least Sargent's *Harlow* attempted to portray the edited facts about the bombshell's life. This *Harlow* veers off-course right from the get-go, presenting the actress as a pious virgin, when she was far from it.

That said, this *Harlow* is more entertaining and infinitely prettier to look at than its rival, due to its sumptuous production values. It has the lavishness of a Ross Hunter production such as *Imitation of Life*. However, the film evokes the sixties, rather than the thirties—from Baker's bouffant-type hairstyles to the over-the-top sets including a circular bed in Manley's bedroom mansion that is more reminiscent of James Bond than Howard Hughes, to the Burt Bacharach–style musical score, to Baker doing what seems to be the Twist on stage during Harlow's personal appearance tour. Perhaps if they were going to present a fabricated look at Jean Harlow anyway, they should have set it in the sixties and offered a story about a fictitious actress. The comparison to Jean Harlow would not have been made and they may have received much better reviews.

The opening is arguably the best segment in this *Harlow*, as the movie studio awakens from its slumber and slowly comes to life. It is beautifully photographed and wonderfully scored by Neal Hefti. The scene excitingly recreates what the vibrant workings of a studio at that time in Hollywood may have been like. Less successful is trying to capture Jean Harlow's life.

Carroll Baker was a bit too long in the tooth and much too thin to make a totally realistic Jean Harlow, but she is made up to resemble her and looks simply stunning. All the gowns and dresses, designed by Edith Head, are gorgeous, save for a hideous beige dress (with matching fur-lined jacket and hat with long veil) that Baker wears when she confronts her husband the morning after the honeymoon night "melee." It looks as if she is going to a funeral, which perhaps was the intention with the death of her marriage. The standout costume for Baker's Harlow is a long, white creation with a scoop neckline and fur-trimmed, short sleeves that looks like an evening gown but is actually a one-piece pant suit.

Like Carol Lynley, Baker delivers an uneven performance. Early on she is totally unconvincing, trying to enact a naïve, wide-eyed, pure innocent being set upon by the big bad wolves of Hollywood. The scene at Jack Harrison's house, as she yells "*Arthur!*" afraid that the movie star is going to make a pass at her, is especially embarrassing. All of the scenes with Connors as Harrison are Baker's weakest—there was just no on-screen chemistry between the pair.

Hayes' script does give Baker some meaty scenes to play, such as when she relives her horrid wedding night to the Landaus. Baker delivers a powerful performance here and arouses sympathy from the audience. In this version, Harlow's wild period begins after the death of Bern a few days after their nuptials. In the Sargent film, she begins stepping out on her husband days after the wedding, but it sticks to the truth of Bern killing himself after almost two months of marriage and does introduce his common-law wife. In this version, Bern offs himself only a few days after their nuptials—with no mention of the other woman.

Other scenes where Baker really excels are when the unhappy movie star begins to crash and burn, trolling for cheap pickups. Particularly good is the part where she drunkenly tells off her agent. This is totally fictitious of course, but these scenes are excellently played by Baker, who always made a more convincing vixen than good girl. This is starkly evidenced in the bedroom scene where she bemoans to Mama Jean her loneliness and her desires to love a man. Baker, still trying to convey a Miss Purity persona for the character, is unconvincing compared to Lansbury doing her doting-mother best.

Too much screen time is given to the annoying Red Buttons as the actress' agent (the film is titled *Harlow* not *Landau*). That is not too surprising, since in the biography Arthur Landau painted himself as Harlow's hero and savior. Buttons' best moment is when he threatens to punch out Paul Bern. You can believe the rage in him. Angela Lansbury makes a more likable Mama Jean than Ginger Rogers, but her sincere performance seems out of place considering the surrounding histrionics. Her Mama Jean is too nice and is much less fun than Rogers' more clinging interpretation. Raf Vallone is quite believable, playing a more sensual Marino Bello compared to Barry Sullivan. While his virility in the bedroom is a topic of conversation between mother and daughter on more than one occasion, there are no heated arguments between Bello and Mama Jean, nor any indication that they divorced before Jean died.

As for the film's leading men, both Michael Connors and Peter Lawford do not make much of an impression. Lawford was much too handsome for the role of diminutive Paul Bern and plays him stiffly. Even his breakdown scene, pleading with Jean to stay his wife, falls flat. Connors is all over the place with an erratic performance. This was not necessarily his fault, as the character (like Zimbalist's William Mansfield) is so undefined for both the actor and viewer. Is he supposed to be Clark Gable or William Powell or a combination of both? No matter who the character is supposed to represent, Connors never clicks with Baker on screen.

Leslie Nielsen is a bit better as the manipulative, stone-faced movie producer, Richard Manley. His character is the outright villain of the piece. After Manley takes a chance and makes Jean Harlow a star, he tries to take sexual advantage of the virginal actress. Nielsen's fans who only know him from his hilarious *Naked Gun* movies of the eighties and nineties would get a kick out of seeing him play such a lech.

As a true movie biography, Joe Levine's *Harlow* is more disappointing than Sargent's *Harlow* since Levine had much more prep time to get his movie produced. He was forever boasting about all the years of research that went into the project. This makes his biopic even more of a failure for all the fiction about the star that it foists onto the public. Even the little things, like using fake titles for Harlow's movies and her movie studio, hurts the picture.

Worse are the known facts about Jean Harlow that were tossed aside. She was married and divorced by the time she was 20 and no virgin, which is what the movie wants the audience to believe. Not surprisingly since he contributed to Irving Shulman's biography, all credit goes to her agent, Arthur Landau, for bringing her to the attention of Howard Hughes and her star making role in *Hell's Angels*. In actuality, the film's co-star, James Hall, reportedly deserved the credit. It was common knowledge that the star abhorred wearing a bra, but that is not even mentioned here due to MPAA interference, as indicated in studio memos. In Sargent's version, though, there are two scenes where it is pointed out.

Once Jean Harlow becomes a star, the film really rolls off the tracks in terms of reality. Harlow is never seen making another movie or shown progressing to a delightful, wise-cracking comedienne. The studio scenes here take place in her over-sized, luxurious bungalow where she exchanges "witty repertoire" with her agent or Jack Harrison. There are no backstage scenes, so the fact that the star was adored by the stagehands is totally ignored. At least Sargent's *Harlow* presented the star as a popular "crew gal," happiest working on a movie set, even while she was dissatisfied with the films offered to her.

Levine's *Harlow* does get credit for showing how Howard Hughes kept Jean Harlow on the road promoting the movie in front of live audiences (and the huge price tag that went with it due to the excessive expenditures by Harlow and her family) and how the billionaire tried to hold her back before she got free of him to make pictures elsewhere. Also, it recognizes that Harlow's movie studio created her blonde bombshell persona. In a series of quick shots, beautifully underscored with the film's opening theme, Harlow transforms with penciled-in eyebrows, her trademark hairdos and slinky wardrobe, and a wandering beauty mark on her face. Here they add it to her lower right chin whereas Lynley sports it on the opposite side.

The film also focused on how tremendously popular Jean Harlow became, with many women bleaching their hair platinum blonde to emulate the sexy actress. The rival version doesn't give the studio any credit for transforming Jean Harlow. In fact, it even includes an early scene where the makeup lady gushes over Jean and tells her that there is not much more that she can do to improve the actress' gorgeous looks.

Both versions of *Harlow* present the Paul Bern impotency theory as to what led to his suicide. Years later, it was purportedly determined that Bern may have killed himself after a chance meeting between Harlow and Dorothy Millette, his common-law wife, who came to see Bern at his home. He may have shot himself after Millette departed.

Levine's film, however, goes one step further, claiming Bern beat his wife on their wedding night, although it is not with a cane as depicted in the Shulman biography. During Harlow's tearful recollection of events to the Landaus, she tells them that her husband pushed her, but she thinks he didn't mean to hurt her. She slammed into the back of the sofa and then fell onto the floor, which caused the bruising on her back. Bern's suicide a few nights later (rather than more than two months later in actuality) sends a hardened, soused Harlow into the arms of any man for sex. This version has no mourning period for Harlow, who immediately starts drinking heavily, as reported by some, but her love of playing craps was excluded.

As Levine's film progresses it gets worse in terms of falsehoods, taking extreme dramatic license as the actress begins boozing it up and trolling for cheap sex. Unlike the rival version where Harlow makes a grand return to Hollywood after studying in New York (which was pure nonsense), finds love with William Mansfield, and dies a happy, respected movie star (which is close to the truth), Baker's Harlow has no such luck. Instead, she remains a drunkard, passing out on the beach where she contracts pneumonia and dies with her agent at her bedside. This is what Levine's *Harlow* wants you to believe. Considering Jean Harlow's last weeks were well documented, this absurd, contrived ending really hurts the movie.

The best way to enjoy this *Harlow*, due to all its biographical inaccuracies, is to treat it as a fictional story of an actress who goes from a virginal bit player to international glamour goddess, but still cannot find love and happiness. This way it remains a colorful, pleasant timewaster, a little more entertaining than the rival version, which, although more factual, still only gets faint praise from most Harlow fans. Neither, of course, comes close to representing the real Jean Harlow beloved by millions.

10

The Aftermath

After both movies had hit the silver screen, the *Ladies' Home Journal* asked, "Have you seen…. *Harlow* (1) or *Harlow* (2)? Pay your money and take your choice right now, between Carol (Lynley) or Carroll (Baker), both solid platinum and a wide screen wide."[1]

With the reviews for both movies in, it seems that all of the adverse publicity both films received due to their warring producers had the critics chomping at the bit, hoping the films would be stinkers so that they could viciously attack them. With poison pens in hand, most did. Philip K. Scheuer covered the making of both movies for the *Los Angeles Times* and his reviews contained both praise and criticism for each. Feeling that some critics went into the screenings already biased, he actually called out his colleagues on this and remarked, "In the present atmosphere of bad feeling, name calling and recrimination, it is scarcely any wonder that reviewers, themselves put on the spot, have been inclined to take a pox-on-both-your-houses attitude toward Bill Sargent's *Harlow* and now Joe Levine's *Harlow*."[2]

Back in the sixties, Carol Lynley threatened to "hold a public burning in the middle of a Beverly Hills Street."[3] Years later, cast and crew, had varying opinions about the two *Harlow* movies. When remembering *Harlow* for her memoir, Ginger Rogers remarked, "Unfortunately, the finished product was very grainy and not too viewable; it was done too fast…. Director Alex Segal didn't have much of a script to work with, but the cast … tried their best."[4] During the mid-seventies, when asked about *Harlow*, Bill Sargent still could not help himself from dinging his rival and quipped, "My picture was the worst movie in history until Joe Levine's came out."[5]

> **CAROL LYNLEY:** I didn't like the movie [Electronovision's *Harlow*]. I didn't like doing it.
>
> **MICHAEL DANTE:** It was just unfortunate that they didn't have the budget to do the job they wanted to do, and that it wasn't distributed properly. It was sad in terms that it wasn't successful at the box office. I really felt Bill Sargent wanted to make a good movie. This was not a bad experience at all. Ed was a great character and I received terrific reviews.
>
> **CAROL LYNLEY:** I think Carroll Baker's *Harlow* is much, much better. It is a movie, which ours really wasn't.
>
> **ROBERT OSBORNE:** I preferred the top tier production values of Joe Levine's *Harlow*. Sargent's version had the look of a quickly done *Matinee Theater* kind of

show. The most fun for me though was watching Mama Jean in each—Lansbury in one and Ginger in the other.

Darrell Rooney: I would say the Baker version is entertaining for the first two-thirds of the movie and more interesting than the end. It hits some marks. The last third is complete and total fiction.

Marvin Paige: I think Carroll Baker's *Harlow* was a stronger project. It was shot in color with a really good cast. It was more of a movie than Sargent's production. I think in both versions there was a bit of fantasy going on. Carol Lynley and Carroll Baker are fine actresses, and I think they both did the best they could under the conditions.

Richard Bennett: Neither *Harlow* was worth the effort I don't think. It's too bad. Jean Harlow was really something. Maybe she wasn't the best actress in the world, but at the same time she was a big star who affected a lot of changes in attitude in the film industry.

With all said and even if the critics just wanted to slam the *Harlows* because they hated all the pre-publicity the films mustered, it is pretty evident that, despite their valiant efforts and professionalism, neither Carol Lynley nor Carroll Baker successfully brought Jean Harlow to life on the silver screen.

Though Lynley and Baker were made to resemble Jean Harlow, neither had her voluptuousness of body or distinctive voice that was needed to play the renowned sex goddess. Their performances could have compensated for this, but they came up short trying to project the qualities that made the blonde bombshell so adored by the public. Comparing the actresses as Harlow really isn't fair, as they essentially played two different characters, who only shared the same name. From the get-go, Lynley's Harlow has had her share of hard-knocks and is experienced in the ways of life, as shown early on when she scams a free lunch from a diner without a trace of remorse. She is feisty or melancholy but rarely happy, always on the defensive battling her mother and stepfather, the studio, and the men in her life. When she tells Step Daddy Dearest to drop dead, she means it. There are too few scenes, however, where Harlow is content and enjoying life, which, by all accounts, she did during the majority of her adult life. It is too bad the script didn't let Lynley play a more nuanced Harlow.

Baker's Harlow is a Cinderella-type—a sweet, hard-working, naïve gal who is shabbily treated by men and Hollywood. When she steals food, she feels much guiltier about it than Lynley's Harlow. Her arguments with Marino ring false (there is less believable conviction here than with Lynley) and she constantly finds comfort in the arms of Mama Jean, the mediator. She is the dependent heroine who can't come to a decision without advice from her mother about sex or her agent about her career. When she overcomes adversity and becomes a big movie star, her life quickly descends into tawdry chaos full of beatings, booze, and cheap sex. These are the scenes where Baker excels. However, as with the other version, the real, happy, content Jean Harlow is nowhere to be found.

One reasonable opinion of the actresses' failure came from Anthony Cassa, writing in *Hollywood Studio* magazine. He felt that since neither of them knew Jean Harlow, they had to impersonate her screen persona and not the off-camera reality.

10. The Aftermath

Both Lynley and Baker were "simply not Jean Harlow" and were trying "to act like Harlow, a person whose natural behavior and personality was never the subject of her film roles."⁶

DARRELL ROONEY: I think Carroll Baker makes a good Jean Harlow. I love her but she was probably too old to have played her. If she would have done it eight years earlier, she would have had more baby fat on her. That is entirely critical but she is still a wonderful Jean Harlow and I feel the best choice to play the role from the pool of actresses of that time. Admittedly, though, she has some missteps like when she is screaming for her agent in Jack Harrison's house. She is not yelling, "*Arthur! Arthur!*" but "*Au-thor!*" "*Au-thor!*" Makes me think, "When are you Midwestern and when are you not?"

Japanese magazine publicity photograph composite featuring "The Two Harlows": Carol Lynley as Jean Harlow and Carroll Baker as Jean Harlow.

As for Carroll's look as Harlow, Jean had inset eyes and part of the genius in photographing her was that her inset eyes had so much more shadow on them because they were deeply set back. They did give Carroll some Jean Harlow-esque eye makeup to make her eyes seem really dark. I liked that but I do not like the sixties eyebrows or hair. I like the ode to Harlow's costumes from her movies, but they tried to do thirties-inspired sixties clothes. And it surprised me how liberally Edith Head borrowed from Jean's movies like *Red-Headed Woman*.

ROBERT OSBORNE: Both Carroll/Carols were about as much like the real Jean Harlow as Hattie McDaniel, mainly because the one thing they lacked—which neither carbon-copy hairdos, costuming or makeup could give them—was sex-appeal. Both are good actresses, but oozing sex was not a quality either possessed on screen.

DARRELL ROONEY: I like Carol Lynley but I think she is unlikable in this movie. She is humorless and always yelling—even being verbally abusive at times. And yet, characters keep saying things like, "Oh Jean Harlow, you are as nice as I heard." *Really*!?! I have not seen it in the movie. This is not Carol Lynley's fault. It is the bad direction and the idea of how they were going to define this character for the film.

As for Carol's look, I think it is barely Jean Harlow–esque even with her wig. There is nothing in her makeup that is beyond the sixties. It is a less successful look. Now the costumes [designed by Nolan Miller], however, are very Jean Harlow, especially the gowns. This has my favorite costume from either movie. It is a white evening gown that has a sort of cape back with fur tails hanging off the shoulders [it is the gown Harlow is wearing when she abandons her husband on their wedding night to go to the Clover Room nightclub]. It was so evocative of the real Jean Harlow in the way she dressed. It was the most successful design of them all.

Over the years, feelings for Levine's *Harlow* have remained largely unchanged. As a biopic about the life of Jean Harlow, it is still considered awful by many. However, it is entertaining, with sumptuous sets and costumes and a fine performance from Carroll Baker. Because it was available on VHS, DVD, and now Blu-ray, it has been in the public eye for years. Darrell Rooney, however, gives it more props in terms of showing Harlow' early life realistically than some of the critics gave it, then and now.

DARRELL ROONEY: This *Harlow* is a nice, big movie. It is in color and has a wonderful musical score by Neal Hefti. It is haunting and sad. There are elements about the film that I think are incredibly successful. I like the first half since it is about Jean Harlow trying to build a career and become somebody—that is interesting.

It also has great casting but it is too bad it is wasted on a script that doesn't work. Angela Lansbury is brilliant. Raf Vallone is perfect. And with Red Buttons you could not have asked for a better Arthur Landau. To me, he is the core of the movie. I wish all that stuff about him here had been true but it is not. I love how they filmed at the Pasadena train station where Jean would take the train from. That is pure thirties Hollywood. There are great things like that in the movie that people like me appreciate.

But there are mistakes. They did not portray Mother Jean correctly. Peter Lawford is the one actor who gives me cringe-worthy moments in this movie and makes me laugh whenever his character of Paul Bern says, "*Give me more time!*" I always start laughing because the scene is just terrible. There is some bad dialog in the movie.

Using false film titles, a made-up movie studio, and disguised characters does not bother me so much since I know it was done for legal reasons. What bothers much more is that the third act does not make sense and delves into Irving Shulman land. Jean Harlow is so frustrated that she goes out sleeping with strange men in San Francisco, which is absolutely not true (her mother and stepfather were with her any time she was there). The movie shifts from a virginal girl trying to be good and save herself for the right man, to trying to sell herself as a sex goddess—one who can't find love or sexual fulfillment and goes bad. Because of that, she must die—overnight of pneumonia. It does not resonate as true on any level.

The death knell is the Arthur Landau character saying, "She didn't die of pneumonia, she died of life." It is melodramatic and silly, as they show all these

Publicity photograph by Bud Fraker of Carol Lynley from *Harlow* (Magna, 1965) wearing a Nolan Miller-designed gown that is the favorite of historian Darrell Rooney from all the Harlow costumes in either film (courtesy Darrell Rooney).

photos of Carroll Baker looking great as Harlow while Bobby Vinton sings the end love song. But I end up not knowing what to feel because none of this makes sense. I do not know what you want me to feel about this person. To me that is where the movie is imperfect but there are still so many great things in it.

Sargent's *Harlow* was only available when it re-ran in TV syndication during the seventies and eighties. It was never released on any video or digital platform until bootleg DVD copies became available during the 2000s.

The highly maligned Electronovision film has received a revisionist look especially when compared to its rival. It has received more recognition for staying truer to the facts about Jean Harlow. Trav SD, on his website called *Travalanche*, states the reasons why he felt that *Harlow* holds up as the better biopic than Levine's film.

TRAV SD: Though it's clearly a shoestring affair made for a fraction of the other one's budget … it does much better on several of the essentials. It gets WAY more of the facts correct … and it's written with a good deal more focus and movement. Where the other film is a soap opera containing numerous scenes featuring people simply talking with no dramatic object of any kind, this one moves along fairly briskly.[7]

Sargent's *Harlow*, however, still had its distractors. Back in December of 1981, when it aired on WTBS, the reviewer in *On Cable* remarked, "Though beautiful, Carol Lynley never achieves the spark or glow of the famed actress who became a fine comedienne. And the slapdash screenplay by Karl Tunberg does nothing to help modern audiences understand and appreciate the platinum blonde screen idol."

Darrell Rooney concurs and argues that just because the film has a sort of check list addressing certain details in Harlow's life, it does not give the film any better dramatic standing today over its rival.

DARRELL ROONEY: I did not find Sargent's *Harlow* particularly entertaining. The movie uses the tropes of that time period in Hollywood to anchor it in that world beginning with having Laurel and Hardy and Al Jolson there at the commissary. Her relationship with William Mansfield is another trope that is so forced and fake. Is he supposed to be an amalgam of William Powell and Clark Gable? *Who is this*? It is nice that they touched on these [Harlow hating to wear a bra, her early marriage, the scenes with Paul Bern's common-law wife and Marie Dressler, etc.], but they do not use them in any particular way that is satisfying. Using a checklist is a good way to describe it. The film is very superficial with no depth to it beyond that. It is not good storytelling.

To me, this movie also suffers from an identity crisis. I do not know if they are making a movie about Marilyn Monroe or Jean Harlow—she goes to study with an acting teacher in New York!?! *Who are you talking about*? I feel this script has more to do with Monroe than Jean Harlow's life. I didn't see Ginger Rogers as Mother Jean's real character. I saw her as someone who was manipulative and would manipulate her daughter but I didn't see her being someone who was guiding her daughter's career.

My biggest problem with this version, apart from I do not know which celebrity they are making a movie about, is in script form, Carol Lynley is given next to nothing to do but be a screaming banshee. She is completely humorless and that is not Jean Harlow. Somewhere, somebody has it in their head that that kind of character is authentically her or is appealing but it is not in any way. I did like those scenes with Jean Harlow backstage with the crew though. I felt they had some grasp of who she was as a person.

Here Harlow becomes a star almost overnight and the movie lost me right there. The ending does not say what she is dying from—at all! Everything is fine and all of a sudden, she faints on the set and then she dies. *Why? We don't know why*. It is very incomplete.

10. The Aftermath

* * *

Once the final box office grosses were tallied, there was a discrepancy with the take for the Electronovision *Harlow*. Sargent announced that his *Harlow* grossed $2 million, slightly more than its budget of $1.5 million, and turned a profit despite the odds stacked against it. He may have quoted the worldwide gross because the movie did not place on *Variety*'s Big Rentals of 1965—meaning it brought in less than $1 million in the states. A.E. Bollengier, vice-president and treasurer of Magna Pictures, commented that despite being locked out of the major chains, *Harlow* did very well in the Midwest and West, which countered its poor performances in some cities such as New York. Per its agreement with Electronovision, Inc., Magna earned 40 percent of the net profits in the U.S. and Canada, and evenly split the profits elsewhere. It also owned world distribution and TV rights.

Unlike Sargent's *Harlow*, Levine's *Harlow* appeared on *Variety*'s list and placed at number 26 with $3 million rentals to date and an anticipated final gross of $3.6 million. It was still short of its $4 million dollar budget. Needless to say, neither film was considered a financial success.

> **CAROL LYNLEY:** There is an old show biz axiom. You make two movies about the same subject and open them around the same time, they both fail. It's like dog chases car and gets run over. There are certain things in show business that are true. And that is one of them.

It is interesting to note that both movies went for the family audience in telling a story about one of the silver screen's most notorious sex goddesses. Why then did they not seek a Sandra Dee or Hayley Mills type for the role of Jean Harlow? Instead, Sargent and Levine cast actresses who were both so determined to shake their on-screen good girl personas, that they had appeared semi-nude in the pages of *Playboy*, and then strangely bragged how their films would not be sexy and salacious. Who wants to see a Disneyfied movie about a sex symbol? Not many, as indicated by the box office grosses.

Realizing that his movie was going to be relegated to secondary theaters due to Levine and Paramount's influence, Bill Sargent might have had a grindhouse hit if he had ramped up the sex and sensationalism. The shoddy Electronovision process just reeked of smarmy, overcoat-clad gentlemen watching the film in a rundown, 42nd Street dive, but more lewdness was needed on screen to get them to fill the seats. Besides some shots of Lynley's cleavage, the audience doesn't even get many glimpses of her legs. Even if his *Harlow* played first run theaters, the cheapjack production values undoubtedly ruined its box office chances, especially during the time of such widescreen, color extravaganzas like *Doctor Zhivago* and *The Sound of Music*.

As for Joe Levine's reasoning for avoiding sex, especially after giving the world *The Carpetbaggers*, it was due to studio pressure. Paramount did not want to challenge the MPAA and tried to keep distance from Shulman's reviled book. However, this backfired in terms of box office receipts. Scholar A.T. McKenna opined in the *Journal of Popular Film & Television*, "The tempering and toning down of *Harlow*, and the strategy of controversy-avoidance, ultimately meant that Levine's film was left without distinction in the marketplace." He makes a good point that without sex and sensationalism to exploit, the only thing that made Levine's version different from Bill Sargent's was that it was filmed in color and featured higher production values. This was not much of an incentive to draw the crowds like *The Carpetbaggers* did with its tagline "You will never see in your life all that you will see in *The Carpetbaggers!*" That movie, as promised, delivered the goods and filled theater seats. *Harlow* did not.

The other advice Joe Levine received was to wait a few months before releasing his *Harlow* to put distance from Sargent's version. This might have helped, but only if Levine had not rushed the film shoot and had given his actors more time to prepare. Also, a better, more factual screenplay was needed if Levine's goal was to make a true biopic of Jean Harlow, as he claimed. In this regard, his major hurdle would have been convincing the lawsuit-wary Paramount Studios to be less cautious about using the real names of people associated with Jean Harlow and the actual titles of her movies. And, of course, he would have had to ramp up the sex to help sell the picture. However, with all the bad press swirling around Shulman's biography, it is highly unlikely that Paramount would have acquiesced and would have most likely stuck to their position of not rocking the boat with the MPAA and anyone alive who was connected to Jean Harlow.

Although both movies failed to become true box office hits, they did influence the fashion and cosmetics world for a very brief period. The Jean Harlow look—with the "pale, white face, the full, braless bosom and the bright, ruby-red lipstick"—was in. Harlow-type dresses, featuring feather capes and plunging necklines, were being offered by one of the top dressmakers, Charles Rose & Associates. Lingerie designer Margie Douglas created slinky, form-fitting negligees, while cosmetic maven Max Factor put out a line of platinum blonde wigs. Beauticians saw an increase in their clients requesting short hairdos à la Jean Harlow. However, the sixties version featured lighter curls or tousled hair, making it more flattering to the woman's face and easier to manage than the thirties do. Although Harlow's hair style was in, platinum blonde was not.

Come awards season, the Hollywood Foreign Press bestowed a Golden Globe nomination on Red Buttons for Best Supporting Actor. It was then reported in *Variety* that Paramount was making an Academy Award push for its *Harlow* in the following categories: Joseph Ruttenberg for Best Cinematography—Color; Edith Head for Best Costume Design—Color; "Lonely Girl" for Best Original Song; and previous Oscar winner (for *Sayonara* in 1957) Red Buttons for Best Supporting Actor. The hopeful actor commented to Sheila Graham, "I've just received word that Paramount is getting behind me for an Oscar nomination for a supporting role.... I am feeling the same heat I felt with *Sayonara*."[8] As anticipated, when Oscar nominations were revealed both *Harlows* were M.I.A. and the heat Buttons must have felt (he lost the Golden Globe to Oskar Werner in *The Spy Who Came in from the Cold*) was perhaps only from sunburn.

The *Harvard Lampoon* didn't overlook the two films and presented a Movie Worst Award to them both. The "From Insult to Injury Award" went to "Carol Lynley as Harlow and to Carroll Baker as Harlow." Surprisingly, neither *Harlow* placed on the *Lampoon*'s list of the Ten Worst Films of 1965.

Carroll Baker did receive some year-end good news. She was voted Favorite Actress in an annual poll of 250,000 randomly selected teenagers from across the country. Favorite Actor for 1965 was Sean Connery. Their win came as a surprise to many. Columnist Dorothy Manners remarked, "There's no particular reason they shouldn't win—except past polls have come up with the likes of Elvis Presley and Debbie Reynolds; Sandra Dee and Tony Curtis.... Now we have James Bond and Jean Harlow on top, which can only mean times are changing. And so are teenagers."[9]

Carol Lynley also received accolades. At the Hollywood Deb Star Ball in January 1966, thrown annually by the Hollywood Makeup and Hair Stylists Guild, she was bestowed a special award "as the former Deb Star to most fully realize the potential she showed when presented at the Ball (1957)."[10] This honor was given to Lynley not for *Harlow*, but for her splendid performance as the harried mother looking for her daughter, who may or may not exist, in *Bunny Lake Is Missing* opposite Laurence Olivier.

In a candid interview regarding Electronovision's *Harlow*, shortly after it was released, Bill Sargent admitted that making the movie was a mistake. Taking responsibility for it, he stated, "As an art picture, forget it; it stinks. We've got a lot to learn. The film could have been and should have been much better. But we did something by design that's never been done before, something very unique." He felt that a lot of the fault belonged with the script, which contained a lot of changes from Karl Tunberg's original submission due to attorney influence in protecting Electronovision from lawsuits. Sargent then went on to offer his somewhat surprising suggestions on how he would have improved his film. "Shooting it in seven or eight days was a mistake. We should have done it in four. Our mistake was not having them [the actors] on the set for two weeks of rehearsal. The shooting schedule in Electronovision is potentially the length of the film and no more."

The producer seemed to be in a very contradictory mood after *Harlow* opened. In some interviews he took accountability for the film's failure—artistically and financially. Other times, depending on his mood, he laid the full blame on his rival. "I make this flat, emphatic, undeniable, not-possible to misquote statement—that is has all been caused by Joe Levine, not indirectly but directly."[11] Sargent went on to say, "Joe Levine has made one honest statement in his life.... He said if he was 25 years younger—with the stupidity in this industry—he could take it over. And he's right. Well, I'm 25 years younger and I could do it if I wanted to, but I don't have the heart for it."[12]

Bill Sargent's longtime associate Lee Savin, one of the producers of *Harlow* (and whom Marvin Paige thought was a very sharp guy), praised his friend for his technology and promotion skills but disagreed with the producer for laying all the blame for the movie's failure on Joe Levine. He remarked, "Bill operates a good deal by the seat of his pants. Sometimes it works, sometimes it doesn't. Like with *Harlow*. We talked and talked about it, but when we actually decided to do it we had exactly seven weeks to deliver it to the laboratory."[13]

Sargent did make a good point that with Electronovision he had brought a new technique to the movie industry that had been stagnant in the last few years. Filmmaking had progressed far less than other major industries. Studios and producers had become complacent ever since they seemed to have conquered television in the fifties with such popular film processes as Cinemascope and Cinerama.

The disappointing box office grosses of *Harlow* made Sargent realize that moviegoers would excuse the less-than-perfect technical aspects of Electronovision for special event programming but not a straight motion picture. He then announced in late May that he was moving ahead with his next production—the Broadway musical *Fade Out, Fade In* starring Carol Burnett and as many original cast members as were available. It was to be produced by the comedienne's husband, Joe Hamilton, and released by Warner Bros. Also on deck was a second *T.A.M.I.* rock and roll concert. To get moviegoers even more interested, he promised that his company would unveil a new system of electronic filming and that it would be a major improvement on Electronovision. Despite *Harlow*'s technical flaws, the major studios were impressed with Electronovision, as negotiations began with Columbia Pictures and United Artists for picture deals.

Now that both movies had been released, the public was hoping the over-exposed *Harlow* wars were finally over—no such luck. The fun really began. As a bemused Carol Lynley cheerfully remarked at the time, "I believe everybody is suing everybody."[14] She was not exaggerating. Sargent stunned the Hollywood community, as aforementioned, when his company, only two weeks after *Harlow* premiered in theaters, filed one of the largest antitrust suits in the history of the motion picture industry. His prior comments pinning *Harlow*'s failure squarely on the back of Joe Levine should have been a warning. Electronovision, Inc., was seeking millions of dollars in damages against eight corporations and two individuals for violating the Sherman-Clayton antitrust acts. Named in the suit (besides Levine, Paramount, and Embassy) were American Broadcasting–Paramount Theaters, Inc.; National General Corp.; Stanley Warner Corp.; Loew's Theaters, Inc.; RKO Theaters, Inc.; Technicolor Corp. of America; and Jack Armstrong, president of National Allied and alternate national director of Independent Theater Owners of Ohio. Per the suit, all were charged with "conspiracy to restrain Electronovision in the production, distribution and exhibition of its film, *Harlow*; to boycott *Harlow* in the theaters of the theater-owning defendants, and to deprive Electronovision of its contractual rights to the services of Technicolor in the processing, developing and printing of *Harlow*."[15] In San Francisco, Magna Pictures filed a separate lawsuit against the same entities.

Paramount, Embassy, and Levine were further charged with conducting "a campaign to discredit its [Electronovision's] *Harlow*, and of inducing exhibitors, by means of unlawful use of economic power and pressure, to refuse to exhibit the plaintiff's *Harlow* thereby monopolizing the best theaters and greatest potential box office revenue for Levine's production of *Harlow*."[16] Charged with conspiring with them in refusing to exhibit Electronovision's *Harlow* were National General, AB-PT, Loew's, RKO, and Stanley Warner. As an individual, Jack Armstrong was charged with joining the conspiracy and "with publicly making false and defamatory statements about Electronovision's *Harlow* even before it was produced, and also urging theater owners ... to boycott the film by refusing to exhibit it."[17] Technicolor was accused of "refusing to abide with an agreement with Electronovision to process, develop, and make prints of the picture"[18] after alleged threats from Paramount, Embassy, and Levine of halting all future business with the lab if they worked with Electronovision. After filing suit, Sargent issued a statement to the press:

> We sincerely regret that we have been forced into this action. Up until now, throughout the years I have been in business, with home entertainment first and now Electronovision I have never sued anyone before. We only took this action because the conspiracy outlined in the complaint was and is so great that, without recourse to law, we cannot function. Unfortunately, as so often is the case, many of the individuals associated with the defendants are fine people with whom we have enjoyed doing business before this, but I intend to pursue this as vigorously as I have ever pursued anything in my life.[19]

Needless to say, the lawsuit scared away the studios that Sargent was trying to work deals with. Columbia and United Artists backed out of their projects with him. Sargent complained, "I get a feeling colder than hell from this industry. On the same day every major's door was closed to me."[20] He also blamed the studios' refusal to work with Electronovision on the company's troubles with the Screen Actors Guild. Jack Kruschen was still complaining to the press that he was owed $2,000 for personal appearances. Sargent once again apologized for the payroll error, claiming all had been paid in full and maintaining that Magna Pictures was responsible for paying Kruschen, not him.

Though *Fade Out, Fade In* faded away due to Warner Bros.' disinterest and Carol Burnett's asking price of $125,000, which proved too high for Sargent to cover, the clever producer was able to get the studio to distribute a filmed version of the stage musical *Stop the World—I Want to Get Off* in 1966. Unfortunately, its original star and co-creator Anthony Newley does not appear. Instead, his London cast replacement, Tony Tanner, fills in opposite Millicent Martin. It was filmed on a single soundstage at England's Pinewood Studios, in color, with an improved film-electronic process called "System 35," which utilized film cameras with electronic viewfinders. Despite these improvements, the movie was not a hit, although it received an Academy Award nomination for Best Scoring of Music—Adaptation or Treatment.

Sargent went on to explain that the iciness he was receiving from the Hollywood community had nothing to do with the poor critical reception of his *Harlow*; "85% of our reviews were good," he boasted.[21] What dream world did he live in? This figure is pure hyperbole and quite the opposite was true. His *Harlow* received, by far, more pans than kudos. Sargent continued contradicting himself after the movie's release and acknowledged the poor notices when he said, "And even though I'm one of the men in this company who agrees with the bad reviews, I'm sure everybody knows you can't make a good one every time. Besides I'm content with our progress."[22]

With financial troubles vexing Electronovision, Inc., Bill Sargent closed the doors to the company in July of 1965. His offices were described as "among the most sumptuous in Hollywood with deep-pile, raspberry-red carpet, and elegant antiques."[23] With cash debts of $150,000, half of which was owed to the government, it was agreed that the best move was to suspend operations. Though *Hamlet* and *Harlow* grossed roughly $4 to $5 million between them, Electronovision's percentage was small. It realized no profit from *Hamlet* due to the distribution deals with Warner Bros., and *Harlow*, per Sargent, was owed $150,000 in profits from Magna Pictures. He was prepared to sue. Magna employee Lamar Criss, who worked as Unit Production Manager on *Harlow*, refuted Sargent's assertion and claimed that his boss, Marshall Naify, was owed "a considerable amount which he advanced above his original investment."[24] This included funds to cover salaries owed cast and crew and $50,000 to free the *Harlow* negative from seizure due to the Sidney Skolsky lawsuit (which Sargent wound up losing when a Superior Court in Los Angeles awarded Skolsky $80,000 in damages for breach of contract). Despite the dire financial predicament, Sargent was still able to look on the bright side and bragged, "Considering we were around only a year, we really shook the town up, didn't we?"[25]

Despite the bankruptcy, Bill Sargent was insisting that the world would see Electronovision productions of more stage plays and musicals in the future. He boasted magnanimously, "I've never been involved with a venture that lost money for myself or my partners. I'm a promoter and a damned successful one."[26] He also pledged that he was through with Hollywood and would never produce a picture there again. He exclaimed, "This industry and town has the best craftsmen in the world, but it's being run by a bunch of jerks, who use intimidation, threats and illegal acts and anything else to literally ---- a producer."[27]

Two months after Sargent closed up shop, Paramount and Embassy each filed a $1 million countersuit against Magna Pictures over its alleged boycott charges against them. The countersuit claimed "unfair competition by Magna on numerous accounts, based on third defense in which Paramount charges Magna and Electronovision with making and releasing their production of *Harlow* despite well-known previous attempts to produce a major and expensive picture for which Carroll Baker had been signed to play Jean Harlow."[28]

Using unfair competition, Paramount also charged Magna with "financing and distribution of an 'inferior' product, released 'a short time in advance of the Paramount film'; to appropriate to themselves the effects of a large volume of pre-production publicity at the defendants' expense, to confuse and mislead the motion picture public and to refrain from taking steps to show the two pictures were not the same."[29] It seems Paramount was grasping at straws with this countersuit considering it is a free market to compete in a democracy and in view of all the separate promotion Sargent did for his film.

In early 1966, it was reported in *Variety* that Premiere Films picked up the rights to sell Bill Sargent's *Harlow* (and all other Magna Pictures' feature films) abroad. However, the title was changed to *Platinum Blonde*, which happen to be the name of one of Jean Harlow's actual movies. No official reason was given, but it was speculated that it was to avoid confusion with Levine's *Harlow*. This prompted *Variety* to quip, "A good thought that, however belated."[30]

In the spring of 1967, Sargent's anti-trust suit versus Paramount and the rest came to trial. Despite Joe Levine's protestations that his rival had "unclean hands,"[31] a settlement was reached out of court between the studio, Sargent, and Magna

Pictures for an undisclosed amount of money. A few months later, the judgment against Sargent versus Sidney Skolsky was overturned by the Court of Appeals. Free and clear of lawsuits, for the time being anyway, Sargent took his share of the settlement and invested it—first in an electronics laboratory in Columbia, Missouri (which burned down) and then two years later in a state-of-the-art recording studio in Salt Lake City.

Despite Sargent's departure from Hollywood, he did not lose contact with some of his associates.

> **MAUREEN GAFFNEY:** I would only see Bill when he would come back into town. One night, he invited Irving Schacht and a few of us out to dinner. Afterwards, we went for drinks at this brand new hi-rise on Franklin just east of La Brea. Bill had this magnificent suite with a balcony. We were drinking but Bill was doing cocaine. He said something to me and I did not like it. I was sassy and spoke back to him. He yelled, "I'll throw you over the fuckin' balcony!" He was coming after me and Irving said, "Don't say another word, Maureen." He was so high.... I thought he just might have thrown me over the balcony.

* * *

Producer Joe Levine was not only in a legal battle with Bill Sargent, but also with his leading lady when she refused to do promotion for *Harlow*. Carroll Baker explains that she declined "because it was just so corny. I was in the same position as a girl who gets involved with a man and does certain things, until it's pretty hard to say, 'Here's where I draw the line.'"[32] She then went on to explain that she lost all enthusiasm for *Harlow* after she lost control of the property and it turned into a picture that she was less than pleased with. Paramount claimed in their suit that Baker was the main reason *Harlow* failed, blaming delays caused by her time off due to illness, which affected her performance and her refusal to promote it.

Despite the lawsuit against her regarding her contractual obligations for *Harlow*, Carroll Baker was under the assumption that her next film for Paramount was to be Joe Levine's production of *Tropic of Cancer* with Paul Newman, and that she was contracted to do five more movies after that. She reported to work on May 19, 1966, under the terms of the pact, but there was no work for her, nor was she paid. The studio insisted that *Tropic of Cancer* was not on the slate and offered her no other film work.

Feeling that she had no other choice, Baker counter-sued for breach of contract in an amount close to $2 million. She blamed her firing on her husband, Jack Garfein, for coercing her to make demands on Paramount when she was sick during the *Harlow* shoot. She also claimed that the studio used her name to drum up interest in *Tropic*, which enhanced its value. First, the studios tried to have the case thrown out claiming there was no contract with Baker, just a simple memo. After that was rejected by the courts, Embassy and Paramount conceded that there was a seven-picture deal, but there was no sub-agreement for Baker to star in *Tropic of Cancer* and the project was shelved anyway.

The lawsuit kept the actress from working for over two years, because she felt that the powerful studio had her blackballed. She explained, "It works in an odd way in Hollywood. Joe Schmoe would have lunch with his cronies and say, 'That bitch—she's nothing but trouble—don't hire her!' Pretty soon I couldn't get work. Then Paramount tried to squeeze me out of my contract and take me for everything I was worth financially and my marriage was breaking up. Add to this the fact that for three years I never had one good word of encouragement from anyone—the press attacked me viciously at every opportunity—I came very close to suicide."[33]

Baker could have worked in television but it was reported that her business manager, Jess Morgan (proxy of Prometheus Productions, where Baker was V.P.) put a moratorium on the small screen for up to five years. He was refusing all offers "in order to protect her corporate percentage interest in *Harlow* and all upcoming pix which will eventually be sold to TV."[34] He felt overexposure, either starring in a series or guest starring on other TV shows, could dilute the value of the sale of her films to television.

While the lawsuit over *Tropic of Cancer* lingered on, Baker was slated to star in a stage production of *Anna Christie*, directed by her husband, at Hollywood's Huntington Hartford Theatre. However, she received notice from Paramount, expecting her to report to the studio "for work on her first of six pictures."[35] It also indicated that she may be assigned to another studio. Speculation was that Baker would be taking the female lead in either *The Spy with a Cold Nose* or *The Caper of the Golden Bulls*, the only two movies on the docket at the time from Embassy/Paramount. She did neither of them—Daliah Lavi was cast in *Spy* and Yvette Mimieux appeared in *Caper*. The actual film the studio had in mind was *The Scene*. Baker was ready to do the movie but only if it was considered her second film of a seven-picture deal. Paramount, however, was still digging in their heels insisting it was the first. Her reps announced that Baker would do the movie only after the courts decided on the lawsuit. It was then announced that she was taking *Anna Christie* to the East Coast for a twelve-week tour.

Baker eventually emerged victorious in her suit against Joe Levine and Paramount, with New York State Supreme Court Justice Arthur Markewich awarding her $200,000. However, her movie career remained stagnant and no major offers came her way.

Due to the unpleasant shooting experience and the subsequent lawsuits, Carroll claimed that she never even saw the entire finished version of *Harlow* until four years later when it was the in-flight movie on a plane she was traveling on from Rome to Buenos Aires. After downing her third scotch on the rocks, Baker decided to finally view it. She was totally surprised that it was not "the bomb" Joe Levine had declared it and wrote, "Well, *Harlow*, poor old thing, I should have been the last person in the world to have shied away from you. After all, whatever blood you had, had come directly from my veins."[36]

11

Harlow's Second Act

On Stage and Screen

The double dose of *Harlow* biopics in 1965 seemed to be enough for mainstream Hollywood with regard to telling the movie star's story. Although the major studios avoided anything to do with the platinum blonde bombshell, she was still fair game for the stage and later low-budget exploitation features. Late in 1965, Billie Dixon played Jean Harlow in the controversial San Francisco stage production *The Beard*. It closed after a single performance but was revived in mid-1966 and was performed at various Northern California universities with Dixon continuing in the lead. Film starlet Alexandra Hay replaced her in the Los Angeles production, but Dixon returned to the role in New York. In between, Pamela Tiffin, a surprising choice, brought Jean Harlow to life in the guise of Kitty Packard in the Broadway revival of *Dinner at Eight*.

The Beard by Michael McClure was a two-character play featuring Harlow and Billy the Kid. According to author Mark Rozzo, "The play had grown out of a piece of poster art McClure had made called *Love Lion, Lioness*, which Dennis Hopper and Brooke Hayward owned. It depicted Billy the Kid and Jean Harlow in the style of a fight poster."[1] It was described as being a "satire on American sexual customs."[2] With Dixon (who began acting at the age of 12 with the Virginia Players in Charlottesville, Virginia) as Harlow and Richard Bright as Billy, the show premiered on December 18, 1965, at the Actor's Workshop in San Francisco. The play has Billy and Harlow in a battle of the sexes permeated with an aura of sexual tension. Per Dixon, the playwright chose these characters because "Michael wanted it specifically Harlow because they both grew up in Kansas where she had become a legend. And Billy the Kid is a folk hero there."[3] In his documentary *The Maze: Haight/Ashbury* televised on KPIX in 1967, McClure remarked that his characters "are together in eternity and it is kind of a Blue Velvet eternity." It was also littered with foul language and ended with a simulated sex act of cunnilingus. It proved too controversial for the venue and quickly closed after only one performance; however, it was reviewed and critic Michael Grieg of the *San Francisco Chronicle* raved that it was the "most effectively upsetting and creatively stimulating work by a local writer that the Workshop has ever presented."

In July of 1966, the play (with the same cast) was revived at the Fillmore West and, once again after only a single performance, the venue got cold feet and cancelled the run. The production then moved to The Committee Theatre, named for the improv group that performed there, and on opening night it was raided by the police. The producer, playwright, and actors were carted off to jail and charged with obscenity. The production then traveled amongst a few universities including Berkeley, Stanford, UC Davis, and Fullerton where, if it was not raided, it stirred up controversy on campus. In a radio interview with Herbert Feinstein in 1967, Dixon revealed that after one performance she was charged with "lewd and dissolute contact in a public place."[4] The ACLU stepped in to help the producer prevail in court.

During this time, it was suspected that Andy Warhol caught a performance of the play and, despite the vehement written objections from the playwright, filmed a movie called *The Beard* starring Gerald Malanga as Billy and Mary Woronov as Harlow. It was never released, however, due to threats of a lawsuit.

A production was then mounted at the Warner Playhouse on La Cienega Blvd. in West Los Angeles. Replacing the original leads were Dennis Hopper and Alexandra Hay. Hopper had been an actor in Hollywood since the fifties but due to his bad reputation was now more photographer than actor. Hay was relatively new to the business. She had just signed a contract with Columbia Pictures and had had small roles in the Matt Helm spy spoof *The Ambushers* starring Dean Martin and the hit comedy *Guess Who's Coming to Dinner?* As opening night approached, Hopper withdrew. It is unclear if he left on his own accord or if the producers let him go but it all centered on a public incident outside the theater. One day, Hopper's wife, Brooke Hayward, left the theater after watching a run-through despite Hopper's pleas for her to stay. Per Mark Rozzo, Hopper became unhinged and he reported, "After she [Brooke] got into the car, he jumped onto the hood and kicked the windshield in while Brooke sat in the driver's seat, aghast. The small crowd of people looking on were no doubt horrified."[5]

Scrambling to fill the role of Billy the Kid, Hopper was replaced by original actor Richard Bright and the show went on. And every night after the curtain came down, the play was raided by the Vice Squad. The actors, McClure, producer Robert Barrows, and director Robert Gist were hauled off to jail just as they had been in Northern California. They were booked on "suspicion of using obscene language and lewd conduct"[6] and released on bail that reportedly ranged from $600 to $1,300 apiece.

In regard to getting arrested nightly, Alexandra Hay remarked at the time, "We got arrested fourteen nights in a row…. It was terrible at first, me in a low-cut satin Jean Harlow dress in a tank with all these horrible women. But it became routine after a while, and they'd just thumbprint us. We'd post bail and on nights when we played two shows, the plainclothesmen would rush us to city prison, book us and rush us back for the second show. The guys at the station looked forward to me coming in every night at 11 p.m."[7]

The play became a cause célèbre, receiving national attention when Barrows filed lawsuits to stop the nightly arrests and to fight the charge that the play was obscene. He prevailed in court and the nightly harassment finally ceased. Even so, Columbia Pictures had enough of the bad press this was bringing their contract player and reportedly demanded that Hay quit, which she did a few weeks later. She was replaced by her understudy, Victoria Hale.

The notoriety that the play brought Hay actually boosted her career. Columbia gave her a major supporting part in the Debbie Reynolds/James Garner comedy *How Sweet It Is* (1968) and then offered her a number of scripts to choose from. The play also brought her to the attention of producer/director Otto Preminger, who was in the audience on opening night. He cast her in a major role in his generation gap comedy *Skidoo* (1969), starring Jackie Gleason and Carol Channing. Then Jacques Demy gave her the second female lead in his homage to the city of Los Angeles in *Model Shop* (1969), starring Gary Lockwood and Anouk Aimee.

Publicity photograph of Alexandra Hay (Columbia, 1967).

When the play closed in LA, Bright and his original leading lady, Billie Dixon, appeared in the Off Broadway production directed by Rip Torn at New York's Evergreen Theatre without any controversy or arrests. It seems the New York City police rightly had more pressing matters to worry about. Torn brought a new perspective to the show and, now with more of a budget, Dixon was able to don a Harlow-style platinum blonde wig instead of using her own hair. Attempting to explain what McClure was trying to say with his play, Dixon opined, "He wants us to see how bleak and empty these characters really are—the idols that the public manufactures and envies."[8]

Lost in the notoriety that the play received for its dirty language, the nightly arrests, and the obscenity debate was the continued negative effect it had on the memory of Jean Harlow. Did fans of the actress really want to watch a sexual act performed on her? Ed Wilcox of the *Sunday News* addressed that issue and commented, "Poor Jean Harlow has really come in for a battering these past few years [starting with *The Carpetbaggers*, then the Shulman bio, and then the two *Harlow* films]. From the sex symbol of the 1930s who made platinum blonde hair coloring famous, she's become a camp symbol for today's youth, who picture her as a frumpy dolt with a personality of a harpy. This is quite a switch for the generation who remember her as an attractive young woman of reasonable talent who died a tragic death of uremic poisoning at the age of 26."[9]

Dixon received mostly positive notices for her performance. Clive Barnes of *The New York Times* commented, "The acting of Billie Dixon, blue-voiced, platinum-haired and Richard Bright ... could no more have been bettered than could Mr. Torn's direction." His review also included a quote from English theater critic Kenneth Tynan, who raved that *The Beard* was "'a milestone in the history of heterosexual art.'"[10]

More reviews included Courtney Campbell of *The Villager* who wrote, "Billie Dixon ... and Richard Bright ... repeat their San Francisco performances with style and assurance." Richard P. Cooke of the *Wall Street Journal* raved, "The performances ... are excellent. Miss Dixon is coldly provocative." Bruce Bahrenburg of the *Newark Evening News* remarked, "The actors do well. Miss Billie Dixon as Harlow is narcissistically vulgar whether demanding her comb to run through her blonde hair or spewing dirty words at her sole companion in eternity." Dixon's good reviews culminated with her receiving an Obie Award for Best Actress.

Publicity photograph of Billie Dixon as Jean Harlow and Richard Bright as Billy the Kid from the Off Broadway stage production of *The Beard*, 1966 (Billy Rose Theatre Division, The New York Public Library for the Performing Arts).

Despite her accolades, Dixon only graced the Broadway stage once as a replacement cast member in the hit comedy *There's a Girl in My Soup* in 1968. On film, she briefly reprised her role as Jean Harlow appearing in *The Beard* during the opening scene in director Agnès Varda's 1969 experimental movie *Lion's Love (... and Lies)*, starring Viva. After bringing *The Beard* to London's Royal Court Theatre, Dixon appeared with the Royal Shakespeare Company in the play *After Hagerty* and had a major supporting role in the British film *The Lady in the Car with Glasses and a Gun* (1970), starring Oliver Reed and Samantha Eggar.

11. Harlow's Second Act

* * *

In 1966, a Broadway revival of the play *Dinner at Eight* was mounted. The movie version featured Jean Harlow in one of her most iconic roles as Kitty Packard, the hatcheck girl who marries a wealthy man. Cast in the part was film actress Pamela Tiffin who was not an obvious choice. Similar to Carol Lynley, she was a successful teenage model who was discovered by producer Hal B. Wallis. He chose her to play the naive ingenue who pursues Dr. Laurence Harvey unaware that her friend, older spinster Geraldine Page, pines for him in Tennessee Williams' *Summer and Smoke* (1961). Billy Wilder then cast her as scatterbrained Scarlett Hazeltine in his hilarious satire on the Cold War, *One, Two, Three* (1961). She is simply wonderful as the Southern belle who drives her guardian, James Cagney as Coca-Cola's man in Berlin, crazy with her antics including eloping with Communist beatnik Horst Buchholz. She earned Golden Globe nominations for both performances.

However, under contract to Wallis, 20th Century–Fox, and the Mirisch Brothers, she became the brunette Sandra Dee starring in films aimed at the teenage set: *State Fair* (1962) with Pat Boone and Bobby Darin; *Come Fly with Me* (1963) with Dolores Hart and Lois Nettleton; two films with James Darren—*For Those Who Think Young* (1964) and *The Lively Set* (1964); and *The Pleasure Seekers* (1964) with Ann-Margret and Carol Lynley. She tried to fight typecasting but once again played the ingenue in *The Hallelujah Trail* (1965), but at least this was an epic western filmed in Cinerama by John Sturges.

Pamela did succeed in progressing to adult roles when she played a spoiled, seductive heiress in the hit Paul Newman detective film *Harper* (1966). Her bikini-clad diving board dance is one of the sixties' sexiest, most iconic moments. Pamela then jetted off to Italy when she was chosen to be Marcello Mastroianni's first American leading lady in the anthology, *Oggi, domani, dopodomani* (1966). There was a caveat though. She had to dye her hair blonde. She had fought the studios for years not to change her hair color but decided this project was worth it. However, she had the hairdressers only bleach the hair on top and kept her natural hair color underneath. The film was temporarily shelved but Tiffin loved being a blonde so much that she dyed her hair fully.

Tiffin no doubt surprised her admirers when she was cast as Kitty. When her agent told her the play's producers wanted her to read for a role, she assumed it was for the part of the debutante daughter and it had no appeal. When she learned it was actually for Kitty, she became intrigued at the chance to play a tough-as-nails type of broad. However, she approached it with mixed emotions, as it would be her stage debut. After working mostly in cinema, Pamela was not sure if she had the confidence to tackle a Broadway role and had previously turned down three plays. She felt her voice was not yet trained and that was one of the reasons she began studying with Stella Adler. But it was her fondness for the thirties that ultimately influenced her decision to audition for Kitty.

Dinner at Eight was written by George S. Kaufman and Edna Ferber and was first produced on Broadway in 1932. It was a comic look at the society set during the Depression. Kitty Packard is the adulterous, social-climbing wife of brusque businessman Oliver Packard. The couple is forever battling and he refuses to accept an invitation to the Jordans' party until he hears that an even richer couple from England will be in attendance. Kitty delivers one of the play's most famous lines, "Politics? You couldn't get in anywhere.... You couldn't get into the men's room at the Astor." The roles were made famous by the aforementioned Jean Harlow and Wallace Beery in the very successful 1933 film version. In the revival, Tiffin acted opposite Robert Burr (substituting for Darren McGavin who switched to the role of a fading film star) as her husband.

Dinner at Eight's cast also included June Havoc and Walter Pidgeon as the hosting couple. A one-time critic of American acting, British Tyrone Guthrie accepted the offer to direct because he found the play to be marvelously written and thought it had a chance of becoming a classic. His prior Broadway shows included *Six Characters in Search of an Author*, *Tamburlaine the Great*, *The Matchmaker* (for which he won a Tony Award for Best Director), and *Gideon*.

Pamela Tiffin as Kitty Packard in the stage production *Dinner at Eight*, 1966 (Photo by Friedman-Abeles ©Billy Rose Theatre Division, The New York Public Library for the Performing Arts).

Stepping into Harlow's shoes was a big risk and undertaking for Pamela Tiffin just one year after Carroll Baker and Carol Lynley had played the blonde bombshell to decidedly mixed reviews. It was surprising to hear from the actress that she tackled the part differently than Harlow and did not try to ape the actress—instead making Kitty softer and gentler. Pamela said, "I didn't see Jean Harlow in the role of Kitty Packard on purpose. I didn't think it would help my performance…. As I see Kitty Packard, she is an intellectually limited child, who marries a rich man, is confused by all his business activities and that is what leads her to infidelity."[11] Considering her whispery, sing-song voice, it is hard to visualize Pamela playing the role any other way.

The play opened on September 27, 1966, at the Alvin Theatre to mixed reviews. As for Pamela, she did not receive unanimous praise, but most of her New York notices were positive and her softer approach to the part was deemed a success. She received the most coverage from critic Norman Nadel of the *World Journal Tribune* who remarked, "Pamela Tiffin is a phenomenal eyeballer. It is not so much her acting … but the combination of that alternatingly babyish and bitchy voice, the whining petulance, the innate vulgarity, and especially the body. Miss Tiffin's legs are stunning, and when she … is hurling herself about that draped and quilted white boudoir, it's enough to take a man's mind off his work."

Critics from outside of New York also weighed in. Richard L. Coe of the *Los Angeles Times* found her to be "touchingly amusing." *Variety* called her "impressive." Edward Sothern Hipp of the *Newark Evening News* said, "[she] offers much more than an exceptionally shapely form." Across the pond, the critic for *The London Times* raved, "Pamela Tiffin reveals unsuspecting talents for vulgarity as the nouveau riche wife."

On the negative side, the Associated Press drama critic William Glover commented that "Pamela Tiffin looks acceptable but proceeds on the regrettable assumption that screeching is acting." George Oppenheimer in *Newsday* called Pamela a "luscious lady who looks somewhat like Jean Harlow," but found her performance to be "far too obvious" and "unreal."

John Gassner writing his annual "Broadway in Review" for the *Educational Theatre Journal* was disappointed with most of the performances in *Dinner at Eight*. Pamela was one of the exceptions and he singled her out saying, "Pamela Tiffin's doll-like but flannel-mouthed impersonation of the lavishly kept but two-timing wife of the business marauder was a sheer delight."

Pamela was proud of her performance as Kitty. She claimed it was stimulating to play such a character and felt she brought newfound vigor to the part. She remarked, "This is the very first time I have been on stage and believe me, it took guts to try. Tyrone Guthrie is such a giant, six feet five, that he found a place for my energy. You know, the way I spit out 'Nerts,' in the play. I give off energy."[12]

Due to her mostly glowing reviews for *Dinner at Eight*, it is not surprising that Pamela Tiffin received a Theatre World Award for her New York stage debut.

Dinner at Eight closed on January 14, 1967, after 127 performances despite a last-ditch effort to save the show by offering two tickets for the price of one. The show lost an estimated $100,000 per Lester Osterman, one of the producers and owner of the theater. It was a financial disappointment considering its all-star cast. At Tony Award time the play was snubbed and did not receive a single nomination. Shortly after, Pamela left her husband, magazine publisher Clay Felker, and jetted off to Rome to begin a career in the Italian cinema.

* * *

In 1968, the *Harlow* bios once again made news when it was announced that two biographical films about Nat Turner, the slave who led a rebellion, were in the works at different studios. Columnists pounced on this and exclaimed it was a bad idea. Emerson Beauchamp of *The Evening Star* would not be the only writer who referenced the two *Harlow* movies to make his point. He remarked, "The Electronovision 'Harlow,' which had quickie written all over it, was completely gruesome, but the Levine version proved a classic demonstration of how to cost many times more money and be equally bad."[13]

The next year, when Judy Garland passed away, the *Harlow* films were yet again resurrected by the press due to chatter from several independent film companies concerning movies about her life story. Syndicated writer Harold Heffernan remarked, "The double Jean Harlow movie fiasco is still too well-remembered, at least in Hollywood trade circles, for even the most eager and reckless quickie promoter to act hastily."[14] He went on to blame the *Harlows* for putting the kibosh on any attempt to bring Marilyn Monroe's life to the big screen. He advised Garland fans to satisfy themselves with seeing her old movies in revival houses.

The dueling *Harlow* film wars would be mentioned again in 1982, after Seattle film critic-turned-author William Arnold wrote a bestselling, well-researched biography about actress Frances Farmer titled *Shadowland*. Reportedly, Marie Yates helped Arnold fashion his manuscript into a book and claimed that she bought all rights outright from him. Movie rights were then purchased by Noel Marshall, an independent producer. Marshall dragged his feet turning the biography into a film, so Mel Brooks' production company, Brooksfilms (along with Marie Yates as producer), usurped him and released the movie *Frances* starring Jessica Lange into theaters—without giving any credit to Arnold's book. A lawsuit was filed by Arnold and Marshall and it raised the question regarding the legal rights of authors who pen books about real people and incidents. Writer Stephen Farber addressed this issue in an article he wrote for *American Film* magazine and used the 1965 *Harlow* bios as an example where, despite all Joe Levine's ranting and raving about Bill Sargent's decision to produce a rival movie, Levine never filed suit—probably because he was advised that it would be a costly matter to win. The only lawsuit filed was by Sargent against Levine and Paramount Theaters conspiring to keep his *Harlow* out of the major chains.[15]

During the William Arnold/Brooksfilm trial, it was alleged that Arnold made up several incidents in the book including representing that Frances Farmer had had a lobotomy. For him to claim copyright infringement, his work had to be fiction. Per the judge in the case it was fiction, despite being marketed as nonfiction. Even so, Arnold still lost the suit.[16]

It was all quiet on the Jean Harlow movie screen front until the mid-seventies when Lindsay Bloom became the next actress to don a platinum blonde wig to portray her in the obscure *Hughes and Harlow: Angels in Hell* (1978) from self-described "schlockmeister" Larry Buchanan.

Buchanan was born Marcus Larry Seale, Jr., and was raised in a Baptist orphanage in Texas. He turned down a ministry scholarship to Baylor University to work in the props department at 20th Century–Fox studios. He got the itch to act and was signed by the studio to a contract in which they changed his name to Larry Buchanan, which he kept for the remainder of his life. He studied filmmaking in the Army Signal Corps and decided movie directing was going to be his path in life, so he stopped acting to make his dream come true.

After directing several religious documentaries for Oral Roberts and writing for TV's *The Gabby Hayes Show*, Buchanan wrote and directed the acclaimed short film *The Cowboy* (1951) and the obscure western *Grubstake* (1952). He then worked as an assistant director to the legendary George Cukor on *The Marrying Kind* (1952).

Settling in Texas, Buchanan's directing career finally picked up steam beginning in 1960 with the mega low-budget horror movie *The Naked Witch*. This was followed by *Free, White and 21* (1963), *Under Age* (1964), and *The Trial of Lee Harvey Oswald* (1964), amongst others.

He signed a deal in 1965 with American International Pictures, the leader of drive-in exploitation movies for young people, to remake (on the cheap in Texas) some of their 1950s low-budget, horror/science-fiction movies for a television syndication package and possible release at the bottom of a drive-in double bill. Among the films he shot on minuscule budgets were *The Eye Creatures* (1965) with John Ashley; *Zontar: The Thing from Venus* (1966) with John Agar; *Curse of the Swamp Creature* (1966) with Francine York; *Mars Needs Women* (1967) with Tommy Kirk and Yvonne Craig; *In the Year 2829* (1967) with Paul Petersen and Quinn O'Hara; and *Creature of Destruction* (1968) with Les Tremayne and Aron Kincaid. In this remake of *She-Creature* (1956) Kincaid played a military parapsychologist who becomes involved with a magician and his lovely assistant, who is transformed into a murderous prehistoric creature. Kincaid was not a fan of Buchanan in the least.

ARON KINCAID: Larry Buchanan was huge in stature and minuscule in the areas of charm and talent. *Creature* has, by far, the worst acting, the worst direction, the worst production values, the worst soundtrack and scoring of any motion picture ever made on this planet! This was the professional low point of my entire career.

It's Alive! (1969) starring Tommy Kirk was the last picture Buchanan delivered to AIP under his remake deal although this was based on a script that the studio never produced. He balked at doing any more of these grade Z, low-budget films. Not surprised by this, Sam Arkoff, one of AIP's top executives, offered him a bigger budgeted feature film. Buchanan proposed his previously written script based on the life of gangster Pretty Boy Floyd and Arkoff agreed to finance it. Buchanan requested a budget of $900,000 and Jack Nicholson to star. He got $300,000 and Fabian Forte, who owed AIP one last film on his contract.

A Bullet for Pretty Boy (1971) was shot on location in Texas with a solid supporting cast including Jocelyn Lane, Adam Roarke, Astrid Warner, and an unbilled newcomer named Morgan Fairchild. For years, there have been unconfirmed rumors circulating about the movie. One was that AIP was dissatisfied with Buchanan's final cut and brought it director Maury Dexter to reshoot some scenes. Another was that Buchanan was fired before the movie was completed and Maury Dexter stepped in to finish it. Unfortunately, in his memoir, Buchanan did not address the issue at all. Whatever occurred, although the movie received mixed reviews from the critics, it was a box office hit. Even so, this was the end of Buchanan's association with the studio.

A few years later, Buchanan scored his biggest critical and commercial success with *Goodbye, Norma Jean* (1974) starring Misty Rowe as Marilyn Monroe. It told the early story of the iconic movie star (convincingly played by Rowe) from her humble beginnings to becoming the platinum blonde sex goddess Marilyn Monroe.

Commenting in his autobiography, Buchanan wrote, "The rhythms of cinema finance continued: losers began dry spells, winners began multiple offers and interest. And so it was following the success of *Goodbye, Norma Jean*, this time, however, I had decided I could no longer stomach the pains of working with no money at all. I determined then and there that I would hold out as long as I could to get a budget of at least $250,000. I knew I could deliver a $2 million look for that kind of change."[17]

Buchanan was offered a lot of films, which he felt were "garbage," and wanted to shoot a script he had been working on about the making of *Hell's Angels* and the relationship that developed between its millionaire producer, Howard Hughes (who had passed away in 1976), and its leading lady, Jean Harlow. To Buchanan's delight, an LA clothing manufacturer came up with $240,000 and the film was greenlit.

When asked why he chose this topic for his new movie, Buchanan explained that he had been researching Hughes' career for a long time and had interviewed his close friend, Hollywood reporter James Bacon, and director Howard Hawks. Rather than doing a lengthy biopic on the millionaire, Buchanan said that he "decided to pick one point, one incident in Hughes' life."[18] Expounding on this, Buchanan said, "I knew from people who knew Hughes … that a lot of the stuff I read about Hughes was bilge. In my research, I couldn't find anybody who had a derogatory thing to say about Hughes. But instead of the whole life story, I thought you could really show more about the man by doing a brief microcosm about his life, setting it in a period before he became a recluse."[19]

The period of Hughes' life that Buchanan chose to highlight on the silver screen was a pivotal junction in Hollywood and the filmmaker's life. He explained, "Hughes wanted to make a talkie and was spending tons of money to do it. Everybody was frantic. Then when he said this girl—Harlow—who was an extra in a Laurel and Hardy short at the time was going to be the star, everybody said he was crazy. And he was. He was always insisting on doing something that was crazy. But the film was a tremendous success both financially and critically."[20]

Buchanan co-wrote the screenplay with Lynn Shubert, who had been a fighter pilot during World War II. Stateside he became an actor appearing on Broadway with Spencer Tracy in *The Rugged Path*. This led to roles in early television programs some of which he wrote. He also acted in and co-wrote with Larry Buchanan the 1952 western *Grubstake* starring Jack Klugman. Shubert transitioned to the teleprompter industry (where he became a leader in the field), but still kept close ties to the creative side of show business. Shubert and Buchanan teamed up again in the seventies on the *Goodbye, Norma Jean* screenplay. Regarding their *Hughes and Harlow* script, the director boasted, "I think we are closer to the truth than the 'researched' versions. You know what research is, don't you? Rewriting someone else's opinion, that's all."[21]

Buchanan's plans to move ahead with his movie drew the irritation of actor/producer Warren Beatty, who was in pre-production for a big budget biopic on the reclusive millionaire. Buchanan then found himself in Bill Sargent's shoes by also upsetting the Hollywood elite with his independent film project. It was like a mini version of the previous decade's *Harlow* wars. However, Buchanan was not the only recipient of Beatty's ire. Executive producer Roger Gimbel had a TV-movie titled *The Amazing Howard Hughes* in production starring Tommy Lee Jones for CBS. Jean

Harlow is seen briefly played by Susan Buckner (best known for playing Patty Simcox in *Grease*). Describing these films as "quick cheapies," Beatty (sounding a bit like Joe Levine did 11 years earlier) felt they would devalue his thoughtful, artistic endeavors to bring Hughes to life on screen. He added, "I think this is a serious subject. No matter what, I'm going to make a serious movie."[22]

Gimbel did not take the criticism lying down and shot back, "Ours is definitely a very serious important effort. This movie will give you a real understanding of Howard Hughes. It will be sympathetic to him."[23] Larry Buchanan, obviously not wanting to make an enemy of Warren Beatty and fight a war-of-words in the press like Bill Sargent had, took a more reserved approach. About *Hughes and Harlow*, he only stated that "It's not exactly a major biography. It's a fun film about two people in love."[24] As for Warren Beatty's movie, it did go into production but not until almost forty years later! *Rules Don't Apply* (a critical and box office disappointment) was released in 2016 starring Beatty as Hughes. Jean Harlow was nowhere to be found in it since the movie began with Hughes's life in 1958 long after she had passed away.

Buchanan's film began shooting in 1977. There was no need to launch a search for an actress to play Harlow, since Buchanan only had one candidate in mind—Lindsay Bloom, who had unsuccessfully tested to play Monroe in *Goodbye, Norma Jean*. The vivacious blonde was familiar to TV watchers as one of the singing/dancing "Ding-a-Ling Sisters" on *The Dean Martin Show* during the 1972–73 season.

Buchanan had first noticed Bloom when he threw a Marilyn Monroe look-alike contest at the Hollywood Palladium. He wrote in his memoir that he and one of the judges, photographer Andre de Dienes, "both liked a beautiful blonde named Lindsay Bloom…. But Lindsay was quite tall and we felt the earliest scenes of Norma Jean in foster homes would not ring true. Reluctantly, we voted for another blonde [Alexis Pederson] who was a page at the ABC television network."[25] Although Pederson resembled Monroe tremendously, she was untrained and mutually parted ways when

Publicity photograph of Lindsay Bloom from the motion picture *Sixpack Annie* (American International Pictures, 1975).

she refused to say some of the risqué lines written in the script. Soon after, Misty Rowe came to Buchanan's attention and won the part.

As for Bloom, she went on to make a few TV guest appearances (*Emergency!*, *Rhoda*, *Wonder Woman*, and *Police Story*) and co-starred in two popular, low-budget, drive-in movies, *Cover Girl Models* (1975) and *Sixpack Annie* (1975) before Buchanan came a-calling again.

> **LINDSAY BLOOM:** I read many times for *Goodbye, Norma Jean* but Misty Rowe got it. That was okay and that's how it goes. I loved Larry and got to know him during this audition process.
>
> My agent got a call from Larry when he was casting *Hughes and Harlow*. He asked me to come in. I was aware of Jean Harlow and they called her the first blonde bombshell back in the day. I knew she was an 18-year-old unknown, who worked in Laurel and Hardy shorts, when she was hired by Howard Hughes to do his movie. I went to meet with Larry and he said, "I was very tempted to cast you as Norma Jean, but Misty Rowe had a quality that I liked. But you are perfect for Harlow and that is why I had to call you back." I auditioned for him and I think another producer. I came back later and read with Victor Holchak, who had already been cast as Howard Hughes, because they wanted to match us up and see how the chemistry was. They then told me I got the part and I was very excited.
>
> It was an honor to get to play Harlow. I was always fascinated with actresses from the thirties and forties. What always stuck in my mind was that I was 26 years old when I was cast and that was the age that she tragically died. I couldn't image being that age playing her and that would be it—that is your full life.
>
> When I got the role, I got a book and read about her. We did not have the Internet then so I researched at the library. I was familiar with Carroll Baker's portrayal of Harlow, which I saw. I knew Carol Lynley had also played her but I did not have access to see her film at the time.
>
> I knew their reviews were not the best, but that did not deter me. I thought it was a great acting challenge for me to play a glamorous movie star. It was the first time I had played someone who actually lived and had been so famous.

Before the movie even began shooting, Bloom had an issue regarding her hair and what the producers wanted her to do that she felt was unacceptable.

> **LINDSAY BLOOM:** My hair is blonde obviously, but they wanted me to bleach it all platinum. I refused because after about a week of bleaching, styling, and curling my hair would break off and I would have about two inches of hair left around my head. When I was cast as Harlow, I was in the middle of shooting an episode of *Police Story* and worked with a very good hairdresser. I told her that I didn't know what to do. She said, 'I can take care of it and get you a couple of good wigs. I can style them for you on the weekends and you can come to my house to pick them up. Just bleach about an inch of the front of your hair around your face.

Buchanan was agreeable to Bloom's compromise and the problem was quickly squashed. Less of a problem was choosing the outfits Bloom would don as Harlow. She immediately hit it off with the costume supervisor and they merrily went off on a shopping spree.

11. Harlow's Second Act

LINDSAY BLOOM: I have to give Lennie Barin, the wardrobe guy, a lot of credit. He found some wonderful, glamorous clothes. I remember him meeting me down on Hollywood Blvd. We went into this warehouse-like building that had these fine period costumes. It was challenging but he kept putting me in these different looks. He was very fey and a bit dramatic and would exclaim, "Oh my god! That looks great on you!" We would tease each other because we had the same initials, L.B. He'd yell, "L.B., get in that outfit!" Another time he said, "I could just put a burlap potato sack on you and you'd look great in it." I replied, "Thank you for the compliment—I think?" It was very fun to dress up as Harlow.

TV actor Victor Holchak, who had already been hired for the role of Howard Hughes, was known to soap opera fans for playing Jim Phillips on *Days of Our Lives*. Due to his look, height (6'4"), and lankiness, Holchak came close to portraying the notorious Hughes twice prior to making this movie. He had been scheduled for the Off Broadway stage production *Howard* but it fell through and had auditioned for the TV-movie, *The Amazing Howard Hughes*, but lost the part to Tommy Lee Jones.

Besides having a physical resemblance to Hughes, Holchak did all the required research to get to know the man. He remarked, "I read all the biographies for this part. But I only read them up to 1935, before the legend started getting out of hand."[26] When asked what he thought was the basis of the short-lived relationship between Hughes and Harlow, Holchak opined, "Hughes didn't trust people. He trusted machines more—airplanes, movie cameras—because he was in control. Harlow was

Publicity photograph of Lindsay Bloom as Jean Harlow from *Hughes and Harlow: Angels in Hell* (PRO International, 1977) (courtesy Lindsay Bloom).

uncomplicated and unpretentious; all she wanted to be was a movie star. She told him so in no uncertain words, and he liked her directness."[27]

Another role Buchanan had to cast was that of legendary director Howard Hawks. Although the character was limited to a single scene, Buchanan felt the still living director should have a say in the matter. He explained, "I needed and wanted his approval … and of course I idolized the man. 'Who's playing Hawks?' he asked when I called him to request a visit. I replied timidly, 'Adam Roarke.' Lucky for me, he not only knew Adam but had directed him in one of his lean and mean westerns [*El Dorado*, 1967]."[28]

The fictitious character of Hughes' righthand man, Billy, was played by David McLean who was best known for his cigarette commercials as the Marlboro Man in the early to mid-sixties, and for his many TV western appearances (*Laramie, Gunsmoke, Death Valley Days, Bonanza, Lancer,* etc.).

> **LINDSAY BLOOM:** I loved working with Adam Roarke. He was a good actor. I had a lot of scenes with David McLean. I recognized him from soap operas [Craig Merritt on *Days of Our Lives*]. He was a great guy and perfect for that part.

Among the crew, Buchanan was able to work again with Nicholas Josef von Sternberg, the son of the acclaimed director, Josef von Sternberg who worked with Marlene Dietrich on six movies including *Morocco*, *Shanghai Express*, and *The Scarlet Empress*. Although his lineage helped, Nicholas had learned his craft at college and had some prior film experience.

> **NICHOLAS VON STERNBERG:** I studied at UCLA with Beverly Mohr, who was the wife of Hal Mohr. He was a cinematographer who shot *Phantom of the Opera* and *A Midsummer's Night's Dream* [and won the Academy Award for each]. He worked on 109 features in total. I got to know him very well and worked with him for about two years. I was an assistant cameraman on a small project and Hal taught me how to love cinematography. He knew my father when he was very young and they grew up together in the business. My dad loaned him one hundred dollars and every time Hal would see him, he would pay him back one dollar. Hal was a wonderful man and teacher. He taught me just about everything he could about cinematography. He gave me some of his equipment—like his viewing glasses—which I used in my own work.
>
> Hal died in 1974 shortly after I started working on *Dolemite*. I was 21 when I was hired. I was originally the production manager and hired myself to be the director of photography. This was my first film and a big thing for me. I never realized that it would still be seen almost fifty years later. After this, through UCLA, I worked on a film called *Kill, Alex, Kill*. I believe I got connected to Larry Buchanan through people who worked on this film. He hired me to be the gaffer on *Goodbye, Norma Jean*.
>
> I was also second camera on *Norma Jean* and shot some footage such as the snuff scene that was used in the film. Larry knew I could shoot because I had already shot a few films before I met him. I don't think he was that happy with the cameraman on *Norma Jean*. I was young, energetic, and really hustled around on the set for Larry. I did not do it on purpose to make an impression, I was just full of energy. That is how I got hired on *Hughes and Harlow*.

Larry Buchanan was quite impressed with the young von Sternberg and described him as "a dedicated craftsman."²⁹ Another reason von Sternberg liked working with the producer/director was because he gave him carte blanche in hiring his crew. Nicholas brought in some talented friends that he had met at school including Lowell Peterson as his camera assistant.

NICHOLAS VON STERNBERG: Larry Buchanan was wonderful and the best person I ever worked for. He really took care of the crew and did not like to shoot long hours. He never wanted to go over twelve hours a day. It was just a pleasure working for him [and] I [did] again on a film called *Mistress of the Apes*.

LINDSAY BLOOM: Larry mentioned many times that Nicholas' father was a famous director and how he liked his directing techniques in making films. Nicholas was very young at the time and just so sweet. He was very easy to work with and I felt comfortable, as an actress, working with him. He knew what he was doing with the camera and lighting. I did a lot of modeling and the camera liked me so that was a good thing. To get a certain feel and look for a period-piece type film can be challenging, I can imagine.

NICHOLAS VON STERNBERG: Lowell Peterson and I became acquainted at UCLA and became close friends. When I started as a director of photography, I relied on Lowell for advice as well as using his help as my camera assistant.

LOWELL PETERSON: I was more of a cinematographer at school than Nick but he landed the movie *Dolemite*. He went and shot that.

NICHOLAS VON STERNBERG: I had my whole crew from before I met Larry. I got to know a bunch of guys who worked on my crew for a number of years and they were terrific … [and] great people. The sound man was Al Ramirez and he worked with me for years. It was just a great experience.

LOWELL PETERSON: This was my and Nick's third movie together. As the director of photography, Nick was in charge of the crew. Larry Buchanan allowed him to pick who he wanted. Nick hired the grip, electric, and camera crews. I ran the cameras—I focused them and put the equipment together. I think we had a second assistant on the film who loaded the magazines. They used a big, old BMCR camera. It was a heavy, ponderous camera to work with.

It was a 25-day schedule, which was quite a lot for a low budget movie. Ron Batzdorff was the gaffer, who is in charge of the lighting. We came up together and worked a lot together with Nick. He later became a very big time still photographer. Ernie Roebuck was Ron's best boy who was the second in charge. He worked on a lot of movies with us too. He became a cinematographer mostly working on low-budget movies.

Nicholas also had a connection to Howard Hughes through his father who worked with him late in his career. Josef von Sternberg directed the Hughes-produced movies, *Macao* (1952) and *Jet Pilot* (1957).

NICHOLAS VON STERNBERG: I think my dad may have known Jean Harlow. I do know he knew Howard Hughes quite well. *Jet Pilot* was not my dad's last movie. That was shot in early 1950 but was not released until 1957. Hughes was such an aviation nut. He wanted to put the latest footage in there and kept updating the planes delaying its release. After shooting *Macao*, Hughes promised my father that he would be able to do anything he wanted to. Hughes really restricted him and obviously he didn't keep his word.

Anatahan (1953) was my dad's final movie and it was shot in Japan. My mother, sister, and I went with him and were there in Kyoto for a year. I was only two years old. I did go on the set a few times and have a picture of myself being held up behind the Mitchell. It was the first time I looked through a camera.

In Joe Levine's *Harlow*, Howard Hughes is a character but there is no indication of a love affair between him and his discovery, Jean Harlow. He unsuccessfully tries to seduce her and then after she becomes a star, prohibits her from working for other studios due to her contract. She later angers him to the point where he releases her to pursue other opportunities. Bill Sargent's *Harlow* has no mention whatsoever of Hughes.

Saying Buchanan and Lynn Shubert took liberties with the life of Jean Harlow would be an understatement. One of the most outrageous claims in the screenplay was that Harlow worked at a bordello dancing with prospective johns when she was down on her luck and was befriended by the establishment's madame. There is also a scene where it is suggested that Harlow did more than dance for a price. Even Levine's *Harlow* with all its fictitiousness did not go this far.

LINDSAY BLOOM: I remember Lynn. He was rather portly and once in a while would come onto the set.

Director of Photography Nicholas von Sternberg, gaffer Ron Batzdorff, and electrical best boy Ernie Roebuck, alongside a prop camera, on the set of *Hughes and Harlow: Angels in Hell*. ©*Lowell Peterson* (courtesy Lowell Peterson).

NICHOLAS VON STERNBERG: Larry didn't have any real feeling for facts. He probably was a fan of both Hughes and Harlow but I think he really liked Jean Harlow. He wanted cheesecake and had Harlow in there all the time.

LINDSAY BLOOM: I don't know who came up with the bordello scenario. When you are an actor, you get a script and you just do it. You don't say, "Hey, that didn't happen and I am not doing that."

The bordello interior scenes (living room, entry hall, dining room, and staircase) were shot at the Morey House (a spectacular Victorian home built by David and Sarah Morey in 1890) in Redlands, California. Scenes were also filmed on location in Redlands amongst the orange groves surrounding the Edwards Mansion (another Victorian home built in 1890) to resemble the landscape as Hughes and Harlow travel to Tijuana. The Morey House was then owned by James Brucker, who also owned Movie World "Cars of the Stars" also in Buena Park. Autos from the collection were supplied for the movie.

Another script oddity was changing the title of Hughes' movie from *Hell's Angels* to *Angels in Hell*. Levine's *Harlow* fictionalized the titles of all of Jean Harlow's movies, including *Hell's Angels*, while in Sargent's *Harlow*, the title *Hell's Angels* was used but the rest of her movies were unnamed. Bill Sargent was able to get away with using *Hell's Angels* without issue, so there must have been a legal reason why Buchanan was hesitant to do so.

NICHOLAS VON STERNBERG: I am not certain, but as far as I know, they changed the title of the movie to *Angels in Hell* because they did not want any copyright infringement.

LINDSAY BLOOM: I also recall that there might have been copyright infringement of some sort so they reversed the title of the movie.

The title change was the least of their worries. When production began on the movie, it hit a snag on day one. Bloom took issue with how she was made up to look like Jean Harlow.

LINDSAY BLOOM: The makeup artist that Larry hired was Ray Sebastian who did not know much about glamour makeup. I went to Larry and said, "Am I supposed to look like this in the entire film?" He said, "There is nothing we can do about it now so let's go film." I agreed but added, "This is not working for me. It is just terrible." I was upset. The scene was Harlow with Mama Jean [Adele Claire] and Marino Bello [Alberto Carrier]. I come in with great news to tell my mother and Bello says I could tell him instead. It was a very dramatic and we shot it. Afterward, I told Larry I had a great makeup artist named Tina Bushelman that I worked with on a film called *Texas Detour* and she knows how to do the glamour makeup. He approved it. She was working nights on a horror film [*The Incredible Melting Man*] and after that would come straight over to do my makeup in the morning. On set, Tina would also style my hair before we put the wig on. The combination turned out very well and it had a good look. I would let Tina take a nap in my trailer afterwards. It made all the difference in the world. Unfortunately, when they looked at the dailies for the first scene later, they realized it couldn't be used so it was cut entirely.

Tina would do my hair and makeup in my dressing room trailer and kept the wigs up on faceless wig heads. One day, she cut out a picture of Jean Harlow and stuck her face on the wig head. I would see Jean Harlow all the time in my dressing room.

LOWELL PETERSON: I knew some of Harlow's movies like *Red Dust* and *Saratoga*, so I knew what she looked like. The hair and makeup were nowhere near accurate. The costumes were bad.

LINDSAY BLOOM: We tried to get the look as close as possible to get a resemblance to Harlow, but my main focus was her personality and essence. I attempted to bring out her sense of humor and wisecracking, which was notorious back in the day. I wanted to project an all-around feel for her. Later, her personality evolved but in that early time frame, she had those attributes that were quite prevalent. That's what I went for. I normally have a good sense of humor.

I really enjoyed the scenes where Harlow meets Howard Hughes. She does not know who he is and then buys him a hot dog thinking he is poor and down-on-his-luck. I also liked the scene where Harlow gets involved in the craps game. I had a lot of fun with it.

As filming continued, the cast, director, and the crew jelled nicely and worked well together. With only a four-week shooting schedule, scenes needed to be set up and shot quickly. Even so, by all accounts, the entire crew did a thoroughly professional job. Another plus was the warm relationship that developed between Lindsay Bloom and Victor Holchak with each other and with Larry Buchanan.

LINDSAY BLOOM: I got along great with Victor and thought he was perfect as Howard Hughes. We became best friends—nothing romantic. He had a wonderful sense of humor and I would joke with him. We enjoyed working together and we were trying to find the right course for the relationship between the two of them from the characters' perspective.

LOWELL PETERSON: I believe this was Victor Holchak's first movie or close to his first movie. He was photogenic and the camera liked him. He was a good guy.

NICHOLAS VON STERNBERG: Lindsay and Victor were wonderful. Everybody got along and there were no big egos on this film. Only after I saw the picture did I realize Royal Dano [as Will Hayes] was in it. That was typical of Larry. He knew a lot about old Hollywood and really appreciated working with me because of my dad. It was such a great film to work on and such a good experience.

LINDSAY BLOOM: Royal Dano was a classic old actor. Our scenes at the movie theater were shot at the Wiltern Theater on Hollywood Blvd. It's still there. We filmed very late at night.

LOWELL PETERSON: I knew of Royal Dano and was happy to see him. I know a lot of film history and had seen Royal in many movies. I enjoyed him and we played Liars Poker on the set with him.

LINDSAY BLOOM: In one of the car scenes, they had a blue screen behind Victor and I and we were supposed to be driving down the road. There were two crew guys on the back bumper bouncing the car up and down. There was an issue with the lighting but they asked us to remain in the car while they corrected it. We were yacking and telling stories. We were laughing and when we started shooting again Victor was about to crack up. We had such a good camaraderie.

I remember another scene when we were walking on the beach in Malibu and we got into a groove together. However, if either of us felt something was not right, we would ask Larry to do it again. Most of the time we would go with the first take unless there was some malfunction of prop or sound.

NICHOLAS VON STERNBERG: I don't remember doing a lot of takes but Larry did work with the actors. He was an actor's director. I remember how he worked with me, particularly about camera angles. I recall him leaving it up to me to make the choices.

LINDSAY BLOOM: Larry was aware of getting things going and to keep it going. However, I remember during first few days on the set, he was always encouraging and would give me a few little things to think about while I was doing different scenes. By about the fourth day, he said, "Lindsay, I don't know what it is you are doing, but whatever it is just keep it up because you are more like Harlow every day." I appreciated that and it was good feedback for me to know that I was on the right track.

LOWELL PETERSON: Larry Buchanan was a sweet guy—good-natured. However, as a director I thought he was sort of slip shod. It was a very low budget movie and it is difficult to make a period low budget movie. It's tough to get cheap locations that look like the thirties.

For Lindsay, though, it was not all fun and games shooting the movie. She knew a lot was riding on her playing the popular Jean Harlow and that her performance would be scrutinized just as Carroll Baker and Carol Lynley's were. Certain scenes proved more taxing than others.

LINDSAY BLOOM: Towards the end of the movie, Howard Hughes is working on his plane and Harlow is trying to talk to him. I was really concerned about this scene and spoke to Larry about it because there was a lot of dialogue. I asked him how he was going to film it. We blocked it out and then he said he wanted me to go up into the plane and fire off the machine gun that was in there. I said, "Really!?! Okay. There are a few challenges here." I went off into a corner by myself and I just sat there trying to, not so much picture what was going to happen, but the why and what I was trying to accomplish as Jean Harlow. I remember saying out loud, "Jean Harlow, if you are listening somewhere in the universe, if you want something done in this scene, feel free to come down and join me." If that was a possibility, I just wanted her spirit to know she was welcome. A lot of people say, "That's weird." But no—you are in a creative space and you are drawing creatively on anything you possibly can to recreate someone's personality. It worked for me anyway.

They called me over when they were ready to shoot. Larry yelled action and I climbed into the plane and was very upset with Hughes. He's all business—his planes are more important than the people. I then remember grabbing that machine gun and firing it off. I was just in a daze because Harlow was really mad and I was in the scene—if you will. It was loud and we were on a big soundstage in Culver City Studios. The sound bounced and ricocheted all over the place. Then I heard applause—the whole crew was clapping. I looked around but didn't hear Larry yell cut and print, but by that time I guessed they liked it. You can't really judge when you are acting—you get into that space. It was quite a day.

Luckily for Buchanan, his co-producers kept a low profile and did not interfere much with the making of the movie. However, that could have been because they had ulterior motives with regard to its distribution, or lack thereof.

NICHOLAS VON STERNBERG: The other producers came on the set once or twice. Bill Silberkleit [*Centerfold Girls, Young Lady Chatterley*] was one of them. He was a guy that Larry knew and the film was done as a tax shelter. We knew that then but didn't realize the full implications of that. I don't think Larry did either.

LINDSAY BLOOM: I met Bill and another producer, Frank Bianchini, at Larry's office one day. I kind of got a bad feeling about Frank—I don't know how else to describe it. I know both of them put up money.

Despite the limited funds and the tax shelter issue hovering over their heads, Buchanan promised the movie would have a multi-million dollar look to it and he was helped by his crew who treated this like they would have any motion picture. Friend and fellow low-budget director Ted V. Mikels [*The Astro-Zombies, The Doll Squad*, etc.] even lent his house for the interior scenes of the home of director Howard Hawks in the movie.

NICHOLAS VON STERNBERG: The budget was a bit less than $250,000. That was considered very low budget at the time. However, George Costello, the production designer, who also was a terrific guy, and I tried to make it look more expensive.

LOWELL PETERSON: I worked with Ted Mikels on a film [*Alex Joseph and His Wives*]. I think Ted was a little more accomplished than Larry Buchanan. I think he got more out of the money that he spent. He was a short guy and he had a sort of "short guy complex." He worked out a lot and was very muscle-bound. Ted was a firecracker kind of guy, whereas Larry was a laid back, good-ole-boy with a much gentler personality.

NICHOLAS VON STERNBERG: Although we had only four weeks to film, Larry would give me time to light the scenes before I would shoot with a Mitchell BNCR with Kodak 5247 film stock, which I liked a lot because it was a very fine grain stock.

LOWELL PETERSON: I believe Nick had Hal Mohr's box of diffusion [filters or gels used to alter the quality of light sources]. Diffusion is something you put in front of a light or a camera lens. If you ever see his film, *A Midsummer's Night's Dream*, the film is so diffused that it is unreal. Every time you see a light source in a frame it is just glowing all around it—it is very beautiful. He was a master of camera diffusion. Nick learned some of that from him.

NICHOLAS VON STERNBERG: I remember lighting the scenes with these very big studio soft lights. When we went on location that was great too. I got to use the soft lights to light the actors and used diffusion on it and used a little too much. When I saw the DVD, which was made from a VHS transfer, the DVD looks a little dark. I shot it with a star filter and a diffusion on top of that. It gave it a sort of nice look—kind of a thirties feel to it. Hal Mohr was a great believer in diffusion, so I inherited that from him.

LOWELL PETERSON: Joe Ruttenberg shot Carroll Baker's *Harlow* and it was very beautiful looking, I thought. It was heavily diffused through the lens. When you see the highlights in the frame, they glisten because they are being picked up by the diffusion on the lens. It also had an excellent [musical] score [by Neal Hefti]. I liked the movie although maybe they didn't get the period look that great either.

Lindsay Bloom credits the talented crew for making it easier for her to get into character, due to the creativity they brought to the set design and costumes.

Lowell Peterson, ca. 1978. ©*Lowell Peterson* (courtesy Lowell Peterson).

Buchanan was lucky to get such a professional bunch of people to work on his picture. He stated, "Imagine, if you will, being given only four weeks to shoot a 35mm color picture, wardrobe and vehicle period circa 1928, featuring World War I dogfights."[30]

>**LINDSAY BLOOM:** I remember the scene where I am walking down the street at Culver City Studios where they set it up with old cars to match the time period. It was when Harlow discovers that the guy she thought was broke and bought lunch for is actually Howard Hughes. I walk up to him and hit him with my purse. However, as I am walking, all of a sudden, the time just dissipates and I thought this must have felt what it was really like for Harlow to have been working at that time. You get into a time warp almost with all the old cars and period costumes—it had that feel. It was a kind of surreal experience to be honest. I often felt the way they dressed the sets and us that it was easy to feel that time period.
>
>**NICHOLAS VON STERNBERG:** We had really great locations. It was an ideal film to shoot for me at that time. The dog fight scenes were from stock footage. We also shot with rear projection using a Mitchell rear projector where we interlocked the camera with it. There was some footage where we had a plane in the foreground and there was stuff in the background occurring, which was projected behind it on a screen. It was pretty much done that way I think in the thirties. Rear projection goes a long way back.
>
>**LINDSAY BLOOM:** When we were out at the airport, a big old stunt guy was dressed up like me because it was supposed to be Harlow in the plane. I said, "Oh my God, Larry! He doesn't look like me at all. His wig looks terrible." Larry replied, "Lindsay, from where I am shooting, it could be Ethel Merman—don't worry about it." He used that line whenever I was overly concerned about something. No

matter what the issue, if he felt it was nothing, he would repeat, "'It could be Ethel Merman—don't worry about it." When shooting finished and we had the wrap party, I received a t-shirt with that phrase on it.

NICHOLAS VON STERNBERG: We did shoot some aerial footage. I got to ride in a plane that took off from Flabob Airport near Riverside. We had an old bi-plane and we shot some footage in it. I was using a handheld Arriflex 2C. It was an open plane and the camera was hanging outside of it. It was the first and last time I ever did that. I also got to ride in another plane and we shot air-to-air.

LOWELL PETERSON: We went to this little airport where they skydived. I am not sure where they got the airplanes. I filmed from the ground. Nick went up and shot some plane-to-plane footage. I believe we were out there one or two days. This was the only time I shot on this film. I was pretty much the assistant for the rest of the movie except this one time. I got a friend of mine to come out to be my assistant.

LINDSAY BLOOM: I think we shot at the airport in January or February of 1977. I still recall the very cold wind. I caught a cold and was sick for the rest of the shoot. I kept fighting and fighting it, but I had a horrific sounding cough—one of those chest-rattlers. I kept pushing myself because I could not be sick. After filming wrapped, I was still ill and had a bad case of bronchitis.

While Lindsay Bloom was battling her illness, Nicholas von Sternberg was still involved in post-production.

NICHOLAS VON STERNBERG: Everything we shot made it into the movie. I timed it in the lab over at MGM. I watched it a few times and I got to sit in on the post-production sound work that was done. I think Larry had a real dream for that film. He really wanted it to succeed and it is really sad that it didn't get shown a lot.

To drum up publicity for the movie, Bloom was sent out to the Movieland Wax Museum in Buena Park, California, where she posed alongside the wax figure of Jean Harlow. Photos of her were printed in many of the national newspapers. Also, Buchanan hired the talented Max Weinberg to cut a trailer for the movie. Weinberg had a sterling reputation and was known as the "Trailer King" in the industry. He worked for many years at United Artists before going independent in 1971. He had created trailers for major films such as *The Apartment, Exodus, The Misfits,* and *The Manchurian Candidate* as well as exploitation trash like *Linda Lovelace for President* and *Dagmar's Hot Pants, Inc.* Regarding his career after leaving United Artists, he stated to columnist John Wilson of the *Los Angeles Times*, "I make good trailers out of bad movies. That's how I make a living. If my trailer is not better than the movie, I'm in trouble."[31]

Weinberg was editing the trailer for Larry Buchanan when the interview took place. He revealed, "This picture I am doing now, *Hughes and Harlow*, and another one, *Empire of the Ants*, are supposed to be released in the next three or four weeks. We haven't got time to play around. We've got to get it out and hope we've found the right selling angles and aimed at the right market."[32] This prompted Wilson to remark, "It appears his skillful editing has managed to give movement and energy to footage that otherwise looks shrill and second-rate."[33]

* * *

Hughes and Harlow: Angels in Hell opens with a limo pulling up to Grauman's Chinese Theatre for the premiere of Howard Hughes' movie *Angels from Hell*. Then the opening credits begin in a title design graphic that is reminiscent of the *CBS Late Show*. When the action picks up, producer Howard Hughes and his film's leading lady, Jean Harlow, are being interviewed about the movie. A phone call from the processing lab sends Hughes on a race to retrieve the final reel from the studio. When Hughes' right-hand man Billy explains to Jean what is happening, she responds, "Oh, shit!" just as a man walks by and gives her a dirty look. When she asks who he is, Billy replies, "Bill Hays of the censorship board," and Jean retorts, "Oh, shit!" Right from the get-go, the audience knows they will be getting a more foul-mouthed, crude Jean, as compared to the Harlows from the 1965 biopics.

As Hughes races to the studio, Billy, from his balcony box seat with Jean by his side, tries to bide time and keeps interrupting Sid Grauman during his welcoming speech. When a frustrated Grauman asks who the "schmuck" in the box is, one of his ushers replies, "Some cowboy who keep Hughes out of trouble." Hughes then returns triumphantly with the final reel and the movie begins. Here scenes from the movie with Harlow are recreated, unlike in the previous *Harlow* films. Jean Harlow's first appearance on screen draws laughter from the crowd causing Hughes and the actress to squirm in their seats. Harlow then quips that she is dying a slow death and that Hughes is going to lose his bet, when he replies that he is surprised that she remembered. Jean responds, "You bet your sweet ass I remember." At this point, there is a flashback to how Hughes met Harlow.

The fiction Buchanan and his writing partner served up was that Hughes (after shooting aerial footage for his new silent movie and watching the dailies) notices the platinum blonde on the set of the comedy-short *Double Whoopee*, where she famously has her dressed ripped off while exiting an automobile. *Hughes and Harlow* shows the playfulness and crass mouth of Harlow either buying lunch for a penniless Hughes (unaware who he is) or playing dice with the crew and Billy.

When Hughes decides to scrap the footage already shot for his silent movie *Angels in Hell* and reshoot with sound, his director tries to dissuade him. After trading insults with Hughes, he is fired and Hughes decides to direct the picture himself. His first order of business is reshooting the aerial footage and finding a new leading lady since the original has a thick foreign accent. He remembers Harlow and asks Billy to find and test her as a replacement. They learn that to pick up some easy money when broke, Harlow works at a local cathouse where Billy is friendly with the madam.

Even though, at first, she is skeptical, Harlow shows up the next day on set to audition. She runs into Hughes again still unaware of who he is. When she finally does realize he is the elusive millionaire, she berates him for sticking her with his lunch tab. As with Sargent's *Harlow*, we see the audition. When she is given her costume to change into, Hughes learns that she doesn't wear a bra or any undergarments. She is horrible during the first take and Hughes pulls her aside. She blames her leading man, remarking, "It's just my luck. I have been rotating my tail for two years as an extra—waiting for a break like this—and I draw a goddamn fairy." Hughes assures her that the actor likes "dames" and knows he is a "tit man." Harlow then ices up her nipples to get him interested. It works and she gets the job.

Howard Hughes (Victor Holchak) and Jean Harlow (Lindsay Bloom) watch the premiere of their movie in *Hughes and Harlow: Angels in Hell* (PRO International, 1977) (courtesy Lindsay Bloom).

That night, Harlow briefly celebrates her good fortune with Mama Jean before rushing out for a night on the town with Hughes, who has nicknamed her "Whitey," obviously due to her platinum blonde hair. While driving to Caliente, Mexico, for authentic Mexican cuisine, Hughes admits he is married. Jean reciprocates, telling him about her teenage nuptials and that her first 50 dollars earned will be going to a divorce. On the way, they stop at a speakeasy where Billy and the crew hang out after a day's filming. There he learns that his stunt pilots have been moonlighting on Howard Hawks' picture with some putting in 24-hour days.

With a hungry Harlow in tow, Hughes makes another detour, this time straight to Hawks' home. Waking the director up at midnight, he accuses him of stealing aerial scenes from his movie to use in his. Before responding, Hawks offers a choice of two drinks to his uninvited guests. A ravenous Harlow shakes her head and quips, "Not unless you can broil it." Hawks then goes on to explain that he did not steal a scene or know that some of the stunt pilots were working on Hughes' film. He agrees to cut the footage and to fire the "the son-of-a-bitch." Impressed, Hughes mentions that his next movie is a gangster picture and offers Hawks the director job.

Jean finally gets her meal when Hughes stops by the home of a Mexican friend named Emiliano, a fisherman. He only knows Hughes as "Sam" and had given him

Lindsay Bloom as Jean Harlow in *Hughes and Harlow: Angels in Hell* (PRO International, 1977) (courtesy Lindsay Bloom).

free fuel and lodging a few years prior after Hughes' plane made an emergency landing on a beach nearby. His wife, Inez, is happy to see "Sam" too and cooks up a late-night feast complete with tequila shots. Before they leave, Hughes slips his friend some money and Harlow is touched by his generosity.

Their evening ends on a deserted beach in the early morning. Harlow confesses she likes "Sam" and is open to a tryst. Hughes surprisingly takes a pass because he is tired of being a joke in Hollywood and knows his movie is good enough to shut up all the naysayers. He counters and says, "You help me with this. You help me bring this thing in and I promise you, when we finish with this, we will tie one on that will make Louella Parsons piss in her pants." Harlow agrees and they seal the deal with a kiss.

The movie then shifts back to the present with Hughes, Harlow, and the audience watching *Angels in Hell* at the premiere. Hughes goes down to the orchestra seats to study Wills Hays' reactions to the on-screen love scene. He thinks Hays is not happy, while Jean feels like she is "going over like a lead balloon" with the audience. She is embarrassed and wants to leave, but Hughes and Billy convince her to stay.

More aerial battle footage screens and the movie dissolves to Hughes and Harlow in the editing room cutting footage. They are interrupted by Hughes' date for the evening and he instructs Jean to go home and get some sleep for the next day's shoot. She reluctantly heads home. Jean then enters her bedroom, strips her clothes off (exposing her breasts), and hops into bed feeling dejected. The film then swings back to the premiere where Billy quips that the plane engine noises are keeping Hays awake. Hughes adds that, for the rest of the audience, it is Harlow's "melons" keeping their attention and wondering (or in some cases hoping) if her dress straps will slip off to expose them. She then says to Hughes that she would have forfeited the bet that night he left her in the editing room when they were interrupted by his date.

Another flashback shows Hughes and his date driving when a distracted Hughes runs over a pedestrian in the safety zone of a streetcar. He lives and changes his story before the sleazy lawyer of Hughes' date can get $20,000 out of Hughes' lawyer for his client's cooperation.

After being released from jail, Hughes goes to Jean and finds her at the bordello fighting off a customer. After punching the guy, Hughes takes her back to the studio. As he silently works on one of the film's airplanes, an irate Harlow vents about Hughes' philandering ways and that she is expected to go home alone and be a good girl. She berates him for chasing "pussy" with his "joystick." Lusting after him and wanting a ride on it herself, she wants to call off their bet and have sex. Frustrated, she then yells, "Would you say something you sadistic bastard! What, are you afraid someone is going to hurt your joystick—you saving it for Lent?" Still not getting a response, she screams that he either needs to "kiss me or kick the shit out of me!" Then she shoots off one of the plane's attached machine guns into the night. The scene ends with her breaking down into tears.

Back in the screening room, Hughes watches from the projection booth as Jean stretches before the blank screen. He realizes then that his aerial footage is missing clouds for contrast to make the scenes look real. While cloud hunting, with Jean in the cockpit, Hughes tells her to drop all the bullshit about going to finishing schools that Jean has been feeding Louella Parsons and start telling the truth. He rightly feels that moviegoers will identify with her true story about being a penniless aspiring actress who came to Hollywood to make it big. He also demonstrates a new gadget he came up with called the automatic pilot.

The movie then shows a montage of clips of scenes from Hughes' film and the post-production. Back at the airfield, one of the stunt pilots, named Charlie, will not take up his plane, feeling that something is wrong with it. When Hughes finds out that he is one of the pilots moonlighting on Howard Hawks' movie, the director calls him out on it and suggests that he may be exhausted from working too much. Hughes takes it up himself, but Charlie is right and Hughes makes a crash landing that lands him in the hospital.

The movie then goes back to the present with the audience watching the aerial footage at the premiere. The movie ends and there is dead silence. After a few seconds, Will Hays claps first and then the audience erupts into a frenzy of applause. Hughes and Harlow sneak off to the airfield and, without filing a flight plan, Hughes takes his plane up. When Harlow asks where they are going, he says, "A certain platinum blonde said if I could make her look good in this picture, she would kiss my ass all the way to Catalina—start puckering." When he says he has perfected the automatic pilot, a skeptical Harlow lies down on the parachutes and Hughes climbs on top out

A bemused Jean Harlow (Lindsay Bloom) joins Howard Hughes (Victor Holchak) on a trek to Mexico for authentic Mexican cuisine in *Hughes and Harlow: Angels in Hell* (PRO International, 1977) (courtesy Lindsay Bloom).

of the frame. The end credits begin to roll as the audience listens to the pair make love.

* * *

Once *Hughes and Harlow* was completed, it was submitted to the Motion Picture Association of America where it was given an R-rating due to its adult language and brief nudity. It then had its premiere and first official public screening in Houston, Texas. It was announced in *The Hollywood Reporter* that the film would be playing in 15 theaters in Houston starting on May 25 and two days later would open in a similar number of theaters in the Dallas-Fort Worth area.

LINDSAY BLOOM: The producers put up the money for Victor and I to fly to Houston for the film's world premiere. It played in several theaters there. Usually when you go to a premiere or on tour to promote a film, they send an advance person a few days ahead of time to set up interviews. When we got there, they hadn't done anything. I was really upset and remember calling my boyfriend (and now husband) Mayf Nutter, who was an actor and country/rock musician, to vent. He said, "Hang on, there's got to be something we can do." He wound up flying down to Houston because he knew a bunch of disc jockeys. We were able to set up some newspaper print interviews too. Mayf got the Old Car Club to come out on the night of the premiere and drive up to the theatre in old period automobiles, which gave it a very nice feel. We got some buzz going.

At the premiere was the first time I got to see the whole movie. While shooting, I was not allowed to view the dailies. I was happy and thought it came out pretty good. It was nice to see it all put together. After it was over, Victor and I did a Q&A with the audience. We made the best of the situation.

Unfortunately for all involved, Buchanan's film did not get a big national release, but it was not shelved despite what he may have been told. He wrote in his book, "Imagine that the crew and cast deliver a slick, professional, entertainment only to learn at the invitational screening at MGM Studios that the whole exercise is … a scam! This meant simply that the product of our efforts would be shelved so that the 'executive producer' rag man would convert his $240,000 to a four-to-one write-off, essentially earning a net of $720,000 without a play date."[34] He pleaded with the investors to change their minds but they would not.

Buchanan felt he owed it to his team to hear the truth directly from him about the other producers' decision. He recalled, "One of the saddest days of my life was when I faced those guys and gals who had gone beyond the pale making a heartfelt film. I had to tell them there was no way I could provide any more work soon. I must confess I choked up a bit when their spokesman rose and announced, 'We're ready when you are, L.B.'"[35] This was an old Hollywood in-joke related to Cecil B. DeMille.

Despite what was conveyed, the film did get a sporadic regional release, popping up in a handful of theaters without much fanfare. Most of the local newspapers did not even send their film critics to review it. It played in Dallas, Amarillo, Atlanta, Seattle, Las Vegas, Miami, Panama City, and Minneapolis, among others, before being pulled from circulation. In Las Vegas, a 1928 Marmon automobile was rented and decked out announcing the movie. The car was used to transport guests from the airport to the premiere at the El Portal Theatre. The film also played in four theaters in Miami and, per *Variety*, grossed a paltry $5,389, as compared to its opening week competition of *Viva Knievel!* ($32,663), *The Van* ($21,925), and a reissue of *Papillon* ($13,046). In the fall of 1977, the movie began popping up as part of a double-bill in Toronto, Canada and in smaller U.S. cities such as Panama City, Florida, and Pocatello, Idaho, before completely fading from the big screen.

Most Jean Harlow historians dispute the romance between Hughes and Harlow and hence feel Buchanan's film was as fictional as the 1965 *Harlow* biopics. Stating why she thinks it was strictly platonic between the pair, Karina Longworth, the author of 2019's *Seduction: Sex, Lies and Stardom in Howard Hughes' America,* commented, "I don't believe Hughes and Harlow did have a sexual relationship. It seems notable that Hughes didn't have sexual relationships with the two actresses who he really put sincere effort into promoting as stars (Harlow and [Jane] Russell). In both cases, I believe Hughes exhausted his attraction to the actress through the voyeurism and obsessive focus on their bodies that he channeled into making *Hell's Angels* and *The Outlaw* and, more significantly, marketing them."[36]

As mentioned, the bordello scenes are ridiculous but another flaw of the movie is the sidelining of fame-grasping Mother Jean and her husband. It is well known that she and Jean were very close and spent a lot of time together. The fact that she (with Marino Bello in tow) would not be at the premiere of Jean's first major movie is preposterous. Although the film is centered around Harlow's relationship with

Hughes, not having her mother at least on the periphery was a mistake—even with the unimpressive Adele Claire in the role.

The car accident portrayed actually did happen but it was about five years after the making of *Hell's Angels*. It was perhaps included to provide a highly dramatic moment. In reality, the pedestrian died. A witness and Hughes' passenger changed their stories exonerating Hughes—most likely after being paid off to do so.

On the plus side, the two leads are quite believable. The physically perfect Holchak makes for a personable, determined Howard Hughes fixated on getting his movie finished and up onto the big screen. He is so focused on this goal that he constantly rebuffs Harlow's sexual advances. This is in line with Karina Longworth's opinion as to what happened between the pair. However, here the duo eventually make love.

Because she got to play Jean Harlow in an important, short period of her life, Lindsay Bloom is able to portray a cruder but happy, full-of-life Harlow closer to what the real-life sex goddess was purported to be like. Harlow knows she could be on the verge of stardom with this picture if it turns out well and those are Bloom's best scenes. However, for dramatic purposes, a frustrated and jealous Jean can't get Hughes into the sack. She is like a cat on a hot tin roof for most of the movie and she explodes in that scene where she exposes her inner self to him in the airplane hangar.

Looks-wise, despite Bloom's praise for her makeup artist and wardrobe supervisor, she resembles the icon much less than Carroll Baker and Carol Lynley. Her wigs seem too full and blown out. Even Bloom's store-bought wardrobe is flimsy and not indicative of the thirties. Her costumes cannot compare to Edith Head's designs for Baker and Nolan Miller's creations for Lynley. But to be fair, they were working with much larger budgets (especially Head) on both of those films.

Because the movie never opened in Los Angeles or New York, come Academy Award nominations time it was ineligible to be considered.

> **LOWELL PETERSON:** I never saw *Hughes and Harlow* and did not know it was barely released because it was used as a tax shelter.
>
> **LINDSAY BLOOM:** It was devasting to me because I worked very hard and thought this would be a career boost. Instead, it was like hitting a brick wall. It took me awhile to get over it.
>
> **NICHOLAS VON STERNBERG:** It was done as a film to be seen by people, but it didn't get released that way. It is really a beautiful movie when you see it. Larry did a nice job. I don't remember who the cutter was [Robert Fitzgerald], but Larry worked with him. They did a good job putting it together.
>
> **LOWELL PETERSON:** I went on to assist Nick as cinematographer on several films including *Mistress of the Apes, Gas Pump Girls,* and *Tourist Trap,* which I think is his best shot movie. He is good with that low-key, sort of film noir lighting.

Although still not available on DVD or Blu-ray, *Hughes and Harlow: Angels in Hell* has been discovered by a few film-related websites and bloggers who have reviewed or discussed the movie in recent years after seeing it on VHS. They are split on their opinions of the movie but all give high marks to Lindsay Bloom's vivacious performance as Harlow.

On *The Biopic Story: The Reel History of Film* website, which lambasted the rival *Harlow* movies and its leading ladies, the positive review ended with "Unlike most of Larry Buchanan's films, this biopic doesn't need the so-bad-it's-good rationale to earn credit. Victor Holchak provides a solid lead as Howard Hughes while Lindsay Bloom delivers the best Harlow yet. And though the bar may be set low by other biopics of this era, *Hughes and Harlow: Angels in Hell* holds its own against *Gable and Lombard, Valentino* and *W.C. Fields and Me.*"

Steven Puchalski, of *Shock Cinema* magazine, did not like the film and remarked, "It's no surprise that a Larry Buchanan film would be cheap, sloppy or idiotically self-important, but the biggest problem is that it is also dull as hell." However, he praised Lindsay Bloom and said, "Bloom doesn't look much like Harlow, but gives her loads of likable moxie."

Writer and filmmaker Peter Hanson, of the *Every 70s Movie* website, wrote, "As co-written and directed by B-movie guy Larry Buchanan, *Hughes and Harlow* offers caricatures instead of people, cheap gags instead of situations, and weak attempts at salt-of-the-earth wit instead of real dialogue. That the picture is mostly watchable can be attributed to the traffic-accident appeal of the real history being depicted, and also to Bloom's zesty performance as a woman who's seen it all but still wants to believe in something better."

Hal Erickson, writing for *The New York Times*, felt a bit differently, and remarked, "Neither Lindsay Bloom nor Victor Holchak are half as fascinating as the real-life characters they portray, and this coupled with a stretched-to-the-limit budget results in a film that never quite reaches its potential. Still, we can't resist that supporting cast: Royal Dano, Adam Roarke...."

* * *

Twenty-six years after *Hughes and Harlow* came and went on the big screen, pop star Gwen Stefani impersonated the blonde beauty in a cameo role in Martin Scorsese's Howard Hughes biopic, *The Aviator*

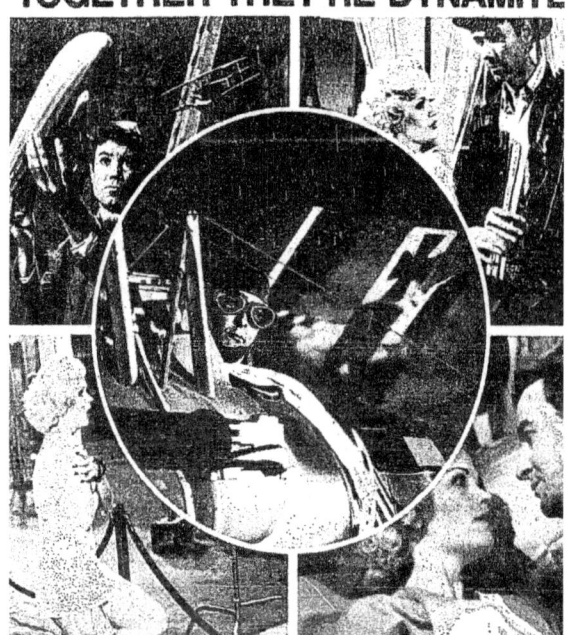

Newspaper ad for *Hughes and Harlow: Angels in Hell.*

(2004). She shows up briefly during the premiere of *Hell's Angels*. In 2014, it was rumored in the press that Mischa Barton, from TV's *The O.C.*, was going to play Jean Harlow in a new biopic but it never came to be.

Jean Harlow's life is just ripe for a good cinematic reboot, especially now that a lot of falsehoods and cover ups have been thoroughly vetted in a number of biographies about the platinum blonde bombshell published since 2000, including *Bombshell: The Life and Death of Jean Harlow* (2000) by Daniel Stenn and *Platinum Girl: The Life and Legends of Jean Harlow* (2003) by Eve Golden. It will be curious to see if Hollywood ever again attempts to tell Jean Harlow's story—and if they get it right.

Biographies—Post Harlows

Irving Shulman went on to author biographies of Rudolph Valentino in 1967 and Jackie Kennedy Onassis in 1972 despite the scathing reviews that *Harlow, An Intimate Biography* received. After receiving a PhD from the University of California at Los Angeles, he returned to fiction, releasing the novels *The Devil's Knee* in 1973 and *Saturn's Child* in 1976. He passed away from Alzheimer's disease on March 23, 1995.

Bill Sargent's recording studio that he opened in Utah was very successful and a number of performers recorded LPs there, including America, the Doobie Brothers, and Billy Joel. Jack Nitzsche also used the studio to record his Academy Award–nominated score for *One Flew Over the Cuckoo's Nest* (1975). It was at about that time when Sargent resurfaced in Hollywood. His decision to come back was due to the fact that he wasn't able to buy a ticket in two different cities to see James Whitmore's sold-out, one-man show *Give 'em Hell, Harry!* Sensing that he could make a lot of money, he bought the rights to the play. After much wheeling and dealing with investors, the play's author, and Whitmore, he released a filmed production, shot in one night and transferred from videotape to film in Theatrovision. This new process was a vast improvement on Electronovision and used nine hand-held cameras spread throughout the theater. The performance was videotaped and then transferred electronically to 35 mm color film.

Whitmore received an Academy Award nomination for Best Actor and the film was a box office hit, reportedly earning $11.5 million on a budget of $3.5 million. Its success impressed The National Association of Theater Owners and they bestowed its "Innovator of the Year Award" on Sargent, honoring his creative marketing of the film. Per David Permut (who helped him put the film together) when riding high, Sargent would utter his favorite expression, "We're shitting in high cotton." Despite this success, Hollywood still wouldn't show him any respect, rejecting his bid to join the Academy of Motion Pictures Arts and Sciences three times and, as of 1975, omitting him from the *Motion Picture Almanac*—considered to be the bible for people working in the film industry. The latter is not too surprising since it is produced by Quigley Publishing and it was Martin Quigley, Jr., in particular, who took Sargent to task for his quickie *Harlow* production ten years prior.

Throughout the seventies, Sargent dabbled in theater productions and was one of the backers of the hit Broadway musical *Beatlemania*. Then, with much ballyhoo, he announced that he was going to film a spear-armed Australian skin diver fighting a 17-foot Great White shark while enclosed in an 80 by 60 feet wire mesh cage in Western Samoa. The wily producer couldn't really justify the idea for this tasteless project, to be titled *Death Match* and broadcast worldwide on closed-circuit television, but candidly admitted, "I am a promoter who's in the business of selling tickets, and if I don't do it, somebody else will."[1] Thankfully, *Death Match* never came to be. Neither did a play about Rudolph Valentino (starring Elvis Presley) at Radio City Music Hall, nor a planned Beatles reunion, in which he offered the Fab Four $50 million to reunite for a one-time, live concert. According to Permut, Sargent only had $2 million in the bank. He asked the producer how they could continue, being $48 million short, and Permut said, "He replied, 'It's a technicality.'"

It was at this time when Sargent reconnected with Maureen Gaffney and Carol Hollenbeck, both of whom had relocated to the Big Apple, Gaffney to pursue a singing career and Hollenbeck a career in theater.

> **Maureen Gaffney:** I was singing at Five's, which was on the west side of Sixth Avenue near 57th Street. I had a cabaret show and Bill, who had a place on Park Avenue, came in late. We went out afterwards for drinks. It was about two in the morning. I was just so hyped up from just coming off the stage and it took time for me to calm down. Bill pretty much told me to shut up and then said, "You had your night—now it's others' turns." He was a character. I was with a man named Bill Lazaro, who was a lawyer and CPA for all the show biz people. I was glad I was with someone because Bill and his girlfriend were doing cocaine.

> **Carol Hollenbeck:** There was a nightclub called Backstage on West 45th Street in the heart of Broadway where we would all hang out. Bill was trying to get involved in the theatre. I was then writing a play. I saw him at Backstage and went up to him. He remembered me and we had another nice conversation. After that, he got involved with James Jennings, who founded the American Theatre of Actors. James had three repertory theatres and named one of them the Sargent Theatre for Bill. Ironically, in the nineties, the play I was developing called *Hometown Premiere* had its sort of production done at the Sargent Theatre. That was weird because, there again, my name got involved with Bill Sargent. The play was based loosely on the premiere of my movie *Eden Cried* in my hometown in 1967.

Making even more money than *Give 'Em Hell, Harry!*, was *Richard Pryor—Live in Concert* (1979), which grossed over $30 million. It was the first movie featuring a comedian doing their stand-up routine. Comparing himself to the major studios, Sargent said, "I'm a prostitute, just like everybody else. I'll extract every penny I can from everybody I can."[2] Unfortunately, his follow-ups to the Pryor film were not nearly as successful—Aram Khachaturian's *Ballet Gayne* (shot in Latvia, its country of origin); the filmed stage production of *Sammy Stops the World* (starring Sammy Davis, Jr., in a revival of *Stop the World—I Want to Get Off* that was reworked especially for the song-and-dance man); and two unreleased, filmed Broadway productions, *Beatlemania* and *Knockout* starring Danny Aiello.

In 1995, a print of Electronovision's *Hamlet* turned up amongst the belongings of the late Richard Burton. His widow, Sally Burton, donated it to the British Institute, which already had two in its collections, though all were supposed to be destroyed. ("I did burn them—at least many of them," confessed Bill Sargent. "We had 971 prints and we only need 500."[3]) It was then learned, through Burton's former manager, that Warner Bros. still had the film negative in its vaults. Having documentation to prove that she owned the rights to *Hamlet* (the original contract stated that ownership of the film would revert to Burton's Atlantic Programmes from Electronovision, Inc. after 90 days from the time the movie was released in September 1964), Ms. Burton was able to get the negative from the studio and have it restored. A deal was made with producer Paul Brownstein who picked up the rights to have the movie re-released in the U.S. and London. Restoration of the movie was left up to Sean Coughlin of Turner Classic Movies. Surprisingly, digitally remastering the soundtrack was more problematic than cleaning up the grainy black-and-white image. A confident Coughlin boasted that the movie would look better today than it did when originally released.

It is too bad no one has taken on restoring *Harlow* in this same matter. It would be wonderful to see an official release on Blu-ray rather than the bootleg, grainy DVD copies that have been circulating for years.

Over the years, Bill Sargent really began putting his *Harlow* down creatively, though not financially. He commented in 1975, "My version of *Harlow* was probably the worst film ever produced, but it made money."[4] In and out of show business during the eighties and nineties, Horace William Sargent III began working on his memoirs shortly before he died on October 19, 2003.

DAVID PERMUT: Everything that is happening today, whether it is James Cameron with his 3-D process for *Avatar* or the Michael Jackson concert film released as an event with a limited run, Bill Sargent was the innovator. I remember sitting with an audience watching *Avatar* and thinking about the time I went with Bill to a warehouse in Culver City in the late Seventies to see a new process called Show Scan developed by Doug Trumble. It had movable seats and took you on these 3-D experiences like a rollercoaster ride. Bill was trying to get financing, but before the demonstration he treated these potential wealthy backers to this sumptuous lunch at Le Dome. Needless to say, most of them got motion sickness and became incredibly ill.

Bill had the first pay cable company in Los Angeles. He broke all kinds of ground, being the first to bring theater to audiences who couldn't go or afford a theater ticket; filming the first rock and roll concert with *The T.A.M.I. Show* and the first comedy concert film with Richard Pryor; and creating a new filming process called Electronovision. Even with reality television, Bill was there first with his idea to film a man fighting a shark to the death. I can probably sell that idea with one phone call to FOX.

You look at all his achievements and they are monumental. In the world today, which is such a corporate environment, there is little room for mavericks, rogues or self-made guys cut from that cloth like Bill. Our industry was founded by those guys. I learned a lot and gleaned a lot from him. He always went up against the system and would tell me, "Make waves—the bigger the better." He did and that was his motto. Bill was a brilliant man and I loved him a lot.

Marshall Naify and **Magna Pictures** were not able to obtain the rights to release John Huston's *The Bible.... In the Beginning*, which they vigorously pursued, and never produced a film about Don Quixote, but continued backing a number of low-budget American films. As with *Harlow*, Naify was credited as "Presenter" on the Arthur Rankin, Jr., animated film *Willy McBean and His Magic Machine* (1965); *The Fat Spy* (1966) a comedy starring, of all people, Phyllis Diller and Jayne Mansfield; and the science fiction adventure *Destination Inner Space* (1966) with Scott Brady and Sheree North. Magna's most notorious release was the gritty, homoerotic *Who Killed Teddy Bear?* (1965) starring Sal Mineo (frequently seen shirtless, in white briefs or a Speedo) as a sexually deviant busboy, who makes obscene phone calls to Times Square discotheque record spinner Juliet Prowse. Magna also continued releasing foreign films such as *Yo Yo* with former Bond Girl Claudine Auger in 1966 and *The Warm Life/La Calda Vita* with Catherine Spaak (the Belgian sexpot Magna wanted to build up à la Ursula Andress or Elke Sommer in the U.S.) in 1967. Obviously, they failed. None of these films were hits, so it is no surprise that Magna ceased distribution, although they did pick up the rights to the Soviet Union's sci-fi film *Solaris* in 1976.

Marshall Naify's main source of income was from United Artists Communications, Inc., one of the largest operators of movie theaters and cable television systems in the U.S. In 1986, he and his brother Robert sold their 51 percent in the company to Tele-Communications, Inc. for $390 million. Marshall kept active in show business as chairman of the post-production company Todd-AO, which Robert ran, and in later years was a prominent thoroughbred horse breeder. He died on April 19, 2000.

Joseph E. Levine just moved on to his next production once *Harlow* wrapped and never looked back—unless it was in a courtroom. His next feature film was *Sands of the Kalahari* (1965) starring Stuart Whitman and Susannah York. As a businessman, he didn't seem to take the competition with Bill Sargent personally, despite his bellowing to the press, and later revealed, "You mustn't bring a picture in on rubber heels. I stole that line from somebody. You have to beat the drums."[5] And boy did those drums get a workout with *Harlow*.

Levine returned to making glossy, trashy melodramas with *The Oscar* (1966), considered one of the worst films of all time, starring Stephen Boyd as a ruthless actor who ruins lives and steps over anyone to win the coveted prize. Levine was also listed as producer or executive producer on a string of movies including *Nevada Smith* (1966; the prequel to *The Carpetbaggers*), *A Man Called Adam* (1966), *The Spy with a Cold Nose* (1966), *Caper of the Golden Bulls* (1967), and *Woman Times Seven* (1967). Riding high, he then sold Embassy Pictures to the Avco Corp. for $40 million to form Avco-Embassy Pictures and stayed on at a salary starting at $200,000 a year. Years later, he confessed it was "a horrible mistake, which made me rich."[6]

One of Avco-Embassy's first releases was the critical darling and major box office smash *The Graduate* (1967). Producer Laurence Turman bought the rights to the novel, but every studio in Hollywood turned him down. He then brought the property, which had director Mike Nichols attached, to Joe Levine, whom Turman described as "an enormously successful schlockmeister" and "a great, flamboyant, throwback salesman."[7] Wanting to produce a prestige motion picture with his new company, Levine agreed to finance the film when Turman promised to bring it in with a budget of $1 million. When Nichols brought his chosen leading man, Dustin Hoffman, to Levine's office for an introduction, the producer thought the actor was the plumber sent over to fix his leaky window. Levine commented that Hoffman was "exactly what Nichols was looking for, someone who did not look like a movie star."[8] *The Graduate* became an enormous hit and an Academy Award winner. Admitting to seeing the movie more than thirty times, the producer remarked, "I was emotionally involved with this movie from the very beginning,"[9] and he deferred to his trusted director regarding all creative decisions in the making of the movie.

Levine then went on to produce such prestige films as *The Lion in Winter* (1968) starring Peter O'Toole and Katharine Hepburn, who won the Best Actress Academy Award for her performance (tying with Barbra Streisand for *Funny Girl*); *Carnal Knowledge* (1971) starring Jack Nicholson, Art Garfunkel, and Academy Award nominee for Best Supporting Actress, Ann-Margret; and *The Day of the Dolphin* (1973) starring George C. Scott. Avco-Embassy also released a mixture of exploitation films, family movies, and foreign films with aggressive marketing campaigns such as the animated *Mad Monster Party?* (1966); *Grazie, Zia!* (1968) with Lisa Gastoni; *Baby Love* (1968) with Linda Hayden; *12 + 1* (1969) with Sharon Tate (in her last role); the biker flick *C.C. and Company* (1970) with Ann-Margret and Joe Namath; and many more, into the seventies and eighties.

In 1974, Levine ended his association with Avco-Embassy. He then formed Joseph E. Levine Presents, Inc. where he boasted in promotional materials, with his typical bravado, that "for the past forty-five years, Joseph E. Levine has towered above lesser moguls of filmdom like a short, bespectacled colossus, making legends, making myths, making instant millions."[10] Up first for the new company was *A Bridge Too Far* (1977), a big budget ($25 million) antiwar film. Directed by Sir Richard Attenborough, it was the story about the tragic Allied paratrooper attack on the Rhine Bridge at Arnhem, featuring an all-star cast including Robert Redford, James Caan, Ryan O'Neal, Sir Laurence Olivier, Sean Connery, Elliot Gould and Liv Ullmann. Levine was blamed for contributing to the bloated salaries of actors driving up movie budgets, but retorted, "Screw it! If a guy can get $500,000 a week, let him get it. If this film is a success, I'll have made a marvelous deal."[11] He did. The film was pre-sold to Europe and TV on the strength of its cast, and despite the mixed reviews, the film made double its budget in the U.S. *Magic* (1978), starring Anthony Hopkins as an actor-turned-ventriloquist who begins to lose his sanity, was Levine's last movie.

During the early eighties, while Levine was reflecting on his long career, Carroll Baker had become either a forgotten memory or, more likely, someone he still had a grudge against. When asked about his working relationships with actors over the years, he responded that he had "gotten along with most people along the way, except that actress, what's her name? Who I starred in *Harlow*."[12] Joe Levine passed away on July 31, 1987.

Larry Buchanan's career never rebounded after *Hughes and Harlow: Angels in Hell* failed. He wrote, "Jane [his wife] and I traveled extensively after the disappointment of *Hughes and Harlow*, taking a sort of reflective hiatus."[13] The couple toured Europe and Egypt. His follow-up movie (kickstarted by a distributor he met in England who wanted a jungle adventure film to sell at the upcoming Cannes Film

Festival) was the ridiculous, but fun, *Mistress of the Apes* (1979). It featured blonde Jenny Neumann as a sort of female Tarzan and *Playboy* playmate and seventies starlet Barbara Leigh (in her last acting role) as a wife searching for her missing anthropologist husband. Sexploitation at its best, the film played a few drive-ins before going direct to the burgeoning video cassette market where it became a long running rental hit.

Buchanan's sporadic eighties output included *Down on Us* (1984) about how the government had a hand in the deaths of Jimi Hendrix, Jim Morrison, and Janis Joplin; and *Goodnight, Sweet Marilyn* (1989), the story of Monroe's death as told by a friend. It starred Paula Lane as Marilyn and used archival footage from *Goodbye, Norma Jean* in flashbacks to her earlier life. Neither did as well as *Mistress of the Apes*.

In 1996, McFarland & Company, Inc., published Buchanan's autobiography *It Came from Hunger! Tales of a Cinema Schlockmeister*. He also began a series of popular one-day filmmaking seminars where he presented, "As much practical information as possible about the reality of making movies on one's own. Film schools cover the artistic and technical aspects; I try to help with the harsh demands of making films in the real world."[14] He was re-editing his movie *The Copper Scroll of Mary Magdalene* that was shelved in the seventies when he passed away on December 2, 2004, in Tucson, Arizona.

Lindsay Bloom's disappointment that *Hughes and Harlow: Angels in Hell* did not get a big national release did not seem to hamper her acting career in the least. After the movie finished shooting, Bloom went on to star or co-star in a number of drive-in movies including *Texas Detour* (1978) with Patrick Wayne and Priscilla Barnes; *French Quarter* (1978) with Bruce Davison and Virginia Mayo; *H.O.T.S.* (1979) with Lisa London; and *The Happy Hooker Goes Hollywood* (1980) with Martine Beswicke. In between, she had a small role in the hit comedy *The Main Event* (1979) starring Barbra Streisand and Ryan O'Neal.

The eighties found Bloom concentrating on television where she popped up in guest-starring roles on many series including *Charlie's Angels*, *Vegas$*, *The Love Boat*, *Sanford*, and *Trapper John, M.D.* Her talent and professionalism landed her the recurring role of Mable Tillingham, the police operator, on a few seasons of *The Dukes of Hazzard* and a short-term role as Bonnie Robertson, the ex-girlfriend of Ray Krebbs (Steve Kanaly) on *Dallas* in 1982.

> **LINDSAY BLOOM:** I read for a couple of Lorimar's shows. Leonard Katzman, who was one of the producers on *Dallas*, liked my work, He said, "I can't give you one of the regular roles, but I will have you back to do something else later." He did and kept his word. I came on after Jock Ewing died. Ray grew his hair long and started drinking at the bar. JR suspects something and is out in the parking lot waiting for us to come out of a bar. We are drunk and he follows us to make sure Ray's wife, Donna [Susan Howard], finds out about us. She does and tries to pay Bonnie off to stay away from her husband. I throw a drink in her face and then she punches me out. Larry Hagman directed that episode. They borrowed this fancy, very expensive fur coat from Neiman-Marcus for Susan to wear. I threw the drink the first time and the cameraman said I threw it too fast. I had to do it again. The wardrobe people

are out there with hair dryers because the coat got wet. The next time I threw it, the liquid hit just under Donna's nose and she started to choke. Larry yelled, "Cut! Cut! Lindsay, that was too good. Try for a happy medium on the left side of her face so we can capture it with the camera." I said, "Okay, Larry!" We finally got it but it took about five takes.

Regarding her punching me, I said, "Larry, do you really think a tough cowgirl like Bonnie would just go down with one punch and not kick that rich gal's butt?" He replied, "I can have her punch you and you can slide down the bar?" I said, "No, that's okay. I will do as the part is written."

Patrick Duffy directed two of my other episodes. I think I did six or seven of them overall. It was a great cast. Steve and I got along wonderfully. Linda Gray, who played Sue Ellen, and I were in the same acting class prior.

Lindsay then co-starred in Showtime's first scripted series, the *Lone Star Bar & Grill,* in 1983. Despite pulling in big ratings with its story of housewives working as hookers out of the saloon, it was cancelled after only one season. After appearing in several TV-movies, she won the highly coveted role of Velda, the secretary to Stacy Keach's private eye in the TV series *The New Mike Hammer* (1984-1987).

Lindsay Bloom as Velda, private eye Mike Hammer's secretary, in "Kill Devil" on *The New Mike Hammer* (Columbia Pictures Television, 1984).

LINDSAY BLOOM: I called it the Velda Marathon. I spent six weeks auditioning. It was ironic, I got the call for the first interview in early July of 1983. My in-laws had been visiting from West Virginia and I put on ten pounds because they were there for two weeks cooking up Southern food with lots of fattening ingredients. After my first audition, my agent said, "Lindsay, they liked your reading but they told me that you need to lose weight." I asked how much weight and was told ten pounds. I said, "Okay, how much time do I have?" He said, "Probably a week to ten days." I knew the recent weight would be easy to get off and knew I could do it. I fasted, drank protein shakes, and started aerobics class.

I had lost the weight by the next audition, but this time they said, "We love the reading and you look a lot better, but you need to lose some more weight." I thought, "For God's sake!" I then added working out at the gym and swimming laps in the afternoon to my routine. I had to focus everything on this because it was an important role. What was really fun for me, and ironic at the same time, that growing up my dad read all the Mickey Spillane novels. I read a lot of those books while I was auditioning for Velda to get tips about her character and personality.

I go back a third time still with my blonde hair and Tim Flack, who was the casting director, said to me, "Lindsay, they really like your reading, which is what's keeping you in, but they just can't see you in the part." I said, "What!?! Don't they have any imagination? Don't they know about hair and makeup?" Tanya Roberts had been cast as Velda in the original pilot. She was not available to do the series because she had bleached her dark hair to blonde and she was in Africa shooting the movie, *Sheena*. I said, "If they want to see Tanya Roberts, let's give them Tanya Roberts." I asked my husband and he said, "Go get your hair dyed. Do whatever to get the part." I went to my hairdresser and we chose a not too dark brown. I went to see Tim Flack after and he said, "No, it has to be darker."

Meanwhile, we are in August of that summer and I then dyed the hair a chestnut brunette. I had my makeup artist Tina, from *Hughes and Harlow*, get me to have a Tanya Roberts look. By this time, it was down to seven of us for the part. It started with hundreds of women that executive producer Jay Bernstein had saw across the country, which was more publicity stunt. I went in to read with Stacy Keach and I guess it went very well. I got a call back to screen test again. Tim told me then that Jay Bernstein was not a fan of mine. Tim told me that Jay said to him, "I don't care how many times you bring that Lindsay Bloom girl back in here, she's not right for the part." At this point I had lost twenty-two pounds, dyed my hair a dark chestnut, and bought the perfect, sexy, electric blue, silk outfit that I thought Velda would wear from a chic Beverly Hills dress shop. I went into the final screen test with two other actresses. One of them was Delta Burke. When I learned that I got the part, I was jumping up and down while on the phone with my agent. It had been a long, drawn-out affair. I think I read for the part nine times. And this is why I called it the Velda Marathon.

All the changes I put myself through lent itself very well for that character. I had a fun time working on the series. It was set in the present day, but they did everything they could to make it feel like the fifties. Before the show came on the air, CBS threw a party. Mickey Spillane was there. Jay introduced us and Mickey said, "There's my Velda. You're great in the part, doll!" I was tickled. He was great fun.

After the TV series ended in 1987, Bloom reprised her role as Velda two years later in the 1989 TV-movie *Mike Hammer: Murder Takes All*. She then stepped away from Hollywood to raise a family with her husband, Mayf Nutter. She resurfaced ten years later in the theatrical feature, *Grizzly Adams and the Legend of Dark Mountain* (1989) starring Dan Haggerty. She vanished yet again only to reappear in 2020 in the indie film *Charlie's Christmas Wish* (2020) starring Toni Hudson and Richard Tyson.

LINDSAY BLOOM: What was interesting about this whole thing, I think it was in April 2018, and I was on Facebook. I am not savvy with it and just scrolling and looking at pictures when I saw I had a bunch of messages. One was from this gal who wrote to me asking if I still acted in movies because she wrote this script and thought there was a part I would be good for. I thought, "What!?!" I did not have an agent but I did have a friend named Jim who handled all my personal appearances. He reached out to her and got a copy of the script. The part was of the mayor of this town and I liked that. I also liked that it was a nice family movie. They flew me down to Canton, Georgia, to film in June of 2018. They had to work around my sales and marketing job schedule. I spent about five days there filming. It was a lot of fun being on location and working with other actors.

Carol Lynley jetted off to England almost the second after *Harlow* wrapped. Producer/director Otto Preminger chose her, over Ann-Margret and Jane Fonda, to play the harried, unstable mother, newly arrived in London, who reports the disappearance of her daughter (who may or may not exist) in the excellent mystery thriller *Bunny Lake Is Missing* (1965). Co-starring were Laurence Olivier as a Scotland Yard inspector, Keir Dullea as her over-protective brother, and Noël Coward as her flamboyant landlord. Preminger was infamous for his bullying tactics with actors (he nearly drove Tom Tryon to have a mental breakdown while making *The Cardinal*), but Carol liked him very much.

CAROL LYNLEY: I had no problems with Otto whatsoever. As a director, he knew what he wanted and I gave him what he wanted. We got along fine. My theory, and I may not be correct, is that Otto was a bit harsher with men. I think the male does not acquiesce as much as the female. I'm couching my words here but trying to be fair. The funniest thing that Keir has said to me about working with Otto was that it took about three years for his voice to become lower again. That gives you an idea of the anxiety he felt in dealing with Otto. Keir didn't really have any personal problems with Otto, it's just that Otto was sometimes combative. The difference between Keir and Tom Tryon is enormous. Tom was nowhere near as good an actor as Keir. Otto took advantage of that. Being the better more confident actor, Keir was able to handle Otto well—and it was a lot to handle.

Carol Lynley as the mother of a little girl, who may or may not exist, in *Bunny Lake Is Missing* (Columbia, 1965).

Though Lynley received very fine notices (for instance, *Variety* said "carrying most of the film on her shoulders.... Carol Lynley is outstanding"), *Bunny Lake Is Missing* received very mixed reviews and was not a financial hit, but it has grown in stature over the years and now is considered a cult classic.

>   **CAROL LYNLEY:** It's about time this film gets its due. I was terribly disappointed when the film was first released. Critics seemed to be reviewing Otto's life and personality, rather than the film itself. I put my heart and soul into that film. Also, Columbia Pictures lost faith in it and instead pushed *The Collector*. A couple of years later, it began being shown in revival houses and has become an art house favorite. The Museum of Modern Art owns a copy and I even introduced the movie at a film festival honoring Laurence Olivier held in New York City. I think the reason it has remained so popular is that it is one of Otto's best films.

After her good reviews for *Bunny Lake Is Missing*, Lynley wisely abandoned the sex kitten image. Unfortunately, she also decided to forsake Hollywood for London, remaining there for about a year and a half. She seemed to have concentrated more on her on-and-off love affairs with TV personality David Frost and actor Oliver Reed than her career, but she found the time to star in the thriller *The Shuttered Room* (1967), based on a story by H.P. Lovecraft, where she looked stunningly gorgeous and was convincingly scared throughout as the inheritor of an old mill (complete with lecherous cousin Oliver Reed and a hideous thing in the attic); and the spy adventure *Danger Route* (1968), playing the double-crossing girlfriend of agent Richard Johnson. At this time, Carol Lynley was one of the actresses Warren Beatty was considering as his co-star in *Bonnie and Clyde* and it was, surprisingly, due to *Harlow*, as he reportedly thought she had the perfect thirties look. This may be true, but according to Carol, he never contacted her or shared the script.

Returning to Hollywood in 1967, Lynley worked in film and television with an equal amount of felicity. She made numerous TV guest appearances and began appearing in made-for-TV films including the very popular *The Immortal* (1969), playing the girlfriend of race car driver Christopher George who discovers that his blood contains antibodies that make him immune to aging and disease. After playing a psychopathic heiress who entraps golfer Paul Burke into a reciprocal murder scheme in *Once You Kiss a Stranger* (1969), a semi-remake of Alfred Hitchcock's *Strangers on a Train* with a sex and sport switch, Lynley became part of ensemble films. Among them were the Dan Rowan and Dick Martin haunted house spoof *The Maltese Bippy* (1969), where she portrayed a secretive college coed, and the road comedy *Norwood* (1970), where she gave an amusing, scene-stealing performance as a foul-mouthed hooker driving cross country with naïve Vietnam vet Glen Campbell.

For Carol Lynley, 1972 was a banner year. She began it as reporter Darren McGavin's woeful girlfriend (and the first to suspect a vampire is terrorizing Las Vegas) in *The Night Stalker*, the highest rated TV movie up to that point. She ended the year as part of an all-star cast in producer Irwin Allen's box office smash *The Poseidon Adventure* (1972), the granddaddy of disaster movies. Carol delivers an especially effective performance as the terrified hot pants–wearing pop singer, Nonnie, who warbles the Oscar-winning song, "The Morning After," and then goes into a state of shock when the ocean liner capsizes.

CAROL LYNLEY: It was a Friday and I went in to meet with Ronnie Neame [the director] and Irwin Allen. We talked about the story and that was it. I went to the beach for the weekend. When I got back home on Monday, my agent was furiously trying to find me. I got the part—they cast me on the spot. I don't know why because they never even gave me a script to read.

We had to do costume fittings immediately. It was so hurried and rushed. Paul Zastupnevich already had Nonnie's look designed with the hot pants and the long vest. However, the one thing I brought to it were the boots. There was going to be a lot of water on that set. Having been a ballet dancer my entire life, I knew that could get dicey. My boots were leather and rubberized underneath. I asked Ronnie and Irwin if I could use my boots because I felt comfortable wearing them. I was also confident that I wouldn't slip in them.

Carol Lynley, ca. 1972 (courtesy Marlin Dobbs).

Despite her recent successes, Lynley never made another big studio motion picture and was, unfortunately, relegated to working in low-budget, independent films (e.g., *The Four Deuces* and *Bad Georgia Road*) and made-for-TV movies. The latter kept her in the public eye since she appeared in several very popular suspense/adventure type-films such as *The Elevator*; the exciting *Deliverance* knock-off *Death Stalk* (a favorite of Quentin Tarantino's); Irwin Allen's *Flood*; *Fantasy Island* (the pilot for the hit series); and *The Beasts Are in the Streets*.

In between, Lynley returned to the stage opposite James Earl Jones in *Of Mice and Men* at the Kennedy Center. Commenting on her role of Curley's Wife, she said, "It's a funny thing, but here I am playing the kind of woman who would have delusions of being another Harlow, and once I played Jean Harlow."[15] She then had a major success on Broadway, triumphantly taking over for Sandy Dennis in the hit Alan Ayckbourn comedy *Absurd Person Singular* with Geraldine Page. Critic Clive Barnes in *The New York Times* raved, "The newcomers slide easily into the play ... and, perhaps best of all Carol Lynley, disenchanted to the point of catatonic withdrawal."[16]

The entertaining remake of *The Cat and the Canary* (1978) should have garnered Lynley kudos for her charming performance as Annabelle West, the sole heir to a fortune who must survive the gloomy night in a creepy mansion—with jealous relatives and a mad man on the loose—to collect her inheritance. A legal dispute, unfortunately, kept the film shelved in the U.S. until 1982 despite an esteemed British cast that included Honor Blackman, Olivia Hussey, Edward Fox, Daniel Massey, and Wendy Hiller.

Carol worked continuously on television until the mid-eighties. You could watch her guesting on such popular series as *Hawaii-Five-0*, *Charlie's Angels*, *The Love Boat*, *Hart to Hart*, *The Fall Guy*, and *Hotel*. She was also a regular visitor to *Fantasy Island*—where she holds the record for most guest appearances.

Lynley was much less active in film, as were most of her sixties contemporaries who now were in their forties. Highlights included *Vigilante* (1982), a hit *Death Wish* knock-off from cult director, William Lustig; *Dark Tower* (1986) directed by Freddie Francis; the thriller *Blackout* (1987), penned by Joseph Stefano (the screenwriter of *Psycho*), where she portrayed one bitch of a cold-hearted mother; and the noir-ish desert road movie *Neon Signs* (1996). In the latter, Barbara McNair and Lynley (à la Thelma and Louise) amusingly played aging, gun-toting thieves who hook up with William Smith for one big score as they drive the desert byroads to Las Vegas.

Carol's last known acting credit was playing a casting director in the short film *Vic* (2006) directed by Sage Stallone, son of Rambo. She was participating in the preparation of the BearManor Media book *Carol Lynley: Her Film & TV Career in Thrillers, Fantasy & Suspense* when she unexpectedly passed away on September 3, 2019, and never saw the finished outcome.

Carroll Baker next turned up again on the big screen two years after the release of *Harlow*. With film work scarce due to her lawsuit with Paramount, she traveled to Vietnam entertaining the troops as part of Bob Hope's USO Tour and made a cameo playing herself as the victim of cat burglar George Hamilton in *Jack of Diamonds* (1967). Her pay was a purported $450 per hour. Then, while attending the Venice Film Festival, she accepted an offer to star in a low-budget Italian movie called *L'harem* (1968). Even though the movie was poorly received, Baker enjoyed the experience so much that she relocated to Italy, leaving her husband back in the States and sending her children to school in Switzerland. A chance encounter with Marilyn Monroe a few years earlier had been prophetic. Baker ran into the waning sex goddess heavily drinking one night and she advised the unhappy star to go to Europe to start a new life where she would be adored. Per Baker, Monroe turned to her and said, "You're right ... but for me it's much too late."[17] It was, but not for Baker, who seemed to strive to take Monroe's place as the newest reigning sex symbol with her recent choice of roles.

Baker enjoyed much success in Europe, starring in sexy Italian giallos such as *The Sweet Body of Deborah* (1968) portraying a wealthy American newlywed whose husband is being haunted by the supposed suicide of an ex-girlfriend; and two for director Umberto Lenzi—*Orgasmo* (1969) where she was cast as a lonely widow enjoying her idyllic time with a younger Lou Castel, until the man's sister arrives, and *So Sweet.... So Perverse* (1969), this time not as a victim, but instead playing the double-crossing mistress of married Jean-Louis Trintignant. She would go on to work for Lenzi again in *Paranoia* (1970) and *Il Coltello di ghiaccio* (1972).

Though the quality of the films she appeared in was lower than in her glory days at Paramount, Baker enjoyed every minute of her time in Europe. "I never lived for

Paranoia (Commonwealth United, 1969), directed by Umberto Lenzi, was one of Carroll Baker's most remembered Italian movies. Baker is shown here with Lou Castel in a steamy shower scene.

today, it was always for tomorrow," she commented. "The marvelous thing in Italy is that what's important is what you are doing today—even if it's a pleasant lunch or watching TV for a couple of hours. You are not so driven here because everyone is slower than you."[18]

Baker kept busy working in the Italian film industry, but found herself mired in films of dubious merit (she was rudely dubbed the "Queen of low-budget, low-grade, low-brows") including *A Quiet Place to Kill* (1970), *Death at the Deep End of the Swimming Pool* (1971), *Captain Apache* (1971), *Silent Horror* (1972), and most memorably *Baba Yaga, Devil Witch* (1973), playing the black-clad title character who lures a beautiful photographer into her bizarre coven.

Carroll returned to the U.S., briefly, when she was cast in *Andy Warhol's Bad* (1977), playing a woman who uses the electrolysis business in her home as a front for her squad of female assassins. Her next U.S. production was the horror movie *The Watcher in the Woods* (1979), which featured her in little more than a cameo as the mother of two teenage girls who contact a ghostly presence in the surrounding forest of their rented English country house, owned by Bette Davis.

Moving to London, Baker began writing her brutally honest autobiography entitled *Baby Doll*, which covers her life up to the time she moved to Italy. Though intimidated at first about the prospect of rehashing her life, she found it surprisingly therapeutic and remarked, "Deep down, I suppose I'd always had some regrets about leaving Hollywood at the height of my career. But after reliving those days through my book, I now know I wouldn't change a thing. I'd do it all over again."[19]

Baker made a triumphant comeback to the silver screen in *Star 80* (1983), playing the mother of ill-fated *Playboy* Playmate Dorothy Stratten. She got the part after a casting director noticed her photo in a newspaper when she came to New York to visit her daughter, actress Blanche Baker. They sent Carroll a copy of the script, which she thought was "marvelous. I'd only vaguely heard of Dorothy Stratten, but when I saw a photograph of her after I'd signed for the role, I was struck by how alike we were. We really could have been mother and daughter."[20]

Playing the mother of a sex symbol caused Baker to reflect on her days as a sex goddess during the sixties. She confessed that she had enjoyed the

No dueling Harlows here. Unlike their producers, once Carroll Baker and Carol Lynley finally met in the nineties, they remained friends until Carol's passing in 2019. Here they are together in 1999 (© Wayne Schulman, courtesy Wayne Schulman).

fabulous lifestyle of drinking champagne at the Four Seasons and riding around in antique cars up to a point, but then it became burdensome. She tired of being told what to say and what to wear. "I was the victim of the last gasp of Hollywood dictatorship and glamour. It was all image, image, image."[21]

The success of *Star 80* led Baker to work steadily in feature films through the early nineties, and among her standouts were the spoof *The Secret Diary of Sigmund Freud* (1984), playing the famed doctor's mother; *Ironweed* (1987), cast as the estranged wife of homeless bum Jack Nicholson; and the comedy *Kindergarten Cop* (1990) in a villainous turn as a grandmother seeking revenge on her drug-dealing son's ex-wife and child who are in hiding. In between, the talented actress and author found time to write two more books—*The Roman Tale*, a novel about the Italian film industry, and *To Africa with Love,* "a true romantic adventure," about Baker's journey through the Dark Continent with a younger lover. Post-1990, Baker mostly appeared in made-for TV movies and episodic television. Her last known acting credit was an episode of TV's *The Lion's Den* in 2003.

Despite working in Hollywood during the same period of time, Carol Lynley and Carroll Baker never encountered each other in person until sometime in the mid-nineties, long after the *Harlow* wars had ceased. Mutual animosity ran rampant between their producers, as they battled each other in person and through the press, but there was none between their leading ladies.

CAROL LYNLEY: I adore Carroll Baker to this day. I think she is a wonderful person and talented actress. When we first met, we laughed, we cried, and I told her that I have been signing autographs for her for years!

When we see each other it's like, "Carol," "Carroll." We jump up and down, and hug and kiss. People sort of back away because they think we're going to get into some sort of cat fight or whatever. I had dinner with her one time in San Francisco. You know, I'm still a fan of hers. I said, "Oh Carroll, you worked with James Dean and George Stevens, such critical people you've worked with. What a great career you've had, and *Baby Doll*. You look so beautiful, Carroll, to this day." And she says, "Oh Carol, shut up!" "No, no, Carroll, I really mean it." We have fun. She's great.

The two hit it off so well that Carol revealed in *Filmfax* magazine, "Though I am not a big fan of horror movies, there is one horror film I would love to do, a remake of *Whatever Happened to Baby Jane?* with Carroll Baker. I would love to work with her. We'd be perfect for the remake and have been shopping it around to various producers."[22] Alas, it never came to be.

Sometime during the 2010s, Carroll Baker relocated back to New York City from California to be nearer to her daughter and her family. As coincidences happen, in 2019, Carol Hollenbeck, whose manager touted her to play Jean Harlow decades prior, met and became friends with Baker.

CAROL HOLLENBECK: You know how life is and can come full circle? A friend of mine, who belongs to the National Arts Club, invited me to hear Carroll Baker read from her new book [*Who Killed Big Al?*]. She was then interviewed by author Foster Hirsch, who is her escort to practically all her public appearances. Interestingly, she did not elaborate or dwell on *Harlow*. She talked about *Baby Doll* and *How the West Was Won*—her movies that were quite big. I met her afterwards and told her I was up for the other *Harlow* with Carol Lynley, who I was always a fan of. That's how we bonded. I did not mention my Regis Philbin connection to her *Harlow*. She was just lovely. I bought her book and we had a nice chat. It was really wonderful. We exchanged emails. She asked me to dinner with her daughter, Blanche Baker, about two months after we met.

She loved Carol Lynley. When Carol passed, it really broke Carroll up. She was so saddened when she lost her. They were very close friends. I was then invited to her ninetieth birthday dinner in Little Italy. She grabbed me by the hand during this and sweetly said,' You stay well. I am losing everybody.' Carroll is really down to Earth and that is why I love her.

Film Credits—Detailed

Harlow

An Electronovision Production, a Bill Sargent production; a Magna Pictures Distribution Corp. release
Filmed in Electronovision
Opening date: May 14, 1965
No official DVD or Blu-ray release as of July 2024

Production Credits: Presenter: Marshall Naify. Producer: Lee Savin. Executive Producer: Brandon Chase. Assistant Producer: Frank Ray. Director: Alex Segal. Screenplay: Karl Tunberg. Music Conductor and Arrangement: Nelson Riddle. Music Composer: Nelson Riddle, Al Ham. Casting Coordinator: Belcourt Artists, Inc. Casting Consultation: Marvin Paige. Production Supervisor: Eddie Dodds. Art Director: Duncan Cramer. Set Decoration: Harry Gordon. Prop Master: Ken Westcott. Makeup: Michael Westmore. Hair Stylist: Mary Westmoreland. Wardrobe: Paul McCardle. Production Assistant: Nanette Elland. Supervising Film Editor: Bill Heath. Film Editor: Leo Shreve. Music Editor: Ed Forsythe. Sound Effects: Jack Finlay. Assistant Directors: Greg Peters, Johnny Wilson, Jim Ford, [not credited: Richard Bennett]. Title Design: Howard A. Anderson Co. Sound: Glen Glenn. Unit Publicist: Martin Roberts. Technical Advisor-Consultant: Don Roberson. Director of Photography: Jim Kilgore. Technical Director: Ray Connors. Video Control: Carl Hanseman. Film Recording Supervisor: S. Dick Krown. Cameramen: John Braislin, Hugh Gagnier, Ernest Hall, Joseph Talosi. Wardrobe Design for Miss Lynley and Miss Rogers: Nolan Miller.

Song "I Believed It All" Words by Al and Marilyn Bergman, Music by Al Ham, Sung by Mary Mayo.

Cast: Carol Lynley (*Jean Harlow*), Efrem Zimbalist, Jr. (*William Mansfield*), Ginger Rogers (*Mama Jean*), Barry Sullivan (*Marino Bello*), Hurd Hatfield (*Paul Bern*), Lloyd Bochner (*Marc Peters*), Hermione Baddeley (*Marie Dressler*), Audrey Totter (*Marilyn*), John Williams (*Jonathan Martin*), Audrey Christie (*Thelma*), Michael Dante (*Ed*), Jack Kruschen (*Louis B. Mayer*), Celia Lovsky (*Maria Ouspenskaya*), Robert Strauss (*Hank*), Sonny Liston (*1st Fighter*), Cliff Norton (*Billy*), John "Red" Fox (*Oliver Hardy*), James Plunkett (*Stan Laurel*), Buddy Lewis (*Al Jolson*), James Dobson (*Counterman*), Paulle Clark (*Waitress*), Harry Holcombe (*Minister*), Maureen Gaffney (*Miss Larsen*), Joel Marston (*Press Agent*), Fred Klein (*Himself*), Nick Dimitri (*2nd Fighter*), Miss Christopher West (*Bern's Secretary*), Lola Fisher (*Nurse*), Ron Kennedy (*Assistant Director*), Brad Olson (*Doctor*), Frank Scannell (*Doctor*), Fred Conte (*Photographer*), Mark Herron (*James Langley*), Catherine Ross (*Wardrobe woman*). Unknown Bit Roles: Jimmy Cross, Denise Frank, Seymour Cassell, Fletcher Fist, Joan Granville, Joe D'Amore, Edwin Mills, Shirley J. Shawn, Len Hendry, James Westmoreland.

Harlow

A Paramount Pictures Corp. Embassy Pictures Corp., Prometheus Enterprises production; a Paramount Pictures Corp. release.

Filmed in Panavision and Technicolor
Opening date: June 23, 1965
DVD release: September 28, 2010, by Olive Films
Blu-ray release: July 23, 2013, by Olive Films

Production Credits: Producer/Presenter: Joseph E. Levine. Director: Gordon Douglas. Screenplay: John Michael Hayes. Based upon the book by Irving Shulman in collaboration with Arthur Landau. Director of Photography: Joseph Ruttenberg, A.S.C. Music: Neal Hefti. Gowns by: Edith Head. Art Direction: Hal Pereira and Roland Anderson. Set Decoration: Sam Comer and James Payne. Makeup Supervision: Wally Westmore. Hair Style Supervision: Nellie Manley. Men's Costumes: Moss Mabry. Dialogue Coach: Leon Charles. Film Editors: Frank Bracht, A.C.E. and Archie Marshek, A.C.E. Unit Production Manager: C. Kenneth DeLand. Assistant Director: Dave Salven. Special Photographic Effects: Paul K. Lerpae. Process Photography: Farciot Edouart. Sound Recording by: Stanley Jones and Charles Grenzbach. Carroll Baker's Hair Styled by: Sidney Guillaroff. Technicolor Color Consultant: Richard Mueller.

Bobby Vinton sings the *Theme from Harlow* ("Lonely Girl") on Epic Records.

Cast: Carroll Baker (*Jean Harlow*), Martin Balsam (*Everett Redman*), Red Buttons (*Arthur Landau*), Michael Connors (*Jack Harrison*), Hanna Landy (*Mrs. Arthur Landau*), Angela Lansbury (*Mama Jean Bello*), Peter Lawford (*Paul Bern*), Leslie Neilsen (*Richard Manley*), Raf Vallone (*Marino Bello*), Peter Hansen (*Assistant director*), Mary Murphy (*Sally Doane*), Kipp Hamilton (*Marie Tanner*), Peter Leeds (*Parker*).

Uncredited Cast (listed alphabetically): Phil Arnold (*Comic Baker*), Jack Baker (*Dance Director*), Bill Baldwin (*Reporter*), Elaine Beckett (*Bridesmaid*), William "Billy" Benedict (*Bespectacled Hero in Movie*), Roxane Berard (*Secretary*), Larry J. Blake (*Editor*), Billy Bletcher (*Policeman*), Joe Brooks (*Assistant Director*), Rand Brooks (*Director*), Robert Carricart (*Director*), Booth Coleman (*Minister*), Roger Creed (*Keystone Kop*), Dennis Cross (*Second Director—Scene 8*), Billy Curtis (*Newsboy*), Bing Davidson (*Reporter*), Robert Dornan (*Photographer*), Fritz Feld (*Window Washer in Movie*), Robert Foulk (*Manny Siver*), Gee Gee Galligan (*Bus Passenger*), Marina Ghane (*Showgirl*), James Gonzalez (*Assistant*), Joe Gray (*Director*), Dan Haggerty (*Police Captain*), Myron Healey (*Rex Chambers*), Harry Holcombe (*Doctor*), Susan Holloway (*Bus Passenger*), Shep Houghton (*Announcer*), Robert F. Hoy (*Tim*), Arline Hunter (*Girl at Theater*), Robert Kino (*Houseboy*), Harry Lauter (*Bus Driver*), Louise Lawson (*Pretty Girl*), Diki Lerner (*Window Washer*), Jo Anne Loren (*Pretty Girl*), Mike Mahoney (*Man from Casting*), Larry D. Mann (*Editor*), Bill McLean (*Still photographer*), Julie Parrish (*Serena Harrison*), William Phipps (*Reporter*), Allan Ray (*Man at Central Casting*), Jack Reitzen (*Reporter*), Benny Rubin (*Director*), Francoise Ruggieri (*Bridesmaid*), Sandra Scott (*Pretty Girl*), Dianne Simpson (*Actress*), Rikki Stevens (*Showgirl*), Claude Stroud (*Bus Passenger*), Lyle Sudrow (*Dave Northcroft*), Romo Vincent (*Pinky*), Guy Way (*Assistant*), Guy Wilkerson (*Comic Hunter*), Edy Williams (*Mail Room Girl*). Bit roles: Ginny Baker, Richard Boyer, Jerry Douglas, Beverly Hills.

Hughes and Harlow: Angels in Hell

A PRO International Pictures release.
Opening date: May 25, 1977
No official DVD or Blu-ray release as of July 2024

Production Credits: Presenter: William B. Silberkleit in association with Frank V. Bianchini and Malcolm Cobrink. Produced and Directed by: Larry Buchanan. Director of Photography: Nicholas Josef von Sternberg. Edited by: Robert Fitzgerald. Screenplay: Lynn Shubert and Larry Buchanan. Associate Producer: Eugene Maday. Technical Advisor: Dr. S. Shearing.

"Escape" and "All the World": Music and Lyrics by Estelle Silberkleit. Sung by Terri Pierce. Music Composed and Conducted by: Jimmie Haskell. Assistant Director: John Curran. Production Manager: Joe Price. First Assistant Cameraman: Lowell Peterson. Second Assistant Cameraman: David Schmier. Stills: Tommy Estridge. Sound Mixer: Al Ramirez. Boom Man: Mark Buckalew. Makeup: Ray Sebastian. Special Makeup for Ms. Bloom: Tina Bushelman. Script Supervisor: Jackie Saunders. Costume Design and Supervision: Lennie Barin. Wardrobe Assistant: Holgie Forrester. Key Grip: Robert C. George. First Grip: Alan Caso. Grip Best Boy: Ray Spadero. Gaffer Best Boy: Ernie Roebuck. Assistant Editor: Linda Sande. Wardrobe: International Costumes. Production Assistants: Tommy Silberkleit, Thomas Keir. Vintage Cars by: Robert Jenson, Cars of the Stars. Art Director: George Costello. Music Scoring Recordist: Ron Malo. Air War Coordination: Antique Areo. Titles and Effects: MGM. Technicolor Color Consultant: Richard Mueller.

Cast: Victor Holchak (*Howard Hughes*), Lindsay Bloom (*Jean Harlow*), David McLean (*Billy*), Charles Aidikoff (*Projectionist*), James S. Appleby (*Pilot*), Wally Berns (*Announcer*), James E. Brodhead (*Lawyer*), Don Brodie (*Director*), Bobby Buchanan (*Pilot*), Adele Claire (*Mother*), David Clover (*George*), Rita Conde (*Inez*), Tony Cortez (*Emiliano*), Brian Cummings (*Assistant Director*), John Curran (*Chase Cop*), Peter Dane (*Director*), Royal Dano (*Bill Hayes*), Richard Dano (*Theater Manager*), Charlie Dell (*Chili Wagon Man*), Dane Denick (*Bartender*), Bud Ekins (*Chase Cop*), Michael Finn (*Drunk*), Clement St. George (*Reggie*), Haji (*Laura*), Jim Hensley (*Police Sergeant*), Stephen Hartman (*Pilot*), Erik Holland (*Nick*), Donald Knapp (*Cabbie*), Stuart Lancaster (*Charlie*), Marius Mazmanian (*French Waiter*), Duncan McLeod (*Lawyer*), Linda Ann Napolitano (*Hat Check Girl*), Nelson Olmsted (*Judge*), Sage Parker (*Flapper*), Terri Pierce (*Chanteuse*), Garth Pillsbury (*Paul*), Adam Roarke (*Howard Hawks*), Walt Robin (*Maitre d'*), Toni Sawyer (*Paul's Wife*), Estelle Silberkleit (*Candy Francis*), Tommy Silberkleit (*Lab Man*), Paula Sills (*Madeleine*), Dave Silverman (*Pilot*), Anthony Sirico (*Frankie Rio*), Sheila Sisco (*Other Woman*), Joel Stedman (*Bruno*), Harry Woolman (*Very Drunk*), Marty Zagon (*Sid Grauman*).

Chapter Notes

Chapter 1

1. Robert Osborne, "Robert Osborne on Jean Harlow," *Now Playing: A Viewer's Guide to Turner Classic Movies*, March 2011, 3.
2. John Stanley, "The Platinum Sex Symbol," *San Francisco Chronicle*, August 15, 1993, 3.
3. *Ibid.*
4. Betty Beale, "Roz Russell's Coat Barely Covers Her," *Washington Star-News*, November 27, 1974, C-3.
5. James Bacon, "Jean Harlow in 'Comeback,'" *The Hartford Courant*, December 13, 1964, 8F.

Chapter 2

1. Thomas M. Pryor, "Plan Film Story of Jean Harlow," *The New York Times*, May 5, 1954, 38.
2. *Ibid.*
3. Tom Coffey, "Cleo Moore Has It and She Shows It," *Los Angeles Mirror*, November 15, 1952, 15.
4. Mike Connolly, "Mike Connolly ... Another Harlow Hopeful," *Pasadena* (CA) *Independent*, August 8, 1954, 42.
5. Louella Parsons, "Hope Talks Contract with Cantinflas," *The Washington Post and Times Herald*, November 20, 1956.
6. Sheila Graham, "Hollywood: Carroll's Sultry, Too," *The Evening Star* (Washington, D.C.), December 11, 1958, B-14.
7. Murray Schumach, "Wald Finds Many Knew Them When," *The New York Times*, May 21, 1959.
8. Stella Stevens, unpublished interview with Shaun Chang, 2005.
9. Hedda Hopper, "Looking at Hollywood: Lee Remick May Star in Film on Jean Harlow," *Chicago Daily Tribune*, August 1, 1959.
10. Louella Parsons, "Joanne Gets 'Jean Harlow' Bid," *The Washington Post and Times Herald*, March 3, 1960.
11. "Murder Probe of Jean Harlow's Spouse Ended," *The Courier-Journal* (Louisville, KY), October 29, 1960, 16.

Chapter 3

1. Lloyd Shearer, "The Real Jean Harlow Story: Everybody Is Capitalizing on the Blonde Bombshell of the 1930s," *Boston Globe*, November 1, 1964.
2. Irving Shulman, *Harlow, An Intimate Biography* (San Jose: iUniverse, 2001), 1–2.
3. Shearer, "The Real Jean Harlow Story."
4. Shulman, *Harlow, An Intimate Biography*, 30.
5. *Ibid.*, 42.
6. *Ibid.*
7. Paul Gardner, "Television: Les Crane's New Program," *The New York Times*, August 4, 1964.
8. Osborne, "Robert Osborne on Jean Harlow."
9. Harry MacArthur, "The Passing Show: Zinnemann's Method Maintains Peace," *The Evening Star* (Washington, D.C.), August 5, 1964, B-6.
10. *Ibid.*
11. Sheila Graham, "Agent's Story of Jean Harlow," *The Miami News*, January 11, 1965, 14A.
12. *Ibid.*
13. *Ibid.*
14. Sheila Graham, "Friends Unite to Destroy Myth: 'Harlow' Book Called Downright Lie," *The Miami News*, January 12, 1965, 15A.
15. *Ibid.*
16. *Ibid.*
17. Associated Press, "Jean Harlow's Father Sues for $3 Million Over Book," *The New York Times*, November 24, 1964.
18. UPI, "Father Brings Suit Over Book on Jean Harlow," *The Hartford Courant*, November 24, 1964.
19. Associated Press, "$5 Million Damage Suit Filed Over 'Harlow' Book," *The New York Times*, May 1, 1965.
20. Herb Lyon, "Tower Ticker," November 26, 1964.
21. "Dell Denied Injunction to Block Harlow Book," *The New York Times*, September 25, 1964.

Chapter 4

1. Marianne Sinclair, *Hollywood Lolitas: The Nymphet Syndrome in the Movies* (New York: Henry Holt, 1988), 101.
2. Richard Warren Lewis, "Baby Doll Grows Up," *Saturday Evening Post*, November 2, 1963, 64.
3. *Ibid.*

4. Don Alpert, "'Baby Doll' Baker Is a Big Girl Now," *Los Angeles Times*, February 24, 1963.
5. Sheila Graham, "Hollywood," *The Evening Star* (Washington, D.C.), November 8, 1964, D-7.
6. Murray Schumach, "Hollywood Candor: Carroll Baker Defends Her Nudity in Films," *The New York Times*, June 14, 1964.
7. Schumach, "Hollywood Candor."
8. Ivor Davis, "This 'Baby Doll' Is a Survivor," *Chicago Tribune*, August 21, 1983.
9. Lewis, "Baby Doll Grows Up," 65.
10. Ibid.
11. Philip K. Scheuer, "Sylvia Girl of Many Aliases in Sad Saga," *Los Angeles Times*, May 4, 1965.
12. Carroll Baker, *Baby Doll: An Autobiography* (New York: Arbor House, 1983), 257.
13. Donna Rosenthal, "Self-Made Mogul Hangs On: Joseph E. Levine, 82, Is Still Wheeling and Dealing," *Los Angeles Times*, July 5, 1987.
14. Katharine Hamill, "The Supercolossal—Pretty Good—World of Joe Levine," *Fortune*, March 1964, 132.
15. Stanley Penn, "Show Biz Success: Energetic Joe Levine Climbs Quickly to Top Ranks of Film Makers," *The Wall Street Journal*, January 22, 1965, 16.
16. Mark Harris, *Pictures at a Revolution: Five Movies and the Birth of the New Hollywood* (New York: Penguin, 2008), 72.
17. Hamill, "The Supercolossal—Pretty Good—World of Joe Levine," 185.
18. Ibid.
19. Ibid.
20. Edward Dmytryk, "Director's Findings: Good Drama Made for Strong Merchandizing," *Variety*, April 22, 1964, 97.
21. "Levine Spikes 'Harlow' Rumors; Pledges Honest, Accurate Picture," *Motion Picture Exhibitor*, January 1965, 11.
22. Baker, *Baby Doll*, 258.
23. Ibid.
24. "Carroll Baker Signed to Play Jean Harlow," *Los Angeles Times*, September 1, 1964.
25. Peter Bart, "Producers Rush 3 Harlow Films," *The New York Times*, September 1, 1964, 28.
26. John Patrick, "Pose in the Nude? Stella Stevens Doesn't Believe in Hiding Her Assets," *New York Sunday News*, July 4, 1965, 4.
27. "2nd Harlow Sought," *The Desert News*, September 8, 1964, B3.
28. Sheila Graham, "Hollywood: Jayne Could Use Harlow Role," *The Evening Star* (Washington, D.C.), September 9, 1964, E-23.
29. Bill Ornstein, "Electronovision to Make 12 Pix at $7.5 Mil Cost," *The Hollywood Reporter*, January 19, 1965, 4.
30. Ibid.
31. Robert Koehler, "Film Clips: Prints of Darkness," *Los Angeles Times*, March 12, 1995, 21.
32. Leonard J. Leff, "Instant Movies: The Short Unhappy Life of William Sargent's Electronovision (1964–65)," *Journal of Popular Film & Television*, Volume 9, 22.
33. "New Process Praised: Electronovision to Bow with Hamlet," *Hollywood Citizen-News*, September 7, 1964.
34. Leff, "Instant Movies," 22.
35. Patricia Davis, "Instant Movies: Young Irish Inventor of Electronovision Has Big Plans for Process," *Lebanon Daily News*, April 2, 1965, 12.
36. Ron McGrath, "Dynamic Bill Sargent: Hollywood Visionary," *San Gabriel Valley Tribune*, December 20, 1964.

Chapter 5

1. Ronald Gold, "Bloody-Pink 'Harlow' War: Sargent Turns to the Attack," *Variety*, May 5, 1965, 5.
2. Ibid.
3. Nan Robertson, "Joseph E. Levine, a Towering Figure in Moviemaking, Is Dead," *The New York Times*, August 1, 1987, 36.
4. Martin Quigley, Jr., "Harlow vs. Harlow," *Motion Picture Herald*, May 26, 1965, 1.
5. Larry Jonas, "Electronovision Put in H'wood Economic Vise, Sargent Avers," *Film Daily*, March 23, 1965, 5.
6. Ibid.
7. "Electronovision Also Goes 'Harlow,'" *Variety*, January 20, 1965.
8. Sheila Graham, "Hollywood," *The Evening Star* (Washington, D.C.), November 3, 1964, A-9.
9. Graham, "Hollywood," November 8, 1964.
10. Clifford Terry, "Presto—Jean Harlow," *Chicago Tribune*, November 15, 1964.
11. Mike Steen, *Hollywood Speaks! An Oral History* (New York: G.P. Putnam's Sons, 1974), 282.
12. Ibid.
13. Baker, *Baby Doll*, 259.
14. UPI, "Reveal Home Looters Aided by Pal in Café," *Chicago Tribune*, December 16, 1964.
15. "Now Hear This! Harlow Pic to Be in Good Taste—Levine," *The Hollywood Reporter*, December 17, 1964.
16. Penn, "Show Biz Success: Energetic Joe Levine Climbs Quickly to Top Ranks of Film Makers," 1.
17. "Two Harlows—Deluxe and Quickie," *Life*, May 7, 1965, 122.
18. Ibid.
19. Ibid.
20. Marjory Adams, "Joseph E. Levine: The Critics Blast His Films, But Filmgoers Flock to Them," *Boston Globe*, January 19, 1965.
21. "Shulman Tells All—Or Nearly All," *Variety*, January 27, 1965.
22. Adams, "Joseph E. Levine: The Critics Blast His Films."
23. Ibid.
24. Emerson Beauchamp, "The Passing Show: 'Harlow' Screenplay; Book on Marilyn," *The Evening Star* (Washington, D.C.), October 3, 1964, 3.
25. Shearer, "The Real Jean Harlow Story."
26. Dick Kleiner, "Show Beat: 'Harlow' Is Oh, So

Clean a Movie," *Park City Daily News*, January 6, 1965.

27. A.T. McKenna, "*Harlow*'s Bridle, or How Avoiding Sex and Engaging the Competition Can Lead to Failure," *Journal of Popular Film & Television*, Spring 2010, 37.

28. *Ibid.*

29. *Ibid.*, 40.

30. Ronald Gold, "Levine Best Showman Since L.B. Mayer But Sargent Wants to Be Just Plain Bill," *Variety*, April 14, 1965.

31. "Skolsky Sues Bill Sargent for $140,000 on 'Harlow' Script Nix," *Variety*, March 10, 1965.

32. "Skolsky Sues on Harlow Pic Pact," *The Hollywood Reporter*, March 3, 1965.

33. "Skolsky Sues Bill Sargent."

34. George Goodman, Jr., "Alex Segal, Pioneering TV Drama Director," *The New York Times*, August 24, 1977.

35. John Crosby, "Alex Segal Finds a Reason for Hope," *The Washington Post Times Herald*, October 30, 1961.

36. *Ibid.*

37. Stephen Bowie, "An Interview with Shirley Knight," *The Classic TV History Blog*, July 1, 2010, http://classictvhistory.wordpress.com/2010/07/01/an-interview-with-shirley-knight/

38. Hedda Hopper, "Jean Simmons Side-Steps the Frenzy of Stardom," *The Hartford Courant*, May 5, 1963.

39. Hedda Hopper, "Peppard Ankles 'Kalahari' Set," *Los Angeles Times,* May 26, 1965.

40. "Wallace Airs 'Harlow' Producers Views on Juxtaposed Radio Tapes," *Variety*, May 12, 1965.

41. Earl Wilson, "Parents Are Scapegoats for Drinking Youths," *The Milwaukee Sentinel*, September 28, 1964, 19.

42. Bob Thomas, "Rita Hayworth Remains 'Selective' in Film Life," *Toledo Blade*, April 1, 1965.

43. Rex Reed, "Angela Lansbury Lands a Movie All Her Own," *The Evening Star* (Washington, D.C.), June 21, 1970, D-5.

44. Sheila Graham, "Hollywood: Vittorio Gassman Is Italy's Olivier," *The Evening Star* (Washington, D.C.), February 7, 1965, E-2.

45. Kevin Thomas, "Connor—New Matinee Idol?" *Los Angeles Times*, March 10, 1966.

46. Tom Lisanti, *Fantasy Femmes of Sixties Cinema: Interviews with Twenty Actresses from Biker, Beach, and Elvis Movies* (Jefferson, NC: McFarland, 2001), 134.

Chapter 6

1. Gold, "Bloody-Pink 'Harlow' War."

2. Dick Kleiner, "Jean Harlow Back in Pair of Movies," *San Antonio Express/News*, May 9, 1965, 7-H.

3. Diane McBain and Michael Gregg Michaud, *Famous Enough: A Hollywood Memoir* (Duncan, OK: BearManor Media, 2014), 169.

4. Tom Lisanti, *Carol Lynley: Her Film & TV Career in Thrillers, Fantasy & Suspense* (Orlando: BearManor Media, 2020), 69, 70.

5. Dan Jenkins, "The Single-Minded Quest of Carol Lynley," *TV Guide*, August 3, 1963, 28.

6. Louella O. Parsons, "Carol Lynley: Still Young and Foolish," *New York Journal-American*, June 6, 1965.

7. *Ibid.*

8. Tom Lisanti, "From Teen Queen to Scream Queen: The Many Faces of Carol Lynley," *Filmfax*, February/March 1997, 58.

9. Leff, "Instant Movies," 27.

10. Philip K. Scheuer, "Electronovision of 'Harlow,'" *Los Angeles Times*, April 13, 1965.

11. James Westmoreland, "The James Westmoreland Story," *The Official Site of Actor James Westmoreland*, August 3, 2011, https://www.jimwestmoreland.com/in-jims-words/the-james-westmoreland-story/.

12. Dorothy Kilgallen, "The Voice of Broadway," *The News Journal*, March 30, 1965.

13. *Ibid.*

14. *Ibid.*

15. Hedda Hopper, "'Harlow' Shaping Up for May Bow," *Los Angeles Times*, April 10, 1965.

16. Mike Fessier, Jr., "Wheeling and Dealing with Bill Sargent," *Los Angeles Magazine*, July 1965, 66.

17. Leff, "Instant Movies," 26.

18. Alex Freeman, "TV Close-Up," *The Hartford Courant*, June 22, 1965.

19. David Lewin, "What a Fight ... This Battle of THE BOMBSHELL Blondes," *South China Sunday Post-Herald*, June 13, 1965, 14.

20. *Ibid.*

21. Scheuer, "Electronovision of 'Harlow.'"

22. *Ibid.*

23. *Ibid.*

24. Lewin, "What a Fight."

25. Harold Heffernan, "'Harlow' May Change Film Industry," *Asbury Park Evening Press*, May 14, 1965, 25.

26. "A Lot to Learn," *Newsweek*, May 31, 1965, 83.

27. Bob Thomas, "Six Days Shooting: Speedy Technique Used for One 'Harlow' Film," *Toledo Blade*, April 15, 1965.

28. *Ibid.*

29. Harrison Carroll, "Behind the Scenes in Hollywood: Jean Harlow on Two Sets," *The New Tribune*, June 2, 1965, 22.

30. *Ibid.*

31. Rose Pelswick, "A 'Harlow' in 17 Days: What Now, Hollywood?" *New York Journal American*, April 18, 1965, 32.

32. George H. Jackson, "An Actor's Viewpoint," *L.A. Herald Examiner*, May 22, 1965.

33. Thomas, "Six Days Shooting."

34. Herb Michaelson, "Harlow—Part II," *Oakland Tribune*, April 22, 1965, 59.

35. "Two Harlows—Deluxe and Quickie."

36. Gold, "Levine Best Showman Since L.B. Mayer."

37. "Wallace Airs 'Harlow' Producers Views."
38. *Ibid.*
39. *Ibid.*
40. *Ibid.*
41. Harold Heffernan, "Sex Symbol Title, Color Scheme 'Theft' Fires Pair," *San Antonio Express*, April 8, 1965, 7-D.
42. *Ibid.*
43. "Wallace Airs 'Harlow' Producers Views."
44. Gold, "Bloody-Pink 'Harlow' War."
45. Jonas, "Electronovision Put in H'wood Economic Vise."
46. Pelswick, "A 'Harlow' in 17 Days," 32.
47. Gold, "Levine Best Showman Since L.B. Mayer."
48. "Two Harlows—Deluxe and Quickie."
49. *Ibid.*
50. "Electro Prez Explains Why Chex Bounced," *Variety*, April 28, 1965.
51. "'Harlow' Suits Start Flying: Magna vs. Para. for $6.3 Mil; SAG Cancels Electronovision," *The Hollywood Reporter*, May 19, 1965, 4.
52. Ronald Gold, "Says Majors in Wall of Chill," *Variety*, June 9, 1965.
53. "Girls Have Chance at Prize in 'Harlow' Film Contest," *San Antonio Express and News*, May 1, 1965, 11.

Chapter 7

1. "Levine's Own Queensberry Credo," *Variety*, May 5, 1965.
2. Peter Bart, "All Is Not Glitter for This Glamour Girl," *The New York Times*, May 22, 1966.
3. Sheila Graham, "Hollywood: End of Dream for Carroll," *The Evening Star* (Washington, D.C.), August 7, 1969, D-17.
4. Sheila Graham, "Hollywood: Cary Grant Calls a Sick Friend," *The Evening Star* (Washington, D.C.), March 31, 1965, C-15.
5. McKenna, "*Harlow*'s Bridle, or How Avoiding Sex and Engaging the Competition Can Lead to Failure," 39.
6. "Levine Spikes 'Harlow' Rumors…," *Motion Picture Exhibitor*, January 1965, 11.
7. Jay Jorgensen, *Edith Head: The Fifty-Year Career of Hollywood's Greatest Costume Designer* (Philadelphia: Running Press; New York: LifeTime Media, 2010).
8. Lisanti, *Fantasy Femmes of Sixties Cinema*, 150, 151.
9. *Ibid.*
10. Art Seidenbaum, "With Wet Cement, White Cadillac, a Film Is Launched: Hollywood Recreates Era of Jean Harlow," *Boston Globe*, March 7, 1965.
11. "Levine Spikes 'Harlow' Rumors…," *Motion Picture Exhibitor*, January 1965, 11.
12. Philip K. Scheuer, "Baker in Bow as Harlow," *Los Angeles Times*, February 26, 1965.
13. *Ibid.*
14. Art Seidenbaum, "With Wet Cement, White Cadillac, a Film Is Launched."

15. William E. Sarmento, "Show Time: Two Harlow Films in Race for the Screen," *Lowell Sunday*, April 18, 1965, 22.
16. Hedda Hopper, "Looking at Hollywood: Arnaz to Do Film on Population Boom," *Chicago Tribune*, April 12, 1965.
17. Hedda Hopper, "Hollywood: Jane Fonda Excited About Newest Offer," *The Hartford Courant*, February 25, 1965.
18. James Bacon, "Carroll Baker: Hollywood's Leading Sexpot a Delightful Person at Home," *The Hartford Courant*, June 21, 1964.
19. Penn, "Show Biz Success: Energetic Joe Levine Climbs Quickly to Top."
20. Rex Reed, "'Baby Doll' Heals Her Hollywood Wounds," *The Washington Post*, February 14, 1971.
21. *Ibid.*
22. Lewin, "What a Fight."
23. *Ibid.*
24. Earl Wilson, "Joe Levine Rivals Mesta," *Los Angeles Herald Examiner*, April 15, 1965.
25. John L. Scott, "Hollywood Calendar: 'King Kong' Connors a Rib-Cracker," *Los Angeles Times*, April 11, 1965.
26. Don Carle Gillette, "Trade Views," *The Hollywood Reporter*, April 13, 1965.
27. Judith Crist, "The Platinum Bomb," *New York Herald Tribune*, August 1, 1964, 31.
28. Carroll, "Jean Harlow on Two Sets."
29. Bob Thomas, "Visit to Harlow Joe Levine Edition," *The Montreal Gazette*, April 27, 1965, 30.
30. *Ibid.*
31. Bob Thomas, "Meanwhile Back on the 'Harlow' Set," *New York Journal American*, April 24, 1965, 8.
32. Baker, *Baby Doll*, 278.
33. McKenna, "*Harlow*'s Bridle, or How Avoiding Sex and Engaging the Competition Can Lead to Failure," 41.
34. Dorothy Kilgallen, "Dorothy Kilgallen's Broadway Notebook," *Sarasota Journal*, May 6, 1965, 26.
35. Dick Kleiner, "All Not Rivalry Over 'Harlow': Film No. 2 Regrets No. 1's Troubles," *Racine Sunday Bulletin*, June 6, 1965, 7B.
36. *Ibid.*
37. Philip K. Scheuer, "Raf Vallone and Image He Wrought," *Los Angeles Times*, March 23, 1965.
38. *Ibid.*
39. Associated Press, "Filmland Relives Wild 30s with 'Jean Harlow' Party," *New York World-Telegram and Sun*, May 24, 1965.
40. Bob Thomas, "Rock Hudson Escapes Bedroom Farces," *The Sun*, June 10, 1965, 7-B.
41. Hedda Hopper, "Looking at Hollywood: Ross Hunter Wants Katharine Hepburn for Film, 'A Very Rich Woman,'" *The Hartford Courant*, May 15, 1965.
42. Alex Freeman, "TV Close-Up: Actress Writing a 'Secret' Book, *The Hartford Courant*, July 6, 1965.
43. Rob Edelman and Audrey E. Kupferberg,

Angela Lansbury: A Life on Stage and Screen (Secaucus, NJ: Carol Pub. Group, 1996).

44. McKenna, "*Harlow*'s Bridle, or How Avoiding Sex and Engaging the Competition Can Lead to Failure," 37.

Chapter 8

1. Leff, "Instant Movies," 27.
2. Emerson Beauchamp, "'Harlow's' Barely Even a Movie," *The Evening Star* (Washington, D.C.), June 5, 1965, 6.
3. "National Box Office Survey," *Variety*, May 19, 1965, 8.
4. "Electrono Pace of 'Harlow' So-So," *Variety*, May 26, 1965, 9.

Chapter 9

1. Sheila Graham, "Carol Lynley Bares Truth." *New York World-Telegram & Sun*, July 1, 1965.
2. Abel Green, "Levine's Luxury Lair Underscores Upbeat," *Variety*, July 14, 1965, 11.
3. "…They Went!," *Variety*, June 28, 1965.
4. "Levine's Scotch-Hop to Chicago; Lively Bally-Rally for 'Harlow,'" *Variety*, June 23, 1965, 19
5. *Ibid.*
6. *Ibid.*
7. Earl Wilson, "It's Controversy Time," *Beaver County Times*, July 20, 1965, B-4.
8. Philip J. Scheuer, "'Harlow' Story Told Again—Less Cheaply," *Los Angeles Times*, August 15, 1965.
9. Harry MacArthur, "The Passing Show: It's Time Again to Think of That Best Film List," *The Evening Star* (Washington, D.C.), December 12, 1965, J-5.
10. "National Box Office Survey," *Variety*, June 30, 1965, 7.
11. "'Harlow' Rousing $23,000 in Philly," *Variety*, June 30, 1965, 10.
12. "Summer Estimates for Paramount," *Variety*, July 7, 1965, 7.

Chapter 10

1. Lois Benjamin, "Have You Heard?" *Ladies' Home Journal*. August 1965, 18.
2. Scheuer, "'Harlow' Story Told Again."
3. Stan Maays, "Meet Carol Lynley: A Living Doll," *The Abilene Reporter News*, September 26, 1968.
4. Ginger Rogers, *Ginger: My Story* (New York: HarperCollins, 1991), 350.
5. *The Evening Star* (Washington, D.C.), September 21, 1975, H-12.
6. Anthony Cassa, "Forgotten 'Baby Doll'— Carroll Baker," *Hollywood Studio Magazine*, October 1981, 28.
7. Trav SD, "Dueling Harlows: Featuring the Battle of the Carol(e)s," *Travalanche*, February 25, 2015, https://travsd.wordpress.com/2015/02/25/dueling-harlows-featuring-the-battle-of-the-carols/,
8. Sheila Graham, "Hollywood: He's Too Young to Be a Father," *The Evening Star* (Washington, D.C.), November 16, 1965, C-7.
9. Dorothy Manners, "Sean Connery and Carol [sic] Baker Selected as Movie Favorites," *Anderson Daily Bulletin*, December 24, 1965, 13.
10. "12 Young Actresses on Deb Star Ball," *The Hartford Courant*, January 2, 1966.
11. Fessier, Jr., "Wheeling and Dealing with Bill Sargent," 32.
12. *Ibid.*, 66.
13. *Ibid.*
14. Graham, "Carol Lynley Bares Truth."
15. "$25-Mil. Antitrust Suit Filed by Bill Sargent," *Boxoffice*, June 14, 1965.
16. *Ibid.*
17. *Ibid.*
18. *Ibid.*
19. *Ibid.*
20. Gold, "Says Majors in Wall of Chill."
21. *Ibid.*
22. *Ibid.*
23. Peter Bart, "Year-Old Electronovision Film Company Closes, but Its President Promises a Comeback," *The New York Times*, July 23, 1965.
24. "Other Side of Coin: Naify Owed by Electronovision, Says Criss in Crossing Sargent Statement," *Variety*, June 7, 1965, 15.
25. Bart, "Year-Old Electronovision Film Company Closes."
26. *Ibid.*
27. Fessier, Jr., "Wheeling and Dealing with Bill Sargent," 32.
28. "Par & Embassy in Electrono Reply," *Variety*, September 29, 1965, 18.
29. *Ibid.*
30. "Sargent's 'Harlow' Sold Overseas as 'Platinum Blonde,'" *Variety*, February 28, 1966, 3.
31. Leff, "Instant Movies," 28.
32. Alfred Friendly, Jr., "An American in Rome: What Ever Happened to Baby Doll?" *The New York Times*, June 29, 1969.
33. Reed, "'Baby Doll' Heals Her Hollywood Wounds."
34. "Reasoning on Carroll Baker Future," *Variety*, September 22, 1965, 7.
35. "Call Carroll Baker Back to Paramount in Midst Stage Run," *Variety*, April 20, 1966, 22.
36. Baker, *Baby Doll*, 279.

Chapter 11

1. Mark Rozzo, *Everybody Thought We Were Crazy: Dennis Hopper, Brooke Hayward and 1960s Los Angeles* (New York: Ecco, 2022), 299, 300.
2. "Producer of 'Beard' Carries Fight to Two-Court Front." *The Van Nuys News*, February 2, 1968.
3. Frances Herridge, "Billie Dixon as 'Harlow'

Talks About 'The Beard,'" *New York Post*, December 13, 1967, 35.

4. Catherine Stott, "Intercourse on Stage: 'Could Be Done if the Two Were Already Partners.' Billie Dixon Talking to Catherine Stott," *The Guardian* (London), March 6, 1970, 8.

5. Rozzo, *Everybody Thought We Were Crazy*, 300.

6. UPI, "Sex Play Is Given Green Light in L.A." *The Times* (San Mateo, CA), January 27, 1968.

7. Barbara Bladen, "The Marquee: Actress Not Afraid to Speak Out," *The Times* (San Mateo, CA), July 25, 1968, 17.

8. Herridge, "Billie Dixon as 'Harlow.'"

9. Ed Wilcox, "'The Beard' Takes the Fuzz on the Chin," *Sunday News* (New York), May 5, 1968.

10. Clive Barnes, "Theatre: Two-Character 'The Beard': Billie Dixon and Bright in McClure's Play," *The New York Times*, October 25, 1967, 40.

11. Daphne Kraft, "Pamela Tiffin No Harlow: Escapes the Shadow," *Newark Evening News*, October 9, 1966.

12. Robert Wahls, "Footlight: Over-Stimulated Pam," *New York Daily News*, October 16, 1966.

13. Emerson Beauchamp, "The Passing Show: Dual Biography Is Nothing New," *The Evening Star* (Washington, D.C.), February 2, 1968, B-8.

14. Harold Heffernan, "The Passing Show: Film About Judy Is a Long Shot," *The Evening Star* (Washington, D.C.), July 21, 1969, B-6.

15. Stephen Farber, "Whose Life Is It Anyway?" *American Film*, May 1, 1982, 39.

16. Matt Evans, "Burn All the Liars," *The Morning News*, www.themorningnews.org/article/burn-all-the-liars, September 2022.

17. Larry Buchanan, *It Came from Hunger! Tales of a Cinema Schlockmeister* (Jefferson, NC: McFarland, 1996), 158.

18. Eric Gerber, "Film Tells How Hughes Mixed Hell with Angels," *The Houston Post*, May 26, 1977, 18B.

19. Jeff Millar, "'Hughes and Harlow' Brief Microcosm of Life," *Houston Chronicle*, May 25, 1977, Section 3, 8.

20. Gerber, "Film Tells How Hughes Mixed Hell with Angels."

21. "Film About Harlow and Hughes Start Team Newcomers Holchak, Bloom," *Boxoffice*, June 20, 1977.

22. Joel Kotkin, "Howard Hughes: Making Movies of the Mystery Man," *The Washington Post*, March 17, 1977.

23. *Ibid*.

24. *Ibid*.

25. Buchanan, *It Came from Hunger!*, 142.

26. Gerber, "Film Tells How Hughes Mixed Hell with Angels."

27. Millar, "'Hughes and Harlow' Brief Microcosm of Life."

28. Buchanan, *It Came from Hunger!*, 159.

29. *Ibid.*, 158.

30. *Ibid.*

31. John Wilson, "Man with a Trailer: Impresario of the Movie Teaser," *Los Angeles Times*, June 20, 1977, E10.

32. *Ibid.*

33. *Ibid.*

34. Buchanan, *It Came from Hunger*, 160.

35. *Ibid.*

36. Bruce Fessier, "Howard Hughes Author to Discuss Sex and Power," *Palm Springs Desert Sun*, January 10, 2019.

Biographies—Post-Harlows

1. "Man-Shark Fight 'Indecent' But He's Sure It's Big B. O.," *Variety*, December 24, 1975.

2. Clarke Taylor, "All-Electronics Entrepreneur," *Los Angeles Times*, December 21, 1979.

3. Fessier, Jr., "Wheeling and Dealing with Bill Sargent," 34.

4. Lou Gaul, "'Harry Filmed by New Technique," *Bucks County Courier Times*, September 25, 1975.

5. Dick Griffin, "Levine: Huckster with Heart," *Los Angeles Times*, June 21, 1966.

6. Rosenthal, "Self-Made Mogul Hangs On."

7. Sam Kashner, "The Graduate: Here's to You, Mr. Nichols," *Vanity Fair's Tales of Hollywood*, Graydon Carter, ed. (New York: Penguin Group, 2008), 170.

8. "Dialogue on Film: Joseph E. Levine," *American Film*, September 1979, 41.

9. Norma Lee Browning, "Levine's Gamble on Mike Nichols Pays Off with 'Graduate,'" *Chicago Tribune*, February 25, 1968.

10. "Dialogue on Film: Joseph E. Levine," 39.

11. Lee Grant, "Joe Levine's Path to 'Bridge,'" *Los Angeles Times*, January 24, 1977.

12. Bridget Byrne, "Jolting Joe Levine," *Women's Wear Daily*, November 31, 1981.

13. Buchanan, *It Came from Hunger!*, 161.

14. *Ibid.*, 179.

15. Tom Donnelly, "'Mice and Men and Carol Lynley, With Homage to Harlow," *The Washington Post*, March 12, 1975, B11.

16. Clive Barnes, "The Stage: Quality 'Takeover' Trend," *The New York Times*, October 9, 1975.

17. Ivor Davis, "This 'Baby Doll' Is a Survivor," *Chicago Tribune*, August 21, 1983.

18. Friendly, Jr., "An American in Rome."

19. Roderick Mann, "The Return of a Grown 'Baby Doll,'" *Los Angeles Times*, June 27, 1982.

20. *Ibid.*

21. Davis, "This 'Baby Doll' Is a Survivor."

22. Lisanti, "From Teen Queen to Scream Queen," 70.

Bibliography

"Actors Guild Ends Film Firm Contract." *Los Angeles Times*, May 19, 1965, p. A8.

Adams, Marjory. "Book of the Day: Biographer Stands Up the Real Jean Harlow." *Boston Globe*, July 8, 1964.

———. "Joseph E. Levine: The Critics Blast His Films, But Filmgoers Flock to Them." *Boston Globe*, January 19, 1965.

Alpert, Don. "'Baby Doll' Baker Is a Big Girl Now." *Los Angeles Times*, February 24, 1963.

"Another 'Going-Together' Party but Par-Embassy Still Just Friends." *Variety*, December 2, 1964.

Archer, Eugene. "Novel by Harlow to Be Published." *The New York Times*, May 29, 1965.

Ashford, Gerald. "Not Technically Proficient, 'Harlow' Film Is Great Drama." *San Antonio Express/News*, May 15, 1965, p. 15-A.

Associated Press. "Clears Set: She Wears Only a Blush in Film Role." *Los Angeles Times*, June 27, 1963.

———. "Filmland Relives Wild 30s with 'Jean Harlow' Party." *New York World-Telegram and Sun*, May 24, 1965.

———. "$5 Million Damage Suit Filed Over 'Harlow' Book." *The New York Times*, May 1, 1965.

———. "Jean Harlow's Father Sues for $3 Million Over Book." *The New York Times*, November 24, 1964.

Backes, Clarus. "Levine Film of Harlow Has Flash—Lots of It." *Chicago Tribune*, June 26, 1965, p. 16.

Bacon, James. "Carroll Baker: Hollywood's Leading Sexpot a Delightful Person at Home." *The Hartford Courant*, June 21, 1964.

———. "Jean Harlow in 'Comeback.'" *The Hartford Courant*, December 13, 1964, p. 8F.

Bailey-Goldschmidt, Janice, Mary C. Kalfatovic, and Martin R. Kalfatovic. "'I Remember It Well': Paul Bern, Jean Harlow, and the Negotiation of Information." *Journal of Popular Culture* 30, no. 3 (Winter 1996).

Baker, Carroll. *Baby Doll: An Autobiography*. New York: Arbor House, 1983.

Barnes, Clive. "The Stage: Quality 'Takeover' Trend." *The New York Times*, October 9, 1975.

———. "Theatre: Two-Character 'The Beard': Billie Dixon and Bright in McClure's Play." *The New York Times*, October 25, 1967, p. 40.

Bart, Peter. "All Is Not Glitter for This Glamour Girl." *The New York Times*, May 22, 1966.

———. "Bishop Proposes New Movie Code." *The New York Times*, March 4, 1965, p. 36.

———. "Film No-How: A Big Scheme Went Blooey." *Des Moines Sunday Register*, August 22, 1965, p. 3-TV.

———. "Films on Harlow Take New Twists." *The New York Times*, October 21, 1964.

———. "How to Try Without Really Succeeding." *The New York Times*, August 1, 1965, p. X9.

———. "Producers Rush 3 Harlow Films." *The New York Times*, September 1, 1964, p. 28.

———. "Year-Old Electronovision Film Company Closes, but Its President Promises a Comeback." *The New York Times*, July 23, 1965, p. 17.

Beale, Betty. "Roz Russell's Coat Barely Covers Her." *Washington Star-News*, November 27, 1974, p. C-3.

Beauchamp, Emerson. "'Harlow's' Barely Even a Movie." *The Evening Star* (Washington, D.C.), June 5, 1965, p. 6.

———. "The Passing Show: 'Harlow' Screenplay; Book on Marilyn." *The Evening Star* (Washington, D.C.), October 3, 1964, p. 3.

———. "The Passing Show: Dual Biography Is Nothing New." *The Evening Star* (Washington, D.C.), February 2, 1968, p. B-8.

———. "The Passing Show: Which Blonde Has the Bombshell?" *The Evening Star* (Washington, D.C.), April 28, 1965, p. B-14.

Beck, Marilyn. "That's Showbiz: Carol Lynley Moves to Quiet Beach Spot." *The Hartford Courant*, January 5, 1968.

Behlmer, Rudy, and Tony Thomas. *Hollywood's Hollywood: The Movies About the Movies*. Secaucus: Citadel Press, 1975.

Benjamin, Lois. "Have You Heard?" *Ladies' Home Journal*, August 1965, p. 18.

"Bill Sargent." [Obituary]. *Variety*, November 3, 2003.

"Bill Sargent Closes Electronovision HQ But Vows to Return." *The Hollywood Reporter*, July 22, 1965.

"Bill Sargent's 'Harlow' Explosive Life of a Blonde Bombshell!" *Movies Illustrated*, June 1965, p.18–23.

Bladen, Barbara. "The Marquee: Actress Not Afraid to Speak Out." *The Times* (San Mateo, CA), July 25, 1968, p.17.

Bowie, Stephen. "An Interview with Shirley Knight." *The Classic TV History Blog*, July 1, 2010. http://classictvhistory.wordpress.com/2010/07/01/an-interview-with-shirley-knight/.
Brookhauser, Frank. "Man About Town: Happy Tour for 'Harlow' Girl." *The Sunday Bulletin*, May 2, 1965, p. 8.
Browning, Norma Lee. "Levine's Gamble on Mike Nichols Pays Off with 'Graduate.'" *Chicago Tribune*, February 25, 1968.
Buchanan, Larry. *It Came from Hunger! Tales of a Cinema Schlockmeister*. Jefferson, NC: McFarland, 1996.
"Bunking a Legend." *Time*, July 23, 1965.
Byrne, Bridget. "Jolting Joe Levine." *Women's Wear Daily*, November 31, 1981.
_____. "No Lark for the Shark." *L.A. Herald-Examiner*, December 9, 1975.
"Call Carroll Baker Back to Paramount in Midst Stage Run." *Variety*, April 20, 1966, p. 22.
Carroll, Harrison. "Behind the Scenes in Hollywood: Jean Harlow on Two Sets." *The News Tribune*, June 2, 1965.
Carroll, Kathleen. "Film Biog of Harlow Is Pretty Dull Fare." *New York Daily News*, May 15, 1965.
"Carroll Baker." *Glamour Girls of the Silver Screen*. http://www.glamourgirlsofthesilverscreen.com/show/18/Carroll+Baker/index.html.
"Carroll Baker Back at Par but Says, 'You Owe Me for the Idle Year.'" *Variety*, June 8, 1966, p. 2.
"Carroll Baker Home Robbed." *Los Angeles Times*, December 12, 1964.
"Carroll Baker: Is She Par Star?" *Variety*, December 29, 1965, p. 4.
"Carroll Baker Signed to Play Jean Harlow," *Los Angeles Times*, September 1, 1964.
Cassa, Anthony. "Forgotten 'Baby Doll'—Carroll Baker." *Hollywood Studio Magazine*, October 1981, pp. 28–29.
"Clarifying the Harlows." *The Progress-Index*, May 24, 1965, p. 4.
Clemeni, Marsha. "World of Women: Harlow Waves Sway Hairdos." *Nashua Telegraph*, July 2, 1965, p. 6.
Coe, Richard L. "One on the Aisle: 'Hamlet' Could Blaze a Trail." *The Washington Post*, September 18, 1964.
_____. "'Rain' Girl Is All Wet." *The Washington Post*, August 3, 1957.
Coffey, Tom. "Cleo Moore Has It and She Shows It." *Los Angeles Mirror*, November 15, 1952, p. 15.
Cohn, Al. "Film About Blonde Bombshell Lands in City with a Dull Thud." *Newsday*, May 17, 1965.
"Columbia Drops Tentative Plans for 'Harlow' Film." *Los Angeles Times*, September 12, 1964.
"Competing Films Re-Enact Jean Harlow's Life." *The Logansport Press*, May 20, 1965, p. 20.
Connolly, Mike. "Mike Connolly ... Another Harlow Hopeful." *Pasadena (CA) Independent*, August 8, 1954, p. 42.
Crist, Judith. "The Platinum Bomb." *New York Herald Tribune*, August 1, 1965, p. 31.
Crosby, John. "Alex Segal Finds a Reason for Hope." *The Washington Post Times Herald*, October 30, 1961.
Crowther, Bosley. "Anthony Dexter Is Valentino in Film Version of Actor's Life Appearing at the Astor." *The New York Times*, April 20, 1951.
_____. "Sensational Sob Stories on Screen." *The New York Times*, July 25, 1965.
Davis, Ivor. "This 'Baby Doll' Is a Survivor." *Chicago Tribune*, August 21, 1983.
Davis, Patricia. "Instant Movies: Young Irish Inventor of Electronovision Has Big Plans for Process." *Lebanon Daily News*, April 2, 1965, p. 12.
"Dell Denied Injunction to Block Harlow Book." *The New York Times*, September 25, 1964.
"Dialogue on Film: Joseph E. Levine." *American Film*, September 1979, pp. 39–47.
Dmytryk, Edward. "Director's Findings: Good Drama Made for Strong Merchandizing." *Variety*, April 22, 1964, p. 97.
Donnelly, Tom. "'Mice and Men' and Carol Lynley, with Homage to Harlow." *The Washington Post*, March 12, 1975, p. B11.
Edelman, Rob, and Audrey E. Kupferberg. *Angela Lansbury: A Life on Stage and Screen*. New York: Carol Pub. Group, 1996.
Edwards, Nadine M. "First Version Now Out: Sargent's 'Harlow' Reflects Hastiness." *Citizen-News*, May 15, 1965.
"Electro Prez Explains Why Chex Bounced." *Variety*, April 28, 1965.
"Electrono Pace of 'Harlow' So-So." *Variety*, May 26, 1965, p. 9.
"Electronovision 'Harlow' Has Arizona Premiere in Yuma." *The Sun*, June 13, 1965.
"Electronovision Also Goes 'Harlow.'" *Variety*, January 20, 1965.
"Electronovision Has Ferrer for 'Harlow.'" *The Hollywood Reporter*, February 25, 1965.
"Electronovision—How It Works." *The Film Daily*, August 10, 1964.
"Electronovision vs. Joe Levine's 'Harlow.'" *Variety*, February 3, 1965.
"Electronovision's WB Deal 'Fades.'" *Variety*, July 20, 1965.
Eleni. "Down All the Years (And Don't Gasp)." *The Washington Star*, May 17, 1977.
"Embassy Replies to Baker Suit." *Variety*, September 1, 1965, p. 4.
Engels, J.A. "Carol Lynley: 30 and Star." *Boca Raton News*, May 25, 1972, p. 6B.
Esterow, Milton. "Harlow, An Intimate Biography." [Review]. *The New York Times*, July 11, 1964, p. 23.
Evans, Matt. "Burn All the Liars." *The Morning News*, www.themorningnews.org/article/burn-all-the-liars, September 2022.
Eyles, Allen. "*Harlow*: Allen Eyles Finds It a Superficial Portrait..." *Films and Filming*, August 1965.
Farber, Stephen. "Whose Life Is It Anyway?" *American Film*, May 1, 1982, pp. 39–41.
Fessier, Bruce. "Howard Hughes Author to Discuss

Sex and Power." *Palm Springs Desert Sun,* January 10, 2019.

Fessier, Mike, Jr. "Wheeling and Dealing with Bill Sargent." *Los Angeles Magazine,* July 1965, pp. 32, 34, 35, 66.

"Film About Harlow and Hughes Start Team Newcomers Holchak, Bloom." *Boxoffice,* June 20,1977.

Flatley, Guy. "Stella Stevens: Toujours 26." *The New York Times,* January 28, 1968, p. D15.

Foster, Frank H., and Robert L. Shook. *Patents, Copyrights & Trademarks.* Hoboken: John Wiley & Sons, 1989.

Foster, James. "Harlowicious Girls Look Jeanuine." *Rocky Mountain News,* April 21, 1965.

Frederick, Robert B. "Electronovision-ary Sargent: From Classicism of 'Hamlet' to Screaming Rock 'n' Rollers." *Variety,* November 18, 1964, p. 4.

Freeman, Alex. "Closeups on TV." *The Arizona Republic,* May 2, 1965, p. C-21.

_____. "TV Close-Up: Actress Writing a 'Secret' Book." *The Hartford Courant,* July 6, 1965, p. 27.

_____. "TV Close-Up: Glamour Girl Wants Peasant Role." *The Hartford Courant,* March 11, 1965, p. 27.

_____. "TV Close-Up: Sinatra Leaves Gotham, Two Models." *The Hartford Courant,* June 22, 1965, p. 23.

Friendly, Alfred, Jr. "An American in Rome: What Ever Happened to Baby Doll?" *The New York Times,* June 29, 1969.

Gaghan, Jerry. "Blonde Lovelies." *Philadelphia Daily News,* April 28, 1965, p. 41.

Gardner, Paul. "Television: Les Crane's New Program." *The New York Times,* August 4, 1964.

Gaul, Lou. "'Harry' Filmed by New Technique." *Bucks County Courier Times,* September 25, 1975.

Gerber, Eric. "Film Tells How Hughes Mixed Hell with Angels." *The Houston Post,* May 26, 1977, p. 18B.

Gillette, Don Carle. "Trade Views." *The Hollywood Reporter,* April 13, 1965.

"Girls Have Chance at Prize in 'Harlow' Film Contest." *San Antonio Express and News,* May 1, 1965, p. 11.

Gold, Ronald. "Bloody-Pink 'Harlow' War: Sargent Turns to the Attack." *Variety,* May 5, 1965, pp. 5, 24.

_____. "Levine Best Showman Since L.B. Mayer But Sargent Wants to Be Just Plain Bill." *Variety,* April 14, 1965.

_____. "Says Majors in Wall of Chill." *Variety,* June 9, 1965.

Goodman, George, Jr. "Alex Segal, Pioneering TV Drama Director." *The New York Times,* August 24, 1977.

Graham, Sheila. "Agent's Story of Jean Harlow." *The Miami News,* January 11, 1965, p. 14A.

_____. "Burton Cast in Film with Old Flame." *The Miami News,* October 7, 1964, p. 20A.

_____. "Carol Lynley Bares Truth." *New York World-Telegram & Sun,* July 1, 1965.

_____. "Cukor Set to Direct Paul Anka in 'Idol.'" *Hollywood Citizen-News,* January 14, 1965.

_____. "Friends Unite to Destroy Myth: 'Harlow' Book Called Downright Lie." *The Miami News,* January 12, 1965, p. 15A.

_____. "Hollywood: Baker-Garfein: Still Status Quo." *The Evening Star* (Washington, D.C.), October 9, 1967, p. D-8.

_____. "Hollywood: Carroll's Sultry, Too." *The Evening Star* (Washington, D.C.), December 11, 1958, p. B-14.

_____. "Hollywood: Cary Grant Calls a Sick Friend." *The Evening Star* (Washington, D.C.), March 31, 1965, p. C-15.

_____. "Hollywood: End of Dream for Carroll." *The Evening Star* (Washington, D.C.), August 7, 1969, p. D-17.

_____. "Hollywood: Fonda Still Young at 60." *The Evening Star* (Washington, D.C.), May 15, 1965, p. 6.

_____. "Hollywood: He's Too Young to Be a Father." *The Evening Star* (Washington, D.C.), November 16, 1965, p. C-7.

_____. "Hollywood: Jane Fonda Gets Nice Round Sum." *The Evening Star* (Washington, D.C.), October 10, 1966, p. C-7.

_____. "Hollywood: Jayne Could Use Harlow Role." *The Evening Star* (Washington, D.C.), September 9, 1964, p. E-23.

_____. "Hollywood: Vittorio Gassman Is Italy's Olivier." *The Evening Star* (Washington, D.C.), February 7, 1965, E-2.

_____. "Hollywood." *The Evening Star* (Washington, D.C.), November 3, 1964, p. A-9.

_____. "Hollywood." *The Evening Star* (Washington, D.C.). November 8, 1964, p. D-7.

Grant, Lee. "Joe Levine's Path to 'Bridge.'" *Los Angeles Times,* January 24, 1977.

Green, Abel. "Levine's Luxury Lair Underscores Upbeat." *Variety,* July 14, 1965.

Griffin, Dick. "Levine: Huckster with Heart." *Los Angeles Times,* June 21, 1966.

Haber, Joyce. "Joe Levine: Call Him Flamboyant." *Los Angeles Times,* May 13, 1968.

Hamill, Katharine. "The Supercolossal—Pretty Good—World of Joe Levine." *Fortune,* March 1964, pp. 130–133, 178, 180, 185.

"Harlow." [Review] *Christian Science Monitor,* July 30, 1965.

_____ [Review] *Cue,* May 29, 1965.

_____ [Review] *Film Quarterly* 19, no. 1, Autumn 1965, p. 62.

_____ [Review]. *The New York Daily News,* July 22, 1965, p. 73.

_____ [Review] *Variety,* May 11, 1965.

_____ [Review] *Variety,* June 23, 1965.

"Harlow Director 'Knew Her When.'" *Boston Globe,* June 20, 1965.

"'Harlow Gals' Here Today." *The Salt Lake Tribune,* April 15, 1965, p. A 12.

"'Harlow' Rousing $23,000 in Philly." *Variety,* June 30, 1965, p. 10.

"'Harlow' Suits Start Flying: Magna vs. Para. For

$6.3 Mil; SAG Cancels Electronovision." *The Hollywood Reporter,* May 19, 1965, pp. 1, 4.

"Harlow Waves Sway Hairdos." *Nashua Telegraph,* July 2, 1965, p. 6.

"Harlow's 2 Films." *The Morning Herald,* May 24, 1965, p. 4.

Harmetz, Aljean. "Innocent Aboard with Joe Levine." *Los Angeles Times,* December 6, 1964.

_____. "Master Promoter—His Fate Is His Fortune." *Los Angeles Times,* September 21, 1975, pp. 1, 34, 36, 38, 42.

Harris, Mark. *Pictures at a Revolution: Five Movies and the Birth of a New Hollywood.* New York: Penguin, 2008.

Heffernan, Harold. "'Harlow' May Change Film Industry." *Asbury Park Evening Press,* May 14, 1965, p. 25.

_____. "The Passing Show: Film About Judy Is a Long Shot." *The Evening Star* (Washington, D.C.), July 21, 1969, p. B-6.

_____. "Sex-Symbol Title, Color Scheme 'Theft' Fires Pair." *San Antonio Express,* April 8, 1965, p. 7-D.

Herridge, Frances. "Billie Dixon as 'Harlow' Talks About 'The Beard.'" *New York Post,* December 13, 1967, p. 35.

Hodgens, R.M.. "Harlow." [Review] *Film Quarterly,* vol. 19, no. 1, Autumn 1965, p. 61.

Holston, Kim. *Starlet: Biographies, Filmographies, TV Credits and Photos of 54 Famous and Not So Famous Leading Ladies of the Sixties.* Jefferson, NC: McFarland, 1988.

Hopper, Hedda. "'Any Wednesday' Waits on Frankie." *Los Angeles Times,* April 12, 1965, p. D2.

_____. "'Harlow' Shaping Up for May Bow." *Los Angeles Times,* April 10, 1965.

_____. "Hollywood: Jane Fonda Excited About Newest Offer." *The Hartford Courant,* April 12, 1965, p. 10.

_____. "Jean Simmons Side-Steps the Frenzy of Stardom." *The Hartford Courant,* May 5, 1963.

_____. "Looking at Hollywood: 'Baby Doll' to Play Film Jean Harlow." *Chicago Tribune,* November 4, 1963.

_____. "Looking at Hollywood: Arnaz to Do Film on Population Boom." *Chicago Tribune,* February 26, 1965, p. B13.

_____. "Looking at Hollywood: Lee Remick May Star in Film on Jean Harlow." *Chicago Daily Tribune,* August 1, 1959.

_____. "Looking at Hollywood: Ross Hunter Wants Katharine Hepburn for Film, 'A Very Rich Woman.'" *Chicago Tribune,* May 15, 1965.

_____. "Looking at Hollywood: Two Take Sordid View of Monroe, Harlow." *Chicago Tribune,* July 3, 1964, p. B3.

_____. "Marilyn to Star in Jean Harlow Film." *Los Angeles Times,* June 4, 1956.

_____. "Peppard Ankles 'Kalahari' Set." *Los Angeles Times,* May 26, 1965.

Houser John G. "'Harlow' Lusty and Busty." *L.A. Herald-Examiner,* May 13, 1965.

"Hughes and Harlow Opening." *The Hollywood Reporter,* May 11, 1977, p. 17.

"Hughes, Harlow Story: Crews Film Movie Segments Here." *Redlands Daily Facts,* January 29, 1977, p. 3.

"In Glitter of 30s—A Harlow." *New York Journal American,* July 13, 1965.

Irvin, Richard. *Judy Garland: The Movie That Might Have Been.* BearManor Media, 2023.

Jackson, George H. "An Actor's Viewpoint." *L.A. Herald Examiner,* May 22, 1965.

"The Jaws of Avarice." *Wall Street Journal,* December 5, 1975.

Jenkins, Dan. "The Single-Minded Quest of Carol Lynley." *TV Guide,* August 3, 1963, pp. 26–28.

Jonas, Larry. "Electronovision Put in H'wood Economic Vise, Sargent Avers." *The Film Daily,* March 23, 1965, pp. 1, 5.

Jorgensen, Jay. *Edith Head: The Fifty-Year Career of Hollywood's Greatest Costume Designer.* Philadelphia: Running Press, New York: LifeTime Media, 2010.

Kashner, Sam. "The Graduate: Here's to You, Mr. Nichols." *Vanity Fair's Tales of Hollywood.* Graydon Carter, ed. New York: Penguin Group, 2008.

Kemezis, Paul. "At the Front with Joe Levine." *The New York Times,* June 13, 1976.

Kilgallen, Dorothy. "Dorothy Kilgallen's Broadway Notebook." *Sarasota Journal,* May 6, 1965, p. 26.

_____. "Jean Harlow Biography Is Stirring up a Storm." *The Washington Post,* July 8, 1964.

_____. "Judy Bows Out as Harlow's Mother." *The Washington Post,* March 30, 1965, p. B6.

_____. "Kim's Gunning for Harlow Biog." *The Washington Post and Times Herald,* March 13, 1958.

_____. "The Voice of Broadway: Levine Plunges on with 'Harlow.'" *The Washington Post,* January 24, 1965, p. A5.

_____. "The Voice of Broadway." *New Castle* (PA) *News,* May 20, 1965, p. 22.

_____. "The Voice of Broadway." *The Mercury* (Pottsdam, PA), May 29, 1965.

Kleiner, Dick. "All Not Rivalry Over 'Harlow': Film No. 2 Regrets No. 1's Troubles." *Racine Sunday Bulletin,* June 4, 1965, p. 7B.

_____. "Jean Harlow Back in Pair of Movies." *San Antonio Express/News,* May 9, 1965, p. 7-H.

_____. "Show Beat: 'Harlow' Is Oh, So Clean a Movie," *Park City Daily News,* January 6, 1965.

Knight, Arthur. "SR Goes to the Movies." *Saturday Review,* June 5, 1965, p. 37.

Koehler, Robert. "Film Clips: Prints of Darkness." *Los Angeles Times,* March 12, 1995, p. 21.

Kopper, Philip. "Blonde Bombshell's Life Distorted in Film Portrait." *Washington Post,* August 6, 1965, p. E6.

Kotkin, Joel. "Howard Hughes: Making Movies of the Mystery Man." *The Washington Post,* March 17, 1977.

Kraft, Daphne. "Pamela Tiffin No Harlow: Escapes

the Shadow." *Newark Evening News,* October 9, 1966.

Lando, Harry. "Sargent Pays Up—& SAG Divorces Him." *The Film Daily,* May 19, 1965.

Lange, Donna. "Second 'Harlow' Version No Real Big Improvement." *The Valley Independent,* August 26, 1965, p. 19.

Leff, Leonard J. "Instant Movies: The Short Unhappy Life of William Sargent's Electronovision (1964–65)." *Journal of Popular Film & Television* 9, pp. 20–29.

Leslie, Ann. "Carol Starts Movie with Olivier, Coward." *El Paso Herald-Post,* 1965.

Letters to the Editors. *Life,* May 28, 1965, p. 19.

"Levine Rushing His 'Harlow' to Market." *Variety,* March 3, 1965.

"Levine Spikes 'Harlow' Rumors; Pledges Honest, Accurate Picture." *Motion Picture Exhibitor,* January 1965, pp. 11, 12.

"Levine-Par 'Only Harlow' Ads Day-Date Electro's Openings." *Variety,* May 12, 1965.

"Levine's Own Queensberry Credo." *Variety,* May 5, 1965.

"Levine's Scotch-Hop to Chicago; Lively Bally-Rally for 'Harlow.'" *Variety,* June 23, 1965, p. 19.

Lewin, David. "What a Fight ... This Battle of THE BOMBSHELL Blondes." *South China Sunday Post-Herald,* June 13, 1965, p. 14.

Lewis, Richard Warren. "Baby Doll Grows Up." *Saturday Evening Post,* November 2, 1963, pp. 61–65.

Lipton, Edward. "Magna Takes Better Turn: Could Net 500G This Year." *The Film Daily,* May 26, 1965, pp. 1, 6.

Lisanti, Tom. "Aron Kincaid: The Beach Boy vs. the Creature of Destruction." *Scary Monsters,* Summer 2019, pp. 12–18.

_____. *Carol Lynley: Her Film & TV Career in Thrillers, Fantasy & Suspense.* Orlando: BearManor Media, 2020.

_____. *Fantasy Femmes of Sixties Cinema: Interviews with Twenty Actresses from Biker, Beach, and Elvis Movies.* Jefferson, NC: McFarland, 2001.

_____. "From Teen Queen to Scream Queen: The Many Faces of Carol Lynley." *Filmfax,* February/March 1997, pp. 56–60, 70.

"Liston Plays Part in Harlow Film." *The Washington Post, Times Herald,* March 20, 1965.

"A Lot to Learn." *Newsweek,* May 31, 1965, p. 83.

Lyon, Herb. "Tower Ticker." *Chicago Tribune,* August 30, 1964.

_____. "Tower Ticker." *Chicago Tribune,* February 2, 1965.

_____. "Tower Ticker." *Chicago Tribune,* May 12, 1965.

_____. "Tower Ticker." *Chicago Tribune,* May 2, 1965.

_____. "Tower Ticker." *Chicago Tribune,* November 26, 1964.

Maays, Stan. "Meet Carol Lynley: A Living Doll." *The Abilene Reporter News,* September 26, 1968.

MacArthur, Harry. "The Passing Show: It's Time Again to Think of That Best Film List." *The Evening Star* (Washington, D.C.), December 12, 1965, p. J-5.

_____. "The Passing Show: Zinnemann's Method Maintains Peace." *The Evening Star* (Washington, D.C.), August 5, 1964, p. B-6.

"Makers of Two Harlow Movies Clash in Suit." *Chicago Tribune,* June 11, 1965, p. B17.

"Man-Shark Fight 'Indecent' But He's Sure It's Big B. O." *Variety,* December 24, 1975.

Mann, Roderick. "The Return of a Grown 'Baby Doll.'" *Los Angeles Times,* June 27, 1982.

Manners, Dorothy. "Sean Connery and Carol [sic] Baker Selected as Movie Favorites." *Anderson Daily Bulletin,* December 24, 1965, p. 13.

Manville, W.H. "Speaking of Money." *Esquire,* April 1967, pp. 50–53.

"Marshall Naify Is Named as Successor to Skouras." *The New York Times,* December 13, 1963, p. 42.

"Marshall Naify Sees UATC Profit in '64." *Boxoffice Magazine,* January 27, 1964, p. 6.

Martin, Betty. "Movie Call Sheet: 'Fade Out' Will Be Filmed." *Los Angeles Times,* May 28, 1965, p. D11.

McBain, Diane, and Michael Gregg Michaud. *Famous Enough: A Hollywood Memoir.* Duncan, OK: BearManor Media, 2014.

McD, Patrick. "Interviews: George Kennedy, Carol Lynley at the Hollywood Celebrities Show." *HollywoodChicago.com,* July 28, 2010. http://www.hollywoodchicago.com/news/11404/interviews-george-kennedy-carol-lynley-at-the-hollywood-celebrities-show.

McGrath, Ron. "Dynamic Bill Sargent: Hollywood Visionary." *San Gabriel Valley Tribune,* December 20, 1964.

McKenna, A.T. "*Harlow*'s Bridle, or How Avoiding Sex and Engaging the Competition Can Lead to Failure." *Journal of Popular Film & Television* 38, Spring 2010, pp. 34–43.

_____. "Joseph E. Levine: Showmanship, Reputation and Industrial Practice 1945–1977." PhD Thesis, University of Nottingham, March 2008.

Michaelson, Herb. "Feh on Thee." *Oakland Tribune,* May 13, 1965, p. 15.

_____. "'Harlow'—Part II." *Oakland Tribune,* April 22, 1965, p. 59.

_____. "The Terrible Ten." *Oakland Tribune,* December 20, 1965, p. 33.

_____. "Women You Can't Forget: Hollywood Discovers Gold in Platinum Blonde Jean Harlow." *Los Angeles Times,* April 5, 1959, p. 48.

Millar, Jeff. "'Hughes and Harlow' Brief Microcosm of Life." *Houston Chronicle,* May 25, 1977, section 3, p. 8.

Mishkin, Leo. "Another 'Harlow' Now on Screen." *Morning Telegraph* (New York), July 22, 1965.

"Murder Probe of Jean Harlow's Spouse Ended." *The Courier-Journal* (Louisville, KY), October 29, 1960, p. 16.

Murphy, A.D. "'Hamlet' to 'Harlow' to Hock." *Variety,* July 22, 1965, pp. 1, 4.

"Naify Puts Magna Into Production; Company Dormant Since 'So. Pacific.'" *Variety,* October 21, 1964, pp. 4, 26.
"National Box Office Survey." *Variety.* May 19, 1965, p. 8.
_____ *Variety.* June 30, 1965, p. 7.
"NATO Will Honor Bill Sargent with 'Innovator' Award." *The Hollywood Reporter,* July 1, 1975.
"New Harlow Story Prepared for Film." *The New York Times,* August 29, 1964, p. 9.
"New Process Praised: Electronovision to Bow with Hamlet." *Hollywood Citizen-News,* September 7, 1964.
"No Time for Sargent's." *Time,* May 28, 1965.
"Now Hear This! Harlow Pic to Be in Good Taste—Levine." *The Hollywood Reporter,* December 17, 1964.
O'Dowd, John. "Rad Fulton (aka James Westmoreland: Back When I Was 'Rad.'" *Classic Images,* January 2023, pp. 13–15, 58–68.
Oliver, Myrna. "Obituaries; H.W. Sargent, Jr., 76; Impresario, Pioneer of Pay-Per-View TV." *Los Angeles Times,* October 26, 2003, p. B20.
Olson, Dave. "Largest-in-Years Oscar Race: 32 Films Loom from 8 Firms." *Variety,* January 12, 1966, p. 5.
"$1-Million Harlow Libel Suit Lost in Missouri High Court." *The New York Times,* December 12, 1967.
Ornstein, Bill. "Electronovision to Make 12 Pix at $7.5 Mil Cost." *The Hollywood Reporter,* January 19, 1965, pp. 1,4.
Osborne, Robert. "Robert Osborne on Jean Harlow." *Now Playing: A Viewer's Guide to Turner Classic Movies,* March 2011, p. 3.
"Other Side of Coin: Naify Owed by Electronovision, Says Criss in Crossing Sargent Statement." *Variety,* June 7, 1965, pp. 1, 15.
Palmer, Raymond E. "Empire Withstands Sex of 'Moses' and 'Harlow.'" *Los Angeles Times,* June 30, 1965, p. C9.
"Par & Embassy in Electrono Reply." *Variety,* September 29, 1965, p. 18.
Parsons, Louella O. "Carol Lynley: Still Young and Foolish." *New York Journal American,* June 6, 1965.
_____. "Hope Talks Contract with Cantinflas." *The Washington Post and Times Herald,* November 20, 1956.
_____. "Jean Harlow Role Still Up for Grabs." *The Washington Post and Times Herald,* December 19, 1956.
_____. "Jean Harlow's Life Bought for Cinema." *The Washington Post and Times Herald,* May 6, 1954, p. 39.
_____. "Joanne Gets 'Jean Harlow' Bid." *The Washington Post and Times Herald,* March 3, 1960.
Patrick, John. "Pose in the Nude? Stella Stevens Doesn't Believe in Hiding Her Assets." *New York Sunday News,* July 4, 1965, p. 4.
Paul, Louis. *Italian Horror Film Directors.* Jefferson, NC: McFarland, 2005.

Pelswick, Rose. "A 'Harlow' in 17 Days: What Now, Hollywood?" *New York Journal American,* April 18, 1965, pp. 32, 33.
Penn, Stanley. "Show Biz Success: Energetic Joe Levine Climbs Quickly to Top Ranks of Film Makers." *The Wall Street Journal,* January 22, 1965, pp. 1, 16.
Petersen, Clarence. "Paperbacks: Real 'Harlow' Out in Soft Cover." *Chicago Tribune,* September 27, 1964.
Pickens, Jessica. "Comet Over Hollywood: Harlow, the Inaccurate Biopic." *The Star* (Shelby, NC), February 6, 2014.
Pollock, Dale. "Sargent Films on the Block." *Los Angeles Times,* January 31, 1980, p. F2.
Pressman, Gregory P. "Harlow at Loew's Orpheum." *The Harvard Crimson,* July 15, 1965.
Pryor, Thomas M. "Fox to Film Life of Jean Harlow." *The New York Times,* June 4, 1956, p. 25.
_____. "Plan Film Story of Jean Harlow." *The New York Times,* May 5, 1954, p. 38.
Quarm, Joan. "'Harlow' Is So Bad It's Almost Satirical Triumph." *El Paso Herald-Post,* May 13, 1965, p. C-4.
Quigley, Martin, Jr. "Harlow vs. Harlow." *Motion Picture Herald,* May 26, 1965, p. 1.
Rautbord, Sugar. "He Fathers a Design 'Dynasty.'" *Chicago Tribune,* October 10, 1984, E8.
"Reasoning on Carroll Baker Future." *Variety.* September 22, 1965, p. 7.
Reed, Rex. "Angela Lansbury Lands a Movie All Her Own." *The Evening Star* (Washington, D.C.), June 21, 1970, p. D-5.
_____. "'Baby Doll' Heals Her Hollywood Wounds." *The Washington Post,* February 14, 1971.
Robertson, Nan. "Joseph E. Levine, A Towering Figure in Moviemaking, Is Dead." *The New York Times,* August 1, 1987, p. 36.
Rogers, Ginger. *Ginger: My Story.* HarperCollins, 1991.
Rosenthal, Donna. "Self-Made Mogul Hangs On: Joseph E. Levine, 82, Is Still Wheeling and Dealing." *Los Angeles Times,* July 5, 1987.
Rozzo, Mark. *Everybody Thought We Were Crazy: Dennis Hopper, Brooke Hayward and 1960s Los Angeles.* New York: Ecco, 2022.
Salmaggi, Robert. [Untitled.] *New York Herald Tribune,* June 11, 1965.
Sar, Ali. "'Mary Poppins,' 'My Fair Lady' Capture Top Honors from Cinema Editors Group." *The News—Van Nuys* (CA), March 18, 1965.
"Sargent Closes Up But Not on Levine." *The Film Daily,* July 22, 1965.
"Sargent Firms Hit by $7,954 in Tax Liens." *Variety,* June 4, 1965.
"Sargent Says Four to Shoot in March." *The Hollywood Reporter,* February 19, 1965, p. 1.
"Sargent Starts 'Stop the World' With Another Electronics System." *Variety,* November 4, 1965.
"Sargent's 'Harlow' Sold Overseas as 'Platinum Blonde.'" *Variety,* February 28, 1966, p. 3.

"Sargent's Electronovision 'Harlow' in Suit Vs. Par., Embassy, Techni." *Variety,* June 16, 1965, pp. 5, 14.

Sarmento, William E. "Show Time: Two Harlow Films in Race for the Screen." *Lowell Sunday,* April 18, 1965, p. 22.

Sauer, Georgia. "Personality Profile: Carol in Focus..." *Chicago Tribune,* December 17, 1972.

"Scene Within a Scene." *The Chicago Defender,* May 22, 1965.

Schallert, Edwin. "Gene Evans Will Star as Butch Cassidy; John Baragrey of 'Carmen' Set." *Los Angeles Times,* June 12, 1954, p. 13.

Scheuer, Philip K. "Baker in Bow as Harlow." *Los Angeles Times,* February 26, 1965, p. C11.

_____. "Electronovision of 'Harlow.'" *Los Angeles Times,* April 13, 1965, p. C13.

_____. "'Harlow' Story Told Again—Less Cheaply." *Los Angeles Times,* August 15, 1965.

_____. "'Harlow' Story—One Down, One to Go." *Los Angeles Times,* May 12, 1965, p. D11.

_____. "'Harlow-Hollywood Film Craze Grows." *Los Angeles Times,* September 25, 1964.

_____. "'Jeanne Eagels' Scorns Sugar-Coated Formula." *Los Angeles Times,* July 21, 1957.

_____. "Kim Novak 'Merges' with Spirit of Jeanne Eagels." *Los Angeles Times,* January 6, 1957.

_____. "Raf Vallone and Image He Wrought." *Los Angeles Times,* Mar 23, 1965, p. C10.

_____. "Sylvia Girl of Many Aliases in Sad Saga." *Los Angeles Times,* May 4, 1965.

_____. "Valentino Film Secrets Out." *Los Angeles Times,* July 16, 1950.

Schumach, Murray. "Hollywood Candor: Carroll Baker Defends Her Nudity in Films." *The New York Times,* June 14, 1964.

_____. "Wald Finds Many Knew Them When." *The New York Times,* May 21, 1959.

Scott, John L. "Hollywood Calendar: 'King Kong' Connors a Rib-Cracker." *Los Angeles Times,* April 11, 1965.

SD, Trav. "Dueling Harlows: Featuring the Battle of the Carol(e)s." *Travalanche,* February 25, 2015. https://travsd.wordpress.com/2015/02/25/dueling-harlows-featuring-the-battle-of-the-carols/.

Seidenbaum, Art. "With Wet Cement, White Cadillac, a Film Is Launched: Hollywood Recreates Era of Jean Harlow." *Boston Globe,* March 7, 1965.

"She Portrays Harlow." *The Port Arthur News,* April 14, 1965, p. 11.

Shearer, Lloyd. "The Real Jean Harlow Story: Everybody Is Capitalizing on the Blonde Bombshell of the 1930s." *Boston Globe,* November 1, 1964.

"Shubert Adds 'Hughes and Harlow' Bio-Pic to Credits." *The Independent Film Journal,* July 8, 1977, p. 23.

"Shulman and Publishers Sue Over a Harlow Paperback." *The New York Times,* August 25, 1964.

"Shulman Tells All—Or Nearly All." *Variety,* January 27, 1965.

"Sidney Skolsky Sues Sargent for $140,000 on 'Harlow' Script Nix." *Variety,* March 10, 1965.

"Sidney Skolsky Wins Electronovision Suit." *Los Angeles Times,* September 7, 1965.

Sinclair, Marianne. *Hollywood Lolitas: The Nymphet Syndrome in the Movies.* New York: Henry Holt, 1988.

"Skolsky Sues on Harlow Pic Pact." *The Hollywood Reporter,* March 3, 1965.

Stanich, Dorothy. "'Harlow' Opens Here; New Technique Outshines Film." *Corpus Christi Times,* May 14, 1965, p. 12-B.

Stanley, John. "The Platinum Sex Symbol." *San Francisco Chronicle,* August 15, 1993, p. 3.

Staskiewicz, Keith. "My Week with Marilyn." *Entertainment Weekly,* August 19/26, 2011, p. 71.

Steen, Mike. *Hollywood Speaks! An Oral History.* New York: G.P. Putnam's Sons, 1974.

Stott, Catherine. "Intercourse on Stage: 'Could be Done if the Two Were Already Partners.' Billie Dixon Talking to Catherine Stott." *The Guardian* (London), March 6, 1970, p. 8.

"Summer Estimates for Paramount." *Variety,* July 7, 1965, p. 7.

"Sweet—And Not So Sweet." *Show,* March 1964.

Taylor, Clark. "All-Electronics Entrepreneur." *Los Angeles Times,* December 21, 1979, p. 48.

Taylor, Frank. "'Beard': Curse for Censor, Kiss for Cast." *The Van Nuys News,* March 1, 1968, p. 24.

"10G Owed Electro 'Harlow' Thesps; SAG Takes Action," *Variety,* May 17, 1965.

Terry, Clifford. "Presto—Jean Harlow." *Chicago Tribune,* November 15, 1964, p. K48.

"...They Went!" *Variety.* June 28, 1965.

Thomas, Bob. "Meanwhile, Back on the 'Harlow' Set." *New York Journal American,* April 24, 1965, p. 8.

_____. "Rita Hayworth Remains 'Selective' in Film Life," *Toledo Blade,* April 1, 1965.

_____. "Rock Hudson Escapes from Bedroom Farces." *The Sun,* June 10, 1965, p. 7-B.

_____. "Six Days Shooting: Speedy Technique Used for One 'Harlow' Film." *Toledo Blade,* April 15, 1965.

_____. "Visit to Harlow Joe Levine Edition." *The Montreal Gazette,* April 27, 1965, p. 30.

Thomas, Kevin. "Connor—New Matinee Idol?" *Los Angeles Times,* March 10, 1966, p. D17.

Thompson, Howard. "Screen: Winner of the 'Harlow' Race." *The New York Times,* May 15, 1965, p. 18.

Thoroughbred Times.com. "Prominent Owner Marshall Naify Dead." http://www.thoroughbredtimes.com/news/printable.aspx.

"$25-Mil. Antitrust Suit Filed by Bill Sargent." *Boxoffice Magazine,* June 14, 1965.

"2nd Harlow Sought." *The Desert News,* September 8, 1964, B3.

"Two Harlows—Deluxe and Quickie." *Life,* May 7, 1965, pp. 118, 121, 122.

Unger, Michael D. "'Harlow' Here Proves Pleasant Surprise." *Newark Evening News,* May 20, 1965.
UPI. "Ben Hecht Story Starts Bern '32 'Suicide' Probe." *The Washington Post and Times Herald,* October 26, 1960, p. 39.
_____. "Father Brings Suit Over Book on Jean Harlow." *The Hartford Courant,* November 24, 1964.
_____. "Reveal Home Looters Aided by Pal in Cafe." *Chicago Tribune,* December 16, 1964.
_____. "Sex Play Is Given Green Light in L.A." *The Times* (San Mateo, California), January 27, 1968.
Wahls, Robert. "Footlight: Over-Stimulated Pam." *New York Daily News,* October 16, 1966.
"Wallace Airs 'Harlow' Producers Views on Juxtaposed Radio Tapes." *Variety,* May 12, 1965, p. 16.
Wedemeyer, Dee, and Daniel F. Cuff. "Sale of Their Company Puts Naifys in Spotlight." *The New York Times,* July 16, 1986, p. D2.
Weiler, A.H. "Riding Screen Cycles." *The New York Times,* May 23, 1965, p. 11.
Westmoreland, James. "The James Westmoreland Story." *The Official Site of Actor James Westmoreland.* August 3, 2011. https://www.jimwestmoreland.com/in-jims-words/the-james-westmoreland-story/.
Wilcox, Ed. "'The Beard' Takes the Fuzz on the Chin." *Sunday News* (New York), May 5, 1968.
Wilson, Earl. "Broadway: Carroll's 'Harlow' and Champagne." *The Evening Star* (Washington, D.C.), July 16, 1965, p. D-8.
_____. "It's Controversy Time." *Beaver County Times,* July 20, 1965, p. B-4.
_____. Joe Levine Rivals Mesta." *Los Angeles Herald Examiner,* April 15, 1965.
_____. "Parents Are Scapegoats for Drinking Youths." *The Milwaukee Sentinel,* September 28, 1964, p. 19.
_____. "Portland's Book Brings Back Wit of Fred Allen." *St. Joseph Gazette,* May 14, 1965, p. 4A.
Wilson, John. "Man with a Trailer: Impresario of the Movie Teaser." *Los Angeles Times,* June 20, 1977, p. E10.

Index

Absurd Person Singular 193
Adams, Marjory 16
Adler, Buddy 12, 14
Adler, Stella 155
After Hagerty 154
After the Fall 49
Alex Joseph and His Wives 170
Alice in Wonderland 90
All the Way Home 49
Allen, Irwin 193
The Amazing Howard Hughes 160, 163
Anatahan 166
Andre, Jackie 84
Andy Warhol's Bad 195
Ann-Margret 60, 61, 65, 155, 187, 191
Anna Christie 151
Anniversary Waltz 59
Arkoff, Samuel Z. 159
Armstrong, Jack 146
The Art of Love 133
Ashford, Gerald 114
Avedon, Richard 14
The Aviator 180

Baba Yaga, Devil Witch 195
Baby Doll 12, 23, 89, 197
Baby Face Nelson 15
Backer, Clarius 130
Bacon, James 160
Baddeley, Hermione 52, 73, 83, 117
Baer, Max 8, 117, 120
Bahrenburg, Bruce 154
Baker, Blanche 196, 197
Baker, Carroll v, 1–4, 12, 23–28, 32–34, 43, 44, 46, 47, 53–55, 58, 62, 69, 73, 76, 77, 87–101, 112–115, 121–123, 126–136, 137–141, 144, 145, 148–150, 156, 162, 169, 179, 187, 194–197
Baker, Jack 113
Balsom, Martin 54, 128, 131
Barin, Lennie 163
Barnes, Clive 154, 193
Barrows, Robert 152
Bart, Peter 34

Barton, Mischa 181
Batzdorff, Ron 166
The Beach Boys 38, 39
Beach Party 39
Beacon, Tony 20
The Beard 4, 151–154
Beatlemania 183, 184
Beatty, Warren 49, 160, 161, 192
Beauchamp, Emerson 115, 157
Beery, Wallace 9, 156
Bello, Jean Harlow (Mother Jean) 5, 6, 8, 10–12, 19, 52, 53, 89, 111, 117, 135, 140, 142, 178
Bello, Marino 6, 8, 20, 52, 53, 89, 98, 117, 135, 178
Bello, Violette H. 20
Ben-Hur 48
Bennett, Richard C. v, 56, 57, 62, 66, 69, 70, 74, 75, 80, 81, 98, 138
Berard, Roxanne 55
Bergman, Alan 110
Bergman, Marilyn 110
Bern, Paul 6–8, 13, 14, 17–19, 47, 54, 117, 119, 134–136
Bernstein, Jay 190
Berry, Chuck 38
Bianchini, Frank 170
The Bible 77, 186
The Big Country 24
Binder, Steve 38
Bischoff, Sam 11, 12
Blackout 194
Bloom, Lindsay v, 2, 4, 161–172, 174, 175, 177–180, 188–191
Blue Denim 59, 60
Blue Hawaii 53
Bochner, Lloyd 52, 117
Boehm, Sidney 46, 47, 101
Bollengier, A.E. 143
Bombshell 8
Bonanza 96
Bonnie and Clyde 192
Bowie, Stephen v
Breakfast at Tiffany's 91
A Bridge Too Far 187
Bright, Richard 151–154
Brownstein, Paul 185

Brucker, James 167
Buchanan, Larry 4, 158–172, 178–180, 187–188
Buckner, Susan 161
A Bullet for Pretty Boy 159
Bunny Lake Is Missing 73, 121, 145, 191, 192
Burr, Robert 156
Burton, Richard 36, 39, 184, 185
Burton, Sally 184, 185
Bushelman, Tina 167, 190
The Buster Keaton Story 40
Bustin, John 113
But Not for Me 24
Buttons, Red 54, 92, 95, 96, 129, 131, 134, 140, 144

Callan, Michael 98
Campbell, Courtney 154
Candy 57
The Caper of the Golden Bulls 150
The Cardinal 60, 61, 98, 191
Carnal Knowledge 187
Carpenter, Mont Clair 5, 20
The Carpetbaggers 17, 24, 25, 28, 31, 32, 41, 43–47, 62, 89, 94, 133, 143, 144, 153, 186
Carrier, Alberto 167
Carroll, Kathleen 113, 114
Cassa, Anthony 138
Castel, Lou 195
The Cat and the Canary 193
Cat Ballou 133
Cat on a Hot Tin Roof 24
Chambers, John 91
Chang, Shaun v, 13
Charlie's Christmas Wish 190
Chase, Brandon 71
Chayefsky, Paddy 88
Cheyenne Autumn 27, 28, 115
China Seas 10
Christie, Audrey 110, 111
City Across the River 15
Claire, Adele 167, 179
Clay, Cassius 35
Coe, Richard L. 157

Index

Cohen, Alexander 36
Cohn, Al 113, 114
Cohn, Harry 13, 34
Cole, Clay 102
College Confidential 15
Colleran, William 36
Il Coltello di ghiaccio 194
Come Blow Your Hon 49
Come On Strong 25
Conners, Michael 54, 55, 92, 95, 98, 101, 127, 128, 131, 135
Connery, Sean 145
Connolly, Mike 12
Cooke, Richard P. 154
The Copper Scroll of Mary Magdalene 188
Costello, George 170
Coughlin, Sean 185
Cover Girl Models 162
Crawford, Joan 7, 10
Creature of Destruction 159
Criss, Lamar 148
Crist, Judith 96, 130
Cronyn, Hume 36
Crowther, Bosley 130
Cukor, George 88, 158
Curran, Pamela 34
Curtis, Tony 15

Dallas 188
Danger Route 192
Dano, Royal 168, 180
Dante, Michael v, 52, 53, 57, 63, 66–73, 80, 112, 119, 137
Dark Tower 194
David, Saul 16
Davis, Sammy, Jr. 184
Day, Janet 84
The Dean Martin Show 161
De Dienes, Andre 161
Dee, Sandra 16, 24, 58, 59, 143, 145, 155
De Havilland, Olivia 53
De Laurentiis, Dino 77
Demy, Jacques 153
Dennis, Sandy 193
Dexter, Anthony 40
Dexter, Maury 159
Dickinson, Angie 22
Dillman, Bradford 51
Dimitri, Nick 70
Dinner at Eight (film) 8, 9, 65
Dinner at Eight (play) 151, 155–157
Dixon, Billie 4, 151–154
Dmytryk, Edward 27, 31
Dobbs, Marlin v
Dr. Jekyll and Mr. Hyde 90
Dr. Kildare 69
Dr. No 115, 133
Dolemite 164, 165
Dorsey, Tommy 52
Double Whoopee 6

Douglas, Gordon 28, 34, 88, 93, 96–98
Douglas, Margie 144
Down on Us 188
Dressler, Marie 8, 52, 117, 142
Duffy, Patrick 189
The Dukes of Hazzard 188
Dullea, Keir 191
Dunning, Bruce 130, 132

Eagles, Jeanne 13
Easy to Love 23
Eden Cried 184
Edwards, Nadine M. 114
Empire of the Ants 172
Erickson, Hal 180
Esterow, Milton 16
Eyles, Alan 132

Fade Out, Fade In 146, 147
The Fat Spy 186
Faulkner, William 11
Feinstein, Herbert 152
Felker, Clay 157
Ferrer, Jose 50
Fields, Freddie 56, 67
Fitzgerald, Robert 179
Flack, Tim 190
Fonda, Jane 191
Forte, Fabian 159
Fontaine, Joan 53
For Those Who Think Young 155
Ford, John 27
Frank, Eugene H. 89
Freeman, Y. Frank 92
From Russia with Love 115, 133
Frost, David 192
Fry, Christopher 48
Fulton, Rad *see* Westmoreland, James

The Gabby Hayes, Show 158
Gable, Clark 7, 8, 10, 24, 54, 95, 120, 135, 142
Gaffney, Maureen v, 57, 58, 65, 72, 84, 85, 149, 184
Garfein, Jack 23, 27, 33, 89, 149
Garland, Judy 3, 50, 51, 62, 66–68, 158
Garroway, David 86
Gas Pump Girls 179
Gassman, Vittorio 53
Gassner, John 157
Gavin, John 51
Geis, Bernie 16
Gemora, Charlie 90
The George Raft Story 40
Gerry and the Pacemakers 38
Giant 23
Gielgud, John 36
Gill, Brendan 16, 132
Gimbel, Roger 160, 161
Gist, Robert 152

Give 'Em Hell, Harry! 43, 183
Glazer, Barney 113
Glover, William 157
Goddard, Mark 81
God's Little Acre 24
Godzilla 29
Goodbye, Norma Jean 4, 159–164, 188
Goodnight, Sweet Marilyn 188
Gore, Lesley 38
The Graduate 186, 187
Graham, Sheila 12, 18, 19, 34, 53, 54, 88, 89, 114, 144
Gray, Linda 189
The Greatest Story Ever Told 115, 133
Greene, Shecky 57
Grieg, Michael 151
Grubstake 158, 160
Guillaroff, Sidney 98
Guthrie, Tyrone 156, 157

Hagman, Larry 188, 189
Hale, Jean 92
Hale, Victoria 153
Hale, Wanda 132
Hall, James 6, 18, 119, 135
The Hallelujah Trail 97, 155
Halsman, Philippe 32
Ham, Al 79, 110
Hamlet 36, 37, 39, 40, 43, 45, 148, 184, 185
Hamp, Ruth 16, 19
Hanson, Peter 180
Hardy, Oliver 6, 142
L'Harem 194
Harlow (Bill Sargent's version) 1–4, 35, 38, 40–46, 48–54, 56–88, 95, 98, 101–120, 122, 130, 132, 133, 135–148, 151, 153, 157, 158, 160, 166, 167, 178, 180, 185, 186, 191, 197, 198
Harlow (Joe Levine's version) v, 1–3, 40–48, 53–55, 57, 58, 69, 76, 77, 87–102, 119, 120–146, 149–151, 153, 157, 158, 160, 166, 167, 170, 178, 180, 186, 194, 197–199
Harlow, Jean 1–181
Harlow: An Intimate Biography 3, 15–21, 32, 44
The Harlow Girls 84–86
Harper 155
Hart, Dolores 60, 155
Hart, Moss 59
Hatfield, Hurd 50, 64, 74, 75, 83, 105, 107–109, 111, 119
Hathaway, Henry 14
Hawks, Howard 160, 164
Hay, Alexandra 4, 151–153
Hayes, John Michael 31, 89, 92, 93, 95, 101, 120, 130, 134
Hayward, Brooke 151, 152

Index

Hayward, Susan 65
Hayworth, Rita 53
Head, Edith 26, 91, 92, 98, 134, 139, 144, 179
Hecht, Ben 13, 14
Hecht, Howard 94
Heffernan, Howard 71, 158
Hefti, Neal 97, 134, 140, 170
Hell's Angels 6, 18, 65, 116, 117, 119, 135, 167, 178–180
Hepburn, Audrey 91
Hercules 29
Herron, Mark 50
Heston, Charlton 98
High Spirits 39
Hipp, Edward Sothern 157
Hirsch, Foster v
Hodgens, R.M. 112, 132
Hoffman, Dustin 187
Holchak, Victor 162, 163, 168, 177, 179, 180
Hold Your Man 8
Holiday for Lovers 49, 60
Holland, Carol *see* Hollenbeck, Carol
Hollander, Gino 28
Hollenbeck, Carol v, 32, 33, 39, 58, 84, 184, 197
Holloway, Susan 55
Hollywood '65 86
Hometown Premiere 184
Hopper, Dennis 151, 152
Hopper, Hedda 11, 13, 16, 27, 73, 94, 99
Hound-Dog Man 60
A House Is Not a Home 31, 53
Houser, John G. 114
How Sweet It Is 153
How the West Was Won 25, 197
How to Murder Your Wife 115
Howard, Susan 188, 189
Hubler, Richard G. 16
Hughes, Howard 6, 7, 11, 18, 31, 54, 89, 119, 134–136, 160, 163, 165–167, 178, 179
Hughes, Mary 39
Hughes and Harlow: Angels in Hell 2, 4, 158, 160–180, 187, 188, 190, 199, 200
Hunter, Arline 55

The Immortal 192
In Harm's Way 133
The Incredible Melting Man 167
Ingram, Rex 40
Ironweed 196
Isherwood, Christopher 101
It's a Mad, Mad, Mad, Mad World 31

Jack of Diamonds 194
Jack the Ripper 29
James Brown & the Famous Flames 38
Jan and Dean 38
The Jean Harlow Story (book) 20, 21
The Jean Harlow Story (proposed film) 11–14, 22, 39, 58
Jeanne Eagles 40, 52
Jennings, James 184
Jessel, George 54
Jet Pilot 165
Johnson, Van 25
Jonas, Larry 114
Jones, Tommy Lee 160, 163
Jorgensen, Jay 91
Journey to the Unknown 73

Kamp, Irene 47
Karp, Jack 28, 32
Katzman, Leonard 188
Keach, Stacy 190
Kilgallen, Dorothy 67, 97
Kill, Alex, Kill 164
Kincaid, Aron v, 74, 81, 159
Kindergarten Cop 196
Klein, Fred 53, 74, 81
Kleiner, Dick 47
Knight, Arthur 113
Knight, Shirley 48, 60
Knockout 184
Kobal, John 5
Koch, Howard 41, 47, 76, 89, 90, 92, 93, 97
Kopper, Philip 130, 132
Kruschen, Jack 52, 74, 83, 113, 147

The Lady in a Car with Glasses and a Gun 154
Landau, Arthur 3, 11, 12, 15–21, 54, 89, 101, 119, 132, 134, 135
Landau, Beatrice 16
Landy, Hanna 128, 129
Lane, Paula 188
Lang, Barbara 14
Lange, Donna 132
Lansbury, Angela 53, 90, 95, 101, 123, 128, 131, 134, 135, 138, 140
The Last Sunset 60, 64
Laurel, Stan 6, 142
Lavi, Daliah 150
Lawford, Peter 28, 54, 95, 98, 127, 131, 135, 140
Lazaro, Bill 184
Lee, Carolyn *see* Lynley, Carol
Leigh, Barbara 188
Lenzi, Umberto 194, 195
The Les Crane Show 18
Levine, Joseph E. (Joe) 1, 3, 4, 25, 28–35, 41–48, 52–54, 57, 62, 69, 76, 77, 79, 82, 87–101, 110, 116, 121, 122, 130, 133, 135, 137, 143–146, 148–150, 161, 186, 187
Lewin, David 70
Lewis, Sanford 111, 114
The Light in the Forest 59
The Lion in Winter 187
Lion's Love (... and Lies) 154
Liston, Sonny 53, 70
The Lively Set 155
Loden, Barbara 49
Logan, George 35
Lone Star Bar & Grill 189
Long Day's Journey into Night 29, 30
Longworth, Karina 178
Lord Jim 115
Loren, Sophia 29
Louise, Tina 13, 24
The Loved One 43
Lovsky, Celia 52
Luft, Joey 51, 66
Luft, Lorna 51, 66
Lumet, Sidney 29
Lynde, Paul 81
Lynley, Carol v, 1–3, 24, 34, 46, 58–75, 92, 102–121, 131, 132, 134, 136–146, 155, 156, 162, 169, 179, 191–194, 196, 197
Lyon, Ben 18, 119
Lyon, Sue 24

Macao 165
MacArthur, Harry 18, 132
MacDonald, Joe 27
Magic 187
Malanga, Gerald 152
The Maltese Bippy 192
Man of a Thousand Faces 40
The Man with the Green Carnation 42
The Manchurian Candidate 53
Manley, Nellie 44, 92
Manners, Dorothy 145
Mannix 55
Mansfield, Jayne 11–13, 22, 34, 186
March, Fredric 90
The Marvelettes 102
Mastroianni, Marcello 53, 155
Mayer, Louis B. 9, 28, 52, 74, 89, 94, 119
Mayo, Mary 110
The Maze: Haight/Ashbury 151
McBain, Diane 24, 58, 59
McClure, Michael 151–153
McElwaine, Guy 67
McGavin, Darren 156
McGrew, Chuck 6, 7
McHale's Navy 64
McKenna, A.T. 143
McLean, David 164
McNair, Barbara 194

Index

McQuade, Tom 5
Michelson, Herb 111, 113
A Midsummer Night's Dream 170
The Mike Douglas Show 85
Mikels, Ted V. 170
Miller, Arthur 12, 22
Miller, Nolan 65, 66, 117, 140, 141, 179
Millette, Dorothy 7, 8, 17, 136
Mimieux, Yvette 24, 58, 150
Mineo, Sal 15, 27, 186
Minnelli, Liza 66
The Miracle 24
Mirisch, Robert 61
Mishkin, Leo 130
Mistress of the Apes 165, 179, 188
Model Shop 153
Mohr, Beverly 164
Mohr, Hal 164, 170
Monroe, Marilyn 11, 12, 14, 22, 23, 27, 62, 65, 88, 114, 142, 158, 159, 161, 188, 194
Moore, Cleo 11, 12, 14
Moore, Terry 34
Morgan, Jess 150
Morriss, Frank 115
Mulvey, Kay 16, 18, 20
My Fair Lady 115, 133

Nadel, Norman 156
Naify, Marshall 45, 77, 148, 185–186
Naify, Robert 186
Neal, Patricia 53
Neame, Ronald 193
Neon Signs 194
Neumann, Jenny 188
The New Mike Hammer 189, 190
Newley, Anthony 147
Nichols, Mike 186, 187
Nicholson, Jack 159
Nicholson, James 159
Nielsen, Leslie 54, 96, 98, 126, 135
The Night Stalker 193
Nightlife 86
Nitzsche, Jack 183
Norwood 192
Novak, Kim 13, 22, 34, 40, 52
Nutter, Mayf 177, 190

O'Brien, Margaret 115
Of Mice and Men 193
Oggi, domani, dopodomani 155
Oliver, Susan 98
Olivier, Laurence 39, 145, 191, 192
Once You Kiss a Stranger 192
One Flew Over the Cuckoo's Nest, 183

One, Two, Three 155
Oppenheimer, George 157
Orgasmo 194
Orsatti, Frank 16
Orsatti, Vic 16
Osborn, Robert v, 5, 18, 137, 139
The Oscar 92, 186
Oscar Wilde 42
Osterman, Lester 157
Othello 39
Ouspenskaya, Maria 52, 113
The Outlaw 178
Outlaw Planet see *Planet of the Vampires*

Pacey, Ann 130
Page, Geraldine 155, 193
Paige, Marvin v, 64–66, 72, 82, 138, 145
Papillon 178
Paranoia 194, 195
Parker, Eleanor 60, 65, 67
Parrish, Julie 54, 55
Parsons, Louella 11, 12, 14, 27, 62
Pascal, John 20
The Pawnbroker 47
Pederson, Alexis 161
Peppard, George 25, 27
Permut, David v, 43, 67, 76, 183–185
Perry, Frank 57
Personal Property 10
Petersen, Clarence 21
Peterson, Lowell v, 165, 166, 168–172, 179, 180
Peyton Place 60
Philbin, Regis 33, 197
Planet of the Vampires 73
Platinum Blonde 7, 148
The Pleasure Seekers 24, 61, 155
Pleshette, Suzanne 65
Police Story 162
Ponti, Carlo 29
The Poseidon Adventure 192, 193
The Potting Shed 59
Powell, William 9, 10, 13, 18, 51, 54, 70, 73, 89, 95, 117, 118, 120, 135, 142
Praturlon, Pierluigi 43
Preminger, Otto 60, 61, 73, 98, 121, 153, 191, 192
Presley, Elvis 53, 145, 184
Pressman, Gregory P. 130, 132
The Prizefighter and the Lady 8
Provine, Dorothy 3, 50, 57
Pryor, Richard 185
Public Enemy 7
Puchalski, Steven 180

Quarm, Joan 113
Quigley, Martin, Jr. 42, 183

Ramirez, Al 165
Ransohoff, Martin 27, 43
Ray, Frankie 57, 58, 73
Rebel Without a Cause 15
Reckless 10
Red Dust 7, 8
Red-Headed Woman 7, 139
Reed, Carol Sir 22, 28, 32
Reed, Oliver 192
Remick, Lee 13
Return to Peyton Place 60, 67
Reynolds, Debbie 90, 145
Richard Pryor—Live in Concert 184
Riddle, Nelson 79
The Rise and Fall of a Star 28
Ritter, Louie 23
Roarke, Adam 159, 164, 180
Robbins, Harold 25, 31
Roberts, Marguerite 34
Roberts, Tanya 190
Roebuck, Ernie 166
Rogers, Ginger 65, 70, 73, 80, 81, 83, 86, 111, 118, 135, 137, 138, 142
Roland, Gilbert 54
The Rolling Stones 38
Room at the Top 52
Rooney, Darrell v, 5–7, 19, 25, 138–142
Ross, Diana 38
Rosson, Harold 8, 9, 120
Rowe, Misty 4, 159, 162
Rozzo, Mark 152
Rules Don't Apply 161
Rush, Barbara 98
Russell, Jane 178
Russell, Rosalind 10
Ruttenberg, Joseph 96, 98, 144, 170

Saint, Eva Marie 12
St. John, Adela Rogers 12, 13, 18
St. John, Jill 49
Salven, David 97
Sammy Stops the World 184
The Sandpiper 132, 133
Saratoga 10
Sargent, William (Bill) 1, 3, 4, 35–46, 48–50, 52, 53, 56–59, 62, 63, 67, 68, 70–73, 76–80, 82–87, 95, 110, 111, 113, 116, 119, 137, 143–149, 160, 161, 167, 183–186
Sarmento, William E. 94
Sauer, Jean-Pierre 43
Savin, Lee 38, 52, 145
Schacht, Irving 58, 149
Scheuer, Philip K. 93, 113, 114, 130, 137
Schulman, Wayne v
SD, Trav 141
Sebastian, Ray 167

Index

The Secret Diary of Sigmund Freud 196
Segal, Alex 48, 49, 52, 59, 68, 70–72, 74, 79–81, 111, 137
Selsman, Mike 60
77 Sunset Strip 52
Shearer, Lloyd 17
Shelton, Abigail 28
Sherwood, Robert 11
Shock Treatment 46, 61, 65
Shubert, Lynn 160, 166
Shulman, Irving 15–22, 32, 34, 35, 44, 46, 47, 89, 93, 101, 122, 130, 135, 136, 140, 143, 153, 183
The Shuttered Room 192
Sidney, George 11
Silberkleit, Bill 170
Simmons, Jean 49
Sixpack Annie 161, 162
Skidoo 153
Skolsky, Sidney 11, 12, 14, 22, 34, 43, 48, 82, 148, 149
Skouras, George P. 45
So Sweet ... So Perverse 194
Something Wild 25
Sommer, Elke 34, 186
The Sons of Katie Elder 133
The Sound of Music 115, 133, 143
Southern, Terry 57
Spaak, Catherine 186
Spillane, Mickey 190
The Spy Who Came in from the Cold 144
The Spy with a Cold Nose 150, 186
Stanich, Dorothy 113
Star 80 196
Star of Midnight 73
State Fair 154
Station Six Sahara 25
Stefani, Gwen 180
Stern, Stewart 15
Stevens, Connie 24
Stevens, George 23, 27, 80
Stevens, Stella 13, 22, 34
Stop the World—I Want to Get Off 147, 184
Strasberg, Lee 23
Stratten, Dorothy 196
Strickling, Howard 16, 18, 19
The Stripper 14, 60
Sullivan, Barry 51, 52, 64, 73, 75, 83, 111, 135
Summer and Smoke 155
The Supremes 38
The Surfaris 81
Suzy 10
The Sweet Body of Deborah 194

Sylvia 28, 46, 54, 112, 132
Synanon 115

The T.A.M.I. Show 37–40, 43, 45, 185
Tanner, Tony 147
Taylor, Elizabeth 23, 24
Terror at Midnight 15
Terry, Alice 40
Texas Detour 167, 188
There's a Girl in My Soup 154
Thomas, Bob 73, 96
Thompson, Howard 112, 114
Three Faces of Eve 24
Tiffin, Pamela 4, 60, 61, 97, 151, 155–157
Today Is Tonight 8, 19
Too Much, Too Soon 24, 40, 51
Torn, Rip 153, 154
Totter, Audrey 64
Tourist Trap 179
The Train 115
The Trials of Oscar Wilde 42
Tropic of Cancer 149, 150
Trumble. Doug 185
Tryon, Tom 191
Tunberg, Karl 48, 68, 77, 113, 117, 120
Turman, Lawrence 186
Turner, Nat 157
Two Women 29
Tynan, Kenneth 154

Under the Yum Yum Tree 34, 60, 61, 65
Unger, Michael D. 113

Valentino 40
Vallone, Raf 54, 92, 98, 123, 128, 131, 135, 140
The Van 178
Van Doren, Mamie 11, 14, 15, 22
Varda, Agnès 154
Vic 194
Vidal, Gore 48
Viera, Mark A. 5
Vigilante 194
Vinton, Bobby 129
Viva Knievel! 178
Von Ryan's Express 133
Von Sternberg, Josef 164–166
Von Sternberg, Nicholas v, 164–172, 179, 180

Wald, Jerry 12, 13
Wallace, Mike 53, 76, 77
Wallis, Hal B. 155
Warhol, Andy 152
The Warm Life 186

A Watcher in the Woods 195
Weinberg, Max 172
Welch, Raquel 57, 73
Weld, Tuesday 15, 24, 58, 59
Wells, Mary 102
Werner, Oscar 144
West, Mae 91
Westmore, Bud 63
Westmore, Ern 63
Westmore, George 63
Westmore, Michael v, 63, 65, 66, 68, 69, 72, 74, 75, 79, 81, 90, 91, 95
Westmore, Monte 63
Westmore, Perc 63
Westmore, Wally 63, 90, 91, 95
Westmoreland, James 64
Westmoreland, Mary 65
Whatever Happened to Baby Jane? 197
What's New, Pussycat? 132, 133
Wheelwright, Ralph 22
Where Love Is Gone 31
Whilby, Bobbie 84
Whitbeck, Frank 16
Whitmore, James 183
Who Killed Teddy Bear? 186
Who's Afraid of Virginia Woolf? 37
Wife vs. Secretary 10
Wilcox, Ed 153
Wilde, Oscar 42
Williams, Edy 55
Williams, John 52
Williams, Tennessee 23
Willis, John 86
Wilson, Carey 20
Wilson, Earl 53, 115
Wilson, John 172
Winters, Shelley 31, 53, 63
Wood, Natalie 15, 30, 51, 65
Woodward, Joanne 14, 24, 60
Woronov, Mary 152
Wynter, Dana 30

The Yellow Rolls-Royce 133

Zanuck, Darryll 34
Zastupnevich, Paul 193
Zec, Donald 130, 132
Zimbalist, Efrem, Jr. 1, 51, 54, 64, 72, 74, 75, 83, 105, 108, 118, 135
Zinnemann, Fred 96
Zinnemann, Tim v, 96–98
Zorba the Greek 115
Zukor, Adolph 92, 93
Zulu 31

www.ingramcontent.com/pod-product-compliance
Lightning Source LLC
Chambersburg PA
CBHW060342010526
44117CB00017B/2933